Creating and Governing Cultural Heritage in the European Union

I0585600

Creating and Governing Cultural Heritage in the European Union: The European Heritage Label provides an interdisciplinary examination of the ways in which European cultural heritage is created, communicated, and governed via the European Heritage Label scheme.

Drawing on ethnographic field research conducted across ten countries at sites that have been awarded with the European Heritage Label, the authors of the book approach heritage as an entangled social, spatial, temporal, discursive, narrative, performative, and embodied process. Recognising that heritage is inherently political and used by diverse actors as a tool for re-imagining communities, identities, and borders, and for generating notions of inclusion and exclusion in Europe, the book also considers the idea of Europe itself as a narrative. Chapters tackle issues such as multilevel governance of heritage; geopolitics of border-crossings and border-making; participation and non-participation; and embodiment and affective experience of heritage.

Creating and Governing Cultural Heritage in the European Union advances heritage studies with an interdisciplinary approach that utilises and combines theories and conceptualizations from critical geopolitics, political studies, EU and European studies, cultural policy research, and cultural studies. As such, the volume will be of interest to scholars and students engaged in the study of heritage, politics, belonging, the EU, ideas, and narratives of Europe.

Tuuli Lähdesmäki is a Senior Researcher and an Adjunct Professor working at the Department of Music, Art, and Culture Studies, University of Jyväskylä, Finland.

Viktorija L. A. Čeginskas is a Postdoctoral Researcher working at the Department of Music, Art, and Culture Studies, University of Jyväskylä, Finland.

Sigrid Kaasik-Krogerus is a University Lecturer working at the Faculty of Arts, University of Helsinki, Finland.

Katja Mäkinen is a Senior Researcher working at the Department of Music, Art, and Culture Studies, University of Jyväskylä, Finland.

Johanna Turunen is a Doctoral Candidate working at the Department of Music, Art, and Culture Studies, University of Jyväskylä, Finland.

Critical Heritages of Europe

Series editors: Christopher Whitehead and Susannah Eckersley, both at the University of Newcastle, UK

The *Critical Heritages of Europe* series seeks to explore the cultural and social politics of the European past in the present. Bridging theoretical and empirical research, the series accommodates broad understandings of Europe – a shifting and historically mutable entity, made both of internal tensions and exogenous encounters, re-imaginings, and influences. 'Heritage' too is taken as an expansive paradigm, made in myriad practices where the past is valorised for the present, from folk traditions to museums and memorials, the management of historic sites and traditions, and everyday matters such as education, political discourse, home life, food consumption, and people's relations with place. Consequently, the series spans a broad array of foci, disciplinary approaches, and ways of investigating and questioning the diverse meanings of European heritages today.

Heritage and Festivals in Europe
Performing Identities
Edited by Ullrich Kockel, Cristina Clopot, Baiba Tjarve, and Máiréad Nic Craith

Dimensions of Heritage and Memory
Multiple Europes and the Politics of Crisis
Edited by Christopher Whitehead, Susannah Eckersley, Gönül Bozoğlu, and Mads Daugbjerg

European Heritage, Dialogue, and Digital Practices
Edited by Areti Galani, Rhiannon Mason, and Gabi Arrigoni

European Memory in Populism
Representations of Self and Other
Edited by Chiara De Cesari and Ayhan Kaya

Populism and Heritage in Europe
Lost in Diversity and Unity
Ayhan Kaya

Food Heritage and Nationalism in Europe
Edited by Ilaria Porciani

Creating and Governing Cultural Heritage in the European Union
The European Heritage Label
Tuuli Lähdesmäki, Viktorija L. A. Čeginskas, Sigrid Kaasik-Krogerus, Katja Mäkinen, and Johanna Turunen

www.routledge.com/Critical-Heritages-of-Europe/book-series/COHERE

Creating and Governing Cultural Heritage in the European Union

The European Heritage Label

Tuuli Lähdesmäki, Viktorija L. A. Čeginskas, Sigrid Kaasik-Krogerus, Katja Mäkinen, and Johanna Turunen

Routledge
Taylor & Francis Group
LONDON AND NEW YORK

First published 2020
by Routledge
2 Park Square, Milton Park, Abingdon, Oxon OX14 4RN

and by Routledge
605 Third Avenue, New York, NY 10017

First issued in paperback 2021

Routledge is an imprint of the Taylor & Francis Group, an informa business

British Library Cataloguing-in-Publication Data
A catalogue record for this book is available from the British Library

Library of Congress Cataloging-in-Publication Data
A catalog record has been requested for this book

ISBN 13: 978-1-03-223625-4 (pbk)
ISBN 13: 978-0-367-14835-5 (hbk)

Typeset in Bembo
by Newgen Publishing UK

Contents

Figures

The copyright of the photographs taken by visitors is owned by the EUROHERIT project, as the interviewed visitors signed consent forms allowing the researchers to photograph their photos and to use them for scholarly purposes.

Authors

Tuuli Lähdesmäki (PhD in Art History and DSocSc in Sociology) is a Senior Researcher and Adjunct Professor at the Department of Music, Art, and Culture Studies, University of Jyväskylä (JYU), Finland. Her research focuses on cultural identities and identity politics, belonging, cultural heritage, strategies of representing, narrating, and interpreting the past, governance of diversities, and populism. Lähdesmäki leads the EUROHERIT (Legitimation of European Cultural Heritage and the Dynamics of Identity Politics in the EU) research project, funded by the European Research Council. She is the PI of JYU's consortium partnership in the DIALLS (Dialogue and Argumentation for Cultural Literacy Learning in Schools) project, funded through the EU's Horizon 2020 Programme. In addition, she is one of the three leaders in JYU's research profiling area, CRISIS (Crises Redefined: Historical Continuity and Societal Change). She has previously worked as an Academy of Finland Research Fellow and as a senior/postdoctoral researcher in projects such as Populism as Movement and Rhetoric, funded by the Academy of Finland. Lähdesmäki has researched as Visiting Scholar at the University of Cambridge, UK, the University of Limerick, Ireland, the University of Pécs, Hungary, and the European University Institute, Italy. ORCiD: 0000-0002-5166-489X

Viktorija L. A. Čeginskas (PhD in Cultural Heritage Studies) is a Postdoctoral Researcher on the EUROHERIT project at the Department of Music, Art, and Culture Studies, JYU. Čeginskas has a PhD in Cultural Heritage Studies from the University of Turku, Finland, and a MA in Contemporary and East European History and European Ethnology from Christian-Albrechts-Universität, Kiel, Germany. In her doctoral dissertation, Čeginskas explored the multi-sited and culturally plural belonging of multilingual adults who grew up in transnational families with three or more languages, based on an ethnographic study that addressed the author's personal situatedness. Her research includes narratives of belonging; the relationship between heritage, emotion, and identity; cultural diversity; multilingual, European, and transcultural identities; and transnational mobility. Čeginskas has previously worked in the public and private sectors in Germany, Lithuania, Estonia, and the Netherlands. ORCiD: 0000-0002-5794-9503

Sigrid Kaasik-Krogerus (DSocSc in Media and Communication Studies) is a University Lecturer at the Faculty of Arts, University of Helsinki. She has previously worked as a Postdoctoral Researcher on the EUROHERIT project at JYU. She specialises in media and communication, identity, and belonging, heritage, critical geopolitics, and European studies in the EU context, especially in Central and East European countries. In 2016, she defended her PhD thesis at the University of Helsinki, Finland, on the construction of Estonian national identity in relation to the EU in the opinion articles of Estonian largest daily paper, *Postimees*, during the country's accession process. From 2015 to 2018, she was a member of the Jean Monnet Module, East within Europe, funded by Erasmus+ at the Aleksanteri Institute, University of Helsinki. ORCiD: 0000-0002-6424-5520

Katja Mäkinen (PhD in Political Science) is a Senior Researcher on the EUROHERIT project at the Department of Music, Art, and Culture Studies, JYU. Mäkinen has a PhD in political science and an MA in art education, both from JYU. Her research focuses on citizenship, participation, identities, and cultural heritage. Mäkinen has applied a conceptual approach to analysing EU programmes on culture and citizenship and examined the EU's participatory governance through ethnographic research. Previously Mäkinen was a junior lecturer in political science and a senior lecturer in cultural policy at JYU. She has been a visiting fellow in the European University Institute, Florence, Italy, and the University of Auckland, New Zealand. She was the convener of the Citizenship Standing Group in the European Political Consortium for Political Research in 2016–2017. She is s co-editor of *Shaping Citizenship: A political concept in theory, debate and practice* (Routledge 2018). She has worked on the projects Politics of Participation and Democratic Legitimation in the European Union, funded by the Kone Foundation, and Muddy Waters: Democracy and Governance in a Multilateral State, funded by the Academy of Finland. ORCiD: 0000-0002-1107-4801

Johanna Turunen (MA in History, MSSc in Sociology) is a Doctoral Candidate in contemporary culture at the Department of Music, Art, and Culture Studies, JYU. In her doctoral dissertation, titled *Manufacturing Transnational Belonging: A Postcolonial Reading of the European Heritage Label*, she analyses the coloniality of European heritage and the post/de-colonial potentialities embedded in the narratives of 'Europeanness' created in the EU's cultural heritage initiatives. She discusses the effects of colonial heritage and eurocentrism and connects them to contemporary phenomena such as racism. Turunen seeks to challenge established and dominant notions of European heritage in order to create space for alternative, less hierarchical, and more inclusive notions. Turunen has a history MA from the University of Eastern

Finland and a Sociology MSc from JYU. Her Master's studies included a period at Ohio Northern University (OH, USA) and a researcher exchange at the Nordic Africa Institute in Uppsala, Sweden. Previously, Turunen has worked in posts related to internationalisation and international academic cooperation at JYU and in the public and civil society sectors in Finland, Namibia, and South Sudan. ORCiD: 0000-0001-6188-4282

Preface

European cultural heritage is a multidimensional research topic. It is the most traditional subject area in Western art and cultural history, and an extremely timely theme in critical scholarship ranging from anthropology to political science. This book is the core outcome of the research project that has explored this challenging topic since 2015, EUROHERIT (Legitimation of European cultural heritage and the dynamics of identity politics in the EU), funded by the European Research Council (ERC). Supported by the ERC Starting Grant received by one of the authors, Tuuli Lähdesmäki, our research team meticulously examined contemporary processes and practices through which the concept of European cultural heritage is formulated and maintained, critically rethought, and developed in Europe today.

The European Union (EU) is a multidimensional research subject. Besides political and legal scholars, researchers with diverse academic backgrounds ranging from anthropology to geography, from media to gender studies, have all explored the EU. Our book adds heritage studies to this variety of approaches.

The EUROHERIT project examines the idea of European cultural heritage in the context of the European Union. It scrutinizes EU heritage initiatives, heritage policies, identity politics, and the notions of European cultural heritage constructed in them. The motivations are two-fold: first, the EU's increased interest in heritage and its potential to impact on social, societal, political, and economic challenges in Europe, and second, the rapidly transforming European multicultural reality and political climate. The project researchers understand EU heritage policies and initiatives as technologies of power in the Foucauldian sense, which both construct notions of European cultural heritage and legitimatize certain European-level policies, on issues such as belonging, identity building, and cultural integration. Hence, EUROHERIT examines the EU as a heritage actor and its policies and initiatives in this field as a heritage regime in Europe.

EUROHERIT combines desktop analysis and ethnographic field research. The latter focuses on the EU's most recent heritage action, the European Heritage Label, drawing on an extensive body of data. Our field research was a major effort by the whole EUROHERIT team. The authors jointly planned, prepared, and conducted it in ten European countries within six months in 2017 and 2018. Challenges included the use of nine languages in the data collection and working on site with experts in a range of fields, from classical archaeology to EU policies, and from composition to archiving work. This extremely positive experience yielded rich data, offering fascinating material for analysis far beyond this book.

The EUROHERIT project is based at the Department of Music, Art, and Culture Studies at the University of Jyväskylä in Finland. Our research team draws on a broad variety of disciplines in the social and political sciences and humanities. This interdisciplinarity is a key feature of the project, and is furthered by Lähdesmäki's individual project EUCHE, European Cultural Heritage in the Making: Politics, Affects, and Agency, funded by the Academy of Finland between 2014 and 2019. Due to an interest in contemporary Europe and its transformation influenced by recent challenges, both EUCHE and EUROHERIT are a part of the University of Jyväskylä's current research profiling area CRISES, Crises Redefined: Historical Continuity and Societal Change, also funded by the Academy of Finland and co-led by Lähdesmäki.

We want to thank the European Research Council and the Academy of Finland for their financial support for our work. The EUROHERIT team is composed of the five authors of this book, but our project was strengthened by a great number of other people: researchers, research assistants, transcribers, and translators, who helped us to collect and process the interview data. We would like to thank the following people for their hard work: Maria Bogdan, Elina Jääskeläinen, Riikka Kalajoki, Miro Keränen, Aino-Kaisa Koistinen, Sofia Kotilainen, Quentin Labégorre, Lorenzo Leonardelli, Bella Lerch, Mila Oiva, Ave Tikkanen, Camille Troquet, Urho Tulonen, Rita Vargas de Freitas Matias, and Anna Vera Veen. We particularly thank all our interviewees working at the European Heritage Label (EHL) sites and in the European Commission for their participation and for enabling our field research. All our survey respondents from the national culture and heritage administration deserve special thanks, as do our other contacts who have provided us with information and helped to facilitate our field research.

The theoretical, methodological, and conceptual development of this book has been strengthened by our cooperation with numerous scholars from other research projects. We are grateful to all of them for inspiring us in our work. This book has been copyedited by Kate Sotejeff-Wilson, who deserves thanks for her detailed work. We also wish to thank Heidi Lowther, our editor at Routledge, for the smooth cooperation in the publishing process, as well as Routledge's anonymous reviewers for their fruitful comments, which helped us develop the book and sharpen our argumentation.

15 June 2019 in Jyväskylä
Tuuli Lähdesmäki
Viktorija L. A. Čeginskas
Sigrid Kaasik-Krogerus
Katja Mäkinen
Johanna Turunen

Acknowledgements

This book was supported by the European Research Council through the EU's Horizon 2020 Research and Innovation Programme under Grant 636177 (EUROHERIT) and the Academy of Finland under Grant SA274295 (EUCHE). This research is part of the University of Jyväskylä's profiling area supported by the Academy of Finland under Grant SA311877 (CRISES). The content of this publication does not reflect the official opinion of the European Union. Responsibility for the information and views expressed therein lies entirely with the authors.

Introduction

Europeanizing cultural heritage

> I believe that developing a sense of European identity enriches and strengthens our local, regional, and national identity and heritage, as you become part of a community of 500 million citizens who have such rich histories and interwoven cultures. By becoming European you will share all of this. I think it is wonderful and inspiring that in today's Europe anyone can take delight in our shared cultural heritage.
>
> (Tibor Navracsics, Commissioner for education, culture, youth and sport, 15 November 2017)

Cultural heritage is a timely topic that has recently been actualized in a new way in Europe. The 2000s have seen growing political interest in creating and promoting a common European narrative of the past and an idea of shared cultural heritage. The European Union (EU) is one of the core promoters of this narrative and idea. In this book, we aim to understand the EU's interest in heritagization and narrativization of the past and to comprehend the processes and practices through which this interest is carried out. We examine EU heritage politics and policies and their implementation in the EU's heritage initiatives, focusing particularly on its most recent action, the European Heritage Label (EHL). The European Commission has envisioned the EHL as the Union's flagship action in the area of heritage. The Commission awards heritage sites with the EHL to promote a specific European significance of cultural heritage, and to strengthen intercultural dialogue and a sense of belonging to Europe and the EU among European citizenry. The main objective of the book is to scrutinize how the idea of shared cultural heritage in Europe is created, communicated, and governed in the EU through the EHL, and with what effects.

There is a substantial body of recent scholarly literature exploring various processes and practices of heritage and remembrance of the past in culturally diverse postmillennial Europe. Some of these studies rely more or less on methodological nationalism, focusing on national cases and contexts, while others seek to examine multiple spatial dimensions of heritage practices and narratives and to investigate interfaces of local, regional, national, and global scales in heritage production (e.g. Ashworth, Graham, and Tunbridge 2007; Lähdesmäki, Thomas, and Zhu 2019; Kockel et al. 2019). Scholars have also focused their analytical gaze on Europe and explored processes and practices of heritage in a contemporary European context. In these studies, the local, regional, national, European, and global or cosmopolitan dimensions of heritage are commonly approached as intertwined and pro-actively producing each other – thus emphasizing the plurality of heritages in Europe (e.g. Pakier and Stråth 2010; Macdonald 2013; Delanty 2017; Lähdesmäki et al. 2019; Whitehead et al. 2019a).

The EU's increased interest in culture and the development of its cultural policy since the Maastricht Treaty – the founding agreement of the EU that is sometimes seen as the start of EU cultural policy, as it adopted an article explicitly focusing on culture – has been broadly examined in academia from diverse perspectives (e.g. Shore 2000, 2006; Littoz-Monnet 2004, 2007, 2012; Sassatelli 2006, 2009; Tzaliki 2007; Näss 2009, 2010; Dewey 2010; Patel 2013; Mattocks 2017). These researchers commonly approach the EU's cultural policy aims as entangled with an attempt to strengthen unification in Europe and to create or foster a European identity. Moreover, scholars have emphasized the complexity of decision- and policy-making in EU cultural policy as well as its symbolic nature due to its "soft law" instruments, such as non-enforceable recommendations and incentives (Dewey 2010). As Dewey (2010, 215) notes, the EU does not exert direct influence on or dictate harmonization of cultural policy at the national level, as the EU member states are responsible for their own cultural policies according to the subsidiarity principle. Therefore, the whole idea of EU cultural policy has been considered controversial. The EU does not officially have an explicit cultural policy, yet its cultural agendas, initiatives, actions, programmes, and policy goals affect both the cultural sector and cultural actors in the member states (Dewey 2010, 116). Several studies of EU cultural policy have scrutinized its discourses and rhetoric, and identified vagueness, limitations, or conceptual contradictions (e.g. Shore 2006; Gordon 2010; Cooke and Propris 2011; Lähdesmäki 2012). Others have critically discussed weak links between ambitious goals and idealistic rhetoric in EU policies and the reality of their implementation (e.g. Mattocks 2017).

The EU's heritage politics, policies, and initiatives have attracted less scholarly attention. However, there are studies examining how the EU has dealt with heritage and used it to advance various policy goals, usually by analysing policy documents, archived reports, and/or interviews with EU policy officers or other transnational actors (Calligaro 2010, 2013; Kaiser 2014; Lähdesmäki 2014a, 2014b, 2016a, 2017; Niklasson 2017; Jakubowski, Hausler, and Fiorentini 2019; Lähdesmäki and Mäkinen 2019; Lähdesmäki, Kaasik-Krogerus, and Mäkinen 2019; Zito, Eckersley, and Turner 2019). Implementation of these policies and initiatives and their impact at local and grass-roots levels have not been analysed sufficiently. Niklasson's (2016) study on EU policies and funding of archaeology is a welcome exception to the limited previous research.

We seek to fill the gap in current research by examining EU heritage politics using in-depth ethnographic methods. Our book is the first published scholarly monograph on the European Heritage Label. It takes an interdisciplinary approach to this EU action and its actors, contents, impacts, and implications are approached utilizing theoretical and conceptual frameworks from heritage studies, cultural studies, political science, cultural policy research, and EU and European studies. In this introductory chapter, we explain the core societal and political contexts of the study, introduce the EHL, describe our methodology and data, discuss the theoretical frameworks, and define the core concepts utilized and developed later in the book.

Transforming commemoration practices in Europe

Since the 1990s, scholars have explored and explained how cultural and social changes of societies have influenced the practices and processes of memory, heritage, and public commemoration (e.g. Gillis 1994; Nora 1998; Clifford 2013). Gillis (1994) has described these changes by dividing the development of Western commemoration practices into three phases: the pre-national, national, and post-national. For him, the current post-national phase is characterized by practices that are more local and/or global and that seek to appeal to people who shape their identities through collectives other than the nation. Similarly, Nora (1998, 614–615) has described how in France the "classical model of national commemoration" began to lose its dominant position in the 1970s and has been replaced by a system of loosely organized and varying commemorative languages. In this new system, Nora claims, the relation to the past differs from the previous model: it is more flexible, loose, voluntary, and in a constant state of developing and transforming. Nora (1998, 614–615) argues that national memory canons have ruptured along with the overturn of the national commemoration model. The role of the state in commemoration processes has diminished and those commemoration practices that still exist at the national level no longer necessarily serve as unifying elements of different collectives within a state.

Societal and cultural changes during the past decades and the transformation of state-controlled memory culture have not wiped out the need and longing for collective remembrance and narratives of the past. Quickly transforming, globalized, and digitalized societies have not lost their interest in the past and preserving its remnants for future generations, quite the contrary (Huyssen 1993; Lowenthal 1996; Harrison 2013a, 2013b). Instead, societies have faced an increasing memory boom with exponential growth in the number of objects and places that are actively identified, listed, conserved, and exhibited as heritage. Macdonald (2013, 2) refers to this "ongoing memory and heritage boom" in Europe by describing how "Europe has become a memoryland – obsessed with the disappearance of collective memory and its preservation".

The increase in commemorating practices and the transformation of the state-led national commemoration model in Europe, particularly in Western Europe, are closely connected (Nora 1998, 616; Whitehead, Eckersley, and Bozoğlu 2019). This transformation has created, if not a power vacuum, at least a new space for another kind of heritage production. It has enabled new actors to enter the realms of memory, in Nora's (1998) terms, and to interpret and narrate the past from divergent and even alternative perspectives that challenge the national canons of memory and heritage. Heritage, memory, and commemoration have become politicized in a new way, enabling diverse actors to influence the politics of the past. Various non-governmental organizations (NGOs), interest groups, commercial actors, and political parties that seek to promote their interpretations of the past and propagate their social, commercial, or political agendas have become more and more active in the realms of memory. One of these heritage actors in Europe is the EU, and its interest in cultural heritage can be viewed against this more general context of memory and heritage booms (Calligaro 2013, 91).

Other recent cultural and social changes, such as the increased significance of social media and the participatory turn in contemporary culture, have bolstered individuals' opportunities to take an active role in commemoration, memorialization, and heritagization. Today, many heritage managers and institutions actively encourage citizens to participate in diverse practices and processes to preserve and promote heritage (Giaccardi 2012; Roued-Cunliffe and Copeland 2017). Moreover, various people and communities have protested against today's memory and heritage regimes that are perceived as fostering one-sided or discriminative memories and narrations of the past – particularly those related to minorities and peoples other than white, Christian Europeans. These "change agents" aim to promote alternative or silenced memories, or to re-narrate and reinterpret past events to form a more inclusive present (van Huis 2019; Turunen 2019a).

Cultural heritage as the EU's response to challenges and changes in Europe today

Despite recent cultural and social changes, the national memory culture has struck back in postmillennial Europe. Various nationalistic groups and political parties have prioritized the national heritage and the commemoration of national memories in their agenda. Particularly in Central and Eastern European EU member states, political forces have actively sought to impose the national state-led commemoration culture. The EU's diversity rhetoric, with its emphasis on the existence of diverse and distinct national cultures in Europe, can be interpreted as feeding this development.

Moreover, the narrative of Europe as a distinct cultural area with its own cultural heritage is attractive to many different groups. In addition to the EU, this narrative is also promoted by European identitarian movements and diverse populist and radical right-wing parties around Europe. Beyond 'the national', these movements and parties also commonly identify with a shared European heritage particularly when they feel threatened by non-European others – immigrants from the Middle East, Africa, and Asia. The idea of a common European heritage is used by these movements and parties to justify their xenophobic, anti-immigration, Islamophobic, and monocultural political attitudes and actions, as well as their selective defence of 'us' Europeans (see Vejvodová 2014; Lähdesmäki 2015, 2019; Brubaker 2017; De Cesari and Kaya 2019; Whitehead et al. 2019b).

In the 2010s, increasing EU interest in a common European narrative of the past and shared cultural heritage can be perceived as a response to the rise of populist, nationalist, and radical right-wing attitudes. Although both sides share an interest in European cultural heritage, their motivation and goals differ greatly. The populist, nationalist, and radical right-wing discourses aim at excluding people by emphasizing 'our' heritage that is not 'yours', if you do not share 'biological-generational' cultural roots in Europe. In contrast, the EU seeks to increase cohesion between diverse people(s) in Europe and thereby strengthen a feeling of belonging to the same community. Cultural heritage is, however, a challenging policy tool for creating inclusion. Although EU's emphasis on common cultural heritage seeks to overcome diverse tensions in Europe, by fostering communality, and creating a positive feeling of belonging to Europe, may simultaneously create new explicit and implicit boundaries and divisions, and exclude some while including others in practice (Turunen n.d.).

In the 2000s, the EU has faced severe challenges – or crises as they have been often referred to in political and media discourses – that have impacted on European societies and politics.: These interrelated challenges range from EU Eastern enlargement to the economic crisis of the Eurozone and European financial markets and from the diverse political crises stemming from the EU's legitimation and democratic deficits to the rise of Eurosceptic political parties who want to exit the common currency zone and/or the EU. The recent 'refugee crisis' with people fleeing a myriad of conflicts and difficult conditions, has exacerbated the political crisis, as contradictory views on how to deal with it exist within the EU and its member states. For a long time, scholars have perceived that the EU is struggling with an identity crisis (e.g. Hoffmann 1994; Weiss 2002; Jenkins 2008). This identity crisis focuses on a difficulty to define what Europe is, what and who belongs to it, who Europeans are, and which elements a European identity or identities could or should be based on in a Europe that is filled with political, material, and symbolic divisions and distinctions (Jenkins 2008; Lähdesmäki 2019).

All these recent challenges affect conceptualizations of cultural heritage in Europe and of how to handle the previous and current narratives of Europe and the European past. The EU has sought to respond to these intertwined challenges by advancing the idea of unity – along with respect and tolerance for diversity – and by enhancing both symbolic and concrete European integration. Culture and heritage serve as political tools in this process (Lähdesmäki 2016a, 2019; Whitehead et al. 2019b). Indeed, presenting the EU as a humanistic enterprise – based on common cultural roots, identity, and shared values – is a means to promote the EU's political legitimacy and its attempts to increase political, economic, social, and cultural integration (Shore 1993, 785–786).

Culture and heritage are not new political tools for the EU. On the one hand, scholars have pointed out how the political actors in the European Community have expected that Europe will experience cultural and social integration as a spill-over effect of successful cooperation in other sectors or policy fields. On the other hand, culture and heritage have been seen as motivating the very foundation of the European Community and, later, the EU (e.g. Rosamond 2000; Sassatelli 2006; Näss 2009).

In addition to culture-related interests during the early decades of European integration, scholars have also emphasized how cultural policy itself has gained prominence in the EU during the 2000s (e.g. Sassatelli 2009; Näss 2010; O´Callaghan 2011; Lähdesmäki 2012). This new interest in culture has included a strong element of the past. In the 2000s and 2010s, the EU launched several new initiatives to foster a narrative of Europe's shared past and cultural heritage (see Figures 0.1 and 0.2). These activities have also been complemented by significant research funding for European history and heritage through the European Commission's Horizon 2020 Programme. The EU's "move to history", as Prutsch (2013, 36) has called it, is a highly future-oriented project: narrations of the past and attempts to foster common cultural heritage in Europe function as building blocks to create a future Europe and to educate a new generation of European citizens. The fundamental utility of the EU's move to history is in its intertwined cognitive and affective nature: it seeks to appeal to people's feelings of belonging, cultural and social attachments, communality, and identity by disseminating knowledge about the European past, as well as by touching people at the emotional level (Lähdesmäki 2014b, 2017, 2019).

The EU has its roots in economic union. Economic interests have also guided the EU's approaches to and uses of heritage in its policy discourses. In EU policy, heritage is often both explicitly and implicitly treated as an asset that can boost tourism, employment, and regional development (Lähdesmäki 2014a; Lähdesmäki, Kaasik-Krogerus, and Mäkinen 2019). It has been seen as having instrumental value that can be used in a global competition for symbolic and economic power and to secure competitive advantages in diverse areas of culture, such as audio-visual production, thereby decreasing the impact of American cultural industries in Europe (Calligaro 2013, 84; Niklasson 2017, 142; Lähdesmäki, Kaasik-Krogerus, and Mäkinen 2019). Moreover, competition for symbolic power continues to keep the EU actively engaged with cultural and heritage conventions and agreements advanced by major transnational

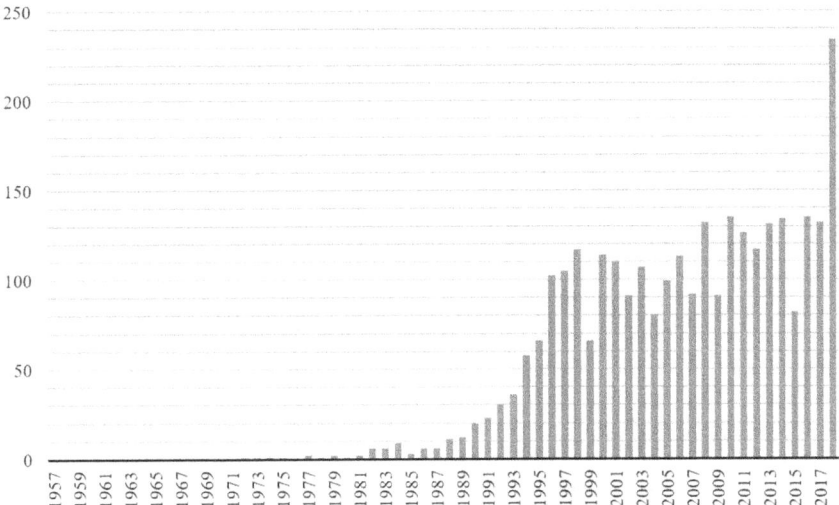

Figure 0.1 The actual increase in the number of documents (n = 2,949) including the search term "cultural heritage" in the EUR-Lex domain "EU law and case law" from 1957 to 2018. Seven hits from 1957 have been ignored as these documents were consolidated versions of the Treaty of Rome dating from 1997 to 2010. Copyright: EUROHERIT

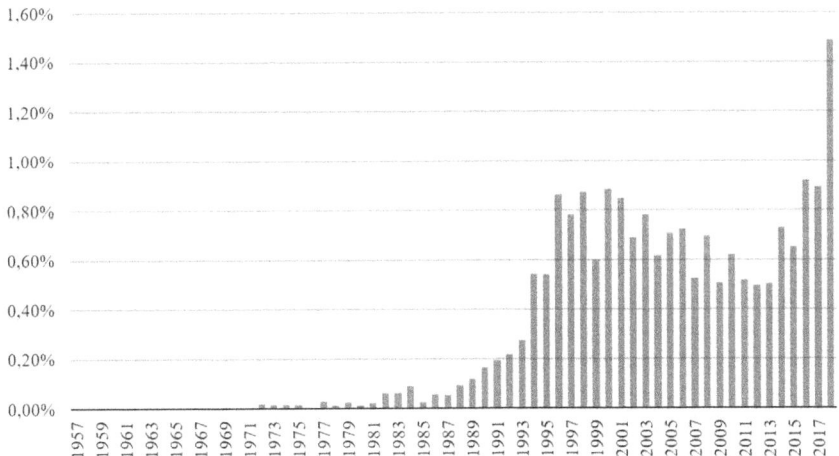

Figure 0.2 The proportionate increase in the number of documents (n = 2,949) including the search term "cultural heritage" in the EUR-Lex domain "EU law and case law" from 1957 to 2018. Seven hits from 1957 have been ignored as these documents were consolidated versions of the Treaty of Rome dating from 1997 to 2010. Copyright: EUROHERIT

organizations, such as the Council of Europe and UNESCO (see Niklasson 2017, 142).

The EU's increased interest in culture and heritage and its attempts to utilize them in policy have not, however, meant a generous budget. Cultural actions are underfunded compared to other policy sectors (Niklasson 2017, 140). The Union's budget for Creative Europe (the programme for cultural and creative sectors for 2014–2020) is €1.46 billion, just 0.1% of the total budget. An attempt is made to compensate for the lack of generous funding with the symbolic nature of EU cultural policy. As Patel (2013, 2) describes it: "[C]ultural policy is designed both to enlarge the scope of EU power and authority and to win the hearts and minds – and not just the hands and muscle – of the European citizens". EU cultural policy is in "the odd position of being at the same time limited in reach and scope, yet distinctively oriented to the ambitious object-ives of identity-building", as Sassatelli (2009, 47) notes. The symbolic nature of the policy is also highlighted by the abstract and affective rhetoric used in policy discourse surrounding it. The EU's appeals to the European cultural area, common past and cultural heritage, and shared European values bring lofty, emotive, and affective tones to the policy discourse, lifting its meanings above the everyday and political sphere of Brussels that is often perceived as distant and bureaucratic (Lähdesmäki 2016b, see also Chapter 3).

New tools for EU heritage policy: The European Heritage Label

Since the late 1990s, the European Commission has launched several cultural programmes and cooperative initiatives that explicitly focus on preserving and promoting heritage. The earliest of them, the Community action programme in the field of cultural heritage – Raphael (1997–2000), was the Commission's first funding programme entirely dedicated to cultural heritage with the aim to engage archaeologists and heritage professionals in its development and implementation. With its focus and aims, Raphael "marked a break with a pre-viously more passive and unstructured engagement with tangible heritage" in EU policy, as Niklasson (2016, 90) notes. Indeed, the EU's previous heri-tage funding instrument, the European Parliament's initiative of the European Historical Monuments and Sites Fund, functioned mainly as financial support for restoring and conserving archaeological and heritage sites, from its pilot phase in 1983 to 1995 (Niklasson 2016, 82–91). During the 1990s, the EU started to cooperate more closely with other transnational actors in the field of heritage. As a result, the Council of Europe's European Heritage Days have been organized in cooperation with the European Commission since 1999, and the Europa Nostra Awards for Cultural Heritage have been awarded in cooper-ation with the Commission since 2002, later renamed as the European Union Prize for Cultural Heritage, and then as the European Heritage Awards in 2018. Europeana, a European digital library, archive, and museum, was initiated by the

Commission in 2005, extending the EU's interest in heritage into timely issues such as digital heritage, digitalization of (non-digital) heritage, and open access.

The EU's fascination with heritage reached a new level with the EHL. This began as an intergovernmental scheme in 2006, initiated by the French Minister of Culture and Communication and supported by the Spanish and Hungarian Ministers of Culture. The initiative was a response to the rejection of the referenda on the Treaty establishing a Constitution for Europe in the Netherlands and France in 2005 (Čeginskas 2018, 33). The main aim of the scheme was to identify and designate sites that "have played a key role in building and uniting Europe" and to promote "a European reading of these sites" instead of their national interpretation (EC 2010a, 15). The ideological and political motive for the EHL scheme was to turn cultural heritage, hitherto framed mainly in national and/or local terms, into a shared transnational European cultural heritage that would function as a basis for "our" (European) identity and feeling of belonging, as the intergovernmental declaration on the EHL indicates:

> We, the European Union Ministers for Culture participating in the European Heritage Label initiative: […] Declare that our heritage in all its diversity is one of the most significant elements of our identity, our shared values and our principles. […] Agree to promote the European nature of cultural assets and the sites which have shaped Europe's history, and to share and raise awareness of the wealth of European Heritage among its people.
> (Declaration on the Initiative for a European Heritage Label 2007)

In 2007, the first series of 42 sites were awarded the Label. The listings of candidate sites were first compiled at the national level by a committee of national heritage experts, and the final decisions on the awards were made by the Heritage Committee of Europe, consisting of the Ministries of Culture and the European Commissioner for Culture or the latter's representative. By 2011, 68 sites from 19 European countries were awarded (see Appendix 1).

The first years of the scheme indicated that the initiative was difficult to implement on an intergovernmental basis due to the lack of coordination and opportunity for operational arrangements (EC 2010a, 18–20; MacCoshan et al. 2009). Critics highlighted the lack of clear criteria for the Label and the diversity of interpretations of the European dimension and European significance in the participating countries (MacCoshan et al. 2009, 18). The European Commission, Parliament, and Council considered the scheme important, however, and in 2008 the Council adopted conclusions to transform the initiative into an official EU action. The decision on the action was finally made in 2011. The sites awarded with the Label during the intergovernmental scheme had to reapply for the EHL according to the new refined regulations and criteria. The majority of sites from the intergovernmental phase of the initiative have not reapplied. Out of the 27 sites that have, only 12 have been granted the EHL under the new criteria (see Appendix 1).

AUSTRIA
• **Archaeological Site of Carnuntum**, Petronell-Carnuntum, 2013
• Imperial Palace, Vienna, 2015
BELGIUM
• **Mundaneum**, Mons, 2015
• Bois du Cazier, Marcinelle, 2017
CROATIA
• Neanderthal Prehistoric Site and Krapina Museum, Hušnjakovo/Krapina, 2015
CZECH REPUBLIC
• Olomouc Premyslid Castle and Archdiocesan Museum, Olomouc, 2015
ESTONIA
• **Great Guild Hall**, Tallinn, 2013
• Historic Ensemble of the University of Tartu, Tartu, 2015
FRANCE
• Abbey of Cluny, Cluny, 2014
• **Robert Schuman's House**, Scy-Chazelles, 2014
• **European District of Strasbourg**, Strasbourg, 2015
• Former Natzweiler concentration camp and its satellite camps (with Germany), multiple, 2017
GERMANY
• Sites of the Peace of Westphalia (1648), Münster and Osnabrück, 2014
• **Hambach Castle**, Hambach, 2014
• Leipzig's Musical Heritage Sites, Leipzig, 2017
• Former Natzweiler concentration camp and its satellite camps (with France), multiple, 2017
GREECE
• Heart of Ancient Athens, Athens, 2014
HUNGARY
• Pan-European Picnic Memorial Park, Sopron, 2014
• **Franz Liszt Academy of Music**, Budapest, 2015

• Dohány Street Synagogue Complex, Budapest, 2017
ITALY
• **Alcide de Gasperi's House Museum**, Pieve Tesino, 2014
• Fort Cadine, Trento, 2017
LITHUANIA
• Kaunas of 1919–1940, Kaunas, 2014
LUXEMBURG
• Village of Schengen, Schengen, 2017
NETHERLANDS
• Peace Palace, The Hague, 2013
• **Camp Westerbork**, Hooghalen, 2013
• Maastricht Treaty, Maastricht, 2017
POLAND
• Union of Lublin (1569), Lublin, 2014
• 3 May 1791 Constitution, Warsaw, 2014
• **Historic Gdansk Shipyard**, Gdansk, 2014
• World War I Eastern Front Wartime Cemetery No. 123, Łużna – Pustki, 2015
PORTUGAL
• **General Library of the University of Coimbra**, Coimbra, 2014

• Charter of Law for the Abolition of the Death Penalty, Lisbon, 2014
• **Sagres Promontory**, Sagres, 2015
ROMANIA
• Sighet Memorial, Sighet, 2017
SLOVENIA
• Franja Partisan Hospital, Cerkno, 2014
• Javorca Memorial Church and its cultural landscape, Tolmin, 2017
SPAIN
• Archive of the Crown of Aragon, Barcelona, 2014
• Student Residence or 'Residencia de Estudiantes', Madrid, 2014

Figure 0.3 A map of sites awarded with the European Heritage Label between 2014 and 2018. Fieldwork sites are bolded and marked with a star. Please note the map is an approximation and is not geographically fully accurate. Copyright: EUROHERIT

Between 2014 and 2018, 38 sites have been awarded the Label under the new requirements (see Appendix 2 and 3). Following the logic of other EU cultural actions (such as the European Capital of Culture that was used as a good example in the preparation phase of the official EHL), the awarding of the Labels is based on applications of local actors. The candidates for the Labels are bi-annually pre-selected at the national level by a national panel, and the final selection takes place by a panel of international experts at EU level, known as the European panel. Finally, the Labels are awarded by the Commission. The EHL is not a funding instrument for the sites as it does not include any regular financing measures. The expected motivation to apply for it relies on its brand value, which is still developing, and the interest in participating in a network of sites promoting the EU's European project through heritage (Čeginskas 2018).

The European Commission seeks to implement various political goals through the EHL, such as advancing integration, economy, governance, and education among European citizenry, as well as increasing a positive image of the EU (Lähdesmäki 2014a). The core political motive for the initiative stems, however, from the EU's politics of belonging. This motive is crystallized in the Commission's (EC 2010b) press release on the forthcoming EHL action:

> The European Union is home to 500 million people. But most don't usually refer to themselves as EU citizens. When asked about their origins, they tend to answer in terms of their nationality. The lack of a strong European identity is seen as a challenge to integration in Europe, but it is hardly surprising. The continent is a vast smorgasbord of languages and customs where countries often seem more different than alike. To give Europeans a greater sense of belonging, the Commission has decided to sponsor the European Heritage Label, a registry of historical sites whose significance transcends national borders.

As the press release indicates, the Commission sought to tackle the 'problem' of a national preference for identification by producing a registry of transnational cultural heritage, to serve as common ground for a sense of belonging to and identification with Europe (Lähdesmäki 2014b). The decision on the EHL action also emphasizes the politics of belonging that it seeks to promote. In the decision, the core objectives of the action are described as "strengthening European citizens' sense of belonging to the Union, in particular that of young people, based on shared values and elements of European history and cultural heritage, as well as an appreciation of national and regional diversity" and the "strengthening intercultural dialogue" (EP&C 2011, 3).

The EHL action focuses on the European layer of meanings. The criteria for awarding the Labels specify how this is framed at the EU level:

> Candidate sites for the label must have a symbolic European value and must have played a significant role in the history and culture of Europe and/or the building of the Union. They must therefore demonstrate one or more of the following:
>
> (i) their cross-border or pan-European nature: how their past and present influence and attraction go beyond the national borders of a Member State

(ii)   their place and role in European history and European integration, and their links with key European events, personalities or movements

(iii)   their place and role in the development and promotion of the common values that underpin European integration.

(EP&C 2011, 4)

The Europeanness of heritage is, thus, defined in the EHL decision as relying on cultural phenomena that are characterized either by border crossing (of national borders in the EU) or European integration. To a certain extent, the attempts to promote a transnational European dimension of heritage undermine dominant national discourses, as the EHL does not define heritage through a singular site, practice, or event in Europe. Instead, the awarded sites give evidence of Europe's interwoven historical processes and dynamic transnational developments (Čeginskas 2018).

The idea of heritage can be understood in the EHL action both in tangible and intangible terms, as evidenced also by the EHL 2030 vision, which lists "archaeological sites, cultural landscapes and natural heritage, historical monuments, places of remembrance, urban quarters, intangible heritage and cultural objects, books and archives" as potential EHL sites (EC 2017, 7). The application guidelines, however, emphasize the material manifestation of this. "[T]here must be a link to a clearly identifiable physical space in which the information and educational activities will be carried out", as the Guide for the Implementation of the European Heritage Label (EC 2014, 4) advises applicants. This requirement effectively concretizes the Europeanness of heritage in the EHL action, attaches 'the European' to specific places and locations in Europe (discussed as "placing heritage" by Lähdesmäki 2016a), as well as highlighting the spatial microscale of European cultural heritage. This requirement can be interpreted as related to the political goals of the action. It seeks to create sites where visitors can spend their time (and money) and, thus, have a positive economic impact, and offer a space for various educational activities that disseminate information about European history and culture and, therefore, educate the next generation of European citizens.

Cultural heritage and the semantics of its Europeanness

The EU rhetoric on a shared cultural heritage in Europe dates to the early decades of the community. This rhetoric gained more institutional strength in the 1990s when it was included in the Maastricht Treaty. Its article on culture emphasizes the Union's role in "respecting [Member States'] national and regional diversity and at the same time bringing the common cultural heritage to the fore" (TEU 1992, 24). According to the article, the EU aims at "encouraging cooperation between Member States and, if necessary, supporting and supplementing their action in [...] conservation and safeguarding of cultural heritage of European significance" (TEU 1992, 24). The same article is included in the Treaty of Lisbon – the current EU treaty in force. In addition to the terms "common cultural heritage in Europe", "Europe's shared cultural heritage", and "cultural heritage of European significance", the EU policy discourse also refers to "European dimension of cultural heritage" or just simply, and most commonly, to "European cultural heritage". One of the core aims of our book is to examine 'the European' in heritage and how it is constructed and narrated through the EHL and in its implementation below the EU level. Our closer analysis of how European significance is framed in the European panel's selection reports has been already published elsewhere (Lähdesmäki and Mäkinen 2019; Turunen 2019b).

A wealth of literature critically discusses the Europeanness of cultural heritage. It has been approached as an intertwined existential, ontological, political dilemma since "heritage is so frequently the grounds for claims relating to an ontological reality in the present", as Whitehead et al. note (2019b, 6). Scholars have emphasized the difficulty in formulating any comprehensive definition of European cultural heritage; even within one society, pasts and heritages are and should be considered as plural (Graham and Howard 2008; Delanty 2010). Attempts to define European cultural heritage are challenged by the diversity of the continent (Larkham 1994, 270) and heterogeneity of Europeans that do not form a singular "European people" (Delanty 2009, 37). Scholars have also asked what might be the European dimension of heritage that goes beyond the mere sum of national icons and identities (Kockel et al. 2012, 5) while still promoting the nation (Sassatelli 2006, 29). In addition to noting the rupture in the classical model of national commemoration, scholars have shown how (nation) states still form the ideological basis, territorialized political sphere, and institutionalized forum of practice for fostering, preserving, and making meaning in cultural heritage (Ashworth 1994, 13; Graham at el. 2000, 259; Graham and Howard 2008). Moreover, states have long endorsed and promoted domestic tourism to sites of perceived national significance, and continue to do so, as these sites are related to the wider social formation of the nation.

The difficulties with the idea of European cultural heritage are also acknowledged by some actors in the European Commission. Particularly our interviews with actors involved in the work of the European panel illustrate firm views on the semantics related to Europeanness of cultural heritage. According to these interviewees (E3; E7), the EHL is not about European cultural heritage but about the "European significance of cultural heritage" or "cultural heritage having a European dimension". Only such concepts were seen allowing for the multi-layered nature of heritage – that is, understanding heritage as including simultaneously interrelated scalar meanings, such as those of 'the European'.

These conceptual differences are mainly about semantics, however, and do not make any major difference to their core focus – 'the European'. In EU policy discourse, all these expressions aim at addressing, discussing, framing, and dealing with European meanings of cultural heritage. The same semantic dilemma can obviously be related to all scales and territorialized notions of

heritage, whether national, regional, or local. In this book, we do not distinguish between the above-mentioned expressions of 'the European' in heritage.
All these expressions in the EU policy discourse and in our field research data
deal with the heritage that is perceived as connected to the idea of Europe. They
are used to construct the idea that 'Europe' and 'Europeans' have some shared
cultural heritage (Lähdesmäki 2016c). In our understanding, the discussions
about European cultural heritage are about a cultural heritage that has a particularly European dimension and significance. The EHL functions as a tool and
an arena to generate and facilitate these discussions, as one of our interviewed
heritage practitioners working at an EHL site (hereafter, 'practitioners'), told us
during our field research (P28):

> I think the institutions who have the Label have some part ... well, not by
> obligation but maybe ... they can serve the institution to make the heri-
> tage known, to remind people what Europe is and what Europe's cultural
> heritage is.

In this book, we follow Delanty's conceptual notion on European heritage.
Instead of searching for any 'factual' or 'true' common layer of meanings in
European cultural heritage, we perceive it in terms of several competing and
contradictory histories and memories, a complex plurality of interconnecting
narratives of the past and the inclusion of new voices, such as those of post-
migration communities (Delanty 2017, 3; see also Whitehead et al. 2019b). For
Delanty (2017, 1), the entanglement of different traditions, histories, and cultures
in Europe produces common reference points and forges European heritage in
new spaces of critical dialogue. The EU heritage policies and initiatives and
their policy rhetoric about European cultural heritage are discursive, narrative,
and performative instances in which European cultural heritage is constructed.
They can be perceived as instances where cultural heritage is Europeanized
(see Delanty 2005; Lähdesmäki, Kaasik-Krogerus, and Mäkinen 2019). The
Europeanization of cultural heritage occurs in EU heritage initiatives through
narrating its meanings as European and connecting heritage sites under the
symbolic "patronage" of the EU (Calligaro 2013, 96).

Box 0.1 Does Europe + the EU equal EUrope?

It has always been difficult to define what and where Europe is, what it
means, and who is perceived as European. With over 60 years of European
integration, the ideas of Europe and the EU have become increasingly
entangled and although the rhetoric of diversity is used extensively,
European identities have mostly been approached as Europe of nations.
While the concept of Europe is often used in a quite unproblematized
way by the EU, it has long been acknowledged that there is an "identity
crisis" (e.g. Hoffmann 1994; Jenkins 2008) at the heart of the Union,

that pivots around the relationships between national cultures, questions of identity and belonging, and the idea of Europe. This identity crisis manifests in the EU's desires to promote belonging of its citizens through heritage and cultural actions, such as the EHL, but recently also in the racialized discourses of Europe's 'refugee crisis' (e.g. De Genova 2018).

Heritage, culture, and memory are important avenues for the EU to resolve this crisis. However, many researchers have shown how, especially in the field of heritage, this can have problematic undertones. In many instances, the EU has positioned itself on the continuum of European history in ways that blur its distinctiveness from Europe (Lähdesmäki 2017). Due to these complexities and transgressions, we want to highlight the distinction and overlaps between Europe and the EU by our choice of concepts – Europe, the EU, and EUrope (for other definitions and uses of the concept see e.g. De Cesari 2017; Niklasson 2017; Turunen n.d.). Whereas Europe refers to the geographical continent and the term EU pertains to the political institutions and member states of the Union, we use the term EUrope to refer to the idea of Europe produced in and through EU initiatives, that is, as conditioned by the EU. The EHL is an official action of the EU with the explicit aim to "bring to life the European narrative and the history behind it" (EC 2019). As such the EHL functions as a prime example of processes aimed at creating and sustaining an idea of EUrope and a joint economic, political, and cultural community of EUropeans. Similar to the innovation of Union citizenship, it aims to foster belonging to the EU.

Ethnography of Europeanization

The study of European cultural heritage and EU heritage policies requires a multifaceted approach due to the complex nature of the processes of Europeanization. We approach our work as an 'ethnography of European cultural heritage' and 'ethnography of Europeanization' in which the focus is not only on heritage sites in/of Europe but also on the idea of Europe itself as an ongoing process and narrative governed by various actors at different levels. Ethnographic research has traditionally been based on three core methods, which also lay the foundation for our data collection: participant observation, interviewing, and the analysis of documents, archival material, and academic literature (e.g. Clifford and Marcus 1986; Culhane and Elliot 2017). In addition, our ethnographic research is heavily influenced by collaborative approaches and by mobile multi-sited ethnography, which is designed to follow the ethnographic object of study through multiple sites and locations.

Our ethnographic research into the idea of European cultural heritage is founded in fieldwork focusing on the EHL. Due to the nature of Europeanization, there is no single location where one can immerse oneself in this idea. Heritage is Europeanized simultaneously at multiple locations and levels, so it requires ethnographic immersion in multiple locales, paying attention to interconnected processes. In order to trace this multifaceted process, we have approached the EHL, a central instrument of Europeanization of cultural heritage, from several vantage points. These include policy, governance, national coordination, individual sites, participating citizens/visitors, and associated processes of narrative meaning-making, such as the exhibitions. This approach is built on the realization that topics like this "cannot be accounted for by focusing on a single site" (Falzon 2009, 1) but require a form of mobile ethnography. Jarzabkowski et al. (2015, 7) note that mobile multi-sited ethnography "prioritizes the phenomenon, such as a particular practice, rather than a particular geographically or culturally-bounded site, demanding instead that the ethnographer follows that actor or practice", thereby demanding immersion in the phenomenon rather than in a specific location.

Due to its scale, this kind of ethnographic research requires collaborative approaches to both fieldwork and analysis. Collaborative researching, thinking, and writing, aimed at sharing insight, can be approached as forms of "knowledge integration" (Franks et al. 2007) as they bring multiple experiences and types of expertise together. In essence, we follow Wasser and Bresler (1996, 6) who perceive the research team as a "[p]owerful interpretative zone [...] where multiple viewpoints are held in dynamic tension as [the] group seeks to make sense of fieldwork issues and meanings". In the following we briefly outline our epistemological approach to collective knowledge production (for more detailed information on intra-team dynamics and collective sense-making, see Turunen et al. forthcoming). These epistemological grounds under-gird not only our interpretative frameworks and analysis, but also the kind of questions we as ethnographers have engaged with.

At the heart of our mobile collaborative ethnography is what Lichterman (2015) has conceptualized as "interpretive reflexivity". It is an active process that seeks to understand the positions of each individual researcher and the positional relationships within the team, but also the more epistemological conditions that influence our knowledge production and the way we know what we know, as individual ethnographers and as a team. Collective practices of interpretive reflexivity make it possible to "show how we came up with the patterns we call meaningful or cultural" (Lichterman 2015, 42), and, more importantly, help to create knowledge that is beyond the scope of a single ethnographer.

The ethnographic field research was conducted at 11 EHL sites in ten countries in autumn 2017 and at the beginning of 2018. These sites are: Alcide De Gasperi House Museum, Italy; Archaeological Park Carnuntum, Austria; Camp Westerbork, The Netherlands; European District of Strasbourg, France; Franz Liszt Academy of Music, Hungary; Great Guild Hall, Estonia; Hambach Castle, Germany; Historic Gdańsk Shipyard, Poland; Mundaneum, Belgium; Robert Schuman's House, France; and Sagres Promontory, Portugal. Some of these sites are broad areas including units and buildings that host cultural, educational, or political institutes and cultural spaces such as archives, exhibitions, or museums. Later in our book, we will discuss more deeply some of these units, such as the exhibition space Lieu d'Europe in the European District of Strasbourg, Franz Liszt Memorial Museum in Franz Liszt Academy of Music, and European Solidarity Centre in Historic Gdańsk Shipyard (see Appendix 5 for the introduction of these 11 case sites). Moreover, we interviewed European Commission policy officers dealing with cultural heritage and a representative of the European panel in Brussels, Belgium.

The fieldwork at each site was carried out primarily by one member of the research team, although some sites were visited by several team members, making it possible to compare observations. Our multilingual research team was able to communicate and conduct interviews at the sites in English, German, French, Italian, Estonian, and Finnish. Additionally, native-speaking research assistants were used at four of the 11 sites (Dutch, Hungarian, Italian, and Portuguese) and a research assistant with native speaker competences at one site (Poland). We would like to emphasize that we are all non-native speakers of English and nevertheless conducted a number of interviews in English with other non-native speakers. In order to do justice to our non-native-speaking interviewees, the quotes from these interviews are sometimes slightly revised in our book regarding the syntax, grammar, and choice of some obviously 'false friends'. These corrections did not affect the content of these interviews nor our analyses of them.

All interviews have been transcribed and, if needed, translated into English. Each translation was reviewed twice, by at least two translators, and by one researcher. When possible, we used translators who had participated in the fieldwork and were familiar with the specific context. Prior to the analysis, the interviews were coded to facilitate easy comparisons both within and between different data sets. In this book, these codes have been simplified, also to ensure the anonymity of our informants. The coded references E1–7 indicate the EU officials and the representative of the European panel, while the codes P1–37 refer to the interviewed heritage practitioners. The coding of the interview partners at the European level and of the heritage practitioners does not disclose their rank, position, department, gender, age, educational background, or precise location. It neither follows the alphabetical order of the heritage sites nor indicates the alphabetical order of the interviewees' names in order to prevent their accidental identification. The visitors are coded according to one of the 11 EHL sites as VS1–11/, followed by a number that expresses the chronological order in which the interviews were conducted at the respective site.

The majority of the interviewed visitors were citizens of the EU core member states, e.g. Belgium, France, Germany, Italy, and the Netherlands (see Appendix 4 for more detailed information on the visitors' backgrounds). While we chose specific EHL sites for our fieldwork based on different criteria, such as the year of awarding, the site's theme, our linguistic competences, and in an attempt to balance the sites according to the North-South, East-West axis, 6 of the selected 11 EHL sites happened to be situated in the aforementioned five countries. Hence the high number of interviewed citizens from core EU countries can be explained by the fact that we (unintentionally) interviewed many 'local' visitors, in terms of national citizens of the country, in which the respective heritage site was located. In this context, it is interesting to note that we did not interview a single Estonian or Hungarian visitor at the Estonian, respectively Hungarian heritage site. We also only managed to conduct one interview with a local at Sagres Promontory. We can only speculate about the lack of local and national visitors at these three sites, whether it was related to the site's specific theme (e.g. Franz Liszt and classic music in Budapest), its location (e.g. the Great Guild Hall is in the middle of the touristic Old Town of Tallinn) or the timing (e.g. the exhibition of Sagres Promontory was closed). Furthermore, our fieldwork findings show that the heritage sites were visited predominantly by visitors with a higher educational background. Although the ratio between the group of interviewed visitors aged between 18 to 50 years (n = 141) and the group of visitors aged between 50 to 85+ years (n = 130) was more or less balanced – as was the proportion between interviewed men and women – we noted fewer visitors aged between their mid-thirties and mid-forties. This could be related to the fact that we conducted our fieldwork outside school holidays, when fewer families visited the heritage sites.

Our data gathering encompassed (a) interviews with key EU heritage officials and a representative of the European panel (n = 7), practitioners working at the selected EHL sites (n = 37), and visitors to these sites (n = 271) (see Appendix 6 for interview questions); (b) photos taken by these visitors at the EHL sites; (c) a survey of national coordinators of the EHL in the selected ten coun-tries (see Appendix 6 for survey questions); and (d) informal discussions with guides (see Appendix 6 for possible questions discussed with them) and various stakeholders of the sites, such as the staff of tourist information centres (nearby).

In addition, the data includes multifaceted observation of these sites (e.g. their exhibition narratives) collected as videos, catalogues, photographs, audio recordings, and notes in field journals and site memos, as well as diverse (multimodal) textual material, such as websites, promotional and educational materials, and policy documents. We asked all 38 EHL sites which were labelled before 2018 to share their EHL applications with us. We were provided with 16 documents. Our data also included a database of 8,299 documents based on a search for the word "heritage" in EUR-Lex, the database of official EU documents.

We utilize all this data in different ways. While some of the nine chapters in this book focus more explicitly on policy documents and interviews, others stem from our observations at the sites. The themes of the chapters, theor-etical frameworks, and concepts have directed our utilization of the data. Therefore, each chapter includes a brief description of the data used and how it was approached and examined. In general, we take a data-driven approach and attempt to understand the construction of European cultural heritage as a complex, multi-dimensional, and many-voiced process. We demonstrate this complexity by utilizing plenty of quotations from our data, thus giving voice to many of the people included in our field research.

Interdisciplinary theoretical framework, core concepts, and themes

This book takes a critical perspective on the recent processes of heritage in the EU and how various actors use these processes to (re-)imagine pasts, identities, communities, Europe, and various symbolic and its concrete borders, and to generate notions of inclusion in and exclusion from Europe. We draw on critical heritage studies, which stem from a paradigm shift away from preservationist and conservationist views of heritage. Rather than asking: What do we do to heritage?, scholars who take this approach have asked: What does heritage do, how and why is heritage used, and with what effects? (e.g. Smith 2006; Harrison 2013a; Lähdesmäki, Zhu, and Thomas 2019; Whitehead et al. 2019b).

In studies extending the preservationist and conservationist paradigm, the concept of heritage has been approached as an act of communication (Dicks 2000), a process of emotional and cultural engagement (Bendix 2009), and a performance and cultural practice of regulation, control, mediation, and negotiation of cultural and historical values and narratives (Smith 2006; Waterton and Smith 2009). In these studies, heritage is emerging when something is narrated, defined, and/or treated as heritage in a specific sociocultural context (van Huis et al. 2019). Critical heritage studies emphasize how heritage is about a political negotiation of identities (Waterton and Smith 2009). It can create and re-create identities by including in and excluding from its realm certain stories, symbols, values, and people. Hence, heritage is an inherently identity political process in which its social and communal meanings and boundaries of belonging are constantly negotiated.

In line with critical heritage studies, we perceive the idea of heritage as political, open to change and struggle, both a source and a result of social conflicts, inclusion, and exclusion (e.g. Smith 2006; Graham and Howard 2008; Harrison 2013a; Lähdesmäki, Zhu, and Thomas 2019). In this view, heritage includes dissonances regarding the stories told through it, the ways the past is represented, and memories used in public spheres (Tunbridge and Ashworth 1996). This dissonance is not only an unforeseen or sometimes unfortunate implication of a certain kind of heritage or process of remembering, but intrinsic to the very nature of heritage (Smith 2006, 82; Graham and Howard 2008, 3; Kisić 2017, 25). Defining, enhancing, and fostering any heritage creates boundaries, excludes people while including some others, and positions objects, interpretations of the past, and people in certain categories. Moreover, we see heritage as an active process, oriented to both the present and future, through which realities are being constructed from the selected elements of the past (Ashworth,

Graham, and Tunbridge 2007; Harrison 2013a; Whitehead et al. 2019b). It includes diverse layers and modes of existence, being an entangled social, spatial, temporal, discursive, narrative, performative, and embodied process.

To examine how the idea of European cultural heritage is created, communicated, and governed in the EHL, this book focuses on four core themes derived from our data: power relations in governance of heritage; geopolitics and bordering through heritage; engagement, participation, and non-participation in heritage; and embodiment, gender, and affective experiences of heritage. These connected themes form the four Parts of the book, each approaching the construction of European cultural heritage through different but interrelated theoretical perspectives. To broaden the analysis of heritage, we use theories and conceptualizations from multilevel and participatory governance, critical geopolitics, the participatory turn in humanities and social sciences, affect theory, and gender studies. All these theories share a critical stance on power relations and processes in which power is used, as well as emphasizing the multiple and multi-layered nature of meanings and of the dynamics of processes in which meanings are produced.

Our entire analysis draws on several core concepts, through which we describe and explain the manifold phenomena occurring and manifesting in our data. Belonging is one of these concepts, and it has been much theorized in scholarly literature (e.g. Antonsich 2010; Yuval-Davis 2004, 2006; Lähdesmäki et al. 2016). The concept has been used to refer both to personal and intimate feelings and experiences and to a shared and collective dimension of engaging in a broader group or community. Stemming from this duality, Yuval-Davis (2006) distinguishes between psychological and political belonging. Inspired by this distinction, Antonsich (2010, 645) perceives the discussions on belonging as structured around two dimensions: "belonging as a personal, intimate feeling of being at home in a place (place-belongingness) and belonging as a discursive resource which constructs, claims, justifies, or resists forms of socio-spatial inclusion/exclusion (politics of belonging)". In this book, we view the feeling and politics of belonging as inevitably intertwined (see Lähdesmäki 2019). Here, politics of belonging is about people in power, who selectively use discursive resources, such as narrations of the past, heritage, and their representations, to create or strengthen a particular embodied feeling of belonging. Belonging includes simultaneous spatial and temporal meanings: it is about attachments in space and time. Belonging can, thus, be seen as a crucial element in the construction of individual and collective identities.

Narration and narratives are an effective means in the politics of belonging: narratives construct reality, evoke affective experiences, and are performative. For us, narration is a form of social action, in which diverse 'mute' cultural phenomena, such as those defined as heritage, are utilized by language, filled with certain meanings, and turned into symbolic markers of groups, communities, and identities (van Huis et al. 2019). People tell stories about themselves in order to give continuity to their existence. Similarly, narratives are used to express and construct shared and public aspects of belonging and identities (Delanty and Rumford 2005, 51). Narratives connect the self and other people, as well as the past and present. However, narratives are always created within a cultural context and order that will "delimit what can be said, what stories can be told, what will count as meaningful, and what will seem to be nonsensical", as Lawler (2002, 242–243) points out. In this, narratives have political potential as they are powerful in structuring and renewing certain cultural meanings and, conversely, foreclosing others (Lawler 2002, 252).

In this book, cultural heritage is understood as thoroughly political. It is plural, constantly changing, and an object of interpretative disputes and power struggles. It is often used to draw boundaries and to form an 'us' or a unity in a context of diversity or conflict. Politics related to cultural heritage is therefore explored here as discourses and practices of aiming to create a certain order and organize human coexistence (Mouffe 2005). We approach politics as aims and goals included in both official policy-making and less institutionalized modes of meaning-making implemented, by various means, actors, and levels. As the core heritage action of the EU, the EHL is about politics as both an institutional political activity and a soft 'politics of meaning'.

Each of our nine chapters emphasizes certain concepts in the exploration of the core themes. These concepts may play a minor role in other chapters as well, thereby forming links between the discussions in the book. In Part 1, we focus on governance of heritage and dynamic power relations included in it. Chapter 1, scrutinizing the governance of European cultural heritage, draws on the concept of multilevel governance. This refers to the complexity of governance in a globalized and networked world in which states are no longer the only or even the key actors in the processes of governance. Multilevel governance is closely related to participatory governance, which aims to better include people in policy processes at different levels of administration. Chapter 2 shifts the focus of governance to the economics and branding of European cultural heritage. It also introduces the concept of neoliberal belonging, in which the aim of governance is to advance the European dimension of cultural heritage and Europeans' feeling of belonging to Europe and the EU through continuous competition.

In Part 2, we explore the geographical dimension of Europe and approach the construction of European cultural heritage through the concepts of scale and multiscalarity. Chapter 3 shows that scale, and transforming and fluid relations between different scalar levels, shape our discussions of 'the European' and the wide range of interdependent yet hierarchical spatialities included within it. Approaching Europe and European cultural heritage in a critical geopolitical context makes it possible to cross spatial and temporal borders in everyday practices. The concept of border and of crossing borders exist on two levels in our book. First, they occur at the geopolitical, public, or official level that is manifested through diverse physical, regulated, and controlled borders and border crossings. Second, borders occur at the private or subjective level, in which they are intertwined with emotive and affective meanings and diverse forms of imaginative border crossings (e.g. Paasi 2011; Dodds, Kuus, and Sharp 2013). Following Paasi's (2005) views, we perceive borders as social, cultural, and political constructs that are never neutral. In terms of belonging, borders are also a common target of politics. Chapter 4 shows the multiplicity of borders and explores them through the concept of bordering. We understand bordering as a practice constituted by a mixture of drawing, erasing, and crossing borders on various scales in Europe and beyond with a focus on social relations where people, regions, states, and Europe are positioned in relation to shifting borders (Müller 2008, 323).

In Part 3, we focus on engagement in heritage through the concepts of participation, heritage dissonance, and community. In the academic research on cultural heritage since the 1980s, the attention has increasingly shifted from objects and collections to the audiences. More and more, scholars are emphasizing that, in addition to professionals and experts, other individuals and groups should participate in discourses and decision-making related to heritage, so that multiple voices and interpretations can be heard (e.g. Macdonald 2005; Murawska-Muthesius and Piotrowski 2015). We understand participation in cultural heritage as a continuum including a wide range of practices. On one end, just visiting a heritage site can be seen as participation. On the other end, visitors contribute to the core activities of the heritage institutions such as collections and exhibitions and take part in decision-making regarding cultural heritage. Our focus is mainly on what aspects of participation are discussed by practitioners at and visitors to the EHL sites, particularly how visitors' own knowledge production concerning heritage is enabled and perceived.

Kisić has conceptualized heritage dissonance not as a problem in itself, but as including "a tension and quality which testifies to the play among different discourses, and opens the space for a number of diverse actions" (Kisić 2017, 31). For her, dissonant heritage functions as a space to further inclusiveness through dialogue among different people, groups, and communities. Chapter 5 illustrates the idea that European cultural heritage encompasses various dissonances, which both include and exclude. In Chapter 6, we focus on community building in the EHL action and discuss how this is implemented using the concept of the heritage community. This concept, introduced by the Council of Europe in 2005, refers to loose communities of feeling and action, drawn together by the heritage that their members wish to value, sustain, and transmit to the future.

European cultural heritage as embodied, affective practices is examined in Part 4. To explore the temporal and spatial hybridity of heritage, in Chapter 7 we introduce the concept of poly-space, that is, experiences of simultaneity of several narrative, spatial, and temporal layers within heritage. The concept stems from a problem with the general conception of place: it often requires drawing boundaries that distinguish a place from other places or spaces. Yet, in our ethnographic field research at heritage sites, we perceived and experienced the crossing and simultaneity of various spatial, temporal, and social boundaries. The connection of heritage to different temporalities can produce a momentary confusing experience – a bizarre moment – and render the heritage site a place that enables individuals to occupy different and changing positions in space-temporality. For us, this is the core dimension of poly-space: it allows people to feel a connection with other people belonging to those layers and, thus, experience belonging and empathy in different spaces and times. Chapter 8 stems from the affective turn in heritage studies: in it, we explore bodies and practices of embodiment at the EHL sites. The concept of affect is crucial to this exploration. In Chapter 9, we focus on how European cultural heritage and the narratives of Europe told at EHL sites are gendered.

The concluding chapter draws together our main findings and interpretations, to discuss the connections between the four core themes of the book. We end by exploring the meanings given to European cultural heritage in EU heritage policy and how Europe is narrated through cultural heritage within the EHL action. Finally, we demonstrate the interconnected nature of narratives, politics, cultural heritage, and ideas of Europe.

References

Antonsich, M. 2010. "Searching for Belonging – An Analytical Framework." *Geography Compass* 4 (6): 644–659.

Ashworth, G. B. 1994. *Building a New Heritage: Tourism, Culture, and Identity in the New Europe.* London: Routledge.

Ashworth, G., B. Graham, and J. Tunbridge. 2007. *Pluralising Pasts: Heritage, Identity and Place in Multicultural Societies.* London: Pluto Press.

Bendix, R. 2009. "Heritage Between Economy and Politics: An Assessment from the Perspective of Cultural Anthropology." In *Intangible Heritage*, edited by L. Smith and N. Akagawa, 253–269. London: Routledge.

Brubaker, R. 2017. "Between Nationalism and Civilizationism: The European Populist Moment in Comparative Perspective." *Ethnic and Racial Studies* 40 (8): 1191–1226.

Calligaro, O. 2010. "EU Action in the Field of Heritage: A Contribution to the Discussion on the Role of Culture in the European Integration Process." In *Cultures nationales et identite´ communautaire: Un de´fi pour l'Europe?*, edited by M. Beers and J. Raflik, 87–98. Berlin: Peter Lang.

Calligaro, O. 2013. *Negotiating Europe: EU Promotion of Europeanness Since the 1950s.* New York: Palgrave Macmillan.

Clifford, J., and G. Marcus. 1986. *Writing Culture: The Poetics and Politics of Ethnography.* Berkeley: University of California Press.

Clifford, R. 2013. *Commemorating the Holocaust: The Dilemmas of Remembrance in France and Italy.* Oxford: Oxford University Press.

Cooke, P., and L. De Propris. 2011. "A Policy Agenda for EU Smart Growth: The Role of Creative and Cultural Industries." *Policy Studies* 32 (4): 365–375.

Culhane, D., and D. Elliott. 2017. *A Different Kind of Ethnography: Imaginative Practices and Creative Methodologies.* North York: University of Toronto Press.

Čeginskas, V. L. A. 2018. "The Added European Value of Cultural Heritage: The European Heritage Label." *Santander Art and Culture Law Review* 2 (4): 29–50.

De Cesari, C. 2017. "Museums of Europe: Tangles of Memory, Borders, and Race." *Museum Anthropology* 40 (1): 18–35.

De Cesari, C., and A. Kaya, eds. 2019. *European Memory in Populism: (Mis)Representations of Self and Other.* London: Routledge.

De Genova, N. 2018. "The 'Migrant Crisis' as Racial Crisis: Do Black Lives Matter in Europe?" *Ethnic and Racial Studies* 41 (10): 1765–1782.

Delanty, G. 2005. "The Idea of a Cosmopolitan Europe: On the Cultural Significance of Europeanization." *International Review of Sociology* 15 (3): 405–421.

Delanty, G. 2009. "The European Heritage: History, Memory, and Time." In *The Sage Handbook of European Studies*, edited by Chris Rumford, 36–51. London: Sage.

Delanty, G. 2017. *The European Heritage: A Critical Re-interpretation.* London: Routledge.

Delanty, G., and Rumford, C. 2005. *Rethinking Europe: Social Theory and the Implications of Europeanization.* London: Routledge.

Dewey, P. 2010. "Power in European Union Cultural Policy." In *International Cultural Policies and Power*, edited by J. P. Singh, 113–126. New York: Palgrave Macmillan.

Dicks, B. 2000. *Heritage, Place and Community.* Cardiff: University of Wales Press.

Dodds, K., M. Kuus, and J. Sharp, eds. 2013. *The Ashgate Research Companion to Critical Geopolitics.* Ashgate: Farnham.

EC (European Commission). 2010a. "Impact Assessment: Commission Staff Working Document" SEC(2010)197, March 9, 2010. Brussels: European Commission.

EC (European Commission). 2010b "Monuments to Europe." Official website of the European Commission, March 9, 2010. Accessed 16 December 2010. http://ec.europa.eu/news/culture/100309_en.htm.

EC (European Commission). 2014. "Guide for the Implementation of the European Heritage Label." Brussels: European Commission.

EC (European Commission). 2017. "European Heritage Label: 2017 Panel Report." Brussels: European Commission.

EC (European Commission) 2019. "The European Heritage Label." Official website of the European Commission. Accessed 15 August 2019. https://ec.europa.eu/programmes/creative-europe/actions/heritage-label_en.

EP&C (European Parliament and the Council). 2011. "Decision No. 1194/2011/EU of the European Parliament and of the Council of 16 November 2011: Establishing a European Union Action for the European Heritage Label." *Official Journal of the European Union* L 303: 1–9.

Falzon, M-A. 2009. *Multi-sited Ethnography: Theory, Praxis and Locality in Contemporary Social Research.* Farnham: Ashgaet Publishing.

Franks, D., P. Dale, R. Hindmarsh, C. Fellows, M. Buckridge, and P. Cybinski. 2007. "Interdisciplinary Foundations: Reflecting on Interdisciplinarity and Three Decades of Teaching and Research at Griffith University, Australia." *Studies in Higher Education* 32 (2): 167–185.

Giaccardi, E., ed. 2012. *Heritage and Social Media: Understanding Heritage in a Participatory Culture.* London: Routledge.

Gillis, J. R. 1994. "Memory and Identity: The History of a Relationship." In *Commemorations: The Politics of National Identity*, edited by J. Gillis, 3–24. Princeton: Princeton University Press.

Gordon, C. 2010. "Great Expectations: The European Union and Cultural Policy: Fact or Fiction?" *International Journal of Cultural Policy* 16 (2): 101–120.

Graham, B., G. Ashworth, and J. Tunbridge. 2000. *A Geography of Heritage: Power, Culture and Economy.* London: Hodder Arnold,

Graham, B., and P. Howard. 2008. "Heritage and Identity." In *The Ashgate Research Companion to Heritage and Identity*, edited by P. Howard, 1–15. Aldershot: Ashgate.

Harrison, R. 2013a. *Heritage: Critical Approaches.* New York: Routledge.

Harrison, R. 2013b. "Forgetting to Remember, Remembering to Forget: Late Modern Heritage Practices, Sustainability and the 'Crisis' of Accumulation of the Past." *International Journal of Heritage Studies* 19 (6): 579–595.

Hoffmann, S. 1994. "Europe's Identity Crisis Revisited." *Daedalus* 123 (2): 1–23.

Huis, I. van. 2019. "Contesting Cultural Heritage: Decolonizing the Tropenmuseum as an Intervention in the Dutch/European Memory Complex." In *Dissonant Heritages and Memories in Contemporary Europe*, edited by T. Lähdesmäki, L. Passerini, S. Kaasik-Krogerus, and I. van Huis, 215–248. New York: Palgrave Macmillan.

Huis, I. van, S. Kaasik-Krogerus, T. Lähdesmäki, and L. Ellana. 2019. "Introduction: Europe, heritage and memory." In *Dissonant Heritages and Memories in Contemporary Europe*, edited by T. Lähdesmäki, L. Passerini, S. Kaasik-Krogerus, and I. van Huis, 1–20. New York: Palgrave Macmillan.

Huyssen, A. 1993. "Monument and Memory in a Postmodern Age." *The Yale Journal of Criticism* 6 (2): 249–261.

Jakubowski, A., K. Hausler, and F. Fiorentini, eds. 2019. *Cultural Heritage in the European Union.* Leiden: Brill.

Jarzabkowski, P., R. Bednarek, and L. Cabantous. 2015. "Conducting Global Team-Based Ethnography: Methodological Challenges and Practical Methods." *Human Relations* 68 (1): 3–33.

Jenkins, R. 2008. "The Ambiguity of Europe." *European Societies* 10 (2): 153–176.

Kaiser, S. 2014. *The European Heritage Label: A Critical Review of a New EU Policy.* Unpublished MA Thesis, University of Illinois, USA.

Kisić, V. 2017. *Governing Heritage Dissonance: Promises and Realities of Selected Cultural Policies.* Amsterdam: European Cultural Foundation.

Kockel, U., C. Clopot, B. Tjarve, and M. Nic Craith, eds. 2019. *Heritage and Festivals in Europe: Performing Identities.* London: Routledge.

Kockel, U., M. Nic Craith, and J. Frykman. 2012. "Introduction: The Frontiers of Europe and European Ethnology." In *A Companion to the Anthropology of Europe*, edited by U. Kockel, M. Nic Craith, and J. Frykman, 1–10. Oxford: Blackwell Publishing.

Lichterman, P. 2015. "Interpretive Reflexivity in Ethnography." *Ethnography* 18 (1): 35–45.

Lähdesmäki, T. 2012. "Rhetoric of Unity and Cultural Diversity in the Making of European Cultural Identity." *International Journal of Cultural Policy* 18 (1): 59–75.

Lähdesmäki, T. 2014a. "The EU´s Explicit and Implicit Heritage Politics." *European Societies* 16 (3): 401–421.

Lähdesmäki, T. 2014b. "Transnational Heritage in the Making. Strategies for Narrating Cultural Heritage as European in the Intergovernmental Initiative of the European Heritage Label." *Ethnologia Europaea: Journal of European Ethnology* 44 (1): 75–93.

Lähdesmäki, T. 2015. "The Ambiguity of Europe and European Identity in Finnish Populist Political Discourse." *Identities: Global Studies in Culture and Power* 22 (1): 71–87.

Lähdesmäki, T. 2016a. "Politics of Tangibility, Intangibility, and Place in the Making of European Cultural Heritage in EU Heritage Policy." *International Journal of Heritage Studies* 22 (10): 766–780.

Lähdesmäki, T. 2016b. "Comparing Notions on European Cultural Heritage in EU Policy Discourse and Scholarly Discussion." *The International Journal of Interdisciplinary Social Studies: Annual Review* 11: 1–14.

Lähdesmäki, T. 2016c. "Scholarly Discussion as Engineering the Meanings of a European Cultural Heritage." *European Journal of Cultural Studies* 19 (6): 529–546.

Lähdesmäki, T. 2017. "Politics of Affect in the EU Heritage Policy Discourse: An Analysis of Promotional Videos of Sites Awarded with the European Heritage Label." *International Journal of Heritage Studies* 23 (8): 709–722.

Lähdesmäki, T. 2019. "European Culture, History, and Heritage as Political Tools in the Rhetoric of the Finns Party." In *European Memory in Populism: (Mis)Representations of Self and Other*, edited by C. de Cesari and A. Kaya, 191–209. London: Routledge.

Lähdesmäki, T. 2019. "European Quarter in Brussels: Constructing a European Lieu de Mémoire." *International Journal of Heritage Studies*. DOI: 10.1080/13527258.2019.1663237.

Lähdesmäki, T., S. Kaasik-Krogerus, and K. Mäkinen. 2019. "Genealogy of the Concept of Heritage in the European Commission's Policy Discourse." *Contributions to the History of Concepts* 14 (1): 115–139.

Lähdesmäki, T., and K. Mäkinen. 2019. "The 'European Significance' of Heritage: Politics of Scale in EU Heritage Policy Discourse." In *Politics of Scale. New Directions in Critical Heritage Studies*, edited by T. Lähdesmäki, S. Thomas, and Y. Zhu, 36–49. New York: Berghahn's Books.

Lähdesmäki, T., L. Passerini, S. Kaasik-Krogerus, and I. van Huis, eds. 2019. *Dissonant Heritages and Memories in Contemporary Europe*. New York: Palgrave Macmillan.

Lähdesmäki, T., S. Thomas, and Y. Zhu, eds. 2019. *Politics of Scale: New Directions in Critical Heritage Studies*. New York: Berghahn's Books.

Lähdesmäki, T., Y. Zhu, and S. Thomas. 2019. "Introduction: Heritage and Scale." In *Politics of Scale. New Directions in Critical Heritage Studies*, edited by T. Lähdesmäki, S. Thomas and Y. Zhu, 1–18. New York: Berghahn's Books.

Larkham, P. J. 1994. "A New Heritage for a New Europe." In *Building a New Heritage. Tourism, Culture, and Identity in the New Europe*, edited by G. J. Ashworth and P. J. Larkham, 260–273. London: Routledge.

Lawler, S. 2002. "Narrative in Social Research." In *Qualitative Research in Action*, edited by T. May, 242–258. London: Sage.

Littoz-Monnet, A. 2004. *The Construction Process of EU Cultural Policy: Explaining Europeanisation and EU Policy Formation*. Oxford: University of Oxford.

Littoz-Monnet, A. 2007. *The European Union and Culture: Between Economic Regulation and Cultural Policy*. Manchester: Manchester University Press.

Littoz-Monnet, A. 2012. "The EU Politics of Remembrance: Can Europeans Remember Together?" *West European Politics* 35 (5): 1182–1202.

Lowenthal, D. 1996. *The Heritage Crusade and the Spoils of History*. Cambridge: Cambridge University Press.

MacCoshan, A., D. Gluck, J. Betts, J. Clark, S. Lee, and N. Pasquier. 2009. *Support Services to Assist in the Preparation of the Impact Assessment and Ex-ante Evaluation of the European Heritage Label: Final Report*. Birmingham: ECOTEC.

Macdonald, S. 2005. "Accessing Audiences: Visiting Visitor Books." *Museum and Society* 3 (3): 119–136.

Macdonald, S. 2012. "Presencing Europe's Past." In *A Companion to the Anthropology of Europe*, edited by U. Kockell, M. N. Craith, and J. Frykman, 233–252. Oxford: Wiley-Blackwell.

Macdonald, S. 2013. *Memorylands: Heritage and Identity in Europe Today.* London: Routledge.

Mattocks, K. 2017. "Uniting the Nations of Europe? Exploring the European Union's Cultural Policy Agenda." In *The Routledge Handbook of Global Cultural Policy*, edited by V. Durrer, T. Miller, and D. O'Brian, 397–413. London: Routledge.

Ministry of Education, Culture and Sport. 2007. "*Declaration on the Initiative for a European Heritage Label.*" January 25, 2007. Madrid: Ministry of Education, Culture and Sport. Accessed 2 August 2011. http://en.www.mcu.es/patrimonio/MC/PatrimonioEur/docs/en_declaracionMinistrosPatEu.pdf.

Mouffe, C. 2005. *On the Political.* London: Routledge.

Murawska-Muthesius, K., and P. Piotrowski. 2015. *From Museum Critique to the Critical Museum.* London: Routledge.

Müller, M. 2008. "Reconsidering the Concept of Discourse for the Field of Critical Geopolitics: Towards Discourse as Language and Practice." *Political Geography* 27 (3): 322–338.

Näss, H. E. 2009. *A New Agenda? The European Union and Cultural Policy.* London: Alliance Publishing Trust.

Näss, H. E. 2010. "The Ambiguities of Intercultural Dialogue: Critical Perspectives on the European Union's New Agenda for Culture." *Journal of Intercultural Communication* 23. Accessed 15 August 2019. www.immi.se/intercultural/nr23/nass.htm

Navracsics, T. 2017. "The Social Role of Education." Speech given at the High-Level People-to-People Dialogue, 15 November 2017, Shanghai. Accessed 15 August 2019. https://ec.europa.eu/commission/commissioners/2014–2019/navracsics/announcements/social-role-education_en

Niklasson, E. 2016. "Funding Matters: Archaeology and the Political Economy of the Past in the EU." PhD diss., Stockholm University.

Niklasson, E. 2017. "The Janus-Face of European Heritage: Revisiting the Rhetoric of Europe-Making in EU Cultural Politics." *Journal of Social Archaeology* 17 (2): 138–162.

Nora, P. 1998. "The Era of Commemoration." In *Realms of Memory. The Construction of the French Past. Volume III: Symbols*, edited by P. Nora, 609–637. New York: Columbia University Press.

O'Callaghan, C. 2011. "Urban Anxieties and Creative Tensions in the European Capital of Culture 2005: 'It Couldn't Just Be about Cork, Like'." *International Journal of Cultural Policy* 18 (2): 185–204.

Paasi, A. 2005. "The Changing Discourse on Political Boundaries." In *B/ordering Space*, edited by H. van Houtum, O. Kramsch, and W. Zierkofer, 17–31. London: Ashgate.

Paasi, A. 2011. "Borders, Theory and the Challenge of Relational Thinking." In *Interventions on Rethinking "The Border" in Border Studies*, by C. Johnson, R. Jones, A. Paasi, L. Amoore, A. Mountz, M. Salter, and C. Rumford. *Political Geography* 30 (2): 62–63.

Pakier, M., and B. Stråth, eds. 2010. *A European Memory? Contested Histories and the Politics of Remembrance.* New York: Berghahn's Books.

Patel, K. K. 2013. "Introduction." In *The Cultural Politics of Europe: European Capitals of Culture and European Union Since the 1980s*, edited by K. K. Patel, 1–15. London: Routledge.

Prutsch, M. J. 2013. *European Historical Memory: Policies, Challenges and Perspectives*. Directorate-General for Internal Policies. Policy Department B: Structural and Cohesion Policies. Culture and Education. Brussels: European Parliament.

Rosamond, B. 2000. *Theories of European Integration*. Basingstoke: Palgrave.

Roued-Cunliffe, H., and A. Copeland, eds. 2017. *Participatory Heritage*. London: Facet Publishing.

Sassatelli, M. 2006. "The Logic of Europeanizing Cultural Policy." In *Transcultural Europe: Cultural Policy in a Changing Europe*, edited by U. H. Meinhof and A. Triandafyllidou, 24–42. Basingstoke: Palgrave Macmillan.

Sassatelli, M. 2009. *Becoming Europeans. Cultural Identity and Cultural Policies*. New York: Palgrave Macmillan.

Shore, C. 1993. "Inventing the 'People's Europe': Critical Approaches to European Community 'Cultural Policy.'" *Man* 28 (4): 779–800.

Shore, C. 2000. *Building Europe: The Cultural Politics of European Integration*. London: Routledge.

Shore, C. 2006. "'In Uno Plures'(?) EU Cultural Policy and the Governance of Europe." *Cultural Analysis* 5: 7–26.

Smith, L. 2006. *Uses of Heritage*. London: Routledge.

Soja, E. 1996. *Thirdspace: Journeys to Los Angeles and Other Real-and-Imagined Places*. Oxford: Blackwell.

Spiller K., K. Ball, E. Daniel, S. Dibb, M. Meadows, and A. Canhoto. 2015. "Carnivalesque Collaborations: Reflections on 'Doing' Multi-disciplinary Research." *Qualitative Research* 15 (5): 551–567.

TEU (Treaty on European Union). 1992. *Official Journal of the European Communities* C191, 1–112.

Tunbridge, J. E., and G. J. Ashworth. 1996. *Dissonant Heritage: The Management of the Past as a Resource in Conflict*. Chichester: J. Wiley.

Turunen, J. 2019a. "Decolonising European Minds Through Heritage." *International Journal of Heritage Studies*.

Turunen, J. 2019b. "A Geography of Coloniality: Re-Narrating European Integration." In *Dissonant Heritages and Memories in Contemporary Europe*, edited by T. Lähdesmäki, L. Passerini, S. Kaasik-Krogerus, and I. van Huis, 185–214. New York: Palgrave Macmillan.

Turunen, J. (n.d.) "Borderscapes of Europe: Cultural Production of Border Imaginaries through European Heritage." Unpublished manuscript.

Turunen. J., V. L. A. Čeginskas, S. Kaasik-Krogerus, T. Lähdesmäki, and K. Mäkinen. Forthcoming. "Poly-Space: Creating New Concepts through Reflexive Team Ethnography." In *Challenges and Solutions in Ethnographic Research: Ethnography with a Twist*, edited by T. Lähdesmäki, E. Koskinen-Koivisto, V. L. A. Čeginskas, and A.-K. Koistinen. London: Routledge.

Tzaliki, L. 2007. "The Construction of European Identity and Citizenship through Cultural Policy." In *Media and Cultural Policy in the European Union*, edited by K. Sarikakis. *European Studies: A Journal of European Culture, History and Politics* 24: 157–182.

Vejvodová, P. 2014. "The Identitarian Movement – Renewed Idea of Alternative Europe." Paper presented at the ECPR General Conference, Glasgow, U.K., 3–6 September 2014. Accessed 15 August 2019. https://ecpr.eu/Filestore/PaperProposal/ff2ea4db-2b74-4479-8175-7e7e468608ba.pdf

Wasser, J. D. and Bresler, L. 1996. "Working in the Interpretive Zone: Conceptualizing Collaboration in Qualitative Research Teams." *Educational Researcher* 25 (5): 5–15.

Waterton, E., and L. Smith. 2009. "There Is No Such Thing as Heritage." In *Taking Archeology out of Heritage*, edited by E. Waterton and L. Smith, 10–27. Cambridge: Cambridge Scholars Publishing.

Weiss, G. 2002. "Searching for Europe: The Problem of Legitimisation and Representation in Recent Political Speeches on Europe." *Journal of Language and Politics* 1 (1): 59–83.

Whitehead, C., M. Daugbjerg, S. Eckersley, and G. Bozoğlu, eds. 2019a. *Dimensions of Heritage and Memory. Multiple Europes and the Politics of Crisis*. London: Routledge.

Whitehead, C., M. Daugbjerg, S. Eckersley, and G. Bozoğlu. 2019b. "Dimensions of European Heritage and Memory: A Framework Introduction." In *Dimensions of Heritage and Memory. Multiple Europes and the Politics of Crisis*, edited by C. Whitehead, S. Eckersley, M. Daugbjerg, and G. Bozoğlu, 1–25. London: Routledge.

Yuval-Davis, N. 2004. "Borders, Boundaries and the Politics of Belonging." In *Ethnicity, Nationalism and Minority Rights*, edited by S. May, T. Modood, and J. Squires, 214–230. Cambridge: Cambridge University Press.

Yuval-Davis, N. 2006. "Belonging and the Politics of Belonging." *Patterns of Prejudice* 40 (3): 197–214.

Zito, A., S. Eckersley, and S. Turner. 2019. "The Instruments of European Heritage." In *Dimensions of Heritage and Memory: Multiple Europes and the Politics of Crisis*, edited by C. Whitehead, S. Eckersley, M. Daugbjerg, and G. Bozoğlu, 50–71. London: Routledge.

Part I

Governing Europe

Chapter 1

Multilevel and participatory governance of European cultural heritage in the EU

Heritage is not only a policy tool for the EU. It is also developing as a policy sector with its own initiatives, policies, and EU officials, which is increasingly addressed and governed in EU policy-making. The EU heritage sector takes a broad cross-sectoral approach, highlighted in the EU's first major heritage-focused policy document, entitled "Towards an Integrated Approach to Cultural Heritage for Europe" (2014). In it, the European Commission presents "Europe's cultural heritage" as an "irreplaceable repository of knowledge and a valuable resource for economic growth, employment and social cohesion", and sums up how the "heritage sector" is in transformation in today's Europe, as it faces diverse challenges and opportunities (EC 2014, 2–4). Since then, heritage – and cultural heritage in particular – has gained an increasingly strong foothold in EU policy, as the EU's own exercise, Mapping of Cultural Heritage actions in European Union policies, programmes, and activities (2017), indicates. The aim of this mapping was to complement the 2014 document and lay the ground for the European Year of Cultural Heritage in 2018. The EU's integrated approach to cultural heritage and recent heritage initiatives have produced broad cooperation between different directorates-general. As one of our interviewees (E4) from the Commission told us, collaboration was particularly intensive during the European Year of Cultural Heritage and generated unforeseen enthusiasm among EU officials.

The development of cultural heritage as an EU policy sector has not (only) been an EU-led process. Certain member states and European transnational organizations have pushed cultural heritage up the EU agenda. Member states have had a crucial role in this process through their EU presidencies since 2010, when Belgium first brought cultural heritage to the spotlight. The Declaration of Bruges (2010), subtitled "Cultural Heritage: A Resource for Europe: The Benefits of Interaction", highlighted cultural heritage's links with various societal sectors and noted how cultural heritage is still managed and preserved on national and/or regional levels, as the EU has limited regulating powers over culture. The declaration emphasized a closer connection between management and preservation of European cultural heritage "vis-à-vis the developments, challenges and opportunities which present themselves within European policy" and suggested incorporating cultural heritage better into the general policy of the EU (Declaration of Bruges 2010, 2). After Belgium, Lithuanian, Greek, and Italian EU presidencies continued to point out the theme of cultural heritage (EC 2014; also E1 and E4). This interest from member states in cultural heritage and increasing the EU's role in it legitimized the Commission's attempts to strengthen its heritage measures. As one of our interviewees (E1) in the Commission said, "a demand from the member states" "gave us the green light" to continue work on these attempts. The impetus for developing heritage as a policy sector is, thus, based on an interdependent interaction between national policy-makers and EU-level actors. "We needed the presidency to choose it as a priority theme", the same interviewee noted.

Various transnational heritage organizations, such as the European Heritage Heads Forum, the European Heritage Legal Forum, and the European Heritage Alliance 3.3, have also been active in raising the profile of cultural heritage on the EU agenda and guiding approaches to it (EC 2014). Moreover, Europa Nostra, the Council of Europe, ICOMOS, and UNESCO have cooperated and interacted with the Commission on various heritage-related issues, most recently during the European Year of Cultural Heritage (2018). These organizations cannot only be seen as lobbyists but as "a kind of representative of the society that helps us to better tailor our policies", as one of our interviewees (E4) from the Commission states. The international heritage organizations take their own initiative to impact the Commission but are also consulted by the Commission, which blurs their position as lobbyists. At the same time, their interest in advancing EU heritage policies, initiatives, and funding legitimizes the EU's heritage-focused activities. As our interviewee (E4) put it, "you can't create something if there is not a real request, a need from the sector" for EU heritage policy-making. The Commission has also consulted heritage scholars and academics regarding policy-preparation activities.

The emergence of EU heritage policy has an impact on the meanings and interpretations of the subsidiarity principle in the governance of culture. The EU does not aim to replace national or regional heritage administrations or control how member states handle heritage. Instead, EU heritage policy reflects both the member states' and Commission's views that common heritage-related challenges exist in the EU, and that sharable best practices and policy ideas should be dealt with at the EU level.

While heritage has been developed as an EU policy sector, it has also become a part of EU governance. EU heritage initiatives, such as the European Heritage Label (EHL), can be seen as practices of governing both the meanings of heritage and people – both practitioners and audiences of heritage (Lähdesmäki 2016). The EU governance of heritage is also about making Europe. Niklasson (2017, 141) has described its twofold mechanism as "making *things* work for Europe" by emphasizing the European significance of heritage sites, and as "making *people* work through Europe" by facilitating cooperation between heritage practitioners. We recognized this twofold mechanism in our data analysis. Moreover, our research of the EHL action brought forth complex power dynamics related to the EU governance of heritage.

Taking the EHL as a case, this chapter examines how European cultural heritage is governed in the EU. The data include our field research interviews with the EU actors and practitioners working at the EHL sites; our survey of EHL national coordinators; the EHL selection reports; 16 EHL applications; and EU policy documents regarding heritage in the EUR-Lex database. Close reading reveals how the decision- and policy-making, governance, power, interactions, and (hierarchical) positions of different actors are manifested and dealt with in the data. The chapter starts from a discussion on multilevel and participatory governance, followed by an analysis of the multi-directionality of EU governance of heritage. We focus on top-down/bottom-up dynamics, power relations, and tensions in the governance of the EHL and how these interact with its management and meaning-making processes. We also discuss EHL networks and how they function. Finally, we explore how the EHL is used to govern various social, societal, and political issues in Europe.

EU heritage policy – combining multilevel and participatory governance

During the past two decades, policy-making and the use of power in the diverse policy sectors in the EU have been broadly explored in terms of multilevel governance (e.g. Hooghe and Marks 2001a; Bache and Flinders 2004; DeBardeleben and Hurrelmann 2007; Piattoni 2009a; Benz 2010; Nousiainen and Mäkinen 2015). This concept refers to the increasing complexity of governance in a globalized and networked world, in which states are no longer the only or even the key actors in all processes of governance (e.g. Hooghe and Marks 2001a; Piattoni 2009a). In multilevel governance, "supranational, national, regional and local governments are enmeshed in territorially overarching policy networks" (Marks 1993, 402–403). However, multilevel governance also functions horizontally, through interaction between different territorial governing bodies and the increased interdependence between governments and non-governmental actors (Bache and Flinders 2004, 3).

The strengthening of EU integration through the Maastricht Treaty speeded up the emergence of this new mode of governance that is based on interdependent and simultaneous acts of governing at different levels. Through the subsidiarity principle introduced in the Maastricht Treaty, the EU sought to regulate the decision-making and processes of governance between the EU and state levels. The Treaty also recognized the multiple levels of governance inside the EU administration (Mäkinen 2018).

The concept of multilevel governance has been firmly established in EU studies (DeBardeleben and Hurrelmann 2007). Researchers have, however, employed it in research with various emphasis as well as identified different phases of how it has been approached in research and how this variance reflects change in the EU (Stephenson 2013). The political essence of multilevel governance has also been interpreted in various ways. Hooghe and Marks have distinguished two different modes of understanding the concept in relation to the EU. The first mode emphasizes multilevel governance as still relying on a relatively stable architecture of non-intersecting memberships between different levels, while the second one sees the relationships between the various levels as more flexible, intersecting, and variable (Hooghe and Marks 2001b; Marks and Hooghe 2003, 2004). The second mode stresses diverse networks between subnational, national, and supranational actors that blur previous demarcations between centre and periphery, state and society, and the domestic and the international (Piattoni 2009b, 163). This is where the democratic challenge of multilevel governance lies. As Piattoni (2009b, 164) noted, "creation of ad hoc networks, which may include, in a rather haphazard way, legitimately constituted deliberative assemblies together with other public and private, individual and collective actors [...] moves beyond a purely representative democracy". Multilevel governance is twofold in nature: it encourages non-governmental actors to participate in governance processes, thus increasing democracy, but simultaneously restricts democracy by complicating governance through equalizing general-purpose jurisdictions (such as national or regional governments) with special-purpose jurisdictions (such as voluntary associations, civil society organizations, and expert committees), thus creating an odd mix of ruling actors (Piattoni 2009b, 164).

The logic of multilevel governance, based on multi-directional, flexible, intersecting, variable, and networked relationships between diverse actors at different levels, characterizes the EU cultural policy. In the EU, the Directorate General for Education and Culture of the European Commission is the motor of cultural policy development but numerous stakeholders, such as international organizations dealing with culture and institutions based on research and information exchange, are involved in setting its agenda and act in various roles and tasks in its policy-making (Deway 2010, 120). Recently, the EU has started to explicitly emphasize participatory governance in its cultural policy discourses and implement it in practice. Similar to multilevel governance, the aim of participatory governance is to involve in policy-making processes diverse stakeholder networks, connecting different actors from the international to the local level.

The close tie between multilevel and participatory governance is reflected in the recent development of EU heritage policy. The aim of the first EU heritage policy was to "strengthen policy cooperation at different levels" (EC 2014, 3), "support new models of heritage governance" (EC 2014, 3), and "continue developing more participative interpretation and governance models that are better suited to contemporary Europe, through greater involvement of the private sector and civil society" (EC 2014, 7). In the same year, the Council of the European Union adopted its Conclusions on Participatory Governance of Cultural Heritage (CofEU 2014, 2) inviting member states to:

develop multilevel and multi-stakeholder governance frameworks which recognise cultural heritage as a shared resource by strengthening the links between the local, regional, national and European levels of governance of cultural heritage, with due respect to the principle of subsidiarity, so that benefits for people are envisaged at all levels.

Moreover, the Conclusions encouraged the member states to "promote the involvement of relevant stakeholders by ensuring that their participation is possible at all stages of the decision-making process" (CofEU 2014, 2). The EU Ministers for Culture agreed to set up an Open Method of Coordination to identify innovative approaches to multilevel governance of heritage involving the public sector, private stakeholders, and civil society, and to enhance cooperation between different levels of heritage governance (EC 2018a, 12). Work on this started in 2015 when the working group on participatory governance of cultural heritage was established. The group consisted of experts from 26 EU member states and Norway, and it met six times during 2015 and 2016. The group published a full handbook of recommendations for policy-makers and cultural heritage institutions. It saw, however, innovative participatory governance formats for cultural heritage as difficult to identify, believing that citizens' broader participation in diverse processes of heritage was still in its infancy (EC 2018a, 13). On the basis of this work and the legacy of the European Year of Cultural Heritage, the Commission released the European Framework for Action on Cultural Heritage in 2018. This framework draws from participatory governance of heritage emphasizing participation in all its five pillars (EC 2018b).

Some EU policy officers whom we interviewed emphasized the need to promote the participatory governance model more in policy-making and management of heritage, particularly in relation to democracy, which is a core value of the Union. As one EU policy officer (E1) noted, heritage is always "a political choice" and a participatory approach is needed as "citizens must be involved" in making these choices. Another EU policy officer (E6) stated:

[C]ultural heritage […] is one of the main issues in European policy related to the quality of democracy, democracy deficit, and, also inequalities, because access to culture […] is one of the main fields of inequalities. So, cultural rights … it is very important that we can see all those developments, also at the international level. The problem with the European Union – we are very much aware of this – it is an issue of competences. So, it is very, very shy on working on cultural issues, both for ideological reasons, saying that we are not a nation state, so we should not have a top-down approach like it happened through the nineteenth century, or in the twentieth century.

As the quotation indicates, the officer perceives heritage in the context of democracy, democratic deficit, inequality, and cultural rights, but recognizes that the Commission is in a difficult position to intervene in this area without perpetrating the top-down model of governance familiar from nation states. Moreover, the Commission is not seen as having competences regarding cultural issues as they belong to the member states' domain. The same officer (E6) noted that citizens' participation in heritage processes is only possible through the involvement of local communities, as "it is illusory to imagine that there can be a sort of a European consultation where European citizens will give their opinion and then we will come up with something consolidated as European cultural heritage". Due to the numerous actors currently involved in heritage processes in Europe, the same officer saw policy-making and management in this area as "absolutely fragmented".

Participatory governance of heritage broadens involvement in multilevel governance by widening its scalar prism to include civil society and their grass-roots actors. Besides, it serves the EU's more general interests and attempts to increase support for its policies – and ultimately its own legitimacy – among European citizens. Participatory governance is a tool to give EU policy-making and governance structures a more human face by moving the power towards the 'lower' levels and allowing citizens to make an impact. In the EHL, this may be, however, only a tokenism, as the fundamental power to define what European significance of heritage is and to label heritage as European stays at the EU level. The modes and effects of participation within the context of heritage sites at the 'lower' levels are explored in Chapters 5 and 6.

Mingling the levels in multilevel governance of the EHL

The multilevel and participatory governance of heritage in the EU generates governmentality in Foucault's terms – governance produces the subjects it seeks to govern. In the case of the EHL, EU governance creates various actors, such as EHL-awarded institutions, their national coordinators, separate contact points offering practical guidance for EHL sites and applicants, national and European selection panels, and networks of these actors, that all participate in valorizing, fostering, and promoting European cultural heritage. These actors have interdependent roles and dynamic power relations in the processes of governing the EHL.

In its preparation phase, the multilevel structure of the EHL action – particularly the national and European levels – was perceived as important for it to function effectively and democratically. According to the Commission, the European level was needed to "ensure both a robust application of criteria and appropriate prominence for the European dimension, whilst also preserving an equitable distribution of sites across the European Union" (EC 2010a, 6). The Commission thought that an "overseeing body at European level" (EC 2010a, 6) would democratize notions of European cultural heritage by transferring decision-making to a panel of independent experts instead of letting the member states themselves decide on the European dimension of heritage.

However, the importance of "a fair geographical distribution of labels across the EU" (EC 2010b, 12) was also pinpointed when arguing that only national pre-selection panels would ensure balanced representation of all member states in the action and, thus, in the making of European cultural heritage. It was seen as important that an equal number of sites be selected from different member states, even though some countries have "a greater pool of relevant sites than others" (EC 2010b, 12). Thus, the same argument – fair distribution and balanced representation – was used to justify both the European and national panels in the EHL selection process.

The multilevel participatory governance of the EHL seeks to engage local heritage actors in the implementation of the action and creating a European cultural heritage from the bottom up. Their crucial role is emphasized by the European panel, as it noted in one of its selection reports (EC 2015, 5):

> The success of the European Heritage Label relies foremost on the willingness of candidate sites to participate; therefore the list of labelled sites will always be different from a theoretical list prepared by experts based upon scientific criteria. The vitality and attractiveness of the European Heritage Label will depend also on how the labelled sites use this recognition themselves.

What kind of power relations are eventually involved in the governance of the EHL, and how do the power dynamics impact on the functioning of the action and the construction of European cultural heritage? The previous research on EU cultural policy (Sassatelli 2006; Sassatelli 2009, 2015; Calligaro 2013; Lähdesmäki 2014a, 2014b, 2014c) has shown how, in EU cultural initiatives, multilevel governance complicates the power relations between macro- and micro-level actors, mingling top-down and bottom-up dynamics.

In the top-down use of power, EU-level actors select emblematic cultural references as representative of European culture and utilize them as symbols of the EU as a civilizational entity in order to humanize the EU and to bring it closer to its citizens, as Calligaro (2013, 103) noted. Bypassing the national level, the EU may present itself as the defender of regional and local cultural heritage and, thus, "develop a model of integration from below" (Calligaro 2013, 115). Indeed, local actors are expected to be interested in taking the initiative to implement several EU cultural actions, including the EHL. The actors are expected to compete locally for the opportunity to participate in these actions, invest their own funds in running them according to the EU's criteria and regulations, promote the EU's aims for the actions, and make the EU more visible at the local level. In this way, the local actors are drawn into the construction of the EU as a cultural entity. The ideological core of this kind of governance is to produce self-creating and self-maintaining European communality, European narratives, and cultural integration in the EU as a 'bottom-up' process (Lähdesmäki 2014c).

The EU's request for self-governance resonates with the Foucauldian understanding of governmentality. Ettlinger (2011, 538) has suggested that Foucault's idea of governmentality or the "conduct of conduct" should be perceived as a "governance of mentalities". In very concrete ways, EHL sites are conditioned to govern themselves both through and towards Europeanization; the EU asks these sites to make Europe prominent in their institutional narratives, creating content for European heritage. The EU urges local actors to use the action to raise national and international awareness of heritage sites, attracting tourists and increasing the sites' possibilities to receive national or European funding. On the local level, however, the EHL is mainly used to underline the specificity and importance of a site. Further possibilities of the action are so far rather modestly utilized. For instance, neither the EHL nor the Year of European Cultural Heritage 2018 has encouraged broader public debate among European citizens on the European significance of heritage (Čeginskas 2018).

Although the EHL decision includes criteria for European significance and a conceptual framework within which local actors have to narrate the meanings and historical roles of the site, they can interpret the idea of Europe and various abstract concepts related to it, such as "a symbolic European value" or "pan-European nature", from their own perspective – and thus use narrative and discursive power in the creation of European cultural heritage (Lähdesmäki 2014b). However, the European panel decides whether the sites have interpreted the criteria and framework correctly. The Commission's and the European panel's discourse on European significance of heritage creates an 'authorized heritage discourse' or AHD, in Smith's (2006) terms. This concept refers to "a wider social practice that has been specifically developed to regulate the management of heritage, often with reference to strict laws and prescriptive procedures" (Waterton and Smith 2006, 13). In AHD, heritage is not only managed and regulated by formal legislation or prescriptive procedures, "but also by a discursive pressure to conform to what appears to be the normalcy" as Waterton and Smith state (2006, 13). AHD also naturalizes its representation and understanding of the past. Smith (2006) describes how this discourse often promotes a consensus approach to history, smoothing over possible conflicts and social differences. The EU-AHD, through diverse EU heritage policy documents, seeks to find common views on Europe's history, advocate certain European narratives, promote the idea of a common cultural heritage, foster shared values, and emphasize notions of Europe as a cultural entity (Lähdesmäki 2019).

The EU-AHD stresses that European cultural heritage is a matter of substance – not of opinion or viewpoint. Some of our interviewees in the Commission and the European panel used this kind of discourse. One of our interviewees (E7) described the work in the European panel stating: "[The European dimension of heritage] is quite complex" but "it is still fact-based", and "among the experts, it is usually quite clear if it [the site] has it or not".

In this discourse, the definition of the European dimension of heritage is clear and unambiguous as it has a legal basis – the decision on the EHL. As the same interviewee (E7) noted:

> a site could actually express a national dimension [...] pretending it is a European dimension of it [the site], but actually, it's not a European dimension, it's a national dimension, tentatively expressed through a European point of view. But then it wouldn't be a European dimension as expressed in the legal basis.

This interviewee describes the members of the European panel as easily identifying the borders of national, European, and other dimensions of heritage. This interviewee told that the European panel had discussed their interpretations of the European dimension of the site only in a few cases, but the panel has always taken unanimous decisions, although its members come from different backgrounds – and European locations. Another interviewee (E3) describes working in the panel as follows: "having said that when we look at things from all perspectives, which we try to do, in our decision-making, there is a consensus".

In the European panel's reports, European significance seems a more flexible, if not even ambiguous concept: the panel's view of this significance is not definite. Whereas the first rounds of applications in 2013–2015 were judged on clear yes/no parameters, the analysis of the unsuccessful candidates in the 2017 panel report shows that these decisions were taken on a spectrum. The 2017 panel report, for example, states that one rejected candidate site "has European significance, [h]owever, these interesting elements are not well articulated or conveyed in the application" (EC 2017, 32) and that another rejected site "has potential, but the application does not demonstrate the level of European significance required under the criteria" (EC 2017, 33, 41, 42). These evaluations show that the panel pays attention to both the symbolic significance of the site and technicalities regarding how this is narrated and contextualized. However, the final reasoning behind the panel's decisions is neither transparent nor easy to decipher.

A good case of changing symbolic value is the Javorca Church of the Holy Spirit in Slovenia. The site application was unsuccessful in 2014, although it was deemed in the panel report as having "potential to deliver a universal positive message of peace and forgiveness" (EC 2014, 36). In a subsequent, and successful, application, its European significance was described as "clearly articulated" (EC 2017, 12) even though the focus or the overall narrative of the site did not change. Ability to define and set the limits of the discourse of European significance places the panel in a position where it can exercise significant power over the whole action and the processes of constructing notions of European cultural heritage. This shows how rhetoric and discursive choices contribute to the definition of European significance.

Our analysis of 16 EHL applications revealed that the European panel's arguments for the sites' European significance in the selection reports in most cases does not directly follow texts in the applications, in which the local actors describe their sites in terms of European significance. Although taking their primary content from the application, the panel significantly reframes and reinterprets the focus of each site. Since 2015, the application form has had a specific section asking the candidate site to summarize their European significance. Not a single panel report repeated this summary but rather produced a narrative collected from other parts of the application. Naturally, since applications were 18–61 pages long, the summary did not reflect their full complexity. The panel's task is to review the application, filter out meaningful bits, and crystallize and conclude on the European significance of the site in its report. Narrative and wordings from the panel reports are used in the Commission's promotional material the sites, such as short videos on the Commission website and YouTube. As the narratives recognized and introduced in the panel reports are not expected to change, they have a crucial role in the EHL action.

Despite their key role in governing cultural heritage in the EU and negotiating its European dimension, Commission policy officers stated in their interviews that they are not intervening in the definition of European cultural heritage or how it should be treated in the member states. They emphasized that "I'm not here to create an authorized discourse on cultural heritage" (E6), "I am not going to tell, and nobody here in Brussels is going to tell Italians [...] or Germans, how they should treat their heritage" (E1), or "we do not impose, we do not decide from the top down" (E4). The officers' view that they are positioned outside power structures reflects the bottom-up ideals of participatory and multilevel governance. In these ideals, the EU policy-making is based on bottom-up suggestions, requests, and initiatives by national, regional, and local actors whose interest in impacting issues at the European level legitimizes the EU actors' governing actions. The officers' view can also be explained by the logic of multilevel governance in general: the use of power is hidden, as it is being used simultaneously by several actors in various ways at various levels. As policy-making in the Commission is profoundly hierarchical, the EU officials may perceive that the power is always somewhere else. As reflected in one of our interviews, "I'm really a policy officer [...], so I know that I will have no influence at all on general European policies" (E6). The EC policy officers are not, however, powerless or 'outside' power structures in heritage-related matters. Their use of power is remarkable in policy-making processes, such as regulations and procedures, and the conceptual choices and discourses involved.

The mingling of bottom-up and top-down power dynamics in the EHL action is also apparent at the level of individual EHL sites, who are supposed to be the core creators of the European dimension and narratives of cultural heritage at the EHL sites. While the EHL panel reports form the basis of the narrative and discursive layer of the action, the action's concrete impact on the narratives and discourses at the sites may be modest. Our interviewees working at EHL sites commonly told us that receiving the EHL award has not had any noticeable impact on their routines. Only two (P24 and P26) of 37 practitioners interviewed recognized some impact. However, all of them did not associate this with any negative effects but considered receiving the EHL as a positive signal. Whether related to the EHL action or not, many of the EHL sites have developed their exhibitions and activities after receiving the Label. Moreover, our interviews and observations revealed that many of the EHL sites started to rethink the meaning and relevance of cultural heritage and approach it more broadly – also in a specific European context and in terms of intangible cultural heritage – after receiving the Label.

In fact, this kind of concrete development of sites is a criterion in the EHL action. In the application, sites have to introduce a "project" to be implemented at the site after being awarded. The project has to include: "raising awareness of the European significance of the site", "organizing educational activities, especially for young people, which increase the understanding of the common history of Europe and of its shared yet diverse heritage and which strengthen the sense of belonging to a common space", "promoting multilingualism", "taking part in the activities of networks of sites awarded the label", and "raising the profile and attractiveness of the site on a European scale" (EP&C 2011, 4). In terms of participatory governance, these requirements seek to Europeanize the sites by top-down regulations that local actors are expected to implement, from the bottom up and (seemingly) on their own initiative. Our field research demonstrated how EHL sites implement these projects in different ways, as many of them are struggling with financial challenges (Čeginskas 2019). The activities organized at the sites commonly focus on their own themes, events, and partnerships, which they already had before the Label.

Although the key focus of the EHL action is on the European significance of heritage and local level as its promoters, the EU-AHD nevertheless constantly refers to and brings out the national scale in the construction of European cultural heritage (see also Abélés 2000; Kaiser et al. 2014; De Cesari 2017). The EHL sites are pre-selected at the national level, followed by the final selection at the EU level. Thus, the national actors are the crucial gatekeepers of European cultural heritage in this process. Even though the action emphasizes overcoming the national meanings of heritage and the European narratives of it, 'the national', either as an operational arena, a building block, or an antithesis of 'the European', is closely intertwined in the EHL action.

Since the launch of the EHL as an intergovernmental initiative in 2007, one of its main goals has been to "reinforce cooperation between European countries" (European Heritage Committee 2007). Although the EHL action emphasizes the importance of active transnational cooperation, it is determined by the national scale: transregional, translocal, or extra-European cooperation do not belong to the explicit discourse or aims of the action. The territorial emphasis is on local sites in distinct European countries. EHL candidates are expected to be either single sites in a particular member state, a composite of "national thematic sites" within one country, or "transnational sites", that is, "the case of sites which are located in different Member States but focus on one specific theme" or "the case of a site located on the territory of at least two Member States" (EP&C 2011, 2). Even the transnational dimension is highlighted in the policy discourse, its implementation is still closely affixed to states. Yet, intention is to cross borders through cooperation between heritage actors from different member states and by interpreting heritage in a transnational European framework.

The national coordinators and contact points have a key role in the governance of the EHL action, although their activeness differs greatly between the member states. While some of our interviewees at EHL sites mentioned communicating actively with their national coordinators, some were not even aware that they had one. Rather than hoping for more involvement from national coordinators, these heritage practitioners wished that the Commission would provide clearer practical coordination and financial support to relieve their strain on human resources and time spent on promoting the European significance of heritage. In other words, they expect clearer governance of the EHL. The core function of the national coordinators, commonly representing Cultural Ministries or other high-level cultural administration bodies, is to govern the action at the national level and organize the national pre-selection of the EHL sites. These coordinators appoint national EHL contact points, commonly representing highest national heritage authorities, to offer practical guidance to the EHL sites. The national coordinators and contact points are examples of the EU policy 'translators' or 'communicators' that the EU cultural actions typically produce below the EU level (see also Niklasson 2016, 267). Through them, the EHL becomes part of a national cultural administration. Our survey revealed that some national coordinators see implementing the Commission's regulations as their core (only) role, while others also aim to add to these regulations further criteria to improve the quality of EHL applications and impact on the thematic content at the sites.

EHL sites are a part of their national and regional cultural and heritage administration. These administrative structures – and financing logic related to them – impact on their activities. Some practitioners (P19 and P17) working at EHL sites in Central and East European countries told us how they consult their national administration (either the Ministry of Culture or other governmental offices) about how the site can or should interpret and communicate history to its visitors, or even ask for its approval on these issues. The national coordinator of eight of the eleven sites included in our field research had suggested the site apply for the EHL, a request which was probably difficult for the sites to refuse.

Naturally, national coordinators' key interest is in 'the national'. In the intergovernmental phase, the European agenda of the EHL initiative was often nationalized in its implementation, particularly in Central and East European countries (Lähdesmäki 2014a). This kind of nationalization occurs in other transnational heritage schemes as well: UNESCO World Heritage listing is based on the national heritage actors and states, who implement the UNESCO's heritage policies within a national framework (Bendix, Eggert, and Peselmann 2012). As Bortolotto (2012, 277) has noticed, each state translates key terms of the UNESCO Convention in different ways, resulting in "domestication of global standards". Similar domestication or nationalization of a supranational agenda occurs within the EHL action. One of our interviewees (P24) from the European Solidarity Centre described this process as follows:

> It came from the Ministry of Culture. It was not an idea of one party, […] the idea was to create the Polish narrative. To show that […] European integration is not something that is only connected to Roman treaties or to Western European consolidation after the Second World War. It is something that is connected also to the process of civic emancipation here, and that Poland is participating in creating modern democracy now for hundreds of years. So the idea was not only to promote one place, the idea was to prepare, I think, four Polish sites that are creating, I would say, a long story, important story of Polish European democracy. So, the first site is the Lublin Union, the second was the Polish Constitution, and the third was the European Solidarity Centre and the shipyard.

The national and European interests and interpretations within the EHL could also include tensions. This concretized particularly in the case of the Great Guild Hall, the first Estonian EHL site in Tallinn. This Gothic building hosts the Estonian History Museum, and its narrative as an EHL is based on two elements: the Hanseatic League whose members used the building during medieval times and the history of Estonians as a small nation occupied and ruled by various European powers. Particularly the latter element raised concerns already in the European panel's selection report. In the first monitoring of the EHL action, the European panel recommended that the site "explain the European significance of the site more robustly" (EC 2016, 15). Our interviews with practitioners at the Great Guild Hall revealed how their understandings of European significance of heritage differed from that of the panel members. The interviewed practitioners considered it odd that the narration of Estonian history could not be simultaneously taken as a European narrative. One interviewed practitioner noted that the criticism created a strange feeling that "we take it [European cultural heritage] as something natural and given". The criticism also triggered antagonism between small (the periphery) and big (the core) European countries. The same interviewee emphasized the Estonian narrative at the site by pointing out how "for a small state the issues, such as our own language and own state, are probably more important than for bigger states where they do not need to everyday think whether they are maltreated or not".

Understandings of the European dimension of heritage do not only differ on different administrative levels of the EHL, but also within the European Commission. The views of the EU actors diverged particularly regarding possible tensions between different dimensions of heritage. Some saw that cultural heritage as such and the ways promoting it may create controversies, whereas others emphasized the positive effects of cultural heritage on societal cohesion. While all interviewed EU actors agreed on the need to tackle a narrow-minded nationalistic promotion of cultural heritage, none of them mentioned the discourse of considering national identities as a challenge for the EU – as it was explicitly stated in the Commission's first press release of the EHL action (EC 2010b). For the interviewees, 'the national' was a central framework to explain their personal views and experiences of cultural heritage. Without being asked, all of them mentioned their nationality and heritage examples from their country of origin. This shows that the national framework continues to dominate public discourse heritage, and its effect on people and their sense of their everyday life should not be underrated.

In general, the interviewed EU policy officers' approach to the concept of cultural heritage commonly reflected that of recent heritage research. For them, cultural heritage was a construct, a process, and included diverse meanings. Some reflected critically on what and how heritage should be dealt with in Europe and in EU policy. As one (E6) noted:

> I think it's a political and moral obligation of the European Union to support critical approaches of cultural heritage. Otherwise, it will be completely used – populated – at museums, by populists. It can start from the best will of different sides, but political populists, nationalists, ethnic tensions, racists, and many other political opinions turn to worse interpretations of the past.

While Commission policy officers envisaged in the interviews how the EU heritage policies could be developed and offered both personal and critical views on cultural heritage and its European dimension, the interviewees directly participating in the work of the European panel were more hesitant to express their personal views or experiences, or to talk about heritage policies beyond the legal framework of the EHL. These actors were reluctant to comment on the political or ideological goals of the action and rather emphasized its function as fostering cultural heritage as such. This reluctance may be affected by the hierarchical structure of EU policy-making. As these interviewees only participated in implementing the EHL action at the EU level, they might not have considered themselves competent to comment beyond their mandate. As one of these interviewees (E7) noted when asked about current challenges in Europe: "It's not my position as an administrator to give my own very personal opinion". The European panel members are not EU policy-makers but heritage experts. This may have affected their responses on the EHL's political, ideological, and societal connections. As our interviewed panel member (E3) said:

> You can't ask cultural heritage to be the medicine for all the diseases. That's not possible. It's true that you see some quotes about job creation or the attractiveness of regions. It's very high in the minds of people. You have very good reports on those kinds of things […] in fact, all this commodification, using cultural heritage for something else, instead of putting people at the core, may not be a good thing. […] Would it help if some politicians would be more aware of how important cultural heritage is for people? Certainly. Would it be useful if politicians would realize that it's not only about commodification? Yes.

In sum, our interview data illustrates how the EHL action is implemented rather independently at different levels. At all levels, our interviewees emphasize that actors above or below them are not intervening in their work, nor do they themselves seek to do so for actors at other levels. In practice, however, all persons involved in the EHL action are closely intertwined in interactive relationships and form loosely organized networks.

Network Europe and hierarchies in the networked EHL action

Multilevel and participatory governance of the EHL action creates diverse relationships between actors included in the processes of governance. These relationships form formal and informal networks through which governance may occur. Network governance is a concept scholars use to describe governance in today's interconnected world (DeBardeleben and Hurrelmann 2007; Sørensen and Torfing 2007; Torfing, Peters, Pierre, and Sørensen 2012). It stems from the notion that "authority structures are often located outside of the machinery of government and are defined by a web of connections of which states are only one part" (DeBardeleben and Hurrelmann 2007, 3). This concept resonates with the notion of a Network Europe (Niklasson 2016) based on deterritorialized relationships between different kinds of people, places, and things. In Network Europe, the EU is just one actor amid other transnational, national, and subnational actors. As Niklasson (2016, 246) demonstrates in her study of EU archaeology and heritage politics, for a long time archaeologists and heritage practitioners have formed a networked cluster of close collaboration between national heritage boards, actors involved in EU-level heritage-related campaigns and actions, and EU-funded cooperation platforms in research and culture.

Similar to many other EU initiatives, networking is a key goal and core mode of action in the EHL, as the decision of the action emphasizes (EP&C 2011, 2, 4, 7). The only concrete measure which the Commission takes to further this is organizing the annual networking meetings for site representatives and for national coordinators. During the first years of the action, separate meetings keep different-level actors apart. The meetings are also closed to outsiders – the organizers clearly emphasized this to our research team when we sought permission to observe some meetings as part of our field research. However, our team gained insights into these meetings from some of their participants from responses to the survey of national coordinators and interviews with site representatives.

The aim of the EHL networking meetings is to increase interaction between the sites and thereafter to enhance the coherence of the EHL action as a bottom-up process. Although our interviewed practitioners had various experiences of these meetings – including scepticism about their usefulness – the meetings can be also seen as proactive. Even if attendees may have had nothing in common apart from being employed at a site that has received the EHL, the annual meetings forged connections between them. Feeding bottom-up networking these meetings may create new collective actors in the EU's multilevel governance of heritage. Indeed, the networking meetings for EHL site representatives have led to action, such as joint funding proposals for the Commission to support further networking between sites. The meetings have also strengthened personal relationships and bilateral or multilateral links between some participants, leading to further cooperation plans. While the site representatives have not necessarily had any previous connections, the national coordinators may have cooperated before the EHL. Particularly in smaller countries, the same officers from the ministries of culture or national heritage agencies manage several international heritage programmes, and also meet each other in relation to these initiatives.

As a mode of governing the EHL action, these networking meetings involve various challenges. The Commission pays the travel costs for one representative from each site to attend. Our interviews show how the meetings often increase the networking of the persons who participate in them, while some other practitioners at the sites may not even know that the meetings take place. The interviewed practitioners commonly saw that the substantial and administrative differences between the sites, as well as the lack of additional funding and human resources, hindered their cooperation. The Commission's networking activities have also created a hierarchy of EHL sites, as some – typically those with the largest resources – have become more active in the EHL network. Our interviewees commonly recognize these sites as network leaders and implicitly, others are seen as passive followers. As one practitioner (P22) stated:

> There are crowd pullers in this network. The expectations towards them are pretty high. There are sites who cling a bit tighter to these crowd pullers, and then there are the absolutely passive ones. Probably this is how it's supposed to be. There always must be some who […] take the lead and organize, others, who help actively, and yet again other ones who just

simply go along. I mean the ones, who are like "yeah, it's okay, just do as you like, it's fine for us". It's the same here. Only that of course here even the crowd pullers don't always agree about things, but that's also like that. And it also makes it a bit difficult that there is no clear assignment and no clear distribution of roles.

The interviewees commonly mention the Imperial Palace in Vienna, Austria, Mundaneum in Mons, Belgium, Lieu d'Europe in Strasbourg, France, and Residencia de Estudiantes in Madrid, Spain as the leaders of the EHL network (see Chapter 2). While some of the sites considered as passive were happy to let them take the lead, some others saw that the imbalance of resources forced the sites into different positions in the network hierarchy. As one our interviewed practitioners (P35) noted: "we aren't all in the same conditions, some of the teams of the other sites have one project team associated to the Label with more people than I have in all the regional department". The active sites have been motivated particularly by the agency that a formal network might give them. As one practitioner from a 'leading' site (P30) said, "an official network [...] would put a frame on it [the EHL], if we had a structure, if we are officially recognized as an EHL network".

Even though the sites experienced various challenges in networking, all of them were networked and cooperated actively with various other international, national, regional, and local stakeholders – including heritage and history organizations, museums, cultural institutions, civil organizations, non-governmental organizations (NGOs), universities, schools, and artists' associations. Many of our interviewees saw other networks as more substantially relevant to their work. As one (P15) noted,

> I met the director of the European Institute for the Cultural Routes, and actually, I was in a kind of dilemma, thinking okay, maybe [...] it has more sense for us to work on a thematic route than to do things in this EHL network.

The EHL as an instrument for governing social, societal, and political issues

Cultural policy is not the only way in which the EU deals with cultural heritage. Indeed, cultural heritage is referred to in EU documents dealing with regional politics, social cohesion, agriculture, and sources of livelihood in rural areas, fishery and environment of coastal areas, environmental politics, sustainable development, EU foreign policy and external relations, cooperation with third countries, social well-being, economy, employment, tourism, research, education, and digitalization (see Sassatelli 2009; Vos 2011; Calligaro 2013; Niklasson 2016, 2017; Lähdesmäki, Kaasik-Krogerus, and Mäkinen 2019). A closer analysis of EU documents indicates that cultural heritage can be used to argue and justify a broad spectrum of EU policy activities (Lähdesmäki, Kaasik-Krogerus, and Mäkinen 2019).

EU heritage policy and heritage initiatives include diverse social, societal, and political goals. Lähdesmäki (2014b) has identified five core focuses in these goals: enhancing cohesion and European integration (see Calligaro 2013, 79); increasing the visibility of the EU and its branding through heritage; educating young people to become pro-European; extending EU governance to culture and heritage; and supporting economic growth through tourism, creative industries, and regional development. This social emphasis in the EU heritage policy resonates with the Council of Europe's Faro Convention (Convention on the Value of Cultural Heritage for Society) launched in 2005. The Council of Europe has a major influence on the development and conceptualization of EU policy discourse. The Council's rhetorical formulations and areas of interest have often been absorbed into EU policy discourse and goals with only a short delay, particularly in questions related to culture (Sassatelli 2009, 43; Patel 2013, 6; Lähdesmäki 2019). One reason for this delay is the cyclic way in which EU policy-making functions. The Commission runs its programmes within five- to seven-year frameworks. Thus, the policy goals that the Commission sets in the framework preparation phase are implemented and make an impact much later. The frameworks direct the discourse and approach to heritage which Commission policy officers take. As one policy officer (E6) said in interview:

> So what was the main issue of the current Commission, and partly of the previous one? It was growth and jobs. It was very important, but you couldn't talk about culture and cultural heritage without trying to explain why they are resources and how they contribute to growth and jobs.

According to this officer (E6), "it is a very rigid system, it's almost like communist planned economies".

Many of our interviewed practitioners had adopted the Commission's policy discourse on the social, societal, political, and economic benefits of heritage. Moreover, the EHL sites have been involved in various social projects and practiced advocacy work in their local communities.

Participation in the EHL action means becoming a part of the EU's political discourse and showcase in field of heritage. The EU-AHD closely links the European dimension of heritage, the institutional history of the EU, and the European integration process, as they are included in the EU's criteria for the Label. Only one interviewed practitioner was critical of this emphasis on the EU's institutional history and promoting the EU. Instead, site representatives often repeated the discourses on Europe and 'the European' that are promoted in EU policy rhetoric. Recurring elements in these discourses include a narrative of the EU as a peace project, lists of values promoted by the EU, emphasis on diversity and interaction of diverse people, and ideas of openness and borderlessness. One our interviewed practitioners (P23) responded to our question of how European significance of heritage could be understood as follows:

> Yeah, [it is] basically the values which unite us: equality, freedom of speech, freedom of the press, tolerance, basically everything that has something to do with democracy, after all. That's what I view as European values, which unite us all, despite all differences in our national characters. But together we agreed on these things, we have equality, we have peace, we have democracy.

The interviewees commonly see their sites as promoters of respect for diversity, tolerance, and openness in the surrounding societies or communities that some of the interviewees described as intolerant, narrow-minded, or withdrawn. Indeed, in populist, nationalist, and conservative political contexts, the EHL sites may even appear too pro-European or EU-minded. This tension has characterized the European Solidarity Centre in Gdańsk, Poland. Some of our interviewees at the Centre noted that even its name has been experienced politically difficult in today's Poland – and not Polish enough. This exemplifies the political border-making and geopolitics of the EHL, discussed in more depth in the next section.

References

Abélès, M. 2000. "Virtual Europe." In *An Anthropology of the European Union: Building, Imagining and Experiencing the New Europe*, edited by I. Bellier and T.M. Wilson, 31–52. Oxford: Berg.

Bache, I., and M. Flinders. 2004. "Themes and Issues in Multi-Level Governance". In *Multi-Level Governance*, edited by I. Bache and M. Flinders, 1–14. Oxford: Oxford University Press.

Bendix, R. F., A. Eggert, and A. Peselmann. 2012. "Introduction: Heritage Regimes and the State." In *Heritage Regimes and the State*, edited by R. F. Bendix, A. Eggert, and A. Peselmann, 11–20. Göttingen Studies in Cultural Property 6. Göttingen: Universitätsverlag Göttingen.

Benz, A. 2010. "The European Union as a Loosely Coupled Multi-Level System." In *Handbook on Multi-Level Governance*, edited by H. Enderlein, S. Wälti, and M. Zürn, 214–226. Cheltenham: Edward Elgar.

Bortolotto, C. 2012. "The French Inventory of Intangible Cultural Heritage: Domesticating a Global Paradigm into French Heritage Regime." In *Heritage Regimes and the State*, edited by R. F. Bendix, A. Eggert, and A. Peselmann, 265–282. Göttingen Studies in Cultural Property 6. Göttingen: Universitätsverlag Göttingen,

Calligaro, O. 2013. *Negotiating Europe: The EU Promotion of Europeanness since the 1950s*. New York: Palgrave Macmillan.

Čeginskas, V. L. A. 2018. "The Added European Value of Cultural Heritage: The European Heritage Label". *Santander Art and Culture Law Review* 21 (4): 29–50.

Čeginskas, V. L. A. 2019. "The Challenges in Creating Visibility of European Cultural Heritage: A Case Study of the European Heritage Label." *Ethnologia Fennica* 46: 109–134.

CofEU (Council of the European Union). 2014. Council Conclusions on Participatory Governance of Cultural Heritage. 2014/C 463/01. *Official Journal of the European Union* C 463: 1–3.

DeBardeleben, J., and A. Hurrelmann. 2007. "Introduction." In *Democratic Dilemmas of Multilevel Governance: Legitimacy, Representation and Accountability in the European Union*, edited by J. DeBardeleben and A. Hurrelmann, 11–14. Berlin: Springer.

De Cesari, C. 2017. "Museums of Europe: Tangles of Memory, Borders and Race." *Museum Anthropology* 40 (1): 18–35.

Declaration of Bruges. 2010. Cultural Heritage: "A Resource for Europe: The Benefits of Interaction." 9 December 2010. Bruges: Belgium's EU Presidency. Accessed 15 August 2019. http://old.europanostra.org/UPLOADS/FILS/Declaration-of-Bruges2010-eng.pdf.

Deway, P. 2010. "Power in European Union Cultural Policy." In *International Cultural Policies and Power*, edited by P. Singh, 113–126. New York: Palgrave Macmillan.

EC (European Commission). 2010a. *"Proposal for a Decision of the European Parliament and of the Council Establishing a European Union Action for the European Heritage Label."* COM(2010)76 final, 2010/0044 (COD). Brussels: European Commission.

EC (European Commission). 2010b. *"Impact Assessment: Commission Staff Working Document"* SEC(2010)197, March 9, 2010. Brussels: European Commission.

EC (European Commission). 2014. *"Communication from the Commission to the European Parliament, the Council, the European Economic and Social Committee and the Committee of the Regions: Towards an Integrated Approach to Cultural Heritage for Europe."* COM(2014) 477 final, 22 July 2014. Brussels: European Commission.

EC (European Commission). 2014. *"European Heritage Label: 2014 Panel Report."* Brussels: European Commission.

EC (European Commission). 2015. *"European Heritage Label: 2015 Panel Report."* Brussels: European Commission.

EC (European Commission). 2016. *"European Heritage Label: Panel Report on Monitoring".* 19 December 2016. Brussels: European Commission.

EC (European Commission). 2017. *"European Heritage Label: 2017 Panel Report."* Brussels: European Commission.

EC (European Commission). 2017 [First Edition 2014]. *"Mapping of Cultural Heritage Actions in European Union Policies, Programmes and Activities."* Brussels: European Commission.

EC (European Commission). 2018a. *"Participatory Governance of Cultural Heritage: Report of THE OMC (Open Method of Coordination) Working Group of Member States' Experts."* Brussels: European Commission.

EC (European Commission). 2018b. *Commission Staff Working Document: European Framework for Action on Cultural Heritage.* SWD(2018) 491 final, 5 December 2018. Brussels: European Commission.

European Heritage Committee. 2007. *"The European Heritage Label: Statement on the European Heritage Label Initiative, 13 February 2007."* Madrid: Ministry of Education, Culture and Sport. Accessed 12 April 2013. http://en.www.mcu.es/patrimonio/MC/PatrimonioEur/RedSitios.html

EP&C (European Parliament and the Council). 2011. "Decision No. 1194/2011/EU of the European Parliament and of the Council of 16 November 2011 Establishing a European Union Action for the European Heritage Label." *Official Journal of the European Union*, L 303: 1–9.

Ettlinger, N. 2011. "Governmentality as Epistemology." *Annals of the Association of American Geographers* 101 (3): 537–560.

Hooghe, L., and G. Marks. 2001a. *Multi-Level Governance and European Integration*. Lanham, MD: Rowman and Littlefield.

Hooghe, L., and G. Marks. 2001b. "Types of Multi-Level Governance." *European Integration Online Papers* 5 (11). Accessed 15 August 2019. https://dx.doi.org/10.2139/ssrn.302786

Kaiser, W., S. Krankenhangen, and K. Poehls. 2014. *Exhibiting Europe in Museums: Transnational Networks, Collections, Narratives and Representation*. New York: Berghan Books.

Lähdesmäki, T. 2014a. "Transnational Heritage in the Making: Strategies for Narrating Cultural Heritage as European in the Intergovernmental Initiative of the European Heritage Label." *Ethnologica Europaea* 44 (1): 75–93.

Lähdesmäki, T. 2014b. "The EU's Explicit and Implicit Heritage Politics." *European Societies* 16 (3): 401–421.

Lähdesmäki, T. 2014c. *Identity Politics in the European Capital of Culture Initiative*. Joensuu: University of Eastern Finland.

Lähdesmäki, T. 2016. "Politics of Tangibility, Intangibility, and Place in the Making of European Cultural Heritage in EU Heritage Policy." *International Journal of Heritage Studies* 22 (10): 766–780.

Lähdesmäki, T. 2019. "Conflicts and Reconciliation in Postmillennial Heritage Policy Discourses of the Council of Europe and the European Union." In *Dissonant Heritages and Memories in Contemporary Europe*, edited by T. Lähdesmäki, L. Passerini, S. Kaasik-Krogerus, and I. van Huis, 25–50. New York: Palgrave Macmillan.

Lähdesmäki, T., S. Kaasik-Krogerus, and K. Mäkinen. 2019. "Genealogy of the Concept of Heritage in the European Commission's Policy Discourse." *Contributions to the History of Concepts* 14 (1): 115–139.

Mäkinen, K. 2018. "Moniselitteinen Monitasohallinta." In *Politiikan tulkinta: Juhlakirja Marja Keräselle*, edited by H-M. Kivistö, K. Kuokkanen, M. Weide, and J. Virtanen, 275–286. Jyväskylä: SoPhi.

Marks, G. 1993. "Structural Policy and Multilevel Governance in the EC." In *The State of the European Community, Vol. 2: The Maastricht Debates and Beyond*, edited by A. Cafruny and G. Rosenthal, 391–410. Boulder, CO: Lynne Riener.

Marks, G., and L. Hooghe. 2003. "Unravelling the Central State, But How? Types of Multi-Level Governance." *American Political Science Review* 97 (2): 233–243.

Marks, G., and L. Hooghe. 2004. "Contrasting Visions of Multi-Level Governance". In *Multi-Level Governance*, edited by I. Bache and M. Flinders, 15–30. Oxford: Oxford University Press.

Niklasson, E. 2016. "Funding Matters: Archaeology and the Political Economy of the Past in the EU." PhD diss., University of Stockholm.

Niklasson, E. 2017. "The Janus-Face of European Heritage: Revisiting the Rhetoric of Europe-Making in EU Cultural Politics." *Journal of Social Archaeology* 17 (2): 138–162.

Nousiainen, M., and K. Mäkinen. 2015. "Multilevel Governance and Participation: Interpreting Democracy in EU-Programmes." *European Politics and Society* 16 (2): 208–223.

Patel, K. K. 2013. "Introduction." In *The Cultural Politics of Europe: European Capitals of Culture and European Union Since the 1980s*, edited by K.K. Patel, 1–15. London: Routledge.

Piattoni, S. 2009a. *The Theory of Multi-Level Governance: Conceptual, Empirical and Normative Challenges*. Oxford: Oxford University Press.

Piattoni, S. 2009b. "Multi-Level Governance: A Historical and Conceptual Analysis." *European Integration* 31 (2): 163–180.

Sassatelli, M. 2006. "The Logic of Europeanizing Cultural Policy." In *Transcultural Europe. Cultural Policy in a Changing Europe*, edited by U.H. Meinhof and A. Triandafyllidou, 24–42. Basingstoke: Palgrave MacMillian.

Sassatelli, M. 2009. *Becoming Europeans: Cultural Identity and Cultural Policies*. New York: Palgrave Macmillan.

Sassatelli, M. 2015. "Narratives of European Identity." In *European Cinema and Television: Cultural Policy and Everyday Life*, edited by I. Bondebjerg, E. Novrup Redvall, and A. Higson, 25–42. Basingstoke: Palgrave Macmillan.

Smith, L. 2006. *Uses of Heritage*. London: Routledge.

Sørensen, E., and J. Torfing. 2007. *Theories of Democratic Network Governance*. New York: Palgrave Macmillan.

Stephenson, P. 2013. "Twenty Years of Multi-Level Governance: 'Where Does It Come From? What Is It? Where Is It Going?'" *Journal of European Public Policy* 20 (6): 817–837.

Torfing, J., G. Peters, J. Pierre, and E. Sørensen. 2012. *Interactive Governance: Advancing the Paradigm*. Oxford: Oxford University Press.

Turunen, J. 2019. "A Geography of Coloniality: Re-Narrating European Integration." In *Dissonant Heritages and Memories in Contemporary Europe*, edited by T. Lähdesmäki, L. Passerini, S. Kaasik-Krogerus, and I. van Huis, 185–214. New York: Palgrave Macmillan.

Vos, C. 2011. "Negotiating Serbia's Europeanness: On the Formation and Appropriation of European Heritage Policy in Serbia." *History and Anthropology* 22 (2): 22–242.

Waterton, E., and L. Smith. 2006. "There Is No Such Thing as Heritage." In *Taking Archeology Out of Heritage*, edited by E. Waterton and L. Smith, 10–27. Cambridge: Cambridge Scholars Publishing.

Chapter 2

Economics and branding European cultural heritage

As noted in the introduction, EU funding is less well developed for culture than for other EU policy sectors, yet the EU has ambitious aims for its cultural programmes, initiatives, and actions. However, EU funding for culture benefits various activities that would otherwise be difficult to implement, particularly by smaller cultural organizations and actors. EU funding facilitates various types of cultural activity, such as cross-border cultural cooperation, mobility of cultural actors between European countries, and activities related to transnational themes. The Union's important role in facilitating cultural border-crossing and transnational interaction was also emphasized by our interviewees from the European Commission. As one of the interviewed policy officers (E1) stated: "culture is always small in terms of budget and so on but without us, there would be almost no cross-border activity. [...] But that's exactly where we step in. In a sense, we are absolutely necessary". The EU funding for transnational interaction does not, however, automatically benefit those cultural actors who might need it most – the small-scale creators of culture outside cultural institutions and other established areas of cultural production. Competition for access to EU funding is tough. Thus, EU funding for culture does not only have positive implications – and this is also well-acknowledged by the Commission. The same policy officer (E1) noted: "we simply do not have enough money. And [Creative Europe] is a programme that has a terrible rejection rate, so we create a lot of disappointed people in Europe".

The EU's attempts to make culture more governable and to make it both a target and an instrument of EU policy objectives has been conceptualized as governmentalization of culture (Barnett 2001), which has increasingly been expressed in line with a neoliberal ethos. Ventura (2012) argues that neoliberalism must be seen as more than just an economic system: it is a cultural structure or a form of governmentality. This entails paying attention to "the way subjects think about the collection of practices, techniques, and rationalities used to govern them and which they use to govern themselves" (Ventura 2012, 2). This neoliberal self-governance, or the "conduct of conduct" in Foucault's terms (translated in Fabion 1994, 337), has also been conceptualized as a "cultural logic" (Jameson 1990) or a "structure of feeling" (Williams 1978). The concept of agency is crucial in understanding these forms of governance. Harvey (2005, 42) argues that the shift to neoliberal policies has been accompanied by a new understanding of agency that is entwined with individuality and competition. As Gershon (2011, 539) expands, "[t]his concept of agency requires a reflexive stance in which people are subjects for themselves – a collection of processes to be managed" or even as a business to run. Accordingly, individuals, or heritage sites, can be approached as competitive actors within the EHL framework.

The EU's heritage initiatives are not funding instruments, but their appeal is thought to lie somewhere else – in their brand value. However, as will be argued in this chapter, the sites are expected to compete for their inclusion in the EHL action and for their visibility in local, national, and international 'brandscapes', and to contribute to building the brand. Although the EHL brand value is seen as one of the main benefits of the action, instead of being its beneficiaries, the sites are tasked with actually constructing it. As such they are entangled into the neoliberal structures of feeling, where they are not only governed, but govern themselves. Engaging in these structures produces a form of 'neoliberal belonging', or inclusion achieved through success in a competitive environment.

The focus of this chapter is on the economic conditions of the EHL action and how these conditions impact its implementation and power dynamic between different EHL actors. The economics of the EHL are closely related to its promotion as a heritage brand, which is still a work in progress. The logic of branding functions within the EHL action, which includes a multi-stage application process, is based on competition for the Label. As the Commission's objective for the EHL action is to increase the feeling of belonging to Europe and the EU among its citizens, and as the heritage sites are required to advance this objective through competition, we show that these conditions are connected to neoliberal belonging. Finally, we discuss the EHL's relation to and competition with other international heritage brands, and how these relations and the competition for visibility and prominence were manifested in our data.

The data used in this chapter include interviews with the EU actors and practitioners working at the EHL sites and information and marketing material collected from the sites. We also asked the professionals and visitors at the sites to tell us what they associate with the design of the EHL logo. These associations are discussed in a separate box. A close reading of this data shows how the topics of funding, benefits of the EHL action, branding, visibility, and competition are discussed and dealt with.

Explicit and implicit EU funding for cultural heritage

The EU's funding instruments for heritage

The European Commission is keen to publicly emphasize heritage – also in economic terms. As Michel Magnier (2018, 2), the Director for Culture and

Creativity at the Directorate General for Education and Culture, states in the Commission's brochure for the European Year of Cultural Heritage:

> Cultural heritage is one of the main sectors supported through Creative Europe and, as part of the programme, it is one of the most represented among the projects selected for financing so far. Between 2014 and 2017, nearly EUR 27 million was dedicated to heritage-related projects.

For four years and to cover all 28 EU member states, this sum does not equal the rhetorical emphasis laid on it in the EU policy discourse. Although the EU's explicit heritage politics has strengthened during the past few years due to new policies, actions, and initiatives focusing on heritage, the explicit funding it allocates to heritage remains modest. Actions and initiatives such as the EHL and the European Heritage Days (jointly run with the Council of Europe), do not include any direct funding for heritage sites or actors. The European Commission allocated €650,000 for the initial implementation phase of the EHL in 2012 but since then the EHL action has not received funding (EP&C 2011; Čeginskas, 2019). In addition to earning a certificate and plaque, only up to 7 of the 30 annually awarded laureates for the EU Prize for Cultural Heritage (as of 2019 known as the European Heritage Awards or Europa Nostra Awards) receive €10,000 each. Other laureates only receive the certificate and plaque.

Although the EU's explicit funding for heritage is underdeveloped, various EU policy sectors that do not primarily deal with culture contribute in heritage funding. In cultural policy research, scholars have made a distinction between explicit and implicit cultural policies (e.g. Ahearne 2009; Throsby 2009; Palonen 2014; Psychogiopoulou 2015). While explicit cultural policies are labelled or articulated as such by the policy makers, implicit cultural policies do not form a coherent administrative entity nor are they primarily meant to impact on cultural matters. Instead, implicit cultural policies are related to other fields that nevertheless have cultural effects (Palonen 2014, 147). Although explicit EU cultural policy has become more active since the turn of the millennium, the policy has been – and still commonly is – implicitly present in a wide range of EU policy sectors. The key channel of implicit EU cultural policy is the distribution of regional and structural funds, which aim to decrease economic and infrastructural disparities between the poorer and richer areas of Europe, and thereby stimulate their competitiveness – though competition for the funds themselves is strong. Regions that have the strongest need for cohesion projects and development in order to reach the average level of well-being in the EU are considered to be more numerous in Central and Eastern Europe (Lähdesmäki 2014a, 16). The EU's regional funds have often functioned as cultural policy tools, as cities and art institutes have managed to secure non-cultural earmarked funds by highlighting employment and enterprise rather than culture in their applications (Palonen 2014). More generally, all EU cultural policies are inextricably intertwined with the economic rationale defining most of the EU's internal policies, so explicit and implicit EU cultural policies may be difficult to distinguish in practice (Psychogiopoulou 2015, 245).

The theoretical division between explicit and implicit EU heritage policy is reflected in the funding instruments. While the EU's explicit funding for its heritage initiatives is modest, implicit funding through regional, structural, and rural development funds has been used for conserving, promoting, and managing cultural heritage in Europe. These implicit funding instruments do not provide substantive input for EU heritage politics, however, unlike the EHL. They do not set the beneficiaries any requirements for promoting a European dimension of values, narratives, or meanings.

These broader funding instruments continue to function as important implicit EU heritage policies (Lähdesmäki, Kaasik-Krogerus, and Mäkinen 2019). For example, from 2007 to 2013, the European Regional Development Fund allocated €3.2 billion to protecting and preserving cultural heritage. Investments in culture and heritage have been used as part of sustainable economic development strategies but can cover a wide spectrum of activities in the public, non-profit, and private sectors. The European Agricultural Fund for Rural Development supports the conservation and upgrading of rural cultural heritage and invested €1.2 billion in this between 2007 and 2013. The European Maritime and Fisheries Fund finances community-led development projects that promote cultural heritage – including maritime cultural heritage – in fisheries areas (EC 2014). Cultural heritage has also received minor funding from the Programme for the Environment and Climate Change (LIFE), the Instrument for Pre-Enlargement (IPA), and the EU programme for the Competitiveness of Enterprises and Small and Medium-sized Enterprises (COSME) (Zito and Eckersley 2018, 9). Moreover, between 2007 and 2013 the EU invested around €100 million in heritage research, and in the Horizon 2020 research programme this funding has even been increased (EC 2017a). For the period 2014–2020, the EU has made available approximately €6 billion for culture and cultural heritage from its cohesion policies (EC 2017a).

Funding the EHL sites

Although the EU finances cultural heritage in various ways, none of these funding instruments seem to really reach the EHL sites. The fact that the sites are expected to finance their EHL activities themselves shows how little the Commission actually values heritage. Many of these sites receive their basic funding from national, regional, and/or local public authorities or foundations. As many of the sites have relatively limited staff – some employ only a couple of people permanently – they do not usually have the resources to apply for EU funding. Successful applications require not only time, but also knowledge and expertise in application techniques and rhetoric (Čeginskas, 2019). Some of our interviewed heritage practitioners mentioned that writing the EHL application was extremely challenging due to their unfamiliarity with such procedures (see also EC 2019, 13). However, some of the sites are large enough to even have their own fundraising units (e.g. the Imperial Palace, Vienna) and have, thus, successfully applied for EU funding to strengthen their activities. The practitioners in some of our field research sites, such as in Carnuntum, Hambach Castle, and Mundaneum, were very aware of external funding possibilities but find the application processes as a time-consuming work that comes on top of their usual site-related tasks.

Regardless of their size, all EHL heritage sites included in our field research wished for explicit funding and/or easier funding structures from the EU to implement the objectives of the EHL action and develop their site accordingly. The interviewed practitioners at most sites were disappointed that the action did not include any financial support, as many of them expected this when it was launched. One of our interviewees (P21) described this disappointment as follows:

> Two years ago, we had a meeting [a network meeting of the EHL sites] in Budapest, where it was mapped what kind of needs the EHL sites have. One common factor was that all are in some sense dealing with memories, either architectural or museumized memories, and therefore for all the themes of preservation, restoration, and conservation are important – and this work is expensive everywhere. So, it would be nice if there would be this kind of practical benefit [from the EHL], to get some advice, some support – but the carpet was pulled out from under the feet of this wish. Each meeting ends in a way that a man in a suit tells how much money Europe has but how this label is not about competing for it.

The European Commission has recently sought to respond to this disappointment by opening a funding call for the EHL sites for "a concrete project, which will consist in creating the conditions for continuous networking, collaboration and training among the European Heritage Label Sites" (EC 2018, 3) with a budget of €500,000. Its stated purpose is to "select a coordinator (a single legal entity or consortium of organisations)" to launch various activities across EHL sites. This funding act, therefore, participates in the governance of the action by selecting coordinator through which the Commission can govern the sites by seemingly delegating the governance to the EHL network itself, thus encouraging a form of self-governance, in the style of participatory governance. The call lists various tasks for the coordinator, ranging from developing and maintaining a multilingual website for the general public to capacity building activities, communication tools, and communication activities to enhance the visibility of the EHL action and sites. Through the call, the Commission simultaneously creates a hierarchy between the sites by categorizing them on an active–passive scale (see Chapter 3). Moreover, the structure of the call creates a hierarchy among the EHL sites: not all of them need to participate, since a minimum of ten EHL sites established in a minimum of five different countries suffice as stakeholders for the application. As with all EU funding instruments, this call is based on competition. The EHL sites are encouraged to compete against each other for funding and for positions within the network.

The Commission decided on the networking funding in 2019. This network, called EHL@N, is coordinated by Burghauptmannschaft Österreich, a subordinate office of the Austrian Federal Ministry for Digital and Economic Affairs responsible for one of Austria's EHL sites, the Imperial Palace. EHL@N includes 19 EHL sites as co-partners as well as associate members.

The EHL as a heritage brand

Brands are an integral part of contemporary culture. Heritage brands that are connected to specific sites, narratives, and histories are increasingly spatial. Designated heritage sites function as experiential environments where people can also consume products. In addition to its touristic and consumeristic logic, heritage branding is also a form of competition, where possessing a high-quality brand title, such as the UNESCO World Heritage Listing, is a sign of success and quality (Poria et al. 2011; King and Halpenny 2014). The competition related to the EHL action brings about a complex power dynamic. It creates competition for attention, visibility, and prominence between heritage sites at the local, national, European, and global levels, as well as between different heritage brands.

Klingmann (2007) has described the spatiality of brands as 'brandscape', a concept that merges physical space, the identity of a place, culture, and brand. The concept resonates with the broader trends to promote the specificity of places in a global competition for attention between cities and regions (e.g. Harvey 2002; Paasi 2009; Olsson 2010; Richards and Palmer 2010). In this competition, attention is expected to be turned into economic development.

Competing for visibility in local, European, and global brandscapes

Many heritage sites are part of their city's or region's brandscape. Heritage includes those appealing, emotional, and affective elements that suit – and are commonly utilized in – place marketing, cultural regeneration, and the business mindset, connected under the term 'experience economy'. During the past few decades, urban planners and marketing experts have increasingly focused on developing appealing experiences in specific places in order to foster their competitiveness and consumption (Schmid 2009; Richard and Palmer 2010; Jakob 2013). As a consequence, various cities have actively sought to offer both their inhabitants and visitors attractive environments, designed for memorable moments and extraordinary experiences (d'Hauteresse 2013). Recently, experience-focused urban planning has increasingly moved from investing in 'hard' location factors, such as constructing impressive buildings, towards 'soft' location factors, such as jointly experienced recreational activities (Allingham 2014). The creation of the EHL action resonates with these trends, and with the entangled scalar power hierarchies in which these changes are taking place.

The EHL action seeks to offer to heritage sites and their host cities or regions an instrument to participate in and respond to the heightened competition for attention between locations, other heritage sites, and leisure activities. For many of the heritage practitioners we interviewed, the Label meant new credibility, and they expected it would influence the ways in which the local administrators of their host cities market and promote heritage sites. The practitioners particularly valued the EHL's international dimension: for them, it indicated a victory in an international competition and, thus, it was seen as higher in brand value than national heritage acknowledgements. As one interviewee (P19) said:

> I have been discussing with certain [local] travel agencies. They say that this [the EHL] is, in a sense, a quality label as someone has given it for a reason. Particularly as it has not been given by [our national actors], it means that it is a [serious] acknowledgement.

The EHL could also be experienced as an acknowledgement for the whole country, due to its competitive European-wide application procedures.

The EHL action contributes to the EU's image-making process and to the creation and development of symbolic resources for the EU. In this way, the EU is 'staging Europe' for various political purposes: as Krumrey (2018, 5) argues, the EU itself is "a product of staging", formed as a result of the EU's attempts to promote cultural history and memory of European integration through dealing with its often neglected historical aspects, such as the Union's own protocols, ceremonies, symbols, and self-image. Krumrey (2018, 6) goes on to note that the EU's own symbolic representation is at the very heart of the real business of its politics. Indeed, studies on EU symbolism have shown how the EU's political reality, was, is, and continues to be constituted through the EU's symbolic representation of itself (Manners 2011).

The EU seems to have two modes of creating and utilizing visual symbolism regarding Europe's heritage, history, and memory. On the one hand, this symbolism seeks to avoid any references to "real" heritage sites or objects in the EU member state. Commemoration of the EU's own protocols, such as the launches of EU treaties, or the creation of the EU's own ceremonies, do not stem from the member state's history or heritage. Moreover, the Euro banknotes are a good example of the attempts to advance a post-national image of the EU by transcending the 'national' realm (e.g. Delanty and Jones 2002; Wintle 2004; Theiler 2005; Fornäs 2011, 2012; Pearson 2013). The visuality of the Euro banknotes is based on architectural motifs of bridges, windows, and doorways that represent different art historical periods in Europe. However, these cultural motifs have been purposefully idealized so as not to depict any real architectural features in any specific European location. The aim is to eliminate national biases that may be caused by borrowing some EU member state's iconography for the EU. The map on the banknotes indicates the spatial framework of their visual aesthetics. Yet EU symbolism also relies on and utilizes national heritage and iconography. For example, the Euro coins have both a national side with symbolism selected by each member state and a European-wide side. Similarly, the EHL follows the logic of selecting certain heritage sites and objects located in some member state as building blocks of 'the European'.

The EU's interest in 'staging Europe' and creating visual symbolism of the Union through heritage is not only related to political interest in strengthening European unity and belonging or positive attitudes to the EU. These interests are also intertwined with economic motives. The EHL was launched as an official EU action in 2011, modelled on the European Capital of Culture (ECOC) action (EC 2010a, 2010b). In the ECOC action, the annually designated cities are expected to gain "enormous benefits for a city in cultural, social, and economic terms, during the year itself and beyond", as the Commission's guidelines (EC 2009, n.p.) for the candidate cities claimed during the years when the EHL action was being developed. According to the guidelines (2009, n.p.), "[i]t is a unique opportunity to regenerate cities, to change their image and to make it better known at European and international scale, which can help to develop tourism". Although the EHL action does not explicitly include similar expectations for active place marketing, cultural regeneration, or developing the attractiveness and competitiveness of the sites, it is based on the idea of a competed-for brand whose value lies in its usability.

Particularly heritage sites that are recognized through awards or labels function as a potential brand resource in a competition for prominence and attention. Different kinds of awards, labels, and listings organized and managed by national or international organizations are based on a branding logic and can thus be perceived as heritage brands. The documents from the preparation phase of the EHL action indicate how the European Commission recognized and promoted the Label's potential as a brand (without however calling it one) from the very beginning. The action's Impact Assessment (EC 2010a) analyzes meticulously how the EHL differs from existing heritage labels, the Council of Europe's Cultural Routes, the EU Prize for Cultural Heritage, and the UNESCO World Heritage List, what value it adds, and how the EHL sites could utilize the Label. The Commission's proposal for the decision on the EHL (EC 2010b, 4) lists its various expected social, societal, and economic impacts:

> These effects would include increased access to heritage sites, notably for young people, increased interest in and knowledge of common European heritage, increased understanding of European cultural diversity, an increase in intercultural dialogue and a greater sense of belonging to the European Union.
>
> Economic benefits can also be expected as the European Heritage Label has the potential to produce positive effects on the local tourism industry,

including the number of people employed. However, the impact on the number of visitors to a site will greatly depend on the quality and credibility the label will acquire and thus on the prestige it will develop over the years.

Of these brands, the UNESCO World Heritage Listing is globally the best known. Various scholars have explored the impact and uses of the UNESCO listing and noted how brand awareness, familiarity, and positive associations with it are of strategic importance in the context of global competition and sustainability of the sites and how they may impact on tourists' willingness to visit the listed sites (Poria et al. 2011; Dewar et al. 2012; King and Halpenny 2014). The status of being listed by UNESCO, which is perceived as a mark of high quality, makes sites easier to promote and position themselves as 'significant' (e.g. Buckley 2004; Li, Wu, and Cai 2008; Shackley 2009; Patuelli et al. 2013; Hassan and Rahman 2015; Caust and Vecco 2017).

Sites as EHL brand makers

Building a strong brand requires strategic planning and systematic work. As the European Commission is a political actor, it is not able to be or interested in being a marketing agent in a large-scale branding campaign for the EHL. The Commission has, however, sought to promote the action through some small-scale measures (that it calls "branding elements" on its website), including an EHL logo, a graphic design charter, poster, leaflets, postcards in multiple languages, and short videos of the sites, published on the Commission's website and on YouTube. As our interviews with the practitioners showed, the sites themselves have very limited opportunities to impact on these branding materials. In the case of Camp Westerbork, the first edition of the Commission's EHL postcards caused confusion among the practitioners working at the site, a memorial commemorating over 100,000 people, mainly Jews, who were deported to Nazi concentration camps, as the EHL slogan "Europe starts from Camp Westerbork" was printed over the image of the memorial. After justified criticism, the site postcard now reads "Europe remembers Camp Westerbork", with a brief explanation of its chequered past on the back. According to the EHL monitoring report (EC 2016, 37), the sites also criticized the fact that locations and their stories are difficult to identify on the postcards.

Further branding measures are left to the individual EHL sites. In accordance with its neoliberal ethos, they themselves are expected to increase their own visibility and awareness of the EHL action as a whole. Our field research indicated that at the sites these marketing measures are rudimentary and mainly limited to the "branding elements" offered by the Commission. During our field research, the sites still commonly offered their visitors booklets, brochures, and leaflets that were created before receiving the EHL and, therefore, did not mention the Label or include the official EHL logo and slogans ("Europe starts here!" and

"Europe starts with you!"). A recent exception to the sites' modest marketing measures is an EHL memory game, initiated by the Burghauptmannschaft Österreich. The game uses the official Commission pictures of the EHL sites. Its instruction sheet includes a brief text by the EU Commissioner for Education, Culture, Youth, and Sport, Tibor Navracsics (2018), stating:

> I congratulate all those who have received the Label and encourage them to make the most of it. I am confident that the European Heritage Label – with the extra visibility it confers – will help them play their educational role as well as foster cultural tourism, bringing direct and indirect economic benefits not only to the communities where they are located but to Europe as a whole.

In this text, Navracsics approaches the EHL as a heritage brand that brings various benefits – if the sites themselves make an effort to utilize it. In our interviews, the Commission officials and the European panel member did not see the EHL as a fully developed brand in the same ways as the Commissioner does. However, they seemed to trust that the awareness, recognition, attractiveness, and prominence of the Label will increase with time. Our interviewees (E3 and E7) who participated in European panels' work emphasized that the EHL is still in its infancy, noting that the public also only became familiar with the UNESCO listing some years after its launch. Both interviewees highlighted the difficulties in promoting the new Label from scratch, as "it was all very theoretical to speak to heritage practitioners managing a site – it was very difficult to make it concrete when there was no list basically", as one of them (E7) described the launch of the EHL action.

All interviewed EU-level actors agreed that both the visibility and the public awareness of the EHL action are poor, but they did not mention increasing funding for the action as a way of improving its visibility. As one of the interviewed EU officials (E5) noted,

> in the end, World Heritage Sites are not funded by UNESCO. But since it has its visibility, then they get funding some other way, like when you have more visibility, you can get more funding – I mean, you can use that brand. It is like a brand, and in that case, the label is not strong enough to be used as a brand. But even the European Capitals of Culture, they don't get that much funding. [...] So, I don't think it is a matter of funding, it is a matter of visibility.

Our field research at the EHL sites demonstrated the heritage sites' unanimous view that the action needs greater visibility and public awareness (see also EC 2019, 12). Thus, both the Commission and the sites agreed on this matter but each seemed to expect the other to take concrete measures to pursue it (see also EC 2019, 13). Some of our interviewed practitioners (P20 and P15) admitted

Figure 2.1 The EHL plaque at the entrance (on the right side of the door) of Alcide De Gasperi House Museum in Trento, Italy. Photo: EUROHERIT

that they have tools to increase the visibility of their sites and the EHL action but have not used them. Two of the sites, the Franz Liszt Academy of Music and the Mundaneum, did not even have the EHL plaque (given to them by the Commission at the official award ceremony) on public display at the time of our field research, although this is an explicit requirement of the action.

The problem of promoting visibility for the EHL is related to the EU's more general lack of common communication arenas and media across Europe. The challenges of the European public sphere have been much discussed in academia for decades (e.g. Habermas 1992; Eriksen 2005; Lauristin 2007; Brüggemann and Schulz-Forberg 2009), and the European Commission has also acknowledged the need to strengthen a common European 'mediascape'. One recent attempt to respond to this need is the Commission's suggestion to increase the European dimension and the EU's ambition in developing a dedicated media channel, Euronews (EC 2017b). However, one of the interviewed officials at the Commission (E4) argued that the promotion of EHL sites is not only hindered by a lack of media, but more generally by a lack of media interest in issues related to cultural heritage. The same official also had the "completely crazy idea" – as the interviewee expressed it – to add pictures of the EHL sites to Euro banknotes as they "have been acknowledged as European […] instead of these fake anonymous places". The official noted that the Union uses symbols of national heritage on Euro coins and that "we could start to put some European heritage somewhere". In this view, branding the EHL intertwines with building the image of the EU and constructing the idea of common European cultural heritage.

Box 2.1 EHL logos and slogans

One of the EU's branding measures for the European Heritage Label is its logo and slogans. The Label had its own logo already during its inter-governmental phase, and some sites, such as Raeren Pottery Museum in Belgium and the Centre Boris Christoff in Bulgaria, have continued to use the old logo as they have not received the official new Label. Some of the sites who have received both labels, such as Robert Schuman House, have also continued to use both logos. The old logo had a clearer visual reference to material heritage, architectural history, and the EU than the new logo that was created when the EHL was turned into an official EU action. In the centre of the old logo is a white Romanesque arch in front of a yellow star on a blue background. The new logo also includes a star, even at its very centre, but it is much inconspicuously formed from the

EUROPEES
ERFGOEDLABEL

Figure 2.2 The EHL logo in Dutch. In the coloured version, the five shapes are lilac, yellow ochre, light green, green, and red ochre, while the text is blue.
Copyright: EUROHERIT

Figure 2.3 Descriptive words used by heritage practitioners working at the EHL sites when asked what they associate with the design of the EHL logo. Copyright: EUROHERIT

Figure 2.4 Descriptive words used by visitors to the EHL sites when asked what they associate with the design of the EHL logo. Copyright: EUROHERIT

white background through the positions of five colourful shapes. The EHL's Graphic Charter (EC 2013, n.p.) states that the logo of the official EHL action "represents diversity of Europe's heritage" and is inspired by the EU flag. It continues: "The diversity that is at the heart of Europe is symbolised by the different shapes and colours of the constituent pieces, which may evoke stones, petals or a footprint … depending on the individual's imagination". The EHL action is also promoted by slogans. "Europe starts here" is aimed at visitors, while "Europe starts with you" addresses heritage practitioners and managers to encourage them to apply for the Label.

In our field research, we asked heritage practitioners and visitors at the EHL sites what they associate with the design of the EHL logo. The most common association among the heritage practitioners stemmed from the logo's different colours (mentioned by 52% of them) and its stones (15%) or shapes (12%) that were interpreted as representing diversity (27%) or differences (12%) between cultures or countries in Europe, simultaneously referring to being together (15%), highlighting things that are common (15%), or forming a unity (6%). These interpretations reflected the discourse that the European Commission has related to the EHL. Many heritage practitioners noted the star in the middle of the logo (15%) and said that the design reminds them of a flower (12%). Moreover, individual associations ranged from the Eurovision Song Contest to NATO, and from Stonehenge to jelly beans. The logo evoked more positive (48%) than negative (24%) associations, though only a few practitioners had ever stopped to think of its symbolism or meanings.

Visitors had similar associations with the EHL logo. In their responses, visitors most commonly highlighted the star in the middle of the logo (32%), its colours (26%), and stones (14%) or shapes (10%) as symbols of being together (12%) and diversity (7%). Compared to the heritage practitioners, visitors paid slightly more attention to the EU flag as a part of the logo. Due to the large number of responses, visitors associated a great variety of interpretations such as an animal pawprint (5%), a flower or petals (6%), different continents (3%), and the founding countries of the EU (2%). The logo also evoked more positive (41%) than negative (17%) associations among visitors.

Neoliberal belonging: Winning at heritage sites

The brand logic and the motivation to compete for exclusive awards is based on their rarity – not everyone receives them. This idea of exclusiveness is contrasted by the future vision for the EHL. In its last selection report, the European panel envisaged that by 2030 the number of the EHL sites will grow to 100 (EC 2017c, 8). The increase in the number of labelled sites would likely raise awareness of the Label but simultaneously make it more common and, thus, decrease its brand value. One of the interviewed practitioners (P23) was already worried that the EHL's exclusiveness was diminishing. The same interviewee had also noticed how other smaller sites and events in the region had sought to benefit from their Label by branding themselves as European through it – and considered this as a negative tendency that endangered the uniqueness of the EHL brand. Practitioners at the Mundaneum and Alcide De Gasperi House said that they were proud that their site was the first to receive the Label in their respective countries. Both sites had also chosen to mention being "the first" in their brochures, and in the case of Alcide De Gasperi House, the "only site of this kind in Italy" (Alcide De Gasperi House Museum 2017, n.p.). The rarity of the EHL was turned into a sign of uniqueness that emphasized the extraordinary distinction of receiving it.

Although the EHL was commonly seen as a merit gained through tough competition, making the most of it is not easy in today's competitive environment. In our interviews, the competition between different tourist attractions was a commonly recognized challenge. Several of our field research sites – such as the Great Guild Hall, Mundaneum, Robert Schuman House, and the European Solidarity Centre – were struggling to get their local marketing authorities or official tourist agencies to promote their EHL award. The reasons for this varied, ranging from a city's interest in promoting only sites that it owns to being an underdog in the competition of prominence for more established heritage narratives or heritage brands, such as the UNESCO listing.

This highlights how the brand value of the EHL is constructed in relation to and competition with other heritage brands. The EHL sometimes has to struggle for attention at the sites themselves, which may have other more established, and thus more useful, heritage labels or awards (see Box 2.2). As a newcomer – with the least recognition – the Label may play a secondary role in promoting the site. The interviewed practitioners stressed the challenge of finding a niche for the EHL in the broader marketing measures of their respective city or region. This challenge is demonstrated by the city and regional tourist brochures in our data, in which UNESCO listing beats less-known heritage brands. As the Tourist Guide Mons (2017, 12), the host city of the Mundaneum, states:

> The province of Hainaut, of which Mons is the capital, holds the national record for sites awarded world heritage status by UNESCO, boasting on impressive 19 classified sites and events. This exceptional density of sites, across such as small area, means that a trip to the Mons Region offers a TREASURE TROVE TO BE DISCOVERED OR REDISCOVERED!

Box 2.2 Competing heritage brands at the EHL sites

With the proliferation of various heritage brands, many prominent heritage sites are nominated for different, at times competing, heritage initiatives. This is also the case with several EHL sites. From our field research sites, certain objects or documents in Camp Westerbork, Mundaneum, and the European Solidarity Centre are included in UNESCO's Memory of the World Register, while Carnuntum is a part of a multinational Frontiers of the Roman Empire World Heritage Site, currently on UNESCO's tentative list. Among our interviewed practitioners at these sites, the UNESCO label was seen as signalling a global significance that does not need to be explained to visitors, while in the case of the EHL "we have to explain what is that, what does it mean, and … so, it means, it takes a little bit more time, a little bit more effort to promote the [our site] in the light of the EHL", as one of our interviewees (P30) notes. Moreover, the Great Guild Hall is in Tallinn's old town, which is on the UNESCO World Heritage List, and the European District in Strasbourg is a part of the city as a whole, which has received the national Ville d'Art et Histoire label. The European District is also close to the historic centre of the city, which has been listed as UNESCO World Heritage.

Before the EHL, the Franz Liszt Academy of Music had received the EU Prize for Cultural Heritage (better known as the Europa Nostra Prize) in the category of conservation, and the FIABCI Grand Prix, awarded by the International Real Estate Federation in the category of heritage. Both these awards and the EHL are highlighted in the Academy's brochure, but in the guided tours at the Academy, only the Europa Nostra Prize was mentioned to demonstrate the significance of the site as heritage in Europe. In the recent brochures of the sites with several heritage awards, the EHL is just one of the many acknowledgements used to convince visitors of their prestige. For example, the European Solidarity Centre lists in its brochure exhibiting "the Boards with 21 Demands […] included in UNESCO Memory of the World Register", being "the first Polish institution to be awarded the prestigious Council of Europe Museum Prize", and "received the Mayor of Gdańsk Special Award for the best architecture project in Gdańsk" – in addition to being "distinguished with the European Heritage Label" (Zapraszamy do Środka 2017, n.p.).

Despite the challenges that the EHL has faced as a new brand in the heritage sector, it has managed to create its own conceptual niche distinguished from other brands, based on the politics of belonging. The EHL action does not emphasize monumental and architectural materiality, natural uniqueness, aesthetic quality, or authenticity of tangible objects – but rather the narratives of Europe, the EU, and belonging to them. As heritage is most commonly defined in national terms (or universal in the case of World Heritage listing), the concept of a European and transnational heritage sets the EHL sites apart from other labels. However, the structure and objectives of the EHL action require local heritage actors to compete against each other and various other actors, within and beyond the heritage sector, for implementing the Commission's objectives. The practices of competition and the logic of branding generally introduce a neoliberal system into heritage, in both the EHL and World Heritage listing as well as in other competed heritage brands. The success of brands is commonly measured against their visibility and recognition that may even become more important for the success of brands than their actual contents.

The brand logic includes a promise of added value: a brand brings specificity, stories, meanings, and contexts that are beneficial to its owners. What added value did the EHL entail to the sites included in our field research? For many of the interviewed practitioners, it created (a feeling of) credibility as an important heritage site at the local, national, and European levels. In addition, some practitioners recognized the instrumental value of the EHL for their attempts to secure funding for their activities or for applying for other more distinguished heritage brands, such as the UNESCO listing in the case of the Sagres Promontory. In this sense, the EHL functioned as a symbolic elevation of the sites – 'winning' the Label highlights their transnational importance, quality, and exclusivity.

The EHL fulfils a dual branding function by addressing both the sites and the EU. This dynamic is planned to work in both directions: the EU brands the sites and the sites brand the EU. By following the EHL's objectives, the sites promote the EU and distinguish it as both a cultural union with historical roots and a political union supporting and interacting with its local and regional actors. At the same time, the European Commission uses the EHL brand in its own image-building rhetoric to create a more human and cultural image for itself.

The difficulties in creating, developing, and utilizing the EHL as a heritage brand reflect the ideological disparity between the heritage and marketing sectors. These sectors have differing goals and mentalities: preservation versus novelty, stability versus change, and value of history versus economic profit. These disparities impact on the development of the EHL action and on how the sites use the Label.

References

Ahearne, J. 2009. "Cultural Policy Explicit and Implicit: A Distinction and Some Uses." *International Journal of Cultural Policy* 15 (2): 141–153.

Allingham, P. 2014. "Art, Media, and Sense-Making in Responsive Urban Environments." *Rask* 40: 31–52.

Barnett, C. 2001. "Culture, Policy and Subsidiarity in the European Union: From Symbolic Identity to the Governmentalisation of Culture." *Political Geography* 20 (4): 405–426.

Buckley, R. 2004. "The Effects of World Heritage Listing on Tourism to Australian National Parks." *Journal of Sustainable Tourism* 12 (1): 70–84.

Brüggemann, M., and H. Schulz-Forberg. 2009. "Becoming Pan-European? Transnational Media and the European Public Sphere." *International Communication Gazette* 71 (8): 693–712.

Caust, J., and M. Vecco. 2017. "Is UNESCO World Heritage Recognition a Blessing or Burden? Evidence from Developing Asian Countries." *Journal of Cultural Heritage* 27: 1–9.

Čeginskas, V. L. A. 2019. "Challenges in Creating the Visibility of European Cultural Heritage: A Case Study of the European Heritage Label." *Ethnologia Fennica* 46: 109–134.

De Gasperi House Museum. 2017. *Brochure*. Trento: De Gasperi House.

EC (European Commission). 2009. *"Guide for Cities Applying for the Title of European Capital of Culture."* Brussels: European Commission.

EC (European Commission). 2010a. *"Impact Assessment: Commission Staff Working Document"* SEC(2010)197, March 9, 2010. Brussels: European Commission.

EC (European Commission). 2010b. *"Proposal for a Decision of The European Parliament and of The Council Establishing a European Union Action for the European Heritage Label"*, COM(2010)76 final, 2010/0044 (COD), 9 March 2010. Brussels: European Commission.

EC (European Commission). 2013. *"Graphic Charter: European Heritage Label."* Brussels: European Commission.

EC (European Commission). 2014. *"Communication from the Commission to the European Parliament, the Council, the European Economic and Social Committee and the Committee of the Regions: Towards an Integrated Approach to Cultural Heritage for Europe"*, COM(2014)477 final, 22 July 2014. Brussels: European Commission.

EC (European Commission). 2016. *"European Heritage Label. Panel Report on Monitoring"*, 19 December 2016. Brussels: European Commission.

EC (European Commission). 2017a. *"European Year of Cultural Heritage 2018. Fact Sheet"*, 7 December 2017. Brussels: European Commission.

EC (European Commission). 2017b. *"Communication from the Commission to the European Parliament, the Council, the European Economic and Social Committee and the Committee of the Regions. Strengthening European Identity through Education and Culture: The European Commission's contribution to the Leaders' meeting in Gothenburg"*. COM(2017)673 final, 17 November 2017. Brussels: European Commission.

EC (European Commission). 2017c. *"European Heritage Label 2017, Panel Report"*, 5 December 2017. Brussels: European Commission.

EC (European Commission). 2018. *"Call for Proposals – EAC/S39/2018: Design and Management of Networking and Capacity Building Activities for European Heritage Label Sites"*. Brussels: European Commission.

EC (European Commission). 2019. *"Evaluation of the European Heritage Label Action: Synopsis Report of All Stakeholder Consultation Activities"*, January 2019. Brussels: European Commission.

EP&C (European Parliament and the Council). 2011. "Decision No. 1194/2011/EU of the European Parliament and of the Council of 16 November 2011: Establishing a European Union Action for the European Heritage Label." *Official Journal of the European Union* L 303: 1–9.

Eriksen, E. O. 2005. "An Emerging European Public Sphere." *European Journal of Social Theory* 8 (3): 341–363.

Faubion J., ed. 1994. *Power: Foucault*. London: Penguin.

Fornäs, J. 2011. *Signifying Europe*. Bristol: Intellect Press.

Fornäs, J. 2012. "European Identification: Symbolic Mediations of Unity and Diversity." *Global Media Journal* 6 (1). Accessed 15 August 2019. www.hca.westernsydney.edu.au/gmjau/archive/v6_2012_1/johan_fornas_RA.html

Delanty, G., and P. R. Jones. 2002. "European Identity and Architecture". *European Journal of Social Theory* 5 (4): 453–466.

Dewar, K., H. du Cros, and W. Li. 2012. "The Search for World Heritage Brand Awareness Beyond the Iconic Heritage: A Case Study of the Historic Centre of Macao." *Journal of Heritage Tourism* 7 (4): 323–339.

Gershon, I. 2011. "Neoliberal Agency." *Current Anthropology* 52 (4): 537–555.

Habermas, J. 1992. *The Structural Transformation of the Public Sphere: An Inquiry into a Category of Bourgeois Society*. Cambridge, UK: Polity Press.

d'Hauteserre, A.-M. 2013. "Val d'Europe: A Pioneering Turn to 'Experience' Planning?" *European Urban and Regional Studies* 20 (4): 435–446.

Harvey, D. 2002. "Art of Rent: Globalization, Monopoly and the Commodification of Culture." In *World of Contradictions: Socialist Register*, edited by L. Panitch and C. Leys, 10–13. New York: Monthly Review Press.

Harvey, D. 2005. *A Brief History of Neoliberalism*. Oxford: Oxford University Press.

Hassan, A., and M. Rahman. 2015. "World Heritage Site as a Label in Branding a Place." *Journal of Cultural Heritage Management and Sustainable Development* 5 (3): 210–223.

Jakob, D. 2013. "The Eventification of Place: Urban Development and Experience Consumption in Berlin and New York City." *European Urban and Regional Studies* 20 (4): 447–459.

Jameson, F. 1990. *Postmodernism, or the Cultural Logic of Late Capitalism*. Durham, NC: Duke University Press.

King, L. M., and E. A. Halpenny. 2014. "Communicating the World Heritage Brand: Visitor Awareness of UNESCO's World Heritage Symbol and the Implications for Sites, Stakeholders and Sustainable Management." *Journal of Sustainable Tourism* 22 (5): 768–786

Klingmann, A. 2007. *Brandscapes: Architecture in the Experience Economy*. Cambridge, MA: MIT Press.

Krumrey, J. 2018. *The Symbolic Politics of European Integration: Staging Europe*. New York: Palgrave Macmillan.

Lähdesmäki, T. 2014. *Identity Politics in the European Capital of Culture Initiative*. Joensuu: University of Eastern Finland.

Lähdesmäki, T. 2014. "European Capital of Culture Designation as an Initiator of Urban Transformation in the Post-Socialist Countries." *European Planning Studies* 22 (3): 481–497.

Lähdesmäki, T., S. Kaasik-Krogerus, and K. Mäkinen. 2019. "Genealogy of the Concept of Heritage in the European Commission's Policy Discourse." *Contributions to the History of Concepts* 14 (1): 115–139.

Lauristin, M. 2007. "The European Public Sphere and the Social Imaginary of the 'New Europe.'" *European Journal of Communication* 22 (4): 397–412.

Lee, C., and R. Bideleux. 2009. "'Europe': What Kind of Idea?" *European Legacy* 14 (2): 163–176.

Li, M., B. Wu, and L. Cai. 2008. "Tourism Development of World Heritage Sites in China: A Geographic Perspective." *Tourism Management* 29 (2): 308–319.

Magnier, M. 2018. No title. In *Creative Europe: Rediscovering Our Cultural Heritage*. Brussels: European Union.

Manners, I. 2011. "Symbolism in European Integration." *Comparative European Politics* 9 (3): 243–268.

Navracsics, T. 2018. "Explaining the European Heritage Label." In *European Heritage Memo.* Vienna: Burghauptmannschaft Österreich.

Olsson, K. 2010. "Cultural Heritage as a Resource in Place Marketing." In *Integrating Aims – Built Heritage in Social and Economic Development*, edited by M. Mälkki and K. Schmidt-Thomé, 251–268. Espoo: Aalto University.

Paasi, A. 2009. "Regions and Regional Dynamics." In *The Sage Handbook of European Studies*, edited by C. Rumford, 464–484. London: Sage.

Palonen, E. 2014. "Assigning Meaning to (EU-)Europe through Cultural Policy." In *The Meanings of Europe: Changes and Exchanges of a Contested Concept*, edited by C. Wiesner and M. Schmidt-Gleim, 144–159. London: Routledge.

Patuelli, R., M. Mussoni, and G. Candela. 2013. "The Effects of World Heritage Sites on Domestic Tourism: A Spatial Interaction Model for Italy." *Journal of Geographical Systems* 15 (3): 369–402.

Pearson, C. 2013. "EUtopia? The European Union and the Parlamentarium in Brussels." *City: Analysis of Urban Trends, Culture, Theory, Policy, Action* 17 (5): 636–653.

Poria, Y., A. Reichel, and R. Cohen. 2011. "World Heritage Site – Is It an Effective Brand Name? A Case Study of a Religious Heritage Site." *Journal of Travel Research* 50 (5): 482–495.

Psychogiopoulou, E. 2015. "Conclusion: Culture and the European Union." In *Cultural Governance and the European Union: Protecting and Promoting Cultural Diversity in Europe*, edited by E. Psychogiopoulou, 237–282. Basingstoke: Palgrave Macmillan.

Richards, G., and R. Palmer. 2010. *Eventful Cities: Cultural Management and Urban Revitalisation*. London: Routledge.

Schmid, H. 2009. *Economy of Fascination. Dubai and Las Vegas as Themed Urban Landscapes*. Berlin: Gebrüder Borntraeger.

Shackley, Myra, ed. 2009. *Visitor Management. Case studies from World Heritage Sites*. Oxford: Butterworth Heineman.

Theiler, T. 2005. *Political Symbolism and European Integration*. Manchester: Manchester University Press.

Throsby, D. 2009. "Explicit and Implicit Cultural Policy: Some Economic Aspects." *International Journal of Cultural Policy* 15 (2): 179–185.

Tourist Guide Mons / Reiseführer Borinage. 2017. Province de Hainaut: Hainaut Tourism.

Ventura, P. 2012. *Neoliberal Culture: Living with American Neoliberalism*. Farnham: Ashgate Publishing Limited.

Williams, R. 1978. *Marxism and Literature*. New York: Oxford University Press.

Wintle, M. 2004. *Europa and the Bull, Europe, and European Studies: Visual Images as Historical Source Material*. Amsterdam: Amsterdam University Press.

Wintle, M. 2009. *The Image of Europe: Visualizing Europe in Cartography and Iconography Throughout the Ages*. Cambridge: Cambridge University Press.

Zapraszamy do Środka/Welcome Inside. 2017. Gdańsk: Europejskie Centrum Solidarności.

Zito, A. R., and S. Eckersley. 2018. "Critical Heritages (CoHERE): Performing and Representing Identities in Europe." *Work Package 1, Work in progress: Framing European Heritage and Identity: The Cultural Policy Instruments of the European Union.* Accessed 15 August 2019. http://digitalcultures.ncl.ac.uk/cohere/wordpress/wp-content/uploads/2018/11/WP1-Eckersley-Zito-1.pdf

Part II

Geo-graphing Europe

Chapter 3

Geo-graphing European cultural heritage

In 2015, the Historic Gdańsk Shipyard was awarded the EHL for the fundamental influence the Solidarity movement (Solidarność) had on the collapse of the Soviet Bloc and the end of the Cold War (EC 2014). One part of the shipyard complex is the European Solidarity Centre that mediates the notion of solidarity and the power of peaceful negotiations through its extensive permanent exhibition. The exhibition proceeds in chronological order, starting with the strikes that began in the shipyard in 1980 and subsequently spread all over Poland. It tells the visitors how, by the end of 1981, the Solidarity movement grew into a nationwide trade union with about 10 million members, and how this period that gave hope for political changes was followed by approximately two years of martial law in Poland. The exhibition concludes by depicting the developments from the second half of the 1980s that led to the roundtable negotiations between Polish government and the Solidarity movement, followed by the first democratic elections in the Soviet Bloc in 1989 and its gradual dissolution. In strictly spatial terms, the same story moves on various scales. The permanent exhibition starts from the atmosphere of the Gdańsk Shipyard, showing the interaction between the workers and the people of Gdańsk. By spreading all over Poland, both the strikes and the Solidarity movement reached the national scale and as a result of international attention and support even attained European and global scales. The exhibition shows how the dissolution of the Soviet Bloc broke up the strict scalar bisection between East and West of the Cold War era.

The exhibition at the European Solidarity Centre is an illustrative example of narrating multiscalar heritage that starts from a single locality and grows to affect European and global scales. As a designated site, the European Solidarity Centre guides us to the EHL as a multiscalar heritage action. This multiscalar approach is highlighted by the EHL website, which states that the aim of the action is the "promotion of the European dimension of the sites and providing access to them" (EC 2019). In this framework, the sites that are already considered to be local, regional, and/or national heritage are made part of 'European heritage' by narrating and putting into practice their 'European significance', which is a key selection criterion of the EHL (EP&C 2011, 4). As Lähdesmäki and Mäkinen (2019, 39, 42) show elsewhere, in the EHL selection reports, European significance is mostly associated with a plurality of territories, connecting various scalar dimensions and their combinations.

The EHL operates within entangled geographical settings and political processes that influence one another and form the basis for multiscalar understanding of heritage. These spatial settings are constituted on various scales and are linked through the circulation of people, goods, and ideas (see also Cohen 2015, 16). Similarly, heritage sites have a strong spatial dimension as they bring various people together. The EHL sites are located all over the EU and the EHL action connects them and their actors on various scales. Therefore, in this chapter, heritage is viewed as geopolitics, in the sense of facilitating the reproduction of certain territorial imaginaries and spatial hierarchies, whereby certain territories are imagined to be superior to others. As this process of 'geo-graphing' aims at making sense of the world, the EHL sites as actors and representations of 'European heritage' help to reproduce and legitimize spatial imaginaries that in turn have an impact on what is seen as 'European heritage' (cf. Koch 2015). This makes the EHL a geopolitical discourse, in which perceptions of both European heritage and European scale are formed in relation to other spatial scales. Instead of representing a static, fixed, or neutral setup, a critical perspective enables us to see all three – heritage, geopolitics, and scales – as a dynamic and entangled process of 'doing' and as in mutual interaction (see also Smith 2006; Harvey 2015, 579; Harvey and Mozaffari 2019). The managers, curators, educators, and other practitioners at the designated sites play a key role in the multiscalar framework of the EHL. Hence, in this chapter, scalar connections and relations are the objects of inquiry. We use our interviews with the heritage practitioners working at the EHL sites to analyze how they engage with the EHL. This enables us to ask which positions the EHL as a geopolitical discourse offers the sites for practicing geopolitics and doing heritage.

The interview data was scrutinized using qualitative content analysis, by coding the interview transcriptions through data-driven logic and clustering the codes into three entities. Based on them, we constructed three interlinked subject positions that enabled us to analyse the potential and limitations of the EHL by making visible both the transformative potential and the scalar hierarchies of heritage. Although the EHL is a very recent action and the current subject positions are most likely to develop over time, neither the action nor the positions are free from the well-established 'background burden' of European scalar hierarchies. We start by discussing two useful critical approaches to the EHL as geopolitics, critical heritage studies and critical geopolitics, followed by the empirical analysis of the practitioners' interviews. We conclude the chapter by discussing the transformative potential of heritage in the framework of geopolitics.

Bringing heritage, scales, and geopolitics together

Both critical heritage studies and critical geopolitics focus on the social world and related imaginaries. In critical heritage studies, heritage is understood as an inherently dissonant social construct, created and shaped by various actors according to political, economic, and social interests (Harrison 2013; Kisić 2017). As we discussed in the introduction, the focus of critical heritage studies is first and foremost on temporal relations. Heritage 'from the past' is seen as a presentist process that is not preserved but formed on the basis of current needs in order to impact on future imaginaries (Harrison 2013, 4; Lähdesmäki, Zhu, and Thomas 2019, 2). In this process "the past valorizes the present and gives to the present a sense of superiority over the very past to which it appeals" (Delanty 2017, 4). In turn, critical geopolitical studies focus on spatial dynamics, such as core-margin (or centre-periphery) relations and related security issues. Studies in 'classical geopolitics' are about dividing the world into powerful 'core' regions and the marginalized and less valuable peripheral regions as well as about gaining control over the 'core'. In contrast, critical geopolitics – which emerged as part of a 'discursive turn' in social and political sciences – explores the power dynamics behind these taken-for-granted territorial divisions. More recent critical approaches, like feminist geopolitics, have broadened the scope of the discipline from territorial entities to human bodies, their safety, and vulnerability. In this book, the embodiment of heritage is discussed in Chapter 8.

Power relations in the EU and/or Europe are often approached in research along East-West and North-South divisions. Critical scholars have framed the Central and Eastern European countries as liminal Europe (Mälksoo 2006, 276) or as simultaneously part of but not fully Europe (Wolff 1994, 7). This notion stems from the eighteenth century, when Eastern Europe became one of the generalized 'others' necessary for Western Europe's self-image (Wolff 1994, 7; Neumann 1999, 143–160). The Central and Eastern European countries continued to be constructed as 'liminal Europe' also after their EU accession (Mälksoo 2006, 2009; Velikonja 2011, 43–44; Ballinger 2017, 52; Komska 2018, 8–10). Therefore, the analytical frameworks of "easternism" (Ballinger 2017, 62) are still useful. Lately the North-South division has gained prominence in the EU context. Particularly in relation to the EU's economic recession, 'irresponsible, irrational, naïve, and chaotic' Southern European countries suffering from economic problems have been juxtaposed in the public discussion with the 'responsible and rational' North which has to 'pay the bill' (e.g. Moisio et al. 2013, 738; see also Dainotto 2007).

Although our research is informed by these geopolitical divisions that are widely used and criticized both in public and academic debates, the divisions are not directly applicable here. Firstly, as Delanty (2017, 21) argues, we have reached a time of post-Western Europe, meaning a "Europe [that] can no longer be defined exclusively in terms of the historical experience of its founding Western European nations". Sticking to East-West or North-South axes reduces the 'big picture' to a binary relationship and in the worst case (unintentionally) fixes and in part homogenizes these spatial poles and relations between them (see also Polynczuk-Alenius 2018, 200). Second, implicitly or explicitly, these divisions mostly focus on the national scale at the expense of the other geographical scales and their entanglements. For instance, the practitioners at two EHL sites, Robert Schuman House and Alcide De Gasperi House, strongly associate themselves as part of (national) peripheries, although being located in 'Western' countries, France and Italy, and part of 'core' Europe, posits them into the core of EUrope. These conflicting scalarities illustrate the variety of multiscalar environments. To avoid unintentional contribution to the preconceived spatial divisions, ready-made categories, and related hierarchies (see Kuus 2013, 32), we shift the focus to the notion of scale and scalar relations (see also Moisio 2011).

Our understanding of scale stems from Lefebvre's (1991) notion of space as a social product (see also Chapter 7). We borrow from Massey (2005, 9) who argues that space is a sphere of possibility that is constituted through various personal, local, national, and global interactions (see Harvey 2015, 583). Hence, we see spatial scales as not fixed but socially produced, transformed, and politically contested by various actors (Marston 2000; Brenner 2001, 604). As Lähdesmäki, Zhu, and Thomas (2019, 3) write, scale and scalar relations are crucial to the process of production and meaning-making of heritage. The EHL is a good example of entangled scalar relations and heritage. Hence, it can be scrutinized as a process of scaling in which multiple spatial units are established and structured in relation to one another with the participation of actors from those different scales (see also Brenner 2001, 600; Lähdesmäki, Zhu, and Thomas 2019, 8, 10). Since the focus of this chapter is on the sites and the heritage practitioners working there, their agency and influence in the context of geopolitical discourse needs to be contemplated.

Beyond issues related to foreign policy and its actors, which are seen as examples of practical geopolitics, scholars of critical geopolitics have emphasized the importance of popular geopolitics, that is, the role of popular culture in legitimizing geopolitical understandings (e.g. Ó Tuathail 1996; Dittmer 2010; Saunders 2017; Saunders and Strukov 2018). Mass media, movies, cartoons, social media, and more have all been analysed as popular geopolitics (Dittmer 2010; Dittmer 2014; Suslov and Bassin 2016; Saunders 2017) whereas heritage sites and museums have frequently been overlooked in the discussions about how geopolitical knowledge is scripted into everyday life (see also Liu, An, and Zhu 2015, 607). Nevertheless, heritage sites are important producers of this knowledge, since they participate in the daily legitimation of geopolitics by simultaneously shaping and fixing people's imaginaries of 'the world'. Such imaginaries help to divide the geopolitical space into 'Europe' or 'the EU' and establish boundaries and relations between what is seen as 'local', 'national', or 'European'. The traditional division between public and private actors does not automatically apply to heritage sites, which are often state owned but act independently from governmental institutions, such as ministries. Hence, heritage sites can be seen to represent a specific mixture of practical and popular geopolitics.

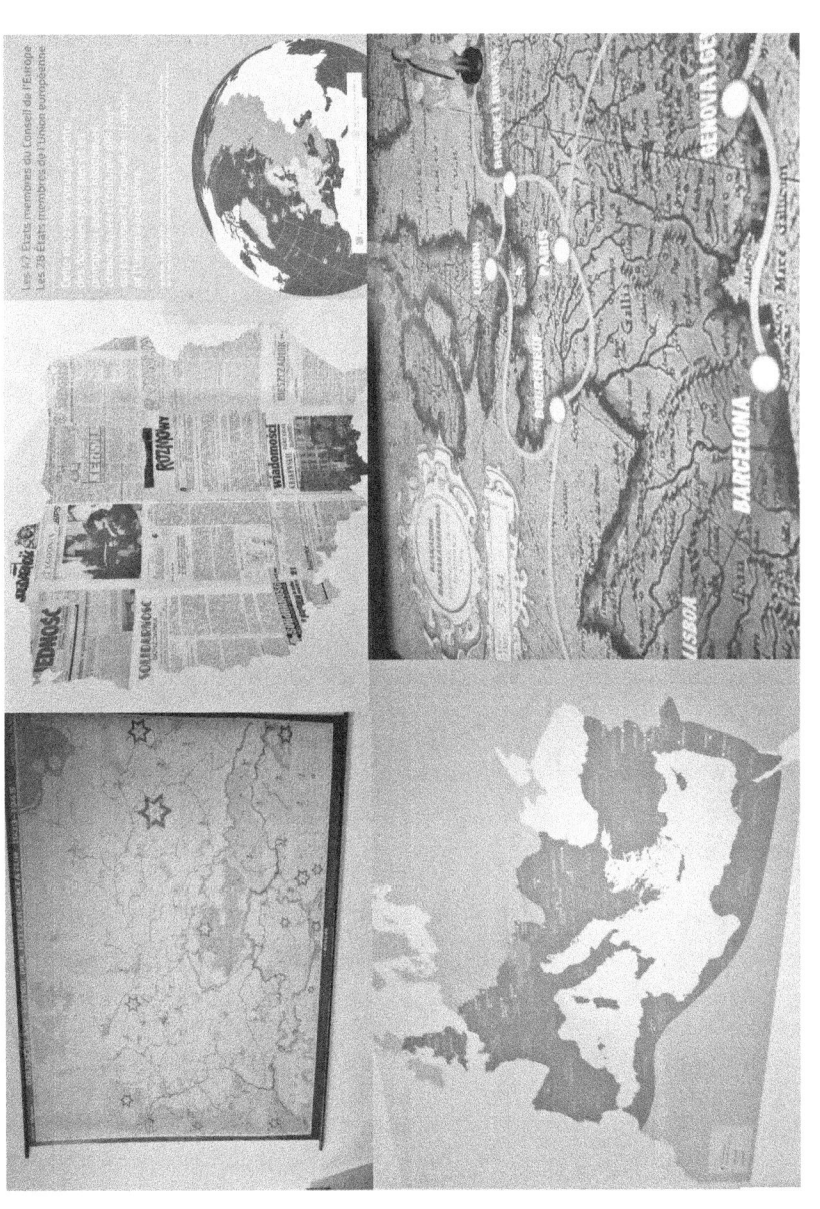

Figure 3.1 Maps presenting various scalar entities are the most prominent exhibits at the EHL sites. This collage consists of the maps displayed in the Camp Westerbork, European Solidarity Center, Lieu d'Europe, Great Guild Hall, and Carnuntum. Photo: EUROHERIT

Engaging with the EHL as a geopolitical discourse

With the designation of the EHL, the heritage sites 'transform' themselves into part of European heritage. In this geopolitical discourse, the heritage practitioners both 'domesticate' the EHL in their sites and simultaneously create substance for the Label (see also Alasuutari 2009; Bortolotto 2012; Kaasik-Krogerus 2019). Therefore, by analyzing which subject positions the EHL offers practitioners, we gain valuable insights into the current developments and the future perspectives of the EHL as a policy action. This also sheds light on practitioners' understandings of the EU and Europe.

A common starting point for all the interviewees was a positive attitude to the EHL, recognizing its importance, and showing willingness to contribute to it in one way or another, at least in principle. On the more practical level, practitioners' preconceptions ranged from enthusiastic gratefulness for the opportunity to participate in the EHL and eagerness to contribute to the action to a more passive or expectant approach. Based on their complementary but partly contradictory attitudes to it, we formulated three subject positions to explain how the practitioners engage with the EHL in their daily practice, understand it, and make sense of it. We call these positions EHL participant, EHL observer, and EHL creator (see Chapter 1 on hierarchy in the EHL network). The practitioners' understandings testify of a wider context from which these three positions stem and to which they contribute.

Analysing the data in terms of these positions enables us to approach the EHL as a network, rather than only the sum of individual sites. These subject positions are not tied to single actors or sites: meaning that neither interviewees nor sites can be categorized as participants, observers, or creators only, but all comprise a mixture of the three. Hence, the approach differs from that taken in Chapter 1, where a hierarchy is identified within the EHL network.

EHL participant

The subject position of EHL participant is connected with the EHL's core idea that the formal award of the Label confirms the European significance of the heritage site. Accordingly, the EHL designation can be interpreted as an act of remarkable recognition, and the award is often received with surprise and a sense of gratitude by heritage practitioners (P6; P31). The EHL participant actualizes in the data in form of a confirmation that the site engages with "European history" (P26), reaches a "European level" (P8; P16), and represents "heritage of European value" (P16), as some of our interviewees stated. This goes together with the assumption that the EHL 'upgrades' the heritage sites from the national to the European scale (P31; P6; P25), which confirms the formal authority of the European Commission in the process as a representative of EUrope. As one of the interviewees said, the EU has high expectations for the network of the sites (P23). Hence, the designation can be interpreted as the fruit of a long period of hard work, as manifested in the application process. This setting enables the sites to use the Label as proof of their competitiveness on the European scale and to raise their credibility, for instance by making it known in other countries (P33) and promoting (national) heritage abroad (P26; P17). The practitioners in this subject position expect that visibility and recognition may lead to greater publicity and (international) reputation that will increase the number of visitors to the sites (P1).

Receiving the EHL has a certain analogy with passing a test or winning a competition: to prove European significance, sites have to fulfil the EHL criteria that make the membership measurable (P18) and therefore give it a notion of 'objectivity'. Since the EHL is still in its initial phase, this position includes the expectation that the sites will develop with the Label. Some heritage practitioners stated their willingness to "live up" to the criteria of preserving and exhibiting the site heritage "on the European level" (P16) and being sufficiently oriented towards Europe (P15). For instance, the story of De Gasperi is developed in the EHL framework from a national narrative into "a story suitable for Europeans", as one practitioner (P4) described it. The use of multiple languages in their work (P28; P30) is another example of how EHL criteria are entangled with the daily practice of the sites. However, the EHL participant position also provides a static understanding of the EHL criteria as a stable basis for perceiving the sites as 'European' now and in the future (P19; P31; P26). As a sign of "belonging to Europe" (P19), the Label stands for 'official' recognition and confirmation of the heritage sites as European. As a side effect, this kind of interpretation enables actors in the heritage sites to see the potential further inquiries about the performance of their EHL sites as distrust expressed by the EU as a supposed authority.

The spatial logic of the EHL participant position stems from the notion that the significance of the site will grow and relates to a sense of superiority produced by the explicit or implicit connections with EUrope and its institutions. According to this logic, the broader scales are assumed to have a higher position in the multiscalar hierarchy, whereas the narrower scales entail a notion of 'limitation'. This approach makes the scales rather fixed entities in a nested spatial hierarchy (Lähdesmäki, Zhu, and Thomas 2019, 5). This recalls the 'Russian doll' model, in which scales are piled up as containers in a hierarchical order that both reflects and forms uneven power relations between social actors (see also Brenner 2001, 606; Lähdesmäki, Zhu, and Thomas 2019, 6, 9). Guided by this logic, our interviewees described the sites as in the process of expanding outward: as being "local and national, but not only" (P6); going "beyond local boundaries and national borders" (P1); or, as one practitioner stated, "you have to go up, and up, and go from local, regional, country, Europe" (P11). In an opposite development within the same process, Europe is reduced to nations (P24) that indicates "throwing away European cultural heritage" and having only national heritage left (P26). To distinguish between 'our' (primarily local or national) location and European scale, the 'EU' and 'Europe' may also be situated 'there'. This way, Europe is mapped as simultaneously both distant and desirable. The way in which some interviewees talk about Brussels as a distant place and a remote actor offers a good example for this. Brussels is referred to as a metonym of the authority of the EU and a central location on the European scale. While doubtless significant and sometimes admired, Brussels also remains distant in this context.

In parallel with the terms 'here' and 'there' that fix the location, the interviews include some examples of how 'upgrading' to Europe is constituted by mobility in both directions. In the process of expanding to a European scale, national actors either 'export' ideas beyond their national scale or 'import' ideas from 'Europe'. Similar mobility expands the European scale into what can be called 'international' or 'universal' scale, but the assumption is also made that European is universal (P31; P16, see also Smith 2006; Bhambra 2009, 81; Lähdesmäki, Zhu, and Thomas 2019, 10). As part of the same process, concerns about Europe's position in the world are expressed in some of the interviews. There are claims like Europe 'should resist' the external pressure of 'becoming too globalized in terms of these multinationals' (P18) or becoming 'crushed between the big global players' (P8). Here, resistance is entangled with the notion of Europe as lacking and/or needing to aim for (political) leadership (P17; P15).

EHL observer

Despite the generally positive attitude towards the Label, the position of EHL observer reflects a slight sense of dissatisfaction with it in daily practice. This manifests as criticism towards different aspects of the action. The name 'observer' indicates a more passive engagement with the action than that of the EHL participant and the EHL creator, without becoming too active or having too high expectations (anymore). The position mediates the lack of reciprocity expressed by some practitioners: while the practical support of the European Commission for the action remains vague and ambiguous, the sites are still expected to be fully committed to the EHL. As discussed earlier, the awarded sites are expected to work hard and commit to the idea(l)s of the EHL. However, as a side effect, the strict selection process also creates expectations towards site membership and the Commission, which are not necessarily met. In some interviews, practitioners openly criticized the fact that cooperation with the Commission is limited to the annual networking conference, whereas responsibility for the EHL has been externalized to the sites without financial support for this (P8; P15; P27, see Čeginskas 2019 and Chapter 2). As one of the interviewees captured the situation, the 'label work' comes 'on top' of all the other practical tasks and without any additional financial or human resources (P22).

The EHL observer position does not challenge the formal superiority of the Commission, and the rules of the 'official' hierarchy are followed in terms of the "European Union as the organization, which is above us" (P27). However, the sites are considered to stand for substantial places whose potential has not yet been sufficiently recognized, supported, and developed in the EHL framework. Hence, the position is accompanied by ironic sentiments towards the gap between the contribution of substance and the official authority of both the Commission and the EU (P21; P24).

The controversy related to this position is acted out by drawing a geographical distinction between the scales and by referring to the rhetoric of 'distant and hierarchical' Brussels as a metonym of the EU and a power centre responsible for the shortcomings of the action. Some practitioners referred to the application process as constituted by "pure European bureaucracy where the sites have to be introduced by using 'correct terms'" and "bureaucratic project language of the European Union" (P19). Characterization of the EHL as "one more European project" (P8) shows that the Label is not the first experience of this kind. In the observer position, the shortcomings are interpreted in the light of the lack of interaction and the way expectations and requests are presented to the sites (P17) in an atmosphere of distrust (P31).

The EHL observer position raises the crucial issue of how to present the sites as both unique and 'European' in the multiscalar context of the EHL. As one interviewee claims, people want to see 'our' specific features, not to hear the same story that can be heard in other places like Germany, England or Brussels (P19). This indicates that sites are willing to make individualized contributions to the European idea instead of promoting institutionalized and "official understandings" of the EU (P15; P19–21). At the same time, the practitioners value networking between the sites, whether now or potentially in future. In both cases networking is understood as a reciprocal process in which some sites exert substantial authority, and may justifiably take the 'unofficial' lead (see Chapter 1). Networks formed through audience engagement, with local people in particular, are considered to be very important. According to many site practitioners (e.g. P19–21; P26; P24; P37, see Čeginskas 2019), the EHL award has not affected the total number of visitors, and the attractiveness of the site is independent of the Label.

The examples show that those who take this position recognize the "official" order of smaller to larger scales as a basis for the EHL framework. The observer position enables the sites to juxtapose the officially central but substantially insignificant European Commission with the 'real' EHL sites or the local environments. The latter are seen to be close to the people and to have substantial relevance in preserving and advancing multiscalar European heritage (P7; P21; P20; P24). To illustrate that, some interviewees used different versions of a birth metaphor, describing the sites as standing for the roots of Europe (P8), the first steps of Europe (P32), and the beginning of Europe – reflecting the official EHL slogan "Europe starts here". In Sagres the practitioners even used the metaphor of the end of Europe and the end of the known world, combining the geographical location and the history of the site (P37). However, the pride that some practitioners take in being awarded the Label may be combined with disappointment. For instance, one practitioner felt that the potential offered by Robert Schuman House as a place where "Europe was dreamed and imagined" had not been developed by the European institutions or used as a representative site for European-scaled diplomatic events (P33).

The position of EHL observer mediates an understanding of the EHL sites as concrete locations of heritage vis-à-vis the European Commission and EUrope. This understanding stems from a more general notion of the local entities, like small towns or villages, as presumably more authentic scenes of events (e.g. P7; P21; P37). Robert Schuman House and Alcide De Gasperi House are good examples of such heritage sites, where visitors are embedded in personalized surroundings that display 'original scenes' of the past and explain the development of the European community. For instance, the house where De Gasperi was born in Pieve Tesino, a little village in the North Italian region of Trentino, close to Austria, was made into a heritage site and museum. The site not only provides factual information about De Gasperi's life and role in the development of the later EU, but visitors have the impression of gaining an 'intimate' insight into his life by visiting the room where he was born. Similarly, Robert Schuman House in the small village of Scy-Chazelles, close to Metz, was Robert Schuman's home until his death in 1963. Visitors can walk among his personal belongings, visit his study and bedroom, and even see the bed in which he died. With their focus on the biographies and personal lives, both heritage sites provide the illusion of a closer and intimate encounter with Europe's past in small, home settings. This presumed closeness supposedly makes such personal and local scales more real for the visitors. Indeed, in order to make people 'feel European', some interviewed practitioners emphasized a need to bring Europe closer to its citizens, instead of expecting local narratives to become Europeanized. Ideally, this process stems from an interaction between the local and European scales – if representatives of the small scales are listened and taken seriously, as one of our interviewees noted (P1).

EHL creator

The position of EHL creator is based on a strong identification with the EHL. As one of the interviewees captured it, "we already see ourselves as a European site [...] so that is part of our identity" (P35). This subject position values defining Europe through heritage and not through the continent (P24), and some actors even expressed willingness to use the opportunities and resources available at the sites to give the EHL an "extra reach" (P22; P33; P14). As one of the practitioners put it, the Label is a present given by the EU and the recipients, the sites, should feel both fortunate and responsible (P30). This position indicates eagerness to introduce the EHL to the audience and to increase the visibility of the Label beyond the sites (P22; P31; P30). For instance, some sites find it important to introduce the Label in their guided tours. As one practitioner explained: "when I make a tour, the EHL is always a huge topic of course, because it really lies close to my heart, and I explain very accurately also about other sites and the network" (P22). Like the other two positions, EHL creator indicates that the sites create substance for the Label. However, instead of focusing on following the criteria or sticking to the official expectations as in the previous positions, practitioners who take this position prioritize issues of substance based on the reciprocal interaction between the sites and the Commission. The position mediates the willingness of the sites to work to promote the EHL as an action of broader societal and public significance (e.g. P36; P35). Referring to the EHL slogan, one of the interviewees said that "'Europe starts with you', it's a responsibility" (P7; also P22).

In practice, this responsibility means developing the sites as 'European heritage'. While EHL observer position includes criticizing the application process as time-consuming, EHL creator position enables the interviewees to see it as a process that enables the applicants to create substance to the Label. This way, 'European heritage' becomes a process of continuous 'doing', instead of 'being' or 'becoming accepted'. The practitioners are prepared to invest time in introducing the heritage sites "in the light of the EHL" (P30). This is exemplified by the statement of the representative of Hambach Castle, who explained how the site practitioners aim to consolidate the EHL framework "much more thoroughly" into their presentation of the European dimension of the Hambach Festival (P23).

In this context, the question is not about upgrading the sites or bringing the EHL 'down' to the local scale but working together in the framework of the action (P23; P33). As one of the interviewees argued, the sites need to promote the Label, rather than expecting it to "give us money" (P34). Like the other positions, the EHL creator stems from the notion that people are more familiar with the sites than with the EHL action. However, in contrast to the other two positions, this realization encourages practitioners to use the familiarity with the sites to promote and strengthen the objectives of the EHL action (P30). The Label is valued for its potential: as one of the interviewees said, the EHL will develop into a strong label with a clear network (P14) where some sites will take the lead (P31; P33). Representatives who mapped their sites as 'not far from Brussels' were especially likely to see Brussels as a point for various EHL representatives to meet, interact, and cooperate.

While the positions of EHL participant and EHL observer are based on vertically moving 'upwards' or 'downwards' on an overlapping scalar hierarchy (upgrading to 'European' or returning to the 'authentic' local), the scalar order included in the views of EHL creator is different: instead of a nested model, the scales form a network of connectivity (see also Brenner 2001; Lähdesmäki, Zhu, and Thomas 2019, 7). On the one hand, the order of scales – from local via national to European and international – is challenged by creating direct connections between local and European scales. Moreover, the local scale has its variety: it can signify a "place dedicated to Europe" like the European District in Strasbourg or refer to local communities as heterogeneous and beyond national boundaries, like the ones near Sagres. Equally, it can map the core places related to the 'founders' of Europe like Robert Schuman House and Alcide De Gasperi House. As one interviewee from the house said, "big ideas and important ideas" can be evoked everywhere, also in small places like Pieve Tesino, a "village of six hundred people in the middle of the mountains" (P1). The interviewee pointed out that this distant and peripheral location that is difficult to access due to limited public transport does not diminish the importance of the site on a European scale (P1). The direct connections created between the local and European scales can in principle empower the sites and their nearby locations (P4). However, unlike in the position of EHL participant, the question here is not about 'upgrading' the scale by seeking for recognition but about contributing to the European scale.

The EHL creator position shows how creating direct thematic connections between the local and European scales is related to understandings about the national scale. Some interviewees favoured "decoupling" the European and national scales in the construction of the European scale, since strong empahsis of the national could cause shortcomings related to inclusivity and variety (P4; P14). Hence, the position makes explicit the idea of forming a European scale that is substantially different from the national one. As argued elsewhere (Turunen, n.d.), in the context of increasing immigration there is a need to imagine and discuss Europe and European heritage also in terms of the translocal scale, making the spaces of multiple cultural traditions explicit (see Anthias 2008). In the EHL context, the notion of the 'translocal' could be one example of the substantial difference between the European and national scales.

At the same time, the EHL creator position enables the sites to extend their scalar boundaries by creating connections to the 'international' or 'universal' scale. In this view, the sites can be present in a locality without being local heritage. As the practitioners from the Mundaneum told us, the heritage of the site situated in Mons is understood as the "DNA of Europe" (P30), "far from being local" but rather European or even universal (P28). However, people who held this position understood the meaning of 'universality' in different ways, depending largely on their mechanisms for creating connections between the EHL actors inside EUrope and with others outside the EU. As some of the practitioners commented, cooperation is not necessarily based on a dialogue but can in principle be used as a channel for promoting the values and heritage of the site in the spirit of a Eurocentric notion of hierarchy of cultures (P37; P34). This is partly connected to the EU's general difficulties in dealing with Europe's colonial past, indicated by the related discussion of how to understand the heritage 'cooperation' between the EU and the other parts of the world in the context of the EHL. As we have argued elsewhere (Kaasik-Krogerus et al. 2018), heritage-related conflicts and controversies are commonly located in the Balkans, the Middle East, or Afghanistan in the interviews, while EUrope is perceived through heritage-related stability and, thus, as a region of safety.

Geopolitics and transformative potential of heritage

Through analysis of the EHL as a geopolitical discourse, we identified three subject positions that we used to examine scalar dynamics and hierarchies related to this discourse. As a result, we could conduct a systematic analysis of spatial power relations and open them up without dividing the sites into pre-existing spatial categories, such as a European 'core' and 'periphery', that tend to confirm or even strengthen power imbalances.

The subject position of the EHL participant enables the actors to value a multiscalar hierarchy, in which the 'European scale', understood as either 'distant' or on 'top', is perceived as superior to the lower scales. In the framework of the EHL, this position stems from an ambivalence between pride in having received the Label on the one hand, since the European scale has been truly 'achieved' as a result of hard work, and, on the other hand, uncertainty due to feeling inferior to the EUropean authority. Instead of facilitating substantial discussion between the various actors, this position contributes to an ambiguous power interplay in the sites' agency, defined by 'having' European significance but 'following' EHL criteria and guidelines. Hence, the understanding of the EHL as a 'quality label' and therefore an 'upgrade' of their significance from a local or national to the European scale, can (unintentionally) strengthen the notion of Eurocentrism in the EU and beyond.

The EHL observer position contains critical notions concerning the claim of reciprocity and interaction between the European Commission and the heritage sites in the framework of the Label. The position is constituted by recognizing the formal 'downscaling' authority of the Commission in relation to the sites as 'lower' scale actors (see Swyngedouw 1997, 148; Lähdesmäki, Zhu, and Thomas 2019, 6). Simultaneously, however, the authority of the Commission is juxtaposed with the substantial superiority of the sites in representing heritage, making the sites the 'real' actors who make a difference in practice. As they are often perceived as authentic scenes of the historical past, the sites are situated on lower scales and therefore assumed to be close to the people. In this position, the ability of the EHL sites to bring the EU closer to the citizens is, however, doubted.

Both the EHL participant and the EHL observer rely on and strengthen the 'Russian doll'–type of scalar order, either by expecting the Label to upgrade their site to a broader European scale or by emphasizing the importance of descending to a less abstract and local scale and, thus, moving the idea of European heritage closer to the people. In both cases, the substantial value of the EHL remains subordinate to the criteria, rules, and regulations of the action. In terms of communication practices, these subject positions focus on listening to and either accepting or questioning the guidance, but not discussing or negotiating its substance. The positions bolster the relations of superiority and inferiority that work both from smaller and concrete to larger and more abstract scales.

The fact that the geopolitical hierarchies are actualized in the context of heritage shows their prevalence and general reach. However, the EHL action is a reciprocal relationship, in which geopolitical hierarchies are brought together with the transformative potential of heritage. The position of EHL creator shows the potential of 'heritage in action', in which interaction and dialogic communication between the Commission and the sites empower and strengthen both the sites' individual agency and their ability to substantially contribute to the EHL action. This position presupposes a polyvocal and dialogic communication between the sites and between the sites and the Commission as equally significant actors, creating substance and promoting meanings of Europe's heritage. The EHL creator does not aim for the recognition on the European scale: this position is based on an understanding that the sites are empowered by substantially contributing to the EHL, which deconstructs the hierarchical order of scales and related power relations (Lähdesmäki, Zhu, and Thomas 2019, 5). Disrupting the scalar order creates new openings, such as 'translocal' alternatives to the 'Europe of nations' or stressing the vagueness of the 'universal' scale. Furthermore, the EHL creator makes explicit the transformative potential of heritage. In contrast, the EHL participant shows how this transformative potential can take the form of transition towards a certain objective (e.g. Europeanizing heritage according to the Commission's guidelines), which is prioritized over processes and practices of (self-)reflection and dialogic interactions in open substantial discussions (see also Offe 1991; Vetik 2012, 12–13).

The difficulties related to broadening the national scale into the European, and the European scale to the universal, call into question the notion that scales are overlapping. There is no agreed understanding of what comes after the European scale, whether this might comprise the 'international' or the 'universal'. This is made explicit by framings such as "more than European" or located "outside European countries" (P16). While seeking to extend their reach, these claims communicate the central position of the European scale and transmit a notion of its expansion in relation to other scales. Although unintentionally, such references may first and foremost strengthen the European scale.

Our final conclusion concerning heritage as a practice of action and 'doing' relates to the engagement of citizens. The agency of the EHL sites and the empowering of the 'local scale' in the logic of the EHL action does not tell us how citizens are or become engaged with heritage at the sites or in dialogue on different scales. Based on the interviews with EHL practitioners, we conclude that this is not necessarily the case. As one interviewee captured it, it is important to 'make people think': "oh yes! Europe is a cool thing and we are all connected with each other" (P22; P1). This leaves questions for the further scrutiny, if the sites' dialogic position with 'Europe' includes an unintended sense of superiority vis-à-vis the citizens and their agency. Therefore it is important to critically examine citizens' engagement with the sites to ensure that the broader public is included in the multiscalar creation of heritage and to avoid unwanted 'top-down import' of the EHL (see Chapters 5 and 6).

References

Alasuutari, P. 2009. "The Domestication of Worldwide Policy Models." *Ethnologia Europaea* 39 (1): 66–71.

Anthias, F. 2008. "Thinking Through the Lens of Translocational Positionality: An Intersectionality Frame for Understanding Identity and Belonging." *Translocations: Migration and Social Change* 4 (1): 8.

Ballinger, P. 2017. "Whatever Happened to Eastern Europe? Revisiting Europe's Eastern Peripheries." *East European Politics and Societies and Cultures*, no. 31: 1.

Bhambra, G. 2009. "Postcolonial Europe or Understanding Europe in Times of the Postcolonial." In *The SAGE Handbook of European Studies*, edited by C. Rumford, 69–86. London: Sage.

Brenner, N. 2001. "The Limits to Scale? Methodological Reflections on Scalar Structuration." *Progress in Human Geography* 25 (4): 591–614.

Bortolotto, C. 2012. "The French Inventory of Intangible Cultural Heritage: Domesticating a Global Paradigm into French Heritage Regime." In *Heritage Regimes and the State*, edited by R. F. Bendix, A. Eggert and A. Peselmann, 265–282. Göttingen: Universitätsverlag Göttingen.

Čeginskas, V. L. A. 2019. "The Challenges in Creating Visibility of European Cultural Heritage: A Case Study of the European Heritage Label." *Ethnologia Fennica* 46: 109–134.

Cohen, S. B. 2015. *Geopolitics: The Geography of International Relations*. Third edition. Lanham, MD: Rowman & Littlefield.

Dainotto, R. M. 2007. *Europe (In Theory)*. Durham, NC: Duke University Press.

Delanty, G. 2017. *The European Heritage: A Critical Re-Interpretation*. London, NY: Routledge.

Dittmer, J. 2010. *Popular Culture, Geopolitics, and Identity*. Lanham, MD: Rowman & Littlefield.

Dittmer, J. 2014. "Towards New (Graphic) Narratives of Europe." *International Journal of Cultural Policy* 20 (2): 119–138.

EC (European Commission). 2014. *"European Heritage Label. 2014 Panel Report."* Brussels: European Commission.

EC (European Commission). 2019. "The European Heritage Label." Official website of the European Commission. Accessed 22 August 2019. https://ec.europa.eu/programmes/creative-europe/actions/heritage-label_en.

EP&C (European Parliament and the Council). 2011. "Decision No 1194/2011/EU of the European Parliament and of the Council of 16 November 2011 Establishing a European Union Action for the European Heritage Label." *Official Journal of the European Union*, no. L 303, 1–9.

Harrison, R. 2013. *Heritage: Critical Approaches*. New York: Routledge.

Harvey, D. 2015. "Heritage and Scale: Settings, Boundaries and Relations." *International Journal of Heritage Studies* 21 (6): 577–593.

Harvey, D. and A. Mozaffari. 2019. "Foreword." In *Politics of Scale. New Directions in Critical Heritage Studies*, edited by T. Lähdesmäki, S. Thomas, and Y. Zhu, ix–x. New York: Berghahn's Books.

Kaasik-Krogerus, S., V. L. A. Čeginskas, T. Lähdesmäki, and K. Mäkinen. 2018. "Drawing, Erasing and Crossing Borders. Negotiating Borders in the EU's Cultural Heritage Policy." Paper presented at ICCPR 2018, Tallinn, August 21–25.

Kaasik-Krogerus, S. 2019. "Politics of Mobility and Stability in Authorizing European Heritage: The Great Guild Hall in Estonia." In *Dissonant Heritages and Memories in Contemporary Europe*, edited by T. Lähdesmäki, L. Passerini, S. Kaasik-Krogerus, and I. van Huis, 157–181. London: Palgrave Macmillan.

Kisić, V. 2017. *Governing Heritage Dissonance: Promises and Realities of selected Cultural Policies.* The Hague: European Cultural Foundation.

Koch, N. 2015. "Gulf nationalism and the geopolitics of constructing falconry as a "heritage sport"." *Studies in Ethnicity and Nationalism* 15 (3): 522–539.

Komska, Y. 2018. "Introduction: A Discontiguous Eastern Europe." In *Eastern Europe Unmapped: Beyond Borders and Peripheries*, edited by I. Kacandes, and Y. Komska, 1–28. New York: Berghahn's Books.

Kuus, M. 2013. "Places of Lower Rank: Margins in Conversations." *Political Geography* 37: 30–32.

Lähdesmäki, T., and K. Mäkinen. 2019. "The 'European Significance' of Heritage: Politics of Scale in EU Heritage Policy Discourse." In *Politics of Scale. New Directions in Critical Heritage Studies*, edited by T. Lähdesmäki, S. Thomas, and Y. Zhu, 36–49. New York: Berghahn's Books.

Lähdesmäki, T., Y. Zhu, and S. Thomas. 2019. "Introduction: Heritage and Scale." In *Politics of Scale. New Directions in Critical Heritage Studies*, edited by T. Lähdesmäki, S. Thomas, and Y. Zhu, 1–18. New York: Berghahn's Books.

Lefebvre, H. 1991. *The Production of Space.* Translated by D. Nicholson-Smith. Oxford: Blackwell.

Liu, C., N. An, and H. Zhu. 2015. "A Geopolitical Analysis of Popular Songs in the CCTV Spring Festival Gala 1983–2013." *Geopolitics* 20 (3): 606–625.

Mälksoo, M. 2006. "From Existential Politics Towards Normal Politics? The Baltic States in the Enlarged Europe." *Security Dialogue* 37 (3): 275–297.

Mälksoo, M. 2009. "The Memory Politics of Becoming European: The East European Subalterns and the Collective Memory of Europe." *European Journal of International Relations* 15 (4): 653–680.

Marston, S. 2000. "The Social Construction of Scale." *Progress in Human Geography* 24 (2): 219–242.

Massey, D. 2005. *For Space.* London: Sage.

Moisio, S. 2011. "Geographies of Europeanization: The EU's Spatial Planning as a Politics of Scale." In *Europe in the World: EU Geopolitics and the Transformation of European Space*, edited by L. Bialasiewicz, 19–40. Ashgate: Farnham.

Moisio, S., V. Bachmann, L. Bialasiewicz, E. Dell'agnese, J. Dittmer, and V. Mamadouh. 2013. "Mapping the Political Geographies of Europeanization: National Discourses, External Perceptions and the Question of Popular Culture." *Progress in Human Geography* 37 (6): 737–761.

Neumann, I. B. 1999. *Uses of the Other: "The East" in European Identity Formation.* Minneapolis: University of Minnesota Press.

Offe, C. 1991. "Capitalism by Democratic Design? Democratic Theory Facing the Triple Transition in East Central Europe." *Social Research* 71 (3): 501–528.

Ó Tuathail, G. 1996. *Critical Geopolitics: The Politics of Writing Global Space.* Minneapolis: University of Minnesota Press.

Polynczuk-Alenius, K. 2018. "The Dialectics of Care: Communicating Ethical Trade in Poland." *Media and Communication* 6 (2): 199–209.

Saunders, R. A. 2017. *Popular Geopolitics and Nation Branding in the Post-Soviet Realm.* London: Routledge.

Saunders, R. A. and V. Strukov, eds. 2018. *Popular Geopolitics: Plotting an Evolving Interdiscipline.* London: Routledge.

Smith, L. 2006. *Uses of Heritage.* London: Routledge.

Suslov, M. and M. Bassin, eds. 2016. *Eurasia 2.0: Russian Geopolitics in the Age of New Media.* Lanham: Lexington Books.

Swyngedouw, E. 1997. "Neither Global Nor Local: "Glocalization" and the Politics of Scale." In *Spaces of Globalization: Reasserting the Power of the Local*, edited by K. Cox, 137–166. New York: Guilford/Longman.

Turunen, J. (n.d). "Borderscapes of Europe." Unpublished manuscript.

Velikonja, M. 2011. "EUrosis: A Critique of the EU Discourse in Slovenia." In *Cultural Transformations After Communism: Central and Eastern Europe in Focus*, edited by B. Törnquist-Plewa, and K. Stala, 17–58. Lund: Nordic Academic Press.

Vetik, R. 2012. "Sissejuhatus." In *Eesti poliitika ja valitsemine 1991–2011*, edited by R. Vetik, 7–22. Acta Universitatis Tallinnensis. Tallinn: Tallinna Ülikooli Kirjastus.

Wolff, L. 1994. *Inventing Eastern Europe: The Map of Civilization in the Mind of the Enlightenment.* Stanford, CA: Stanford University Press.

Chapter 4

Heritage and bordering
Unity in diversity and difference

Borders have a key role in contemporary debates and geopolitical imagination about Europe. The ideals and practices related to creating a sense of unity by making 'borderless spaces' inside the EU are entangled with proliferation and enforcement of borders, even through erecting walls to secure them (see also Rumford 2008, 53, 59, 60). Borders are not equal: they treat people in different ways and promote selective mobility at different speeds. For some, borders represent barriers slowing down or stopping their movement, while for others they signify gateways enabling their passage (Casas-Cortes et al. 2015, 57; see also Kinnvall 2016). Borders that have real and concrete effects for some people can seem invisible for others, who may not even recognize their existence (Rumford 2008, 41–42; see also Yuval-Davis, Wemyss, and Cassidy 2018, 230). The growing variety of approaches to borders concerns the actors engaged in bordering. In addition to nation-states, the EU has a prominent role in 'border work'. Simultaneously, ordinary people participate in the everyday processes of bordering (Rumford 2008, 17, 39; Yuval-Davis, Wemyss, and Cassidy 2018) through their daily interactions within their communities and society at large.

Since culture and cultural heritage are important intermediaries in the processes of bordering, the prominent role of borders in Europe is felt in the framework of making European heritage. The decision of the EHL action specifies that candidate sites have to show their cross-border or pan-European nature that goes beyond national borders, and transnational sites are expressly stated as eligible (EP&C 2011, 4). Various transnational sites have applied, and one, the former Natzweiler concentration camp and its satellite camps, located in France and Germany, was awarded the EHL in the 2017 selection round. Furthermore, several EHL sites are situated in border areas and/or deal explicitly with simultaneous drawing and erasing of borders, as well as with advancing and restricting cross-border mobility. Good examples include Robert Schuman House (France), Alcide De Gasperi House (Italy), Sagres Promontory (Portugal), the Great Guild Hall (Estonia), Camp Westerbork (the Netherlands), and Archaeological Park Carnuntum (Austria). Moreover, sites like the Village of Schengen in Luxembourg or the Pan-European Picnic Memorial Park in Hungary are presented in the European panel's selection reports as a symbols of "free movement of goods and passport-free travel" (EC 2017, 17) or a "borderless Europe" (EC 2014, 20; see also Lähdesmäki and Mäkinen 2019, 39). In addition to these symbolic references, the exhibitions at EHL sites commonly contribute to the geopolitical imagination of Europe with the use of maps and common references to borders (Turunen, n.d.).

On this basis, we approach the EHL as a geopolitical discourse where bordering is constituted by a mixture of drawing, erasing, and crossing borders on various scales in Europe and beyond (see also Yuval-Davis, Wemyss, and Cassidy 2018, 229–230). As Chapter 3 showed, in these processes of bordering, the European scale of heritage and geopolitics is constructed by connecting 'the European' to various other scales (see also Dittmer and Gray 2010, 1673). The idea of European heritage contributes first and foremost to creating, maintaining, and crossing (symbolic) borders, while forming ambiguous local, national, European, and global communities. European geopolitics, in turn, is related but not limited to the EU's 'hard' border practices and controls. Both notions are characterized by a contradictory process: the strengthening and securing of some borders and the simultaneous loosening of others. The ambiguities of bordering and border practices have been an inherent part of the EU since its very beginning when the cross-border experience of its 'Founding Fathers' (like Robert Schuman and Alcide De Gasperi) advanced the opening of internal borders (see Kaasik-Krogerus et al. 2018) and when the strength of the external (Eastern) borders was mediated in the context of the Iron Curtain metaphor and related border practices. The Iron Curtain has also been memorialized as European heritage by awarding the intergovernmental EHL in 2011 to a network of German sites related to it.

There has been a turn both in critical heritage studies and geopolitical studies towards everyday practices, experiences, and interactions. In critical heritage studies, the focus of research has shifted from conservation to 'conversation', towards dialogue and interaction (Waterton and Dittmer 2014; Kisić 2017; Lähdesmäki 2017) whereas critical geopolitical studies have extended their scope from states and political unions to human interaction and to how ordinary people experience and take part in geopolitics (Dittmer and Gray 2010, 1673–1674; Koopman 2011). Geopolitics researchers are paying increasing attention to how people produce geo/space in their daily interactions (see Massey 2008, 14–15). Accordingly, everyday life is anticipated to have a greater impact than narratives of political heroism on new European (geo)politics (Dittmer 2012, 119; see also Cram 2009).

In the spirit of this turn, in this chapter we bring together museum exhibitions as 'texts' and the agency of ordinary people to analyze how visitors to EHL sites take part in bordering in the process of 'doing' heritage (see also Dittmer and Gray 2010; Koopman 2011; Smith 2015). As the visitor interviews engage with people's perceptions of both the site and the idea of European heritage, they are approached as a dialogic process of meaning-making between the sites and the visitors. In a close reading, we inquire into how bordering takes place in the visitor interviews and how the interviewees use it to engage with the EHL and more generally Europe. Since the EU promotes the notion of 'unity in diversity' and the EHL is deemed to strengthen citizens' sense of belonging to the Union, we scrutinize bordering from the perspective of intertwined notions of unity, diversity, and difference. Visitors form and manage these notions in two directions: a sense of belonging to EUrope is sometimes entangled with an understanding that EUrope belongs to them (see also Balibar 2009a, 192–193; Yuval-Davis, Wemyss, and Cassidy 2018). In the conclusions, we discuss how this process of bordering enables people to make sense of Europe, its current realities, imagined ideals, and possible future scenarios.

Bordering in the service of unity, diversity, and difference

Borders have been defined as social, cultural, and political constructs that are both made meaningful and exploited by human beings as part of the institutionalization processes of territories (Paasi 2005, 22). The etymology of the word 'border' accords two controversial meanings to it: circumscription (Andrén and Söhrman, 2017, 3) in terms of cooperation, and exclusion as contested practices (Laine 2016; Andrén and Söhrman 2017, 3). As such, borders can imply the idea of exclusive belonging and often lead to restrictive policies on immigration and movement in social and geopolitical frameworks (Kendall, Woodward, and Skrbis 2009, 93).

During past decades, scholars have expanded the notion of border as a territorial 'edge' to include wider and multiple understandings of mobile bordering practices as a 'normal' and thus invisible part of everyday life (e.g. Parker et al. 2009, 586). Borders have become spaces where issues like unity, diversity, difference, change, and continuity are debated and enacted: they can be mapped as multifaceted, complex, and dynamic multiscalar entities that have symbolic and material forms and are maintained by various actors in different bordering practices (see also Laine 2016). Hence, bordering is not about "things in space" (Breglia 2006, 89) but social relations where people, regions, states, and Europe are positioned in relation to these shifting borders (see also Müller 2008, 323).

The imaginaries of EUrope are characterized by controversies and ambiguity (see also Jenkins 2008, 166): EUrope as a polity that distinguishes between clear inside and outside borders (Dittmer 2014; see also Bachmann and Sidaway 2009) is entangled with 'fuzzy' imaginaries constituted by non-contiguous space. For instance, some non-EU countries and areas are embedded within 'European space' (like Switzerland and Kaliningrad) whereas France and Spain possess territories that are located outside Europe (Rumford 2008, 33). This phenomenon is inherent in the EHL heritage sites. For instance, numerous visitors engaging with the Sagres Promontory on the Atlantic coast characterize the heritage site – reflecting the narrative told by the site itself – both as a place where Europe starts and ends and as a place from which the 'discoveries' and 'explorations' to other continents set out in the past centuries.

Rumford (2008) has used the idea of "European cosmopolitan borders" to describe how increasing free mobility and border crossing is contributing to the multiplicity of borders and the lack of clear separation between being inside or outside European space. However, not all European borders are cosmopolitan and not all groups of people experience them as such (Rumford 2008, 54, 67). Different groups of people both participate in and experience European bordering differently. The EUropean reality of borders draws on a two-way process where, on the one hand, the EU's idea of openness is endorsed by not possessing a closed space or clear borders within the EU and Schengen area (Balibar 2009b, 6–7), and, on the other hand, these attempts entangle with strong multi-layered border making and guarding that affect the mobility of certain groups (see also Scott 2009, 233).

Approaching borders as something to be crossed, allowing mobility, and seeing this as part of the idea of Europe is a key aspect of the EHL. The EU's 'Founding Fathers' emphasized the importance of culture for the economic and political rapprochement of European countries as early as the 1950s (Schuman 2010), as the EHL narrative highlights. Robert Schuman House explains that this was partly due to the 'Founding Fathers'' personal and family experience of borders as everyday zones of cultural exchange and mutual influence. According to the exhibition at Robert Schuman House, Schuman's vision of a peaceful Europe and cooperation between different European nationalities after the Second World War stemmed from his personal experience of permeable borders and his conviction of a possible cooperation and peaceful cohabitation between people living in the borderland. Similarly, numerous interviews with visitors to EHL sites located in internal border areas indicated that they easily engage with the notion of the border area as a uniting factor across state borders and sometimes also in terms of a 'birthplace' of Europe. Some of these visitors to the former houses of Alcide De Gasperi and Robert Schuman engaged with the life stories of both personalities as being from the border area and 'between' nations and cultures. According to one visitor to Alcide De Gasperi House, as she is half-Moroccan and half-Spanish, she could easily engage with the story of De Gasperi who had lived in the border area between two cultures. Hence, borders create an area that can be understood as a borderland, a space of cultural exchange and social interaction.

Such experiences and understandings of borders have an impact on the daily life of contemporary EU citizens, resulting in and from the creation of four freedoms – free movement of goods, capital, services and persons – across borders and the political ideal of Europe being 'united in diversity'. The Schengen Agreement signed in 1985 facilitated the crossing of internal EU borders and advanced the effortless day-to-day experience of borderlands in Europe. The fact that the village of Schengen, where the agreement and the Schengen Implementation Convention were signed, received the EHL in 2017 shows that attempts to cross, overcome, or erase borders are valued as European heritage. In this context, the EU's internal borders have at least partly become acknowledged as a zone of encounter in terms of active, everyday interaction and exchange that contribute to strengthening a notion of unity. Similarly, while moving within 'Schengenland', few identity markers show that one has actually left the EU, for instance when travelling from Copenhagen to Oslo (Risse 2003, 490). A similar idea is mediated by the images on Euro banknotes showing imaginary bridges, gateways, and windows that communicate the openness and connectivity of Europe (Shore 2000, 115). Since these images are from different time periods, they advance a sense of historical continuity between the current EU and Europe of past centuries. As part of European heritage, the ideas of both continuity and openness are constitutive to creating a sense of unity among EU citizens. Paradoxically, this does not necessarily make the construction of bordered spaces insignificant in people's minds and lives. In everyday life, borders are commonly understood as representations of images and imaginations related to the performance of banal daily routines and practices (Strüver 2005). For example, as a starting point for a trip or a holiday, borders can be a gateway for openings and opportunities (Rumford 2008, 60, 67).

In today's Europe, the ambiguous idea of border crossing is accompanied by parallel processes of dissolving and fortifying EU borders in the name of both promoting unity in diversity and emphasizing cultural differences. Tearing down the Iron Curtain as a border between the East and the West in order to 'unite both sides in diversity' has been followed with securing 'Fortress Europe' by strengthening of external borders with the help of various border management techniques (Leontidou 2004, 607). Paradoxically, fortifying the (primarily external) borders of EUrope can be seen as a process that creates a 'special' space. Rumford (2008, 61–63) writes about the EU's 'border work' that reaches beyond its external borders and 'stretches' European space to both Eastern partnership countries (Scott 2009) as well as the Mediterranean (Laïdi 2005 quoted from Bialasiewicz 2012, 844). The EU's attempt to foster a common European heritage is an example of strengthening the borders on a more symbolic and cultural level (Andrén and Söhrman 2017, 1). Despite the widespread claim during the EU Eastern enlargement that the candidate countries have 'always belonged to Europe culturally and historically', scholars have pointed out challenges related to incorporating 'Eastern' heritage into the 'joint European' one (see also Beck and Grande 2007, 3; Jones and Subotić 2011). Hence, the ambiguities of bordering are exemplified in the process of negotiating the ideals of diversity and openness as part of European heritage in the EU, with the intention to promote these ideals outside the EU (e.g. the Joint Communication of the European Commission and the European External Action Service, entitled Towards an EU Strategy for International Cultural Relations) and to protect the European heritage from 'foreign' influence that is supposedly 'different'.

In sum, borders and bordering constitute a resource for a sense of belonging in the EU, including the notions of inclusion and exclusion, and experiences of access and participation (Anthias 2008, 8; Rumford 2008, 66). While inclusion can be easily associated with erasing borders for creating unity, exclusion refers to non-belonging. The EU motto 'united in diversity' reflects the simultaneous attempts to foster and govern diversity, making it a good example of the process by which the scope of 'our' diversity and difference from 'the Others' are negotiated.

Four categories of bordering

Next, we will examine the processes of bordering through a more detailed reading of our visitor interviews. Since we did not specifically ask about borders in the interviews, the first phase of our analysis mapped any explicit references to borders (e.g. use of terms like 'borders', 'boundaries', and 'frontiers') in the data. This gave us an initial understanding about the scope of bordering in the interviews. In the next phase, the analysis was widened to include implicit references to borders (e.g. travelling, moving, differences, connections, and 'distant' places and people).

We drew an analytical distinction between spatial and temporal dimensions of bordering. Interviewees expressed temporal dimensions of bordering in relation to the relevance or irrelevance of borders in the contemporary world or Europe. The process of drawing, crossing, and dissolving (real and imagined) borders in the present is often linked in the interviews to other periods in the past and future. Bordering has a spatial dimension: borders can be used to unite, connect, or distinguish 'Europe' or the EU from other scales (such as the local, regional, national, or global), and their actors. As part of this process, the notions of 'inside' and 'outside' EUrope and its border regions are negotiated in the data by making a distinction between what is and what is not Europe. Our data indicated that the national and European scales are tightly intertwined, since the interviewees often simultaneously spoke from a national and European perspective.

The mapping of spatial and temporal dimensions resulted in the formation of four analytically distinct but partly overlapping categories of bordering in the data: (1) borderless Europe, (2) internal borders, (3) external borders, and (4) borderless world. In each category, we identified two subcategories. The visitors' practices of explicit and implicit bordering were sometimes ambiguous. When talking about borders, interviewees made more clear statements and drew lines, but did not necessarily do this when discussing issues implicitly related to bordering. Hence, cases of implicit bordering show how these categories are blurred: there is no fixed 'inside' and 'outside', but the same phenomena and processes can be located both within and without. At the core of the bordering process, in the borderscape, the scope and significance of what is internal and external, as well as the temporal axis of bordering, are negotiated (cf. Turunen n.d.). The data shows a tension between

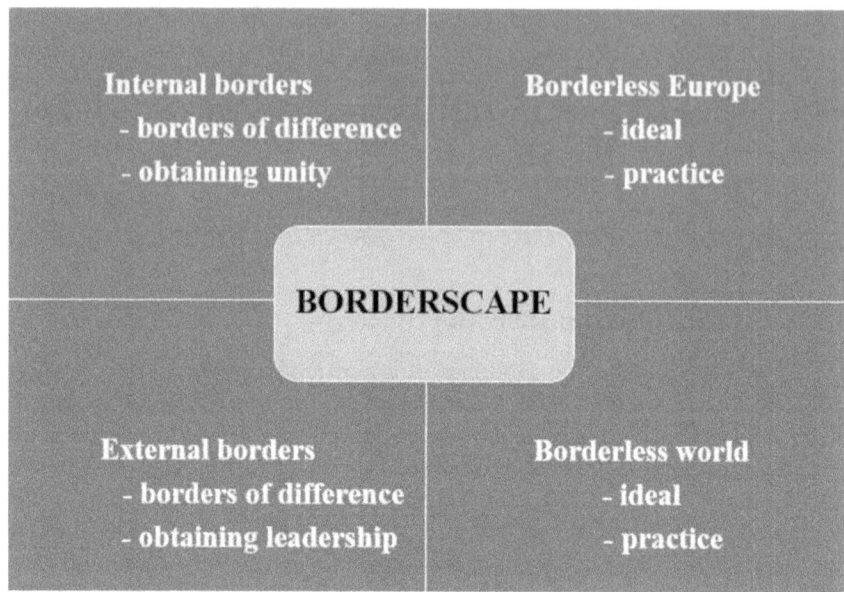

Figure 4.1 Categories of bordering formed on the basis of the visitor interviews at the EHL sites

a teleological assumption about moving from meaningful borders towards the notion that borders will either no longer be needed, or that they will 'return'.

Borderless Europe: Something old and something new

> So, travelling into Germany, we just visited Hamburg last week. And, well, 70 to 80 years ago, it wasn't possible to just drive up to Hamburg and just visit the city. We were in war with [Germany]. It's changed that much.
>
> (VS3/22)

This quotation is from a US citizen visiting Europe with his partner. Before arriving at Camp Westerbork in the Netherlands, where they were both interviewed by our team, they spent some time travelling in Europe. The quote above touches on the idea of 'borderless Europe' from two perspectives. Borderless Europe is an (unattainable) future oriented ideal, that did not exist in the past and that for some is still out of reach. At the same time, for the couple we interviewed, borderless Europe already exists as a practice. There is a tension between these positions that plays out especially in temporal terms. While practice can lead towards the ideal, the normative, utopian notion embedded in ideals remains always out of reach – as a desirable objective not yet achieved in practice. Both ideal and practice communicate a strong sense of unity.

To start with the former, the vision of Europe as a united entity without borders mediates and contributes to a subcategory, the borderless ideal. It is notable that borders arise in this subcategory first and foremost in a symbolic sense as barriers that characterize people's views and understanding of Europe. The interviewees who engaged with such a borderless ideal tried to envision Europe as a single unified space (VS1/1). Inherent to this vision is the idea of sharing common elements, like values or a "European mindset", across national scales and borders and constructing Europe together, with others (VS7/1; VS3/4). Emphasizing connections to other people is interesting, as the idea of being European is often associated in the interviews with open-mindedness (e.g. VS2/16; VS2/17). Open attitudes are juxtaposed by some interviewees with a national mindset focused on maintaining integrity of borders, advocating for closure and disintegration, or referring to dangers embedded in people's thinking that their identity "ends at the border" (VS7/18; also VS8/8). The need to think beyond national spheres is further emphasized by calls to look beyond the historical East-West and North-South dichotomies. As one visitor argued, "you must be able to count on Europe, meaning we shouldn't be West and East in a dualist way" (VS10/8).

Parallel to the notion of sharing a common vision of and for Europe runs a narrative about cooperating to create and facilitate unity in Europe (VS9/8; VS9/9). Here the focus is on future achievements. Different spheres like economics or politics indicate the condition of not being 'there yet', a work in progress that is expected to continue (VS6/1; VS11/36; VS3/3). In sum, the borderless ideal is first and foremost future oriented, and its visions and imaginaries are constructed against the present condition. The aim is to achieve certain ideals related to Europe, shared and worked for by 'Europeans'. However, this approach also highlights how borderless Europe as a normative utopian state always remains an ideal.

In contrast to the borderless ideal, borderless practice is constituted by an understanding that a Europe without borders exists as an everyday reality and interaction of its citizens. The main argument for a borderless Europe used in the interviews is based on one of the four freedoms of the EU. Most often these interviews invoked the free movement of people, or "freedom of travelling" (VS3/26) as captured by one visitor to Camp Westerbork. As the interviewees put it, since the "borders are open" (VS3/24; also VS11/33), people can "cruise around all Europe" (VS7/10) and go to different places. Some interviewees also mentioned the Schengen Agreement in this context as a contract that makes state borders inside EUrope invisible (VS4/17; VS7/5; VS7/6).

The interviewees gave various examples of mobility: travelling as a tourist and visiting different countries, benefitting from the Erasmus educational exchange programme, and working abroad. The common denominator for these experiences is opportunity to encounter other people from foreign countries and experience different languages and cultures (e.g. VS1/12; VS2/8; VS4/16; VS5/6; VS8/12; VS10/20; VS10/21). Their experiences connect either to notions of rupture between contemporary and past phases of 'Europe' or to notions of continuity that see contemporary Europe as the result of a longer development. In the interviews, both notions are constructed as part of contemporary reality and substantiated by examples from people's everyday lives. For instance, the ruptures emphasize how certain aspects of travelling have become easier. As one interviewee put it, "a hundred years ago, you couldn't do this, or at least with much more difficulty" (VS1/12). On the other hand, the opportunity to travel freely was taken for granted by younger interviewees as they had never experienced travel before the Schengen Agreement came in force (VS1/15;VS10/8;VS10/9).

Furthermore, the visitor interviews show that Europe's present unity is often contextualized in terms of historical continuity. The notion of unity was perceived as dating back to distant history, "moved across the whole continent through all centuries and millennia" (VS2/9) and embodied in "traces" of the past that can still be found in contemporary Europe (VS2/7). Several visitors constructed the notion of contemporary Europe as one, with its borders and regions being in flux, but still as inherited from antiquity (VS5/1;VS7/2;VS8/18) and argue that a lot has been shared in Europe since "that time" (VS2/4; VS3/31). For example, visitors to Carnuntum frequently drew parallels between a borderless Europe and the Roman Empire that was "everywhere" and spread across at least half of Europe.

In sum, the interviews make explicit the positive features of borderless Europe and the ways in which citizens benefit from it. Simultaneously, 'borderlessness' as a state that becomes part of 'normality' is entangled with a certain 'border blindness': people do not necessarily become aware of the existence of borders that are invisible in their daily lives (Rumford 2008, 41–42). On the one hand, the contemporary borderless reality of EU citizens is juxtaposed with the hindered mobility in the past, such as the heritage of the Second World War. On the other hand, there is an implicit assumption about the universality of free movement without recognizing those who are not able to move freely in Europe, like people seeking asylum in the EU, or those who cannot benefit from freedom to travel for economic reasons and who most probably do not engage with the sense of unity created by borderlessness.

Internal borders: Debating unity, diversity, and difference

> I think that's something we also have in Europe, where we still have borders in between the countries, but they are still linked together, and united.
>
> (VS4/7)

As indicated by this quotation, there was a trend in the interviews to discuss the continuing importance of Europe's internal borders. In this category the interviewees referred to both concrete borders between the countries and more abstract or symbolic ones that are seen to exist between Europe's manifold 'cultures'. While the condition of 'borderlessness' was cherished, maintained, and constructed directly in relation to a notion of unity, the category of 'internal bordering' is more heterogeneous. It shows the complexities of negotiating notions of unity, diversity, and difference within Europe. The concepts of diversity and difference in relation to unity are used in the data in two ways: either as synonyms, or to distinguish between enriching diversity and challenging or even problematic difference. Both can contribute to forming the condition of 'unity in diversity' but larger differences are also seen as a threat to unity.

As revealed in numerous interviews, European and non-European visitors alike consider that both cultural diversity and challenging difference are manifested in Europe's distinct languages, cultures, history, and heritage. Although potentially causing tensions, these aspects are seen as the key characteristics inherited from the past that constitute contemporary Europe and which therefore need to be protected and conserved (e.g. VS2/12). Discussions on difference and diversity are also understood as entangled with ideas of sharing commonality and similarities across European countries. As one interviewee put it, being different but also similar is "our strength" (VS1/2), which can be learned through direct interaction and encounters with different cultures, as other interviewees argued (VS2/15; VS8/13). While the statements in this category reflect perceptions of the cultural and linguistic differences inherited from Europe's past as a challenge or obstacle to unity, they nevertheless often argue in favour of encouraging diversity and overcoming significant differences. On the basis of this controversy, we formulated two subcategories: borders of difference and obtaining unity.

In the subcategory borders of difference, explicit connections between the past and the present are created on the basis of two-fold mobility. On the one hand, the interviewees referred to the differences inherited from centuries long past that are seen to create a path dependency towards certain developments in the EU. As one of the interviewees put it, unity is difficult "if you look in the past at how much war there was between the different countries" (VS3/9). In the contemporary EU, the differences reveal themselves to visitors in the form of the different interests and behaviour of its member states (e.g. VS1/5) and accordingly as a lack of unity, both linguistic and cultural, that would be comparable to that within a single country (e.g. VS7/8).

On the other hand, the internal differences of the EU are interpreted in this category as "turning back" (VS1/2), referring to a process, where the presumed unity of the near past is replaced by increasing differences (VS2/11). There are direct and indirect references in the data to various 'crises' of Europe – particularly to economic hardships and the support and financial loans given to some member states as part of the attempt to solve the crises of the Eurozone (VS6/9; VS4/10; VS4/11). Some of our interviewees also pointed out challenges regarding the principles of democracy, like freedom of the press (VS7/2) or respecting the law (VS2/10). Additionally, the rise of nationalism and the extreme right across Europe, as well as the recently reinstated border controls and new fences in some European member states, both of which create a more abstract sense of 'closing up Europe', were seen to hamper cohesion and unity (VS5/6;VS9/10). As one of the interviewees noted: "we now live in times when Europe is shaky, and this worries me a lot" (VS10/1).

In this subcategory, some interviewees referred to the EU Eastern enlargement as an event that has extended Europe's space but also brought borders back into the EU by markedly increasing the difference and thereby decreasing the unity of the Union (e.g. VS9/2). Visitors from 'older' EU member countries described the Central and Eastern European member states of the EU as 'different' (VS5/16), since they "have such a different culture that we have here in the Benelux and in France and Germany" (VS3/7). Some visitors emphasized the presumed 'Asian' influence of the East European member states, by for instance claiming that Eastern European countries "have always been buffer countries between a European model of civilization and a more Asian model of civilization" (VS1/9). While the visitors voiced perceived cultural differences, referring like one visitor to "Eastern culture" (VS1/11), underlying arguments include economic reasons and work competition by the unwanted influx of "workers from the East" (VS10/15). Such comments not only refer to geographical distinctions but also allude to existent hierarchical dimensions of the EU. For instance, some interviewees talked about lowering bars so that "everybody could be part of the European Union" (VS3/9) or mentioned that it was a mistake to incorporate too early nation-states that still struggled with their past and related economic and political problems (VS5/9; also VS8/5;VS8/18;VS8/20). As concerns the future, some visitors voiced expectations of the 'Eastern countries' eventually unifying with 'central Europe' (VS1/9), suggesting that Europe's core is represented by the founding members of the EU.

While in the subcategory of borders of difference the agency of the interviewees was limited to making observations and/or expressing concerns related to borders, they took a more active approach to the idea of obtaining unity and their visions of the ideal situation. As one interviewee claimed, despite a lot of differences, people are working hard together for the unity of the EU even if the goal is sometimes hard to achieve (VS1/1). In general, the existence of various cultural and political differences was acknowledged without constructing an either/or distinction between differences and unity. Many interviewees recognized both differences and similarities as well as things that Europeans share, like values and history (e.g. VS5/22;VS5/23).

Furthermore, some interviewees noted that while Europe as a whole is created by a mixture of differences (VS8/11) and diversity (VS2/16;VS1/1) this does not prevent Europe from 'working' (VS8/23) as seen in the EU. Hence, a shared understanding of having various differences can actually contribute to the sense of unity (VS1/1). Unsurprisingly, the most common way of picturing differences in this subcategory was to draw from and contribute to the notion of a Europe of nation-states (see also Abélès 2000; De Cesari 2017; Turunen, n.d.). The interviewees emphasized that even in a joint Europe, countries and nations have their own cultures and histories (VS2/1) that should be cared for (VS7/21), hence emphasizing the need to preserve differences and avoid the homogenization of Europe's cultural diversity (e.g. VS9/16).

Unity was communicated in the interviews as a work in progress where ongoing action was supposed to contribute to both the present and the future imaginaries of united Europe (VS2/8). On a more concrete level, the question for many visitors is about coming together to cooperate and act jointly (e.g. VS2/16; VS6/6). One of the interviewees likened the attempt to create unity in Europe to making music in an orchestra, where the diverse tones and instruments play together and make it sound beautiful (VS6/5). To make explicit the efforts required to fulfil the ideal of a united Europe, interviewees used expressions like 'working hard' and 'figuring things out' (VS1/1; VS7/5).

In sum, the past has an important, but not a uniform, role in constituting an understanding of 'unity in diversity' in the process of bordering. On the one hand, there are references to the common past as existing in the background and enabling people to relate the idea of unity to notions of continuity with the past. On the other hand, many visitors emphasized the importance of taking conscious decisions and joining forces across borders to overcome past conflicts and differences in order to create unity. Europe's unity is perceived as a work in progress in which the final goal is not being or becoming the same or homogeneous but being together despite countless differences. Unity is therefore both a lost and future utopia: an ideal condition that contemporary Europe seems to recede from and a future task and political choice to bring and keep the countries together.

External borders of difference

> [W]e lately visited Africa, and the difference is huge. Then you're happy to be European and to be able to live a life like this.
>
> (VS7/20)

In this quotation the visitor from Belgium juxtaposes Europe with Africa to simultaneously highlight differences between them and create a sense of unity among fellow Europeans. The example illuminates how constructions of unity and difference mutually influence one another and work in processes of bordering: they help to strengthen a sense of internal unity by excluding the ones outside as 'different'. In our data, the claims about differences are made by visitors from countries inside and outside the EU; members of both groups recognize differences during their visits to the EHL sites. In terms of external borders, we formulated two subcategories based on the relevance given to the temporal aspect in the process of bordering: borders of difference and obtaining leadership.

Borders of difference is a subcategory characterized by a rather static perception in which numerous interviewees (sometimes implicitly) juxtapose Europe, or more specifically the EU, with the features, practices, and heritage that characterize distinct geographical and cultural areas. Various regions were mentioned in the interviews, starting from continents like Africa or Asia and ending with single countries like India, Singapore, or Russia. In some interviews, this distinction was broadened to include people either by claiming that for instance Canadians, Australians, or Americans are different from Europeans (VS9/8) or by referring to people's distinctive mentalities across different parts of the world (VS9/14). The observations were largely made by the interviewees who have travelled outside the EU and experienced these places to be 'different from Europe'. To capture the difference, visitors tended to point out issues like "diverse lifestyles and cultures" on different continents (e.g. VS2/16). As one Japanese interviewee explained, the fact that there are not many Christians in Japan makes it culturally very different from Europe (VS5/3; also VS9/25).

The visitors sometimes mediated differences by referring to the import-ance of a sense of home, which they usually associated with having a deeper knowledge and understanding for a certain place. Some interviewees with a European background argued it is easier to feel at home in Europe than in Asia, Africa, or "even America" (VS3/25; VS3/27). They also created a link between geographical distance and knowledge about other places. Frequently visitors claimed that the further one goes from Europe, the more difficult it becomes to understand the culture, customs, and practices of the foreign and new surroundings as they become more different from home (VS2/7; VS9/14; VS9/23). The process works both ways – understanding culture and cus-toms in Europe is also assumed to be more difficult for visitors from outside Europe (VS11/12). European visitors often claimed that (longer) stays outside Europe have transformed their sense of belonging to a home country into a sense of feeling European, as the global context diminished the significance of national and cultural differences between European countries and cultures. As part of the bordering process, the entangled experience of distance and diffe-rence may contribute to strengthening the notion of European unity. In the words of one interviewee, "the further away you are from Europe, the more you become European" (VS2/19). The data also shows variation in how visitors experience and conceptualize difference. On the one hand, some interviewees emphasized that they did not want to create oppositions but facilitate a com-parison with other geographical and cultural regions (VS9/18; VS9/20; VS9/21). On the other hand, the difference between 'comparison' and 'opposition' is rather vague: comparison based on presumed characteristics may result in a stereotypical juxtaposition of what Europe is and what it is not. For instance, one interviewee stated that due to the differences he perceived, Turkey was not part of Europe for him (VS5/9).

While distinctions are made between different but parallel entities in the sub-category borders of difference, the next subcategory, obtaining leadership, is constituted by the hierarchical perceptions of superiority and inferiority that are negotiated in the process of bordering. Unlike the rather static construction in borders of difference, the perceived hierarchies in the second subcategory make visible the key role of the temporal aspect in notions of difference and unity.

Practices and processes that are in the past of some parts of the world may still be part of the present in other (e.g.VS5/19).These other parts of the world may be rather close places like the Middle East or former Yugoslavia (VS2/8). Especially the visitors to Camp Westerbork created a link between Europe's (dark) past and the present of some other areas of the world.The claim 'never again' related to the experiences of Second World War and Holocaust in Europe is juxtaposed with the fact that similar events are happening now, albeit outside the EU borders. These examples show how visitors make sense of these contemporary events outside the EU without creating a link to the practice of contemporary EUrope. Furthermore, in temporal terms of bordering, Europe is shown to be 'ahead' of some other areas. In this context, the superiority of contemporary Europe is (implicitly) indicated and sometimes also criticized (e.g.VS3/22).

The obtaining leadership subcategory refers more explicitly to an open power struggle between states and/or regions in the world with an aim of 'winning the game' (VS9/16;VS9/27). Claims made in this subcategory included that Europe has to stand up for democracy against "despotic countries" (VS7/5), preserve its position among the "big blocks of nations" (VS7/23) or even fill the position of a "world leader" (VS8/1). Interestingly, these positions were voiced by both European and non-European visitors alike.The examples were guided by a strong temporal dimension. The future imaginary of a stronger Europe in relation to other great powers stems both from the past, when "Europe was much stronger" (VS4/11) and from the current situation when it is positioned as inferior to the other 'great powers', like China or the United States. The necessity of bringing unity in order to achieve political goals was emphasized. For instance, several visitors explicitly referred to the United States having managed to 'unite' the states 'long ago'; consequently, Europe could or should do that too in order to become stronger (VS1/8;VS10/8;VS11/22;VS6/1).The aspect of unity concerns issues like economic integration of European states but also concerns diversity in general.While one interviewee pointed out that Europe could learn from how India or some African countries handle their many languages in the everyday context (VS9/28), the multitude of languages in Europe, especially compared to official monolingualism in the United States, was also seen by some as an issue that needs to be 'solved' before achieving unity between European countries, since having many official languages tends to make things complicated within the EU (VS3/9;VS6/9;VS4/5).

Borderless world

> I just feel like a person of the world. That's all. I'm just a person of the world. I could live in the United States and I could live in the Netherlands. That's all.That's it. I don't feel tied to a particular country.
>
> (VS3/21)

The quotation indicates the core of this category: the world is experienced as one entity and instead of a juridical basis, the citizenship of this world is constituted by experiences. Consequently, the process of bordering in this category shows how the external borders of EUrope, or any other territory, become obsolete. Like the category of borderless Europe, this category is constituted by the subcategories of ideal and practice. The first subcategory, based on the dreams and expectations formulated by the visitors, moves on an abstract level by emphasizing universality and related imaginaries. In the second, bordering is put into a temporal context, starting from past developments and heading towards future prospects.

In the data, the borderless ideal subcategory is constituted more as a state of mind or an understanding of the world than an actual part of the social reality. The interviewees did not claim that the world is borderless but envision the positive aspects of this ideal as part of their worldview. For instance, the notion that European identity tends to create borders between people was questioned (VS3/22). Similarly, distinguishing between inside and outside of Europe (VS3/21) was challenged as a practice that could cause exclusion (VS6/10). Some interviewees were also critical of juxtaposing Europe with other areas (e.g. VS9/1; VS10/3) and a notion of superiority related to that (VS3/28). One example of this is making a distinction between the EU as a fixed entity and Europe as a wider community that does not have clear borders. This contributes to widening of the membership of the EU and spreading some of its principles, like the four freedoms (VS2/19; VS6/22; VS7/22). The geographically limited area of diversity is widened beyond Europe, imagining that "a world state defined by the UN" could exist in the future (VS7/2).

The borderless ideal is largely based on the principle of universality and an assumption that certain universal issues and characteristics make borderless space possible, in Europe and beyond. One example of this view is given by a visitor who interpreted the exhibition in Alcide De Gasperi House. The interviewee told us that De Gasperi's ideas about paying attention to problems and social issues are universal and can be spread all over the world. In this subcategory, people are seen to be the same all over the world, for instance, willing to take care of children and elderly people and mostly doing good things (VS3/29). Although meant to increase inclusivity, the scope of the principle of universality remains problematic in this context. Since the interviewees did not elaborate on their position, they did not consider that different people may face different borders and not all of them experience cosmopolitan borders (Rumford 2008, 54, 67). Therefore, while envisioning a future imaginary of a borderless world as an 'end goal' and the ideal to "work for" (VS10/23), the fact that the starting point and the road towards this is not the same for everybody was usually not taken into account (see also Beck and Grande 2007, 1–27).

The practice subcategory draws on past experiences that can be either similar or interrelated. Concerning past similarities, the narratives mediated by the EHL sites may help the visitors to realize that similar stories are told outside the EU, too. Commenting on the exhibition in Camp Westerbork, one inter-viewee explained that since the United States has had a slave trade and has a huge population of migrant workers, great similarities can be found between the narratives of Camp Westerbork and narratives in the United States. The visitors to the Historic Gdánsk Shipyard also stated that people from different parts of the world could relate to the rise of the Solidarity movement in Poland, a process that created a wide sense of unity.

In addition to similar experiences, some interviewees traced back to the common roots and heritage that are supposed to create unity across the borders in the world (e.g. VS9/22). These claims referred to different processes of mobility, to the people who have come to and left Europe. The interviewees noted, for instance, that we all come from Africa (VS9/27) and many cultures have been imported to Europe (VS11/28). Hence, contemporary Europeans probably have ancestors from very distant places without necessarily being aware of this (VS9/28), so it is important to be receptive to other cultures today (VS9/10), as some of our interviewees stated. Moreover, some of the interviewees claimed that individuals with European roots "made America great" (VS5/14; VS5/13) and emphasized how European influences can be observed in different parts of the world (VS7/19). This process was seen to continue in today's world that gets smaller and smaller, as one interviewee noted (VS2/17), in relation to globaliza-tion that makes the borders meaningless and creates similarities and homogen-eity in Europe and beyond (VS5/23; VS10/23; VS6/17).

Although past connections were discussed in a rather general level and a positive or a neutral way, the interviews included a few critical mentions of past attempts to extend the borderless space beyond Europe in the form of colonization and related exploitation of resources (VS7/12; VS11/21). For instance, Sagres Promontory is seen in the data as a place on the "edge of Europe" characterized by the attempts to "find other worlds" and make them part of Europe in a process of conquest (VS11/33). These examples indicate the power hierarchies related to bordering and the idea of borderlessness. These hierarchies were also recognized by some of our interviewees: the Europeans' past experiences of their continent as the 'centre of the world' are supposedly different from the ones of the people in former colonies (VS7/12; VS9/23). The interviewees, however, situated these experiences largely in the past without creating explicit links to power hierarchies in contemporary Europe (see De Genova 2017, 18).

In sum, this category of bordering reveals an ambiguous process constituted by, on the one hand, the principle of universality and an ideal of unity and, on the other hand, a variety of past and present experiences of what borderlessness means and stands for. In the framework of European heritage and more pre-cisely the EHL, the cleavage between the abstract ideals of borderlessness and the complex and controversial practices of bordering could be better addressed in the narratives of the EHL sites by including different viewpoints and encour-aging debates on borders and about unity, diversity, and differences.

Bordering and the hierarchies of the European inside and outside

Engaging with the EHL sites shows the variety and scope of everyday bordering. On the one hand, a lack of borders appears in the data as both an ideal and an ongoing practice: either borders do not matter (any longer) or there is a vision and sometimes also a 'strategy' for getting rid of them. On the other hand, interviewees take existing borders for granted and accept them as part of contemporary reality. In this case, the borders guide the aims of obtaining internal unity of the EU or the EU's leadership in the world. Borders create differences and divisions, but differences also legitimize and justify the borders, make them 'natural' and taken for granted. Exclusive and 'different' categories of inside/outside as well as other spatial and symbolic hierarchies are accepted along with borders. This shows their strength: borders are accepted and they matter, although they are also criticized and not necessarily liked.

The analysis of bordering made visible hierarchies both inside and outside the EU. The problematic 'difference' inside the EU was linked to issues like the Union's Eastern enlargement, which shows where the EU's simultaneous outside and inside borders were and are located. The analysis confirms what other scholars have pointed out: turning external borders into internal ones is a multifaceted and complex process (see Dzenovska 2013, 410–411; Dzenovska and De Genova 2018, 10–11). Taking external borders for granted goes together with taking the "world hierarchy" and a competition for leadership of it for granted, too. Many of our interviewees saw Europe as possibly inferior to the existing 'great powers'. The need to strengthen the EU to cope in global competition was discussed in the interviews, but without creating connections between the European present and its colonialism. The latter is basically missing from the bordering discourses in our data, since it is mentioned only couple of times and as a past phenomenon without contemporary relevance.

The fact that borders were not idealized in our data indicates that visitors at the EHL sites do not represent European citizenry as a whole. For instance, there were no explicit claims for strengthening external borders (i.e. Fortress Europe). Our analysis of bordering shows multiplicity of borders but does not shed too much light on the different allocation of rights to various people by these borders (Casas-Cortes et al. 2015, 57). Everyday bordering practice indicates 'border blindness', that is, an inability to see that borders address people in different ways or do not even concern everybody. Our analysis demonstrated how bordering took place in discussions on about universal ideals or values. Despite their claimed 'universality', these views largely mediate Eurocentric values and practices (see also Smith 2006; Lähdesmäki, Zhu, and Thomas 2019, 10). Apart from questions such as who does and does not move across borders, what is missing in our data is an enquiry about who is in control of this movement (Yuval-Davis, Wemyss, and Cassidy 2018, 231). The EHL could create a dialogic space to raise these issues and strengthen the agency of the people.

Of the four categories of bordering, the strongest agency for people in Europe is provided by the notion of a borderless Europe where citizens both benefit and work for borderlessness. The interviewees highlighted the outcomes of this work by juxtaposing borders in the past with the options offered by a borderless Europe today. The agency of citizens could be strengthened in relation to internal bordering by empowering those who do not yet benefit from borderless Europe. While some interviewees challenged Europe's external borders from a universal point of view as 'citizens of the world', the EHL could contribute to this challenge by offering other options to critically explore these external borders, for instance engaging with multi-voiced narratives related to them. Past and present experiences and events can be negotiated and used to create and question future imaginaries of Europe. Moreover, bringing different narratives together could help to challenge the static vision of the rest of the world as 'just different' from Europe and/or as living in a time that is already in the past for Europeans. The relations between borderless Europe and people seeking asylum in Europe were very rarely discussed by our interviewees. Instead of designating the EHL to 'immigration sites', the existing sites could create spatial and temporal continuity and connections to make the topic present in various contexts.

Finally, since heritage is largely about future imaginaries, a shift from looking for similarities and differences as something inherited from the European past to an approach of 'doing' heritage could be strengthened in the framework of the EHL. Without diminishing the importance of past experiences, it is essential that the notion of 'too big differences inherited from the past' does not guide people dealing with the issues of borders, heritage, and Europe today. Heritage has the transformative potential to help contemporary citizens to meet the challenge of dealing with the past, making both the past and contemporary interaction between 'inside' and 'outside' Europe more explicit and negotiable.

References

Abélès, M. 2000. "Virtual Europe." In *An Anthropology of the European Union: Building, Imagining and Experiencing the new Europe*, edited by I. Bellier and T. M. Wilson, 31–52. Oxford: Berg.

Andrén, M. and I. Söhrman. 2017. "Introduction." In *Cultural Borders of Europe: Narratives, Concepts and Practices in the Present and the Past*, edited by M. Andrén, T. Lindkvist, I. Söhrman, and K. Vajta, 1–17. New York: Berghahn's Books.

Anthias, F. 2008. "Thinking Through the Lens of Translocational Positionality: An Intersectionality Frame for Understanding Identity and Belonging." *Translocations: Migration and Social Change* 4 (1): 5–20.

Bachmann, V. and J. D. Sidaway. 2009. "Zivilmacht Europa: A Critical Geopolitics of the European Union as a Global Power." *Transactions of the Institute of British Geographers*, no. 34: 94–109.

Balibar, E. 2009a. "Europe as Borderland." *Environment and Planning D: Society and Space* 27 (2): 190–215.

Balibar, E. 2009b. "Ideas of Europe: Civilization and Constitution." *Iris* 1 (1): 3–17.

Bialasiewicz, L. 2012. "Off-Shoring and Out-Sourcing the Borders of EUrope: Libya and EU Border Work in the Mediterranean." *Geopolitics* 17 (4): 843–866.

Beck, U. and E. Grande. 2007. *Cosmopolitan Europe*. Cambridge, UK: Polity.

Breglia, L. C. 2006. *Monumental Ambivalence: The Politics of Heritage.* Austin: University of Texas Press.

Cram, L. 2009. "Introduction: Banal Europeanism: European Union Identity and National Identities in Synergy." *Nations and Nationalism* 15 (1): 101–108.

Casas-Cortes, M., S. Cobarrubias, N. De Genova, G. Garelli, G. Grappi, C. Heller, S. Hess et al. 2015. "New Keywords: Migration and Borders." *Cultural Studies* 29 (1): 55–87.

De Cesari, C. 2017. "Museums of Europe: Tangles of Memory, Borders, and Race." *Museum Anthropology* 40 (1): 18–35.

De Genova, N. 2017. "Introduction: The Borders of "Europe" and the European Question." In *The borders of "Europe": Autonomy of Migration, Tactics of Bordering*, edited by N. De Genova, 11–35. Durham, NC: Duke University Press.

Dittmer, J. and N. Gray. 2010. "Popular Geopolitics 2.0: Towards New Methodologies of the Everyday." *Geography Compass* 11 (4): 1664–1677.

Dittmer, J. 2012. Graphic Narratives of Europe. In *Remappings. The Making of European Narratives*, edited by O. Chenal and B. Snelders, 111–119. Amsterdam: European Cultural Foundation.

Dittmer, J. 2014: "Towards New (Graphic) Narratives of Europe." *International Journal of Cultural Policy* 20 (2): 119–138.

Dzenovska, D. and N. De Genova. 2018. "Desire for the Political in the Aftermath of the Cold War". *Political In/Of Europe* 2018 (80): 1c15.

Dzenovska, D. 2013. "Historical Agency and the Coloniality of Power in Postsocialist Europe", *Anthropological Theory*, no. 13: 394–416.

EP&C. 2011. "Decision no. 1194/2011/EU of the European Parliament and of the Council of 16 November 2011 Establishing a European Union Action for the European Heritage Label." *Official Journal of the European Union*, no. L303: 1–9.

EC (European Commission). 2014. *"European Heritage Label. 2014 Panel Report."* Brussels: European Commission.

EC (European Commission). 2017. *"European Heritage Label: 2017 Panel Report."* Brussels. European Commission.

EC (European Commission) 2019. "The European Heritage Label." Official website of the European Commission. Accessed 21 August 2019. https://ec.europa.eu/programmes/creative-europe/actions/heritage-label_en.

Jenkins, R. 2008. The Ambiguity of Europe. *European Societies* 10 (2): 153–176.

Jones, S. and J. Subotić. 2011. "Fantasies of Power: Performing Europeanization on the European Periphery. *European Journal of Cultural Studies* 14 (5): 542–557.

Kaasik-Krogerus, S., V. L. A. Čeginskas, T. Lähdesmäki, and K. Mäkinen. 2018. "Drawing, Erasing and Crossing Borders. Negotiating Borders in the EU's Cultural Heritage Policy." Paper presented at ICCPR 2018, Tallinn, August 21–25.

Kendall, G., I. Woodward, and S. Zlatko. 2009. *The Sociology of Cosmopolitanism, Globalization, Identity, Culture and Government*. New York: Palgrave and MacMillan.

Kinnvall, C. 2016. "The Postcolonial has Moved into Europe: Bordering, Security and Ethno-Cultural Belonging." *JCMS: Journal of Common Market Studies* 54 (1): 152–168.

Kisić, V. 2017. *Governing Heritage Dissonance: Promises and Realities of Selected Cultural Policies.* Amsterdam: European Cultural Foundation.

Koopman, S. 2011. Alter-geopolitics: Other Securities are Happening. *Geoforum*, no. 42: 274–284.

Lähdesmäki, T. 2017. "Cultural Heritage in Today's Europe: Challenges and Opportunities." Paper presented in the Dissonant Heritages: Contestation of Meanings and Uses of Memory in Today´s Europe workshop, Florence, Italy, April 27–28.

Lähdesmäki, T. and K. Mäkinen 2019. "The 'European Significance' of Heritage: Politics of Scale in EU Heritage Policy Discourse." In *Politics of Scale. New Directions in Critical Heritage Studies*, edited by T. Lähdesmäki, S. Thomas, and Y. Zhu, 36–49. New York: Berghahn's Books.

Lähdesmäki, T., Y. Zhu, and S. Thomas. 2019. "Introduction: Heritage and Scale." In *Politics of Scale. New Directions in Critical Heritage Studies*, edited by T. Lähdesmäki, S. Thomas, and Y. Zhu, 1–18. New York: Berghahn's Books.

Laïdi, Z. 2005. *La Norme Sans la Force.* Paris: Presses de la Fondation Nationale des Sciences Politiques.

Laine, J. P. 2016. "The Multiscalar Production of Borders." *Geopolitics* 21 (3): 465–482.

Leontidou, L. 2004. "The Boundaries of Europe: Deconstructing Three Regional Narratives." *Identities: Global Studies in Culture and Power* 11 (4): 593–617.

Massey, D. 2008. "Esipuhe". In *Samanaikainen tila*, edited by Massey, D., 13–16. Tampere: Vastapaino.

Müller, M. 2008. "Reconsidering the Concept of Discourse for the Field of Critical Geopolitics: Towards Discourse as Language and Practice." *Political Geography* 27 (3): 322–338.

Paasi, A. 2005. "The Changing Discourse on Political Boundaries: Mapping the Backgrounds, Contexts and Contents." In *B/ordering Space*, edited by H. van Houten, O. Kramsch, and W. Zierkofer, 17–31. London: Ashgate.

Risse, T. 2003. "The Euro Between National and European Identity." *Journal of European Public Policy* 10 (4): 487–505.

Parker, N., N. Vaughan-Williams, L. Bialasiewicz, S. Blumer, D. Carver, R. Durie, J Heathershaw et al. 2009. "Lines in the Sand? Towards an Agenda for Critical Border Studies." *Geopolitics* 14 (3): 582–587.

Rumford C. 2008. *Cosmopolitan Spaces: Europe, Globalization, Theory.* London: Routledge.

Schuman, R. 2010. *For Europe.* Geneva: Nagel Editions SA.

Scott, J. W. 2009. "Bordering and Ordering the European Neighbourhood: A Critical Perspective on EU Territoriality and Geopolitics." *TRAMES* 13 (3): 232–247.

Shore, C. 2000. *Building Europe: The Cultural Politics of European Integration.* London: Routledge.

Smith, L. 2006. *Uses of Heritage.* London: Routledge.

Smith, L. 2015. "Theorizing Museum and Heritage Visiting." In *The International Handbooks of Museum Studies: Museum Theory*, edited by A. Witcomb, and K. Message, 459–484. Chichester: John Wiley & Sons.

Strüver, A. 2005. *Stories of the "Boring Border": The Dutch-German Borderscape in People's Minds*. Münster: LIT-Verlag.

Turunen, J. (n.d.). "Borderscapes of Europe." Unpublished manuscript.

Waterton, E. and J. Dittmer, J. 2014. "The Museum as Assemblage: Bringing Forth Affect at the Australian War Memorial." *Museum Management and Curatorship* 29 (2): 122–139.

Yuval-Davis, N., G. Wemyss, and K. Cassidy. 2018. "Everyday Bordering, Belonging and the Reorientation of British Immigration Legislation." *Sociology* 52 (2): 228–244.

Part III

Engaging Europe

Chapter 5

Participation

Inclusive and exclusive heritage

Through the EHL, the idea of European cultural heritage is created and governed with the goal of promoting intercultural dialogue and belonging to the EU. In the following two chapters, we examine citizens' engagement with this 'European cultural heritage' in the exhibitions and activities at the EHL sites through a key concept for achieving this goal: participation. We analyse the dynamics of participation in the EHL framework and the ways in which it produces both inclusive and exclusive notions of cultural heritage and Europe. The aim is not, however, to explore in detail how participation is promoted in the sites' practical activities as we did not have the possibility to attend the workshops and projects organized by the sites to a sufficient extent to be able to compare and analyse.

When cultural heritage is understood as a social and discursive construct constantly created and shaped by various actors according to their political, economic, and social interests, participation is central to it. Several scholars have emphasized that discourses on cultural heritage are not only about the past, but also about utilizing selected aspects of the past to design scenarios for the future based on present concerns (e.g. Turnbridge and Ashworth 1996; Graham, Ashworth, and Turnbridge 2000; Smith 2006; Graham and Howarth 2008; Harrison 2013; see our Introduction). As the EHL offers an arena in which to remember different pasts in order to shape the present and the future – with young people as its target audience – it is worth examining who is able to participate in the discussions in this arena. Ideally, participation in the sphere of cultural heritage includes activities through which different memories can meet and entangle (see Stanković 2016; Delanty 2017a). Such participation enables critical thinking and multiple perspectives, imagining and discussing alternatives, and finding grounds for acting collectively (Kisić 2016, 140).

As earlier pointed out in this book, cultural heritage is inherently political. Residents, local businesses, public administrators, and elected representatives may have competing ideas about the use, protection, and dismantling of cultural heritage (on heritage and commodification, see Kirshenblatt-Gimblett 2006; Macdonald 2013). Participation therefore always includes power struggles between diverse interests and actors. This "heritage dissonance" (Kisić 2016) is increased by the participatory shift that broadens and diversifies the actors involved in defining, selecting, interpreting, and safeguarding heritage and opens up the space for contestations and discord (Kisić 2018, 136).

Related to this participatory shift, scholars of new museology and other similar strands of thought (e.g. Vergo 1989; Macdonald 2005, 2007; Applegate Krouse 2006; Hooper-Greenhill 2006) have for a long time emphasized both the important interaction between heritage institutions and communities and the active role of visitors as meaning-makers rather than mere consumers as well as empowering silenced groups, like women, minorities, and indigenous people (e.g. Macdonald 2005, 2007; Applegate Krouse 2006; Hooper-Greenhill 2006; Murawska-Muthesius and Piotrowski 2015). Various studies on participation in heritage processes and practices (e.g. Sandell 2003; Watson and Waterton 2010; Adell et al. 2015; Bidault 2018) emphasize that citizens should have the right to produce knowledge about and define cultural heritage. They should be able to influence what kind of stories are told at heritage sites and in memory organizations, and how they are told. "People who interact with cultural heritage in varied and sometimes unexpected ways, who share specific memories about a site or a story, also have a crucial say" as Bidault (2018, 76) notes. This is related to the idea of the "critical museum" (Murawska-Muthesius and Piotrowski 2015; see also Kirshenblatt-Gimblett 2019): museums are increasingly seen as critical actors and contributors to debates, which can empower the powerless and redress social inequalities. In order for museums and heritage sites to act as change agents (van Huis 2019), they need to be places of participation for a wide range of visitors and citizen-driven activities.

Participation in heritage processes and practices has been increasingly emphasized in cultural heritage policies at local, regional, national, and European levels. Several policy documents indicate that participation is high on the EU heritage policy agenda (see Chapter 1). One of the specific objectives of the European Year of Cultural Heritage (EYCH 2018) was to "promote innovative models of participatory governance and management of cultural heritage, involving all stakeholders, including public authorities, the cultural heritage sector, private actors, and civil society organisations" (EP&C 2017, 5). In its report regarding the integrated approach to cultural heritage (proposed earlier by the European Commission), the European Parliament (EP 2015, 12) highlighted the importance of taking a multi-perspective, democratic, and participative approach to the past. The Council concluded that "the adoption of a locally rooted and people-centred approach to cultural heritage [and] participatory approaches" (CofEU 2014, 1) are central in several EU actions, including the EHL. Interestingly enough, questions about participation are hardly visible in the policy documents regarding the EHL itself (e.g. the decision of the action in 2011, the European Panel reports from 2013, 2014, 2015, and 2017, and the European Panel report on monitoring the EHL in 2016). It is thus necessary to take a close look at the empirical realities to see how and to what extent the participatory approach is present in the EHL framework.

Because the EHL is embedded in the EU's participatory governance (see Chapter 1), and because participation at EHL sites takes place within cultural heritage institutions, we look at it as part of participatory governance. This form of governance aims to create closer connections between citizens and administration by involving citizens in governmental processes through various participatory practices that are increasingly organized by different levels of administration (Papadopoulos and Warn 2007; Saurugger 2010; Lindgren and Persson 2011; Michels 2011; Moini 2011). Several layers of EU participatory governance are involved in the EHL, from the EU institutions and the national, regional, and local authorities to the staff members and visitors of the sites. The EHL framework limits the activities of those involved in it, but actors may also challenge the top-down approach through the alternative interpretations they give to cultural heritage and the ways of dealing with it (see Chapter 1).

Participatory governance is characterized by governmentality, a typically liberal and neo-liberal style of governance. Through different technologies of agency, it aims to produce subjectivities, guide the conduct of citizens, and thus engage them in fulfilling the objectives designed by the administration (Foucault 1991; Cruikshank 1999; Dean 2010). Due to their position at the intersection between the administration and citizens, the interrelation of participatory practices with democracy is contested (e.g. Nousiainen and Mäkinen 2015). This is because participatory practices can guide participation in two directions. They may offer opportunities for more direct democracy, include elements from grassroots activities, and promote citizens' participation in decision-making. Moreover, civil society actors may be involved in them either as organizers or participants. As such, they can be viewed as part of civil society activity, and thus as central components of democracy. Participatory practices therefore have the potential to support democracy as people's rule in which participation means making claims, being involved in decision-making, and changing the decision-makers when needed. However, participatory practices are often limited to networking, developing expertise, or organizing events and activities, and the conditions of participation in them are defined by the administration, in order to legitimate its goals rather than contest them and open new space for debate and action.

This complexity of participation in the framework of participatory governance is explored in this and the following chapter: how are aspects of both democratization and governmentalization manifested in the EHL? We focus on the forms, aims, effects, and limitations of participation in the EHL action, asking who are allowed, invited, and expected to participate, where, and how. Based on a qualitative close reading of the interviews with the practitioners and visitors at the EHL sites, we investigate what meanings are given to participation and what roles are endowed to citizens by the interviewees.

In this chapter, we investigate the ways in which the EHL sites both enable and limit participation. In what follows, we first introduce the theoretical framework that helps us to understand the past in the plural and guides our analysis.

We then investigate whether and how the visitors are encouraged to define and construct cultural heritage in the exhibitions and other activities organized by the EHL sites and the roles given to visitors and their meaning-making. Finally, we examine how the interviewees see the limits of participation: what problems and shortcomings arise in terms of participatory governance related to the EHL. We conclude by discussing the ideas of belonging, inclusion, and exclusion implied by the participatory practices of the EHL sites.

Pluralist remembering in the context of heritage dissonance

The concepts of heritage dissonance and inclusive heritage discourse, both developed by Kisić (2016, 2018), are used here to make sense of the forms of participation at the EHL sites, and of the inclusive and exclusive heritage narratives and practices related to them. In addition, we draw on the notions of politics of the past (Stråth 2000; Hodgin and Radstone 2003), agonistic remembering (Cento Bull and Hansen 2016), and remembrance (Winter and Sivan 1999).

As discussed earlier, heritage dissonance refers to the idea that heritage is not only constructed and fluid but also inherently contested. Kisić (2018, 135) connects heritage dissonance to radical democracy and to the "democratic opening of heritage" towards all social actors: this "democratic opening" redefines heritage "as a plural and therefore conflicting ground – the space where the meanings of the past and visions of the future might compete and collide". Conflicts and contestations are understood as relevant conditions for radical or agonistic democracy (Mouffe 1992, 2000, 2005). Against this backdrop, it is crucial to ask whether heritage sites, through their participative practices, can create space for dissent and debate, and thus for democracy.

We understand inclusive heritage discourse (Kisić 2016) as a channel enabling participation in the context of heritage dissonance. By facilitating a dynamic and pluralist understanding of the past, inclusive heritage discourse provides space for heritage dissonance – that is, different memories, interpretations of the past, and meanings given to heritage. Inclusive heritage discourse can be perceived as an arena, in which participation and heritage dissonance mutually build up each other. It offers an alternative to the authorized heritage discourse (AHD), as defined by Smith (2006; see Introduction), as it recognizes the active agency of various groups and includes their insights in producing and using cultural heritage (Kisić 2016, 281). As such, an inclusive heritage discourse has the potential to promote intercultural dialogue, one of the two key aims of the EHL. Kisić (2016) has developed inclusive heritage discourse in the context of heritage related conflicts in the former Yugoslav republics, although intercultural dialogue need not necessarily refer to difficult situations. In the EHL documents, however, the notion of intercultural dialogue is not further elaborated (see Box 5.1).

As noted, our investigation into the ways of participation at the EHL sites also leans on the ideas of politics of the past, which we see as a broader context for heritage dissonance. The past is always remembered, interpreted, and used in a myriad of ways by a variety of actors (e.g. Stråth 2000; Hodgin and Radstone 2003), and this precisely makes heritage inherently dissonant. Which aspects of past are chosen to be remembered and retold, and which are left in silence and oblivion, is a complex political process. In this respect, the field of memory can be(come) a battlefield (Passerini 2003). Whose interpretations and meanings achieve a dominant position, and who has the opportunity to participate in the production of meanings in the first place, are therefore of utmost importance. In these processes, competing narratives of the past need to be heard. Discussions about the past should pay attention to discontinuities and ruptures, to enable dissonant interpretations to emerge without excluding those who do not identify with the dominant story. Agonistic remembering, suggested by Cento Bull and Hansen (2016) is reflexive and dialogic and takes into consideration the contexts, agencies, and emotions related to the past. It does not smooth over struggles and controversies, but it does not build fixed us-them constellations, either. As such, it can allow heritage dissonance to become visible. The agonistic remembering and inclusive heritage discourse can be seen as two entwined ways of dealing with heritage dissonance.

The EHL aims at highlighting a European dimension of heritage, which makes the interplay of collective and individual memory important. It is relevant to explore whether the EHL sites allow for a space in which "personal memories interact and intertwine with other personal memories, and are shaped by the collective (or cultural memories) related to different groups to which a person belongs" (Stanković 2016, 6). The term remembrance is often used in the context of heritage and draws attention to the articulation of individual and collective remembering, instead of assuming a collective memory necessarily shared by individuals (Winter and Sivan 1999). By emphasizing processes and practices of remembering, it refers to a multi-perspectivist approach to the past, which can help to prevent oversimplifying or creating an unequal bias to interpretations of the past, and thereby strengthen the potential for diverse heritage and a more understanding society (Stanković 2016, 6–10). Such a multi-perspectivist remembering stresses the need for various individuals and groups to participate in producing interpretations of the past. Delanty (2017a) suggests a pluralist (instead of particularistic or universalistic) idea of memories, that allows new conceptions and narratives of heritage to emerge from the encounter and entanglement of different memories.

Drawing on this pluralist understanding of the past, we discuss below what kind of participation has been made possible at the EHL sites and how this has been done. We explore whether and how the sites encourage visitors to make their own interpretations about the sites, the past they deal with, and the idea of cultural heritage itself, and what roles are given to visitors and their interpretations.

BOX 5.1 Intercultural dialogue in the EHL

In the decision that establishes the EHL as an EU action, the main objectives are "(a) strengthening European citizens' sense of belonging to the Union [and] (b) strengthening intercultural dialogue" (EP&C 2011, 3). Neither of the two goals is clearly defined in the official EHL documents, such as the panel reports, in which both aims are mostly discussed implicitly. The goal of creating belonging is discussed in the documents through the concept of European significance of cultural heritage, as the sites are required to communicate "at the European level" their "European dimension", "pan-European nature", and their contribution to "European history and culture and European integration". The goal to promote intercultural dialogue can be found implicitly in the official documents in discussions defining the European significance of the heritage sites as interaction across borders and between several territories or population groups (such as linguistic or religious groups), or through transnational exchange of values and principles in different spheres of intellectual life (Lähdesmäki and Mäkinen 2019).

The concept of intercultural dialogue emerged in the EU's policy discourses in the early 2000s, but the dialogical approach to intercultural encounter can be traced back to the UNESCO programmes in the 1980s and the Council of Europe initiatives in the 1990s. The European Year of Intercultural Dialogue was celebrated in 2008; one of its goals was to raise awareness of the concept itself. The EC's motives for launching the year stemmed from EU Eastern enlargement, immigration, and globalization, all of which were seen to evoke a need to know different cultures better. The concept has been adapted to the EU's policy discourses both in its internal and external affairs; either explicitly, or indirectly, by referring to the need to develop intercultural skills and competencies and create dialogue between people in multicultural environments. It has been embedded in the areas of culture, citizenship, multilingualism, education, training, and sport. For example, in the 2010s, the Culture Programme (2007–2013) and Creative Europe (2014–2020) have emphasized intercultural dialogue. Furthermore, in its policies on refugees and migrants, the EU uses intercultural dialogue as a core concept to deal with differences in diversified societies (Lähdesmäki et al. forthcoming).

In the EUROHERIT fieldwork, we asked both the heritage practitioners and EU officials whether, in their opinion, cultural heritage can be used to promote intercultural dialogue. Some of the interviewed EU officials embedded the idea of intercultural dialogue in the core of cultural heritage. As one of them suggested, cultural heritage could be understood as the product and result of this dialogue (E4). Another recognized that there are conflicting interpretations and uses of cultural heritage but that in some cases cultural heritage can become a symbol of dialogue between different values, traditions, and cultures (E5).

The EU officials perceived that intercultural dialogue can be understood as an exchange between the EU and a non-member state. It was also seen as a dialogue helped by cultural heritage between countries in difficult situations; Northern Ireland, the Balkans, and the Middle East were mentioned as places where projects related to intercultural dialogue had been carried out. According to the interviewees at the EU level, intercultural dialogue can be collaboration, focusing on preservation and other common interests in the field of cultural heritage and cooperation among national cultural institutes in Europe, or in the framework of the EU's Culture Programme. They linked intercultural dialogue with the promotion of peace, tolerance, and cultural diversity and emphasized the role of knowledge and education in combating prejudices but did not give any EHL-related examples of intercultural dialogue.

The interviewed practitioners considered it possible that the EHL sites where they worked could have a role in intercultural dialogue but not all of them were able to give concrete examples. Several sites nevertheless organize workshops, projects, and other events, in which – often young – people from different backgrounds can meet, thus enabling intercultural dialogue within their own society. Some practitioners – for instance from the Hambach Castle, Mundaneum, and the Historic Gdańsk Shipyard – saw that intercultural dialogue is inherent to their site's narrative. One of the practitioners recognized the unequal positions of cultures, problematizing the concept of civilization and noting that hierarchies of knowledges and cultures still exist (P37). The same practitioner suggested intercultural events as a way to reflect on and dissolve prejudices against cultures which experience discrimination.

The question of what the cultures that are supposed to be in dialogue actually are is not raised in the EHL documents, nor was it discussed in our fieldwork interviews. On the whole, the concept of intercultural dialogue is rather invisible in the EHL framework, despite its central position as one of the two main objectives of the EHL. The mutual relationship between the two goals is not discussed, either. It is not clear whether they are interrelated or separate, or why the concept of intercultural dialogue gets so little attention compared to the emphasis on the 'European significance' of cultural heritage.

Contradicting meanings and interpretations

Both practitioners and visitors at the EHL sites play a role in the EU's participatory governance. As they participate in different ways, they also hold different power positions. As members of the AHD, heritage practitioners have a hegemonic position to interpret, narrate, and present the past. However, there is always space for several interpretations, and both participatory and non-participatory exhibition practices and events give visitors new opportunities to interpret and make sense of the sites and their narratives. Based on our interview data, the EHL sites encourage visitors to voice their own interpretations to varying degrees, but it remains unclear whether the visitors' interpretations are incorporated into the exhibitions and other activities at the sites.

The interviewed heritage practitioners bring up examples of various ways in which visitors can participate in giving meanings to cultural heritage and to topics related to the EHL sites. As one practitioner pointed out, "the museum means completely different [things] for these different categories [of visitors]" (P4). Several practitioners agreed with their colleague's idea, expressed as follows: "we want to be a place where they [visitors] can find their own opinion [...] we don't give them the right answer" (P26). Such conceptions of a heritage site as an implicit forum of debate refer to the potential of an inclusive heritage discourse that provides a channel to agree and disagree with others about heritage and to "express memories, feelings, interests and attachments to heritage in a dialogical way" (Kisić 2018, 137). How this potential is realized depends on several factors from the concrete means available in the exhibitions and activities of the site to the visitors' willingness to express their own interpretations.

Practitioners said that the EHL sites could engage visitors more actively through various interactive practices in their exhibitions, such as a puzzle about the European map, interactive stations, or augmented reality. Both practitioners and visitors viewed interaction between guides and visitors as a way of creating space for dialogue and thus enabling the visitors to share their own interpretations. For both parties, interactive activities at the sites are fun and counterbalance the text-heavy exhibitions. The use of audio recordings and visual materials or the opportunity to engage with concrete objects increase emotionality: they make the site more feelable, tangible, and thus more comprehensible. According to the interviewees, such elements of audience engagement involve the visitors actively with the site and can stimulate their interest in it, and in heritage in general.

In addition to the exhibitions, activities organized by the EHL sites can provide space for visitors of various ages to concretely and actively participate. These activities include festivals, projects, theme weeks, workshops, concerts, conferences, lectures, book presentations, commemorations, discussions, films, theatre, dance, food events, pageants, documentaries, and radio programmes.

These events most often take place directly at the site but occasionally at other locations, and they often involve cooperation with other actors, such as the town, municipality, or associations.

In these practices, the visitors' role and influence can vary. According to many of our interviewed practitioners, participation enables visitors to make their interpretations heard. For instance, the Historic Gdańsk Shipyard offers a programme aimed at young people, which "is prepared by young people and they participate in the whole process of [its] preparation", as the site seeks to show them that "their own voice is very important for us" (P26). Heritage sites can deliberately utilize the meaning-making power of their visitors. In particular, local people can directly participate in the core activities of organizing exhibitions and events, by handing over material to the archives and collections and by sharing their stories. In this way, their own meaning-making may have some impact for the site, as one practitioner noted.

> All things, which we have in our archives [...] the people give to us. Like [...] this, you know, they come in and [say]: "look, I have some super documents, maybe you need them in your archives". Or [they give] some photos, et cetera. [...] And once they come in with these documents, they come in also with their stories. Personal stories about why they have these documents.
>
> (P25)

Sharing personal stories or objects is a way to create direct interaction and mutual exchange between the individual visitors and the sites, which can result in a win–win situation for both the individual and the heritage site in question. Heritage practitioners often consider such direct exchanges and interactions as rewarding, in the sense that the visitors "tell us their story and make us richer", as one practitioner pointed out (P27). Such exchanges enable memories to entangle (Delanty 2017a; Stanković 2016) and make space for remembrance as an interplay of individual and collective remembering (Winter and Sivan 1999). Visitors' contributions can make the heritage narratives and interpretations more polyvocal at the heritage site.

Similarly, Lieu d'Europe initiated a project with a school in the immediate neighbourhood, with the objective that the young pupils produce a brochure that explains "their impression and version of Lieu d'Europe to other young people" (P15). The practitioners at Camp Westerbork are also interested in encouraging and utilizing their visitors' interpretations. Speaking about a special assignment for student groups visiting the heritage site, one practitioner explained how such a mutual interaction could look.

> So we say, "ok, this is our new exhibition. We want to tell this story especially for people who are fifty years or older, and you are our brain camp and [you will] feed us with your ideas – we feed you with the historical

insights and sensibilities". And they think out of the box, and we try to create new forms of interaction.

(P14)

Based on the practitioners' accounts, through participatory projects organized by the sites, the participants can influence the ways in which heritage is presented at the sites. Moreover, they can share their own interpretations of the site in question with other people.

Even if the heritage sites aim at encouraging visitors to enter into mutual dialogue with them, the main objective remains educating the visitors instead of providing them with opportunities to reconstruct heritage and change the ways it is presented at the site. The practitioners sometimes conceptualized their interaction with their visitors as a "transmission of the information" (P32), in terms of a simple one-way communication to inform visitors about the "historical facts". This is exemplified in a description by a practitioner about the interaction between the visitors and the site, which is limited to basic interaction and service, covering ticket sales and issuing information brochures and maps at the entrance desk (P32). Such approaches reflect an elitist idea of a heritage institution as an authority defining and transmitting the "grand canons" of cultural narratives, aiming to "civilize" and "discipline" the public (Bennett 1995; Murawska-Muthesius and Piotrowski 2015). For example, some of the interviewed practitioners assumed that citizens neither have enough understanding of (and for) cultural heritage nor should they be given free rein to act upon it. They viewed the promotion of European heritage as "the task of each citizen" but at the same time they pointed out that "it's good to receive a bit of initiative and guidance from above, so that it becomes clear to everyone, what Europe means and what kind of different cultural heritage exists", as one of the practitioners denoted (P22). However, the same practitioner recognized the importance of participation as such: "this works only if everyone participates, but such initiatives as the EHL hopefully help to strengthen the awareness of the citizens and help them to get involved" (P22). This practitioner envisioned the EHL as a tool of participatory governance, which helps the citizens to become actively involved in heritage matters.

Based on the practitioners' views, the sites can offer facilities for activities to be organized *by*, *with*, or *for* the citizens. The double meaning of participation characteristic to participatory governance is thus present in their accounts. The sites have the power to take the initiative and select the participants and the ways of enabling participation, but the participants themselves also decide how to use the participatory practices. The multiple roles of heritage sites in relation to visitor activities were reflected in a practitioner's explanation that the site sometimes only gives the immigrants a gathering place but it can provide also other support for their activities or it can organize culture days for immigrants itself (P26). The sites empower citizens to have an impact on the narratives and activities of the sites and beyond, but they can also invite citizens to participate in a pre-defined frame without real opportunities for influence.

The meanings given by the visitors to the sites and their topics may conflict with the ones provided by the sites, indicating that heritage is inherently dissonant. People with personal experience of the historical periods discussed at the sites sometimes tell site staff that their own interpretations contradict with those of the exhibition, arguing that the narrative of the site is "wrong" and "false" (P27), or not reflecting "their story" (P25). These conflicting interpretations of the past reveal that visitors to a heritage site also claim ownership of the narrative and site, showing that they care about it and the past that it represents. They exemplify the idea of agonistic remembering (Cento Bull and Hansen 2016) recognizing the competing narratives and interpretations of the past that may contest the dominant ones. As such, they manifest the multiperspectivist understanding of the past in plural.

However, interviewed visitors who did not participate in any of the specific projects organized by the site did not mention they were actively encouraged to produce alternative interpretations, and only a few visitors explicitly pointed out that their own perception contradicted the narrative of the site. This can be due to various reasons. First, the sites may enable various interpretations, leaving it unnecessary to challenge one main narrative. Second, the sites may exhibit a canonized narrative of local and/or European history, included in national canons and disseminated through school curricula, that their visitors see as "correct". Third, people who usually visit heritage sites may tend to relate to the stories told there. Fourth, the narratives are presented in such an authoritative way and the heritage institutions have such a hegemonic position in the production of meaning that questioning them and thus shaking the consensus is not an option. In such an institutionalized framework, visitors may have adopted their roles as receivers or guests so effectively that their participation in it is inevitably formalized and does not spur them to challenge the narratives of the sites. This raises the question of how empowering and inclusive the narratives and practices of the sites are, and whether they allow disagreement and participation with an "emancipatory and democratic potential" (Kisić 2018, 137).

Some of the practitioners explicitly acknowledge heritage dissonance, meaning that the concept of heritage itself is plural and constantly changing. In the quotation below, the diversity of opinions, perspectives, and interpretations is appreciated as an indispensable aspect of heritage, keeping it alive.

> The same concept of heritage, especially when speaking of the immaterial heritage, is an elusive concept that no one can probably claim to define once and for all and for this very nature it is a continuous game in discussion. And fortunately! Because this keeps it alive, but at the same time interpretable, constantly interpretable and therefore admits diversity by its very essence: a diversity of opinions and perspectives.
>
> (P4)

In line with this, one of our interviewed visitors pointed out that "it's important to approach [cultural heritage] quite critically" (VS2/17). According to this visitor, cultural heritage is "not something we picked up naturally, but someone later said: 'this will be our history and that's on what we base our present culture as well as our claims to power'" (VS2/17). The visitor remarked on the close relation between heritage and power and emphasized that everyone should be able to give their own meanings to the past instead of adopting the dominant conceptions. These views imply the core question of participatory governance: the tension between the top-down approach of the authorized heritage discourse and bottom-up approach of inclusive heritage discourse. In general, however, it was not common for the interviewees to explicitly discuss the controversies and power struggles regarding cultural heritage and the uses of the past.

As a dissonant construct, cultural heritage can be used to create boundaries and exclusive narratives. This was discussed by some of the heritage practitioners but not so much by the visitors. According to one practitioner, cultural heritage can sometimes be "used as a weapon [...] to define 'us' and to define who we are in these borders" (P9). Thus, it has great potential, but it also risks being used to define "us" in an exclusive way. Drawing borders between "us" and "them" can be interpreted as community construction (see Chapter 6) that includes some people and excludes others. Even the core term of the EHL action, "European cultural heritage", suggests a common – and hence potentially exclusive – culture instead of diversity, as one practitioner pointed out (P33). The same practitioner asked how it is possible to award the EHL to only some sites when Europe is everywhere (P33), pointing out that the EHL framework necessarily excludes several heritage sites and their stories from its common European narrative of the past. Furthermore, some of the visitors remarked that the stories told at the sites are "not only about Europe" (VS4/9) but address global or universal themes. Framing them all as European manifests appropriation of selected aspects of the past and excludes other aspects. The interviewed practitioners, however, also think that heritage can be used for telling more inclusive stories, as the following quote explains.

> But it has to be broadened, this view of the heritage we have. To point out that this cultural heritage is a heritage of many cultures. [...] It's a mixture of people coming here, staying, and moving around. [...] They have roots everywhere. We all have. So, [...] you could say that [in a] way we have the same cultural identity. [...] a way to point out that we have things in common. And that it's not the thing that divides us. I think that's the main thing we could use this cultural heritage for.
>
> (P9)

While the practitioners welcome most of the initiatives from their audiences, they also mention examples of such activities that they consider unwelcome civic participation. This includes demonstrations of far-right groups on the commemoration day of the Hambach Festival at Hambach Castle and Catholic groups coming to pray in Robert Schuman House. This activity appears as bottom-up participation of the wrong kind that is not encouraged but rather tolerated by the practitioners. This unintended participation reveals conflicting uses of and meanings given to the sites and their history, and thus refers to agonistic remembering and heritage dissonance. According to the practitioners, the sites can allow this kind of activities, such as demonstrations, but only on a small scale and without disturbing other visitors and normal activities, and if they conform with the law of the land. In the spirit of inclusive heritage discourse, and reflecting their narratives concerning free speech, these practitioners emphasized that their sites are places of dialogue and open to everyone. In this sense, citizens' participation and contribution to meaning-making of heritage can been seen as a process where the boundaries of what is European heritage are negotiated.

Limits of participation

As we have discussed before, it is of crucial importance, who can be involved in making decisions about defining, selecting, interpreting and presenting cultural heritage. In this respect, our analysis reveals a major limitation of participation at the EHL sites. None of the practitioners or visitors mentioned citizens' participation in decision-making concerning cultural heritage in local, national, EHL, or any other context. Instead, they use expressions like "bring alive", "keep alive", and "energize" when describing the citizens' role in heritage matters. Perhaps this shows that the role of citizens is to participate in a limited, pre-defined framework, in order to animate heritage sites and heritage that has been defined somewhere else, rather than to be proactive on the essential questions of heritage.

Participation is conditioned by the ways in which the sites communicate about their activities and who they address in their websites and promotion material. One of the interviewed practitioners talked about "very complicated communication" between the visitors and the site as an institution. In the interviewee's words: "it's an institutional communication, so it can put some barriers between us and the visitors" (P33). These problems are typical for participatory governance in which communication, or at least the initiative for it, is often rather top-down than bottom-up and may create barriers between the institution and the citizens who are asked to participate.

The barriers to communication link to the broader issue of accessibility. Who is addressed at and invited to heritage sites, and who is able to visit them? The obstacles to access may be physical, linguistic, or socio-economic. It has been noted that a typical visitor to heritage sites does not represent the average population regarding gender, age, and educational and socio-economic background (e.g. EC 2013b; see Appendix 4 for the background data of our interviewees).

Minority groups, people living in poverty, and people with disabilities can have limited access to cultural heritage. This, in turn, can be used against them and as a way to control and marginalize these groups. Such discrimination may decrease their capacity to participate in the cultural life of society and exercise citizenship (Bidault 2018, 78). Access is needed to participate; according to Anthias (2002; 2009), it is a pre-requisite for belonging.

The cost of an entrance ticket may be a barrier, while free entrance enhances accessibility, as one of our interviewed visitors pointed out: "it is good that it is open for the public. That we can go by ourselves and that it is free. I think is important, it doesn't put a barrier to the entry" (VS4/4). Thus, free and easy entrance to heritage institutions increases access and may be the first step to active participation in heritage. It may contribute to the importance of cultural heritage in the society, as another of our interviewed visitors noted: "I think particularly of the free entrance in the museums for youngsters until 26 years old. That was something that allowed students, youngsters, to open themselves to culture and discover museums more easily" (VS4/5).

The way in which exhibitions are constructed and how they tell the story of the EHL sites may pose challenges to participation and the meaning-making of heritage. The lack of interactivity is discussed by both visitors and practitioners in our data. Together with a lack of prior knowledge, it may hinder access to the content of a site and thus prevent active participation and meaning-making. Exhibitions based on long texts can create distance since they are "not very engaging", as one practitioner pointed out (P33). Instead, the same practitioner wished "to have something more interactive and more dynamic" (P33) in the exhibitions. Also, some visitors criticized the exhibitions at the EHL sites for being too text-heavy. However, not all visitors felt this way. The heritage sites need to consider the needs of several types of visitors and use various channels of interaction.

One obstacle to visitors' active participation and meaning-making in heritage may be the languages used at the EHL site. During our fieldwork, we noted that several sites limited their exhibitions to very few languages. If their visitors do not know any of those, it is difficult for them to interpret or give input into the exhibition, as many of our interviewed visitors stated. The language barrier may prevent visitors from participating in activities, events, and other interactive practices at the site, as one of the interviewed visitors described.

> Sorry, interactive activities, they are mainly for the Dutch speakers. [...] So, clearly some multimedia in different languages could help, if you want to use these [sites as] a European [...] heritage. Otherwise you keep [the heritage] for just Dutch speakers. There were very few things in English, very few things in the drawers [at the exhibition]. There is just English and German as foreign languages.
>
> (VS3/31)

The practitioners we interviewed would like to increase the number of languages at their sites, as they are expected to according to the decision of the EHL action, but the sites do not have enough resources for this. For the practitioners, multilingualism indeed represents "Europe", as one of them expressed it: "if any visitor is going out from here with the idea that he can read in different languages the same text, for us it's like if he said 'oh, actually, it's Europe here'" (P33). Using several languages is seen as a way to make the memory and history of the sites "truly European" and display their story in a form "suitable for Europeans", as one practitioner noted (P4). For the same practitioner, presenting the heritage and the narrative of the site in several languages broadens the meaning of the site from the local to the European level: "our challenge is to make the cultural heritage that is connected to [our site] a European heritage" (P4). Using several languages may influence activities and audience participation. As the same practitioner continued: "to empower our multilingual attitude can bring us to have a more European attitude also in the way we organize our events and in the way we look for new audience for our activities" (P4). In sum, multiple languages and multilingualism are conceptualized in our data as a central characteristic of Europe, and hence it is seen as crucial for a heritage site with "European significance" to be multilingual. On the other hand, the lack of a common language is often seen as an obstacle for developing the public sphere or a shared identity in Europe, and for our interviewed visitors, the multiplicity of languages in Europe was both a strength and a problem (see Chapter 4).

Participation may be limited because not all population groups participate in an equal way. EHL sites often interact "with those who already participate in the public life of the community" attached to organizations operating in the field of the site, as one of the heritage practitioners noted (P1). This practitioner stated that the visitors are "very often people who are already aware of these issues [exhibited at the site]" (P1). This is typical in other contexts of participation, too. Such bias can also be interpreted positively, as noted by another practitioner: "then you have people who want to participate, which is great" (P15).

Participants in activities related to Europe organized by or at the EHL sites may be particularly Europe-minded, and according to one practitioner, "if you want to have proposals from young people for Europe, it's also interesting to listen to those euro-enthusiastic people" (P15). Nevertheless, the same practitioner felt that people without much knowledge of Europe are in fact a more interesting audience for the site and its activities.

> I just began a theatre project with two artists, and a specific group of fif-
> teen-year-old people who are, let's say, quitting school and maybe doing [a
> traineeship before going to a vocational school]. And they are in between.
> […] So, they are in a specific programme, and I just began kind of a theatre
> workshop with them. We'll continue with a new workshop in a few weeks,

and that gives me the idea that those young people who I think don't really care about Europe, they are a much more interesting public than all those who come to our brilliant conferences and who already know a lot about Europe, and who already are convinced that Europe is needed for our society.

(P15)

Some of our examined EHL sites have attempted to fill the knowledge gap for local citizens and educate them about European issues by arranging events that "open a place for sharing things with citizens [who] can re-explore themes [concerning the European integration] that have become [...] more and more distant for them", as one practitioner noted (P4). The aim is to start from people's own concerns so that the events meet both "the interests of those who already have specific knowledge and interests in European issues and of those who still don't have this knowledge" (P4). For this practitioner, this allows citizens with poor knowledge of European issues to "find a moment of engagement and begin to realize that there are issues that concern and can also interest them" (P4).

A lack of prior knowledge can hinder access to the narratives of the sites, as observed by one of the interviewed visitors: "I have a feeling that you need some basic information already before you come here. Because if you don't have any information about Europe, about the European Union, the institutions, et cetera, it's a little bit confusing, I guess" (VS4/6). Visitors' ability to interpret, challenge, and contribute to the narratives of the sites can be limited by insufficient or unclear information given at the site if they cannot compensate for it with their existing knowledge.

The distance between decision-makers and participants is a core question of democracy in general and participatory governance in particular. According to a practitioner, the discussions about the idea of European cultural heritage are far removed from everyday life and "they risk becoming elite speeches" (P1). This practitioner remarked that "not everyone has the opportunity to relate to this heritage" (P1). While the same practitioner saw that "an active role can also involve associations of the third sector or the citizens", the interviewee acknowledged that "these topics [...] are always spoken about at a very high level, or at least in a group of experts, and everyone at the lower levels is automatically excluded from certain types of reflections" (P1). When asked whether cultural heritage is important in society today, one interviewed visitor confirmed that, in their view, "these stories of cultural heritage are highly political. For common people, like me, it does not necessarily speak to me" (VS4/12).

Active participation also requires resources that not everyone has. One practitioner emphasized that "[e]veryone should be able to get closer to culture" (P1) and criticized the fact that participatory projects related to Europe are often targeted to those who already have opportunities to be active in these matters. Instead, the interviewee continued, "[w]e should help those who do not have these possibilities [...] Europe should approach those who do not have these possibilities" (P1). As these quotes indicate, many of our interviewed practitioners had an interest in expanding access to their site and involving new audiences in their activities.

EHL and the governance of participation

Similarly to other memory institutions, the EHL sites have the potential to create feelings of both enrichment and alienation (Young 2003, 204). Therefore, it is crucial to examine these possibilities and limits of participation in terms of inclusion and exclusion (see Tlili 2008). Exclusion from cultural heritage means that citizens cannot "participate in decisions regarding their own cultural heritage, or cultural heritage with which they have a particular relationship", including interpreting, preserving, safeguarding, critically reviewing, storing, and displaying cultural heritage (Bidault 2018, 78). In cultural heritage policies and practices, the ways of seeking inclusion usually lean on the cluster of participation, community, and the bottom-up approach. For example, Kisić (2016, 26) believes that "the use of participative methods of heritage making, management, and interpretation such as discussions, evaluations, oral histories, personal collecting, crowd-collecting, crowd-curating and artistic interventions" can become the basis for a more inclusive, plural, and participatory heritage policy.

Our interview data indicates that interactive practices included in the exhibitions and in the pedagogic and other activities organized by the EHL sites provide visitors with opportunities for participation – at least in terms of engaging with the story told at the EHL site. Earlier analyses of participatory policies in the field of cultural heritage have indicated that a consensus-driven participatory approach may limit the possibilities for contestation and opposition, and thereby endow a decorative or tokenistic role for the participants (Adell et al. 2015). Such an approach depoliticizes both participation and cultural heritage and does not open up new space for diversity and debate necessary for democracy. For example, if transmitting information about the past is a central aim of the heritage sites, they primarily see their visitors as receiving audiences and objects of education rather than proactive producers of heritage. Our data does not include explicit reflections on who has the right to narrate the past and how it should be done. Interviews with practitioners show that some of the EHL sites use the visitors' own interpretations about the site and the past it deals with, but in general, practitioners do not discuss the effects of the visitors' meaning-making and knowledge production on the sites. Although there is in principle room for disagreement and conflicting arguments in the activities of the EHL sites, the interviewed visitors rarely explicitly challenged the conceptions the sites offer, which confirms the sites' underlying aspiration for consensus, so typical of participatory governance.

The interviews revealed several limits on participation common in participatory governance. Sometimes the interaction between the site and its audiences is complicated or reduced to top-down communication to inform visitors. The exhibitions may not be interactive enough to encourage the visitors to participate and interpret actively. Not everyone may have the resources required for participation, for example due to the low number of languages sites use. Furthermore, participants tend to already be active in issues related to the site or public life. The distance between decision-makers and citizens limits both traditional and non-traditional forms of participation, including participatory governance. Policy instruments such as the EHL are constantly coined to bridge this gap, but based on the interviews, citizens play no visible role in decision-making regarding the EHL. By both practitioners and visitors, participation in heritage is not discussed as a way for the various audiences to contest and redefine meanings of heritage or to claim profound changes in the exhibitions and activities of the EHL sites.

As part of the EU's participatory governance, participatory practices organized by the EHL sites have a problematic relation with democracy, and they can end up strengthening the AHD. As participation in the context of participatory governance differs from citizen-driven activism and social movements, it perhaps cannot be expected to produce counter-narratives and make a significant contribution to democracy. But the participatory practices organized by the EHL sites also have a potential to generate inclusive heritage discourse and to approve the idea of heritage dissonance that Kisić (2018, 135) links to radical democracy. To support these goals, the sites can include existing civic activities, either in heritage or other spheres, and encourage new civic activity to emerge. In such activity, the fixed roles of practitioners and visitors which characterize participatory governance should be changed to enable equal participation and to open up space for debate. A pluralist conception of the past can be another way to promote reconceptualizing and re-narrating Europe's cultural heritage so as to resist hegemonic meanings. The participatory practices stemming from such an intrinsically political conception of cultural heritage understood as thoroughly dissonant can encourage dissensus over consensus and emphasize the diversity of heritage. They may thus make visible multi-vocal, silenced, oppressed, or dominated interpretations of heritage and, through initiating public debate about the manifold meanings inherent to heritage, contribute to a democratic and inclusive vision of belonging.

References

Adell, N., R. F. Bendix, C. Bortolotto, and M. Tauschek, eds. 2015. *Between Imagined Communities and Communities of Practice: Participation, Territory and the Making of Heritage.* Göttingen: Universitätsverlag Göttingen.

Anthias, F. 2002. "Where Do I Belong? Narrating Collective Identity and Translocational Positionality." *Ethnicities* 2 (4): 491–514.

Anthias, F. 2009. "Thinking Through the Lens of Translocational Positionality: An Intersectionality Frame for Understanding Identity and Belonging." *Translocations: Migration and Social Change* 1 (4): 5–20.

Applegate Krouse, S. 2006. "Anthropology and the New Museology." *Reviews in Anthropology* 35 (2): 169–182.

Bennett, T. 1995. *The Birth of the Museum: History, Theory, Politics*. London: Routledge.

Bidault, M. 2018. "Heritage and Participation as Matters of Human Rights." In *Heritage is Ours: Citizens Participating in Decision Making*, edited by A.-M. Halme, T. Mustonen, J.-P. Taavitsainen, S. Thomas, and A. Weij, 74–85. Helsinki: Europa Nostra Finland.

Cento Bull, A., and H.L. Hansen. 2016. "On Agonistic Memory." *Memory Studies* 9 (4): 390–404.

CofEU (Council of the European Union). 2014. "Council conclusions on participatory governance of cultural heritage." *Official Journal of the European Union* C 463: 1–3.

Cruikshank, B. 1999. *The Will to Empower*. Ithaca, NY: Cornell University Press.

Dean, M. (1999) 2010. *Governmentality. Power and Rule in Modern Society*. Reprint, London: Sage.

Delanty, G. 2017a. "Entangled Memories: How to Study Europe's Cultural Heritage." *The European Legacy* 22 (2): 129–145.

EC (European Commission). 2013a. "*European Heritage Label 2013. Panel Report.*" Brussels: European Commission.

EC (European Commission). 2013b. "*Special Eurobarometer 399. Cultural Access and Participation.*" Brussels: European Commission. https://ec.europa.eu/commfrontoffice/publicopinion/archives/ebs/ebs_399_en.pdf.

EC (European Commission). 2014. "*European Heritage Label 2014: Panel Report.*" Brussels: European Commission.

EC (European Commission). 2015. "*European Heritage Label 2015: Panel Report.*" Brussels: European Commission.

EC (European Commission). 2016. "*European Heritage Label: Panel Report on Monitoring.*" Brussels: European Commission.

EP&C (European Parliament and the Council). 2017. "Decision (EU) 2017/864 on a European Year of Cultural Heritage (2018)." *Official Journal of the European Union* L 131: 1–9.

EP (European Parliament). 2015. *Report: "Towards an Integrated Approach to Cultural Heritage for Europe" (2014/2149(INI))*. *Committee on Culture and Education*. Rapporteur: M. Diaconu, 24.6.2015.

EP&C (European Parliament and the Council). 2011. "Decision No 1194/2011/EU of the European Parliament and of the Council of 16 November 2011 Establishing a European Union Action for the European Heritage Label." *Official Journal of the European Union* L 303: 1–9.

Graham, B., G. J. Ashworth, and J. E. Turnbridge. 2000. *A Geography of Heritage: Power, Culture and Economy*. London: Arnold.

Graham, B. and P. Howard. 2008. Heritage and Identity. In: *The Ashgate Research Companion to Heritage and Identity*, 1–18. Burlington, VT: Ashgate.

Hall, S. 1999. "Whose Heritage? Un-Settling 'the Heritage', Re-Imagining the Post-nation." *Third Text* 13 (49): 3–13.

Harrison, R. 2013. *Heritage: Critical Approaches*. London: Routledge.

Hodgin, K., and S. Radstone, eds. 2003. *Contested Pasts: The Politics of Memory*. London: Routledge.

Hooper-Greenhill, E. 2006. "Studying Visitors." In *Companion to Museum Studies*, edited by S. Macdonald, 362–376. New York: Blackwell.

van Huis, I. 2019. "Contesting Cultural Heritage: Decolonizing the Tropenmuseum as an Intervention in the Dutch/European Memory Complex." In *Dissonant Heritages and Memories in Contemporary Europe*, edited by T. Lähdesmäki, L. Passerini, S. Kaasik-Krogerus, and I. van Huis, 215–248. New York: Palgrave Macmillan.

Kirshenblatt-Gimblett, B. 2006. "World Heritage and Cultural Economics." In *Museum Frictions: Public Cultures / Global Transformations*, edited by I. Karp, C. Kratz, L. Szwaja and T. Ybarra-Frausto, 161–202. Durham, NC: Duke University Press.

Kirshenblatt-Gimblett, B. 2019. "Agents of Transformation: The Role of Museums in a Changing World." Keynote lecture in the 14th international SIEF congress Track Changes: Reflecting on a Transforming World in Santiago de Compostela, April 17.

Kisić, V. 2016. *Governing Heritage Dissonance. Promises and Realities of Selected Cultural Policies.* Amsterdam: European Cultural Foundation.

Kisić, V. 2018. "Heritage in the Era of Plurality". In *Heritage is Ours: Citizens Participating in Decision Making*, edited by A.-M. Halme, T. Mustonen, J.-P. Taavitsainen, S. Thomas and A. Weij, 134–140. Helsinki: Europa Nostra Finland.

Lindgren, K.-O. and T. Persson. 2011. *Participatory Governance in the EU.* Basingstoke: Palgrave Macmillan.

Lähdesmäki, T., A.-K. Koistinen, and S. Ylönen. Forthcoming. *Intercultural Dialogue in European Education Policies: A Conceptual Approach.* New York: Palgrave Macmillan.

Lähdesmäki, T., and K. Mäkinen. 2019. "The "European Significance' of Heritage: Politics of Scale in EU Heritage Policy Discourse". In *Politics of Scale: A New Approach to Heritage Studies* Lähdesmäki, edited by T. Lähdesmäki, Y. Zhu, and S. Thomas, 36–49. New York: Berghahn Books.

Lähdesmäki, T., T. Saresma, K. Hiltunen, S. Jäntti, N. Sääskilahti, A. Vallius, and K. Ahvenjärvi. 2016. "Fluidity and Flexibility of "Belonging": Uses of the Concept in Contemporary Research". *Acta Sociologica* 59 (3): 233–247.

Macdonald, S. 2005. "Accessing Audiences: Visiting Visitor Books." *Museum and Society* 3 (3): 119–136.

Macdonald, S. 2007. "Interconnecting: Museum Visiting and Exhibition Design." *CoDesign* 3 (1): 149–162.

Macdonald, S. 2013. *Memorylands: Heritage and Identity in Europe Today.* London: Routledge.

Manzo, L. C. and D. D. Perkins. 2006. "Finding Common Ground: The Importance of Place Attachment to Community Participation and Planning." *Journal of Planning Literature* 20 (4): 335–350.

Michels, A. 2011. "Innovations in Democratic Governance: How Does Citizen Participation Contribute to a Better Democracy?" *International Review of Administrative Sciences* 77 (2): 275–293.

Moini, G. 2011. "How Participation Has Become a Hegemonic Discursive Resource: Towards an Interpretivist Research Agenda." *Critical Policy Studies* 5 (2): 149–168.

Mouffe, C. 1992. "Preface: Democratic Politics Today." In *Dimensions of Radical Democracy: Pluralism, Citizenship, Community*, edited by C. Mouffe, 1–14. London: Verso.

Mouffe, C. 2000. *The Democratic Paradox.* London: Verso.

Mouffe, C. 2005. *The Return of the Political.* London: Verso.

Murawska-Muthesius, K. and P. Piotrowski. 2015. *From Museum Critique to the Critical Museum*. London: Routledge.

Nousiainen, M. and K. Mäkinen. 2015. "Multilevel Governance and Participation: Interpreting Democracy in EU-programmes." *European Politics and Society* 16 (2): 208–223.

Papadopoulos Y. and P. Warn. 2007. "Are Innovative, Participatory and Deliberative Procedures in Policy Making Democratic and Effective?" *European Journal of Political Research* 46 (4): 445–472.

Passerini, L. 2003. "Memories Between Silence and Oblivion." In *Contested Pasts: The Politics of Memory*, edited by K. Hodgin and S. Radstone, 238–254. New York: Routledge.

Sandell, R., ed. (2002) 2003. *Museums, Society, Inequality*. Reprint. London: Routledge.

Saurugger, S. 2010. "The Social Construction of the Participatory Turn: The Emergence of a Norm in the European Union." *European Journal of Political Research* 49 (4): 471–495.

Smith, L. 2006. *Uses of Heritage*. London: Routledge.

Stanković, I. 2016. *Vision Document: Valuing Heritage as Learning and Entertaining Resources*. Cultural Base. https://culturalbase.eu/archive/.

Stråth, B., ed. 2000. *Myth and Memory on the Construction of Community: Historical Patterns in Europe and Beyond*. Brussels: PIE-Peter Lang.

Tlili, A. 2008. "Behind the Policy Mantra of the Inclusive Museum: Receptions of Social Exclusion and Inclusion in Museums and Science Centres." *Cultural Sociology* 2 (1): 123–147.

Turnbridge, J. E. and G. J. Ashworth. 1996. *Dissonant Heritage: The Management of the Past as a Resource in Conflict*. Chichester: John Wiley.

Watson, S. and E. Waterton, eds. 2010. Special Issue on Heritage and Community Engagement. *International Journal of Heritage Studies* 16 (1–2): 1–159.

Vergo, P. 1989. *The New Museology*. London: Reaktion Books.

Winter, J. and E. Sivan. 1999. "Setting the Framework." In *War and remembrance in the twentieth century*, edited by J. Winter and E. Sivan, 6–39. Cambridge: Cambridge University Press.

Young, L. (2002) 2003. "Rethinking Heritage: Cultural Policy and Inclusion." In *Museums, Society, Inequality*, edited by R. Sandell, 203–212. Reprint, London: Routledge.

Chapter 6

Constructing communities through heritage participation

States and other entities continue to use cultural heritage in their attempts to construct communities and produce identity and a sense of belonging. Since both participation and community have become core concepts in heritage making (Adell et al. 2015, 8), in this chapter, we explore what kind of heritage communities are constructed through the notions of participation in the EHL context. We examine participation in the conceptual framework consisting of the interrelated concepts of identity, belonging, and community.

The assumption that heritage is closely linked with identity is widely shared in the AHDs (Smith 2006; see Introduction) of heritage professionals. However, the relation between heritage and identity is loaded with tensions (see Introduction). In AHDs, heritage is often seen as "inevitably contributing to all that is 'good' in the construction of national or group identity", but because of their tendency to "fossilise and 'preserve' heritage as unchanged and unchangeable" (Waterton and Smith 2010, 12), heritage management processes may essentialize identity, thereby ignoring that both identity and heritage are constantly changing and (re-)constructed. In identity-building processes, cultural heritage becomes an instrument of drawing boundaries that can be used to exclude as well as include.

The concepts of belonging and identity are tightly interrelated but scholars draw analytical distinctions between them (Yuval-Davis 2006; Antonsich 2010; Anthias 2013; Guibernau 2013; Lähdesmäki et al. 2016; see also Introduction). Both can be understood as dynamic processes constantly constructed by various actors with intersecting elements such as values, languages, practices, and symbols. Both can be used to create attachments with others or establish boundaries at individual and collective levels.

European identity is commonly appealed to in EU rhetoric. The entire EU cultural policy has aimed at promoting European identity since its inception. The notion of European identity is, however, deeply controversial, as highlighted in the scholarly literature on EU cultural policy (e.g. Shore 2000; Sassatelli 2009; Patel 2013) and on European identity (e.g., Delanty 1995, 2005; Risse 2003, 2006; Bruter 2003, 2004, 2005; Herrmann and Brewer 2004; Mayer and Palmowski 2004; Beck and Grande 2007; Antonsich 2008; Pichler 2008;

2009). EU cultural policy documents also use the concept of belonging. We have seen that the EHL sets its main goal in "strengthening European citizens' sense of belonging to the Union" (EP&C 2011, 3). The EHL thus exemplifies the EU's politics of belonging as a political project "aimed at constructing belonging in particular ways to particular collectivities that are, at the same time, themselves being constructed by these projects in very particular ways" (Yuval-Davis 2006, 197).

Belonging and identity are crucial to the idea of community. Communities are often defined through their location and through cultural elements that the members supposedly share. Such "imagined communities" (Anderson 1999) can also be understood as communities of memory, highlighting that communities are composed by their past (Bellah et al. 2008, 152–154). While participation is closely linked to identity and belonging, it indicates a different aspect of membership in a community. Paying attention to participation and collective action sheds light on the politics and power relations intrinsic to community (Delanty 2006, 4; Yuval-Davis 2006, 206–207; Watson and Waterton 2010b, 2). Membership of society relies on participation in various spheres, such as education, training, work, social activities, cultural life, and political decision-making (Newman et al. 2005, 44). All of them shape people's roles and belonging in a community, but not everyone has equal opportunities to participate. In Chapter 5 we discussed that the core question regarding heritage in terms of participation is who is included in and excluded from the process of decision-making about what heritage is and is not (see also Waterton and Smith 2010, 10). This links to the question of whether participation is sometimes used to assimilate "excluded communities into an understanding of traditional definitions of heritage" rather than to broaden definitions of cultural heritage to include hitherto excluded groups and "serve a diversity of cultural and historical experience" (Waterton and Smith 2010, 11).

Community has been a buzzword since the last decades of the twentieth century. Community has been perceived as being lost or in crisis and simultaneously as a solution for all kinds of social problems from crime to poverty (Delanty 2006, 5, 72; Waterton and Smith 2010, 6). In these discourses, community is often linked to participation and participatory governance. Not surprisingly, the success of participatory experiments has coincided with social fragmentation in several societies (Lappalainen 2017, 120–121). However, enthusiasm about communities is nothing new: the emergence of modern society raised concerns about the disintegration of community (Delanty 2006, 15), and in the 1930s, the revival of community was viewed as a cure for manifold social problems (Nousiainen 2016).

In the heritage sector, community is frequently addressed in policy and numerous other discourses (Crooke 2006; Watson and Waterton 2010; Adell et al. 2015). It is often used as a tool for heritage practitioners, policy makers, and scholars to "manage and make sense of 'others'" (Waterton and Smith 2010, 5). Indeed, community was invented as a sector of governance in the 1990s in the 'third-way' style of government of Tony Blair and the British Labour Party. In this 'governmentalized' discourse, notions of community are produced to legitimize decisions and policy lines, and to create and control citizens as dutiful members of the community. Nonetheless, governmentalization may also include potential for community empowerment, as scholars have pointed out (Rose 1999a, 167–184; Rose 1999b; Delanty 2006, 87–90; Miller and Rose 2008, 88–94). The EU heritage policy, including the EHL, can be interpreted as an instrument of this governmental communitarianism, in which cultural heritage is to construct community – similarly to how nation states have used and continue to use cultural heritage in their nation building processes.

Our interest here lies in how different conceptions of community are constructed and in the meanings given to communities in the discussions on participation related to cultural heritage. We see communities as more than simply pre-existing and necessarily positive "seemingly homogeneous collectives" (Waterton and Smith 2010, 5) defined by location, ethnicity, class, education, religion, or any other factor. Our point of departure is "a politically engaged and critical conceptualisation [of community]; one that engages with social relationships in all their messiness, taking account of action, process, power and change", as suggested by Waterton and Smith (2010, 5). According to this conceptualization, community is "(re)constructed through ongoing experiences, engagements and relations, and not all these need be consensual" (Waterton and Smith 2010, 8). Indeed, the policies and practices regarding cultural heritage, ranging from the international organizations, such as the UNESCO and the Council of Europe, to local contexts, formulate the conceptions of community and community engagement in a highly controversial way (e.g. Adell et al. 2015).

The Framework Convention on the Value of Cultural Heritage for Society, adopted in Faro, introduced the concept of heritage community (Council of Europe 2005). This concept refers to individuals and groups alike who wish to preserve and mediate specific cultural heritage to the subsequent generations. According to the Faro Convention, "every person has a right to engage with the cultural heritage of their choice, while respecting the rights and freedoms of others" (Council of Europe 2005, 1). The Convention thus conceptualizes heritage engagement as a right (see Zagato 2015, 142–144) and links it to the right to participate freely in cultural life, enshrined in the United Nations Universal Declaration of Human Rights (1948). Article 12 of the Faro Convention is titled "Access to cultural heritage and democratic participation". According to it, everyone should be encouraged to participate in "the process of identification, study, interpretation, protection, conservation and presentation of the cultural heritage [and] public reflection and debate on the opportunities and challenges which the cultural heritage represents". The same article continues that "the value attached by each heritage community to the cultural heritage with which it identifies" must be taken into consideration and that the voluntary organizations are seen not only "as partners in activities [but also] as constructive critics of cultural heritage policies". (Council of Europe 2005, 5.) In Article 7, "Cultural heritage and dialogue", the Council of Europe stresses the respect for diversity of interpretations and suggests establishing "processes for conciliation to deal equitably with situations where contradictory values are placed on the same cultural heritage by different communities" (Council of Europe 2005, 3–4). These articles acknowledge that heritage is dissonant and interpretations of it can cause controversies between different actors, or "heritage communities". The participation of individuals and groups in the field of cultural heritage is seen as important and their role is understood as both affirming and criticizing cultural heritage policies.

The Council of Europe and the EU launched a joint project called "The Faro Way" as a contribution to the European Year of Cultural Heritage in 2018, related to its key initiative on social innovation and participation (The Faro Way 2018). The objective of the project is to promote the role of civil society and communities in heritage governance and to increase the number of European states signing and ratifying the Faro Convention. In the EHL framework, the concept of heritage communities is used in the panel report in 2017, with an explicit reference to the Faro convention, as the EHL sites are envisioned to "reveal heritage communities of people, who are proud to interpret their past within the wider framework of European culture and history" (EC 2017, 7, 26). The European dimension of cultural heritage is strongly highlighted in this understanding of heritage communities that are seen as "custodians of [the EHL sites'] European significance" (EC 2017, 7).

In this chapter, we first discuss whether the members of local communities around the EHL sites form a specific heritage community and how their participation contributes to activities and practices of defining cultural heritage at the sites. Since the official EHL documents strongly emphasize the 'European significance' of heritage and its uses for creating 'European belonging', we then investigate how the idea of a European community is constructed at the EHL sites and how it engages European citizens. Finally, we explore the link between affects and visitors' participation in heritage at the EHL sites as well as community building related to it, as constructed in the interviews. In conclusion, we discuss the implications of these community constructions in relation to the notions of belonging and identity in the participatory governance of the EHL. The analysis is based on a qualitative close reading of the interviews with heritage practitioners and visitors at the 11 EHL sites.

Building local communities

Relations between the EHL sites and the surrounding population are shaped by several factors, which manifested in the interviews with local visitors. We define visitors who indicated that they live or have lived in the close surrounding of the EHL sites as local. In these interviews, we recognize the construction of two interrelated types of communities. In the following, we first discuss a local community attached to the site as a physical place and then another type of community based on the identification with the themes of the site. Finally, we discuss how the heritage practitioners see the relations between their EHL sites, the local audiences, and the communities constructed around them.

The following quote from an interview with a visitor to Camp Westerbork who spent his childhood near the camp indicates that local visitors may feel strong ownership over a site through their memories about the place.

> I thought I belonged to the camp. I belonged to it, in that sense that we experienced it after the war. But that confrontation with the post-war remnants, like the batteries... we played on those.
>
> (VS3/20)

The close relation with the site is based on this visitor's personal childhood memories of playing in the place itself. As an adult, he found the place very emotional and sad, even though he said it was a beautiful place to live. Similarly, a local visitor to Mundaneum conceptualized his earlier experiences of the building as part of his current relation to the site. He felt "closer and attached to the architectural heritage of the museum [as] they have kept the same atmosphere" (VS9/23) in the building. Based on their memories of the place, people are able to construct communities of memory (Bellah et al. 2008, 152–162) around the EHL sites. These memories can relate to the place itself, and to its previous meanings and uses, but also to its current use as a heritage site.

Some heritage practitioners brought up how people living in near the EHL sites develop a strong, homelike relationship with the place through their own memories. As one noted:

> [T]o a lot of people, it is 'my Hambach', 'our castle'. For them, it simply belongs here and triggers childhood memories, which are changing – and that may be dramatic in some ways because they've played here on the ruins as little kids, and now it's all valuable, high-quality, and fancily renovated and developed, so, of course, it's sad for many, but others are glad about it. So, it's polarizing.
>
> (P23)

The practitioner shows that the transformation of places over time influences the relation between the site and the people living in its vicinity. Indeed, the transition of the site and its function is perceived differently by each member of the local population. Many local inhabitants are glad that a place with a multilevel history is turned into a heritage site and may become frequent visitors. However, some consider this transformation as problematic, and perhaps connect it with a loss of their ownership of the place and its past. In addition, the heritagization of places can cause practical problems, such as increasing traffic, as some practitioners reported, prompting concrete changes. For example, Sagres Promontory had been a popular destination for the local population for picnics and other activities, but after it was given an official nation-wide heritage status in the 1980s, it became inaccessible outside fixed opening hours. The site managers are aware of such possible concerns. Many reported that they have put effort into establishing good relationships with the neighbourhood, which has had a positive impact on the local attitude towards the heritage site. Such heritagization processes are often accompanied by increasing tourism, which may diminish the ownership of the local communities over the sites. However, the public recognition sites receive as attractive tourist destinations, may strengthen their cultural value and economic significance in and for the local communities (e.g. Kirshenblatt-Gimblett 2006; Poria et al. 2011; Patuelli et al. 2012).

A heritage site can be part of the everyday environment of the local inhabitants, and be a place of work, study, or leisure. For example, Sagres Promontory is a daily environment for those who come there for fishing. A fisherman who has visited the place "hundreds of times" spoke of his close relationship with the environment of the site. For him, it was "[t]he most beautiful place on earth", "world heritage" and "a paradise" that is important "[f] or the fishermen and for people who would like to have a walk" (VS11/6). Thus, a specific notion of community can be constructed around the EHL sites through local people's ordinary activities. For example, local students use the archive centre in Mundaneum regularly for reading and studying, or the area around Camp Westerbork can be a local destination for a walk or a bike ride. In this respect, the sites can be and become meaningful on a local level. Constructed through the everyday activities of the locals, the core of this kind of "lived-space-community" (Lefebvre 2002, 39, 362) is the physical location. Physical place serves as an arena that enables people to come together, encounter each other, act collectively, attach symbolic meanings, narratives, and emotional sentiments to material, and forge the environment in order to manifest these meanings and narratives through it. Physical places are thus significant elements for constructing a notion of community.

A community can also be based on the story of the site around which it is constructed. Several local visitors expressed that they deeply identify with the narratives of the sites. As the place and content of heritage sites are inextricably entangled, living near a site and knowing about the people, life, and places around it may facilitate identification with the site and increase a sense of ownership of the narrative told there. As one interviewed visitor from the region to Alcide De Gasperi House noted, "here in this museum, I feel like home, because it tells a story that […] I have already lived in my history" (VS1/10). The geographical vicinity and sometimes entangled personal memories and family ties make the topic of the site feel close. As a visitor from Camp Westerbork noted: "it still is my history, because I live so close by to it. […] I do consider it part of us" (VS3/16). Similarly, a local visitor to Alcide De Gasperi House explained how his bonds with region and landscape contributed to his identification with the site narrative:

I feel personally and strongly related to the political figure of De Gasperi: he lived a few kilometres from my birthplace and his political efforts and results are fundamental in my political and social vision. We also share the same attachment to the Province of Trento and the love for nature and mountains.

(VS1/16)

The geographical closeness, nature, mountains, and the figure and message of Alcide De Gasperi all help build a close relation between this visitor and the site. By highlighting their personal identification with the narratives of the sites, local visitors discursively build a community of meaning related to the EHL sites. The visitors create meaning in their interpretations of the topics raised at the sites, and this meaning is contextualized by the place itself.

Similar types of community construction can be recognized in the interviews with the heritage practitioners. The practitioners aim to foster the relationship between the locals and the site through the place itself. For example, one practitioner working in the Robert Schuman House explained that while some locals come to visit only the garden, their interest in the site may grow, so they may also visit the home museum. Finally, they start bringing other people to the site, which indicates that they have developed a notion of ownership over it. The garden is used for activities at Robert Schuman House, combined with a visit to the home museum. Thus, the sites try to attract locals through the place itself, by utilizing the importance and familiarity of the setting.

The practitioners also see that the heritage sites are important to locals because of the themes addressed there. Sometimes idealizing this, they think that local people are proud of the past of their home area and the sites can be significant in their identification processes. For example, locals see Hambach Castle as "first of all home" and "an identity symbol", as one of the practitioners explained (P22). She went on to say that locals are "[p]roud of the fact that here […] was the cradle of German democracy" (P22). The past is seen as strengthening the bond between the local population and the site in this case.

Most of the sites seek to include local people in their activities by organizing cultural programmes and events specifically for and with them, such as Christmas parties or workshops with the local schools or offering free entrance once a year (P8). The sites are also present at local events, and, according to a practitioner, "this kind of interaction links the museum to local activities" (P1). For instance, the Historic Gdańsk Shipyard has community-building projects encouraging people to get involved in the local area. As one of its practitioners explained, "we want to start [making] people think about their own environment and what they can do around their home" (P26).

Through such activities, the EHL sites wish to promote community construction around them, "to collect the community around the museum or in the museum and also only to stay together and to reflect together", as one practitioner explained (P4). These accounts reflect the idea that "the new museum, stemming from a critique of the standard authoritarian treatment of the spectator as a passive recipient, should work more closely with its audiences, with particular local communities" (Murawska-Muthesius and Piotrowski 2015, 5). This means that memory institutions have to listen to the concerns of local communities, in active dialogue and exchange with them.

As discussed in Chapter 5, the practitioners welcome the local population and their initiatives for cooperation and wish to establish direct relationships with them. According to one practitioner, this is "the only way to convey what we want to do with the museum and also to understand what people would like to see in the museum" (P4). According to another, "there are definitely stimuli that come from people who live in that place and that represent their everyday experience so, for sure, the local population will contribute to this" (P1). The same practitioner told us about a retired person who "is involved in various cultural activities in the area and works as a guide voluntarily […] to make herself available to the community" (P1). Thus, practitioners see local people as active on the site and in the communities around them.

Nevertheless, the practitioners see themselves and their sites in the guiding role as facilitators in the construction of communities. The following quotation exemplifies the view that people need supervision by heritage experts in order to communicate about and 'recognize' heritage.

> The local people first of all, they don't know how to tell this story. They don't have the means, and they come to us as museum experts or heritage practitioners and ask advice how to make exhibitions and how to tell the stories of all those people. You need also, I think and that's why I said top-down [previously], people who can advise you what is the heritage and why is it so special, because it might mean maybe something more than what people initially think.
>
> (P10)

In a similar vein, Hertz (2015) has analyzed how the guidelines of the UNESCO Convention for the Safeguarding of Intangible Cultural Heritage advice states to sensitize communities, groups and individuals to the importance and value of their cultural heritage in order for them to be able to act upon it. Heritage practitioners admittedly have expertise in exhibiting and telling stories about the past. However, this kind of top-down approach, typical for participatory governance despite its aim to engage citizens in administration, can exclude important interpretations and meanings given to the past. After all, the EHL sites could be places in which local people can "talk about a piece of history that is theirs", as one of the practitioners stated (P1).

A short geographical distance and close relation to the place can make the content of a site more relevant and sometimes more sensitive to locals. Some practitioners acknowledged that local visitors may have a contradictory relation to the sites, feeling even accused by sites dealing with difficult history.

According to them, the locals may give the site slightly different meanings than other visitors and their interpretations may also differ from the main narrative of the site, as we discussed in Chapter 5.

The EHL sites often attempt to create interaction with the locals by organizing events that deal with familiar themes, as the interviews with the practitioners indicate. At Alcide De Gasperi House, for example, European integration is discussed in close connection to local themes. A Europe-themed festival for the local schoolchildren indicates the strategy of the site to "walk with two legs" (P4), that is, to emphasize both the European and the local dimension. This combination of the European and the local exemplifies how both practitioners and visitors see "local" in the framework of "European", particularly in border regions and smaller, more remote places, such as Robert Schuman House and Alcide De Gasperi House. For some of the interviewees, the category of European provides a transnational perspective on heritage that is perceived as more inclusive than the national one. But the local and European can also contradict. The following quote from a practitioner interview reveals conflicting interpretations about the place by the local population and the staff.

> I guess for the neighbours it is a piece of local heritage, because this house dates back to the eighteenth century, it has a story, they defended the house when it could have been sold [and] transformed into a hotel. So, for the neighbours this house and the park belongs to the local heritage. [...] it's true that the neighbours consider this place [...] rather a local piece of heritage, but there are quite a few, and other people, for them it's obvious that what we have to say is European. It's a European narrative, it's not a local narrative.
>
> (P15)

This quote refers to the contradiction that some members of the local population tend to regard the building with its materiality as a piece of local heritage, while as an EHL site, the site promotes a European, not a local, narrative. So, a multiplicity of meanings can be attached to one place and it may be difficult to balance two contradicting heritage narratives. An example of reconciling the local and international scales is provided at another site. A visitor to Mundaneum connected the building to the city of Mons: "But the building is part of the history of the city. So, what you don't have through the collection, you have it through the building itself" (VS9/22). The building and its history are local, so the visitor feels close to Mundaneum even though the content of the site is not predominantly local. And in reverse: although the sites themselves stand on particular places, locals give them various meanings and interpret them in varying spatial frameworks. Hence, the communities constructed and perceived by the locals around the EHL sites can be located not only on local scale but also regional, national, European, or global.

Building European communities

Culture is part of the EU's politics of identity and belonging, practiced in relation to citizens, member states, and non-member states. Culture, and its European dimension, were presented as the core factors in integration by the Committee on a People's Europe, whose reports have been seen as an important milestone in promoting the role of cultural issues in political and economic integration (Shore 1993 and 2000, 25; Shore and Black 1996, 286). These reports explicitly aimed at making the European community more tangible for citizens through everyday life, values, and symbols (Committee on a People's Europe 1985, 10, 22–23, 29). The introduction of a flag, hymn, and Europe Day, all proposed in the reports, ended up in the Treaty of Lisbon as symbols of the EU – although only as a separate declaration not signed by all the member states (Lisbon Treaty 2007, 267). The objective was to create a sense of belonging and to present Europe as a community formed by people and not only by economic integration. The EHL can be interpreted as an instrument in these discursive, symbolic, and practical attempts to 'bring Europe closer to the citizens'. The Label follows a long tradition of using culture to create a European identity and belonging. In this process, cultural heritage is used as a technology of proximity (Walters and Haahr 2005) for creating sense of belonging and thus promoting the legitimacy of the EU integration – however, this is currently being strongly questioned in Europe.

A central context of participation in our interview data is indeed the so-called 'European construction'. Our interviewees commonly envisaged Europe, European identity, and the EU as under construction. We asked them how they interpreted the official EHL slogans "Europe starts here" and "Europe starts with you". The interviewees had various conceptions of European community and belonging to it – although it was not always clear whether they were referring in their responses to Europe or the EU. Particularly the latter slogan stimulated discussion of participation as a way of belonging to the European community in the making, as we will see below.

Both the practitioners and visitors recognized the potential of cultural heritage to enhance belonging to Europe. Concerning the role of the EHL in this process, one interviewed practitioner pointed out that the EHL action is an attempt to create belonging to Europe with cultural means, but "we have to work all together […] for giving a sense to this" (P32). Another practitioner agreed that the EHL provides a network but said that the network as such did not "make you feel more a part of Europe", but rather the dialogue within it did (P1). Several practitioners understood the EHL sites as facilitating a sense of belonging to Europe or as "ambassadors" "pass[ing on] the knowledge of what is a heritage, what is Europe and […] the wealth of Europe" (P33). This concerns especially sites directly related to the EU, such as Robert Schuman House, Alcide De Gasperi House, and the European District of Strasbourg. Europe is often an explicit topic of activities organized by many of the sites.

These activities connect cultural heritage to current questions, such as Brexit or migration. Indeed, the sites can help "the citizens of Europe to feel more European", as one practitioner reasoned, particularly if they "become a bit more interactive, where you can touch things with your hands, not places where you are told only about experiences" (P1). This practitioner thus called for exhibitions that enable visitors' active participation at the site and also for "[a]ctions [that are] more direct and more on a daily basis" (P1). The same ideas were mediated by some of the visitors. A visitor who finds it "hard to really grasp what Europe is" experiences the European District of Strasbourg as "a direct physical representation of Europe" (VS4/17). While it often seems to her that EU matters "don't concern me at all", in this site she feels that

> here it sort of shows that there actually is sort of a human dimension behind it. There's a physical building where actual human beings work, doing the stuff that you read about in the news, and you can watch them.
> (VS4/17)

Some of the interviewed practitioners and visitors claimed that the EHL sites represent something more than themselves, understood as a seedbed for the European dimension. They saw the sites as symbols of "bigger, mixed, transregional" (P23) history with "connecting factors" (P23) shared with other heritage sites, or even a "universal experience" (P27). In other words, they represent a broader and more open conception of community than the national communities, which were perceived as narrow by many interviewees. Both practitioners and visitors commonly connected the idea of European identity to values such as freedom, democracy, peace, equality, and human rights, and the EHL sites were experienced as reminders of these values and of the importance of acting for them. It was also common for the interviewees to conceptualize European identity through cooperation and exchange of culture, ideas, and opinions across state borders. Another prominent way of conceptualizing European identity in the interviews was through the peace project. All of these elements were seen as building blocks of the European community under construction. Both practitioners' and visitors' views, thus, resonate with the EU's common narrative of the European project.

Feeling "more European" is closely connected to the notion of European identity. One of our interviewed practitioners described "being European" as one of the several identifications persons may have. A heritage site such as a museum can tell about this "multi-layered idea of identity", he claimed.

> By communicating a complex idea of identity, a multi-layered idea of identity that allows people to remain themselves while being European, the idea that being European does not mean being anything else than what you already are, but simply recognizing a level in which you are together, [...] it's about concentric circles [...] It's not that one thing excludes the

other, it's not that one thing suffocates the other, they are floors of the same building and this is a thing that the museum tells better than many lessons. (P4)

Many of the practitioners took it for granted that something like a European identity exists and they themselves share it. Several visitors shared this view, while some of them were more hesitant. The practitioners commonly emphasized that they did not want to define Europe for visitors. Quite the opposite, they argued that the EHL sites can make space for a debate about Europe. As one of these practitioners claimed: "we are here to create the debate, [...] to give [...] positive and negative information, so that people can participate in the debate" (S4/1). According to another practitioner, the site does not aim to "give an absolute definition of the meaning of what Europe is" since "[t]he idea of Europe is not coming from an unequivocal concept of Europe, everyone has their own message" but rather attempts to send the message that "everyone can do his bit" (P1).

The conception of Europe as constantly being constructed is repeated in the interview data. "Europe is still at work, and we want you to be part of this construction", as one of the practitioners said (P15). According to another, "[the slogan] 'Europe starts with you', it's for making Europe really interesting for people, for showing them that they are real members of the European Union. And Europe can be constructed with them, too" (P32). In other words, being involved in 'European construction' may strengthen participants' ownership of the 'European project' and their belonging to EUrope. But the visitors may also need "help" to feel European cultural heritage "inside themselves", as another practitioner put it (P10). Hence, while such calls may provide inspiration for visitors' active participation in EU integration, visitors may not be expected to reflect critically on the multiple and transforming meanings of Europe. This is a common drawback in participatory governance.

Also for the visitors, the slogan "Europe starts with you" implied the importance of participation in this construction process. They felt that it invited them personally to participate in the activities of the site and, above all, in 'constructing' Europe. "Europe starts [...] from the participation of citizens to Europe", as one visitor noted (VS1/2). For the visitors, the slogans simultaneously refer to acting for and belonging to Europe or the EU. They felt that "the slogans are asking me to participate in this community to which I belong" (VS1/7) and were convinced that "each one of us has a relevant role in the creation of the European belonging" (VS3/31). The slogans were also interpreted as a reminder that "Europe is inside of us" (VS1/1) and that it starts "in my heart, so generally the way how I live here" (VS2/15). Based on the slogans, the visitors understood Europe as a "community of people, more than a community of things and places" (VS3/22) with components that go beyond concrete matters such as the economy, including more abstract or imagined elements like solidarity.

The visitors to the home museums of EU founding figures particularly interpreted the slogan "Europe starts with you" as an invitation to continue 'European construction', conceived as a process started by Robert Schuman and Alcide De Gasperi. The visitors to these sites repeatedly emphasized that "it's up to us to continue creating a Europe" (VS10/3) and to spread the message of the EU founding figures. Through their involvement, citizens can bring to the constantly changing European project something that the current European community does not represent. As one the visitors to Alcide De Gasperi House noted, "we must feel part of a project to understand [...] the importance of how to change Europe, because [...] I feel it is no longer de facto represented by the current European community" (VS1/13).

The notion of Europe under construction is demonstrated by the ways in which the interviewees explicitly discussed the EU as a community in the making. They sometimes distinguished between the current EU and the future EU they would hope to see. Many visitors criticized the current EU or considered it to be "certainly a bit in crisis", as one visitor put it (VS1/8) but saw citizens' participation as a way of improving it. According to both visitors and practitioners, participation in activities organized by the EHL sites can contribute to this: "we can learn [...] the idea of participation [...], to do something to make a better Europe", as a visitor noted (VS1/3). A participant in a project organized by Alcide De Gasperi House emphasized the value of such projects in terms of citizens' direct participation: "it's very important for us as citizens [...] that we [...] will do something for Europe" (VS1/2).

Some visitors explained their own active contribution to constructing Europe from the bottom up. As one them noted, "I also feel spurred on to bring something of mine to this community" (VS1/7). These visitors explicitly contested the top-down approach: "we should not be [a] customer of someone else that [...] deliver this European spirit. So, we are the ones who make Europe" (VS3/31). According to their bottom-up approach, "[i]t can't be only few people that decide. Instead everyone can maybe say his opinion and participate, get involved", as another visitor stated (VS1/4). These visitors acknowledged the role of institutions and that Europe is made "both from above and below" but emphasized that citizens should not "let the process of Europeanization be totally something that is imposed on you from above", as one of them claimed (VS1/9). Europe is here envisioned as a community of active citizens who participate in community building in a concrete way.

Despite the slogans' invitation, the EHL sites do not always succeed in their aim to inspire visitors to participate in constructing Europe: "I don't feel that very activated by it. It's more a passive reception of information" (VS4/6). The visitors may not find enough material about the role of citizens in the sites: "I didn't feel any highlight of the initiatives of the European citizens" (VS4/12). Indeed, when asked about the responsibilities of promoting cultural heritage in Europe, few practitioners mentioned citizens' activities. Some of them replied firmly within the framework of participatory governance: "when we [teach] people what European heritage is, people, the citizens of Europe, have to speak to others about that" (P33). In such a top-down conception, the relation to citizens is rather paternalistic than interactive, and citizens are defined as first receivers and then distributors of the information given by the sites.

In the EHL action, the EU's power to name and define is used to produce and legitimize the idea of European cultural heritage – and thereby a European community, or EUrope. Since the notion of European cultural heritage implies a conception of common roots and a shared past, it can be used to build a direct relation to citizens, bypassing the member states. Because of this implication, the idea of European cultural heritage is a powerful way of forging a European community and belonging. Thus, the EHL is a tool in the EU's politics of belonging (Yuval-Davis 2006) aiming to govern diversity in Europe and to seek legitimacy. Participatory practices organized in the EHL sites manifest this community construction at the grass-roots level (see Box 6.1).

Box 6.1 Examples from participatory practices: Hands-on exercises on building Europe

Pedagogic activities form the core of the outreach actions at several EHL sites. This reflects the task given to the EHL sites of "organizing educational activities, especially for young people, which increase the understanding of the common history of Europe and of its shared yet diverse heritage and which strengthen the sense of belonging to a common space" (EP&C 2011, 4). The pedagogic activities, often organized in collaboration with schools, focus on a wide range of topics, such as current socio-political phenomena, citizenship education, and the past that the site in question deals with. Commonly they concentrate on the idea of Europe and the attempts to construct a European community, following the EHL objective of "strengthening European citizens' sense of belonging to the Union, in particular that of young people" (EP&C 2011, 3).

According to one of our interviewed practitioners from Hambach Castle, Europe is the most popular topic in the pedagogic programme of their site (P22). Instead of learning about the institutions acting at the European level, their workshops dealing with Europe are about the question of belonging to Europe, reflecting on whether the participants feel European and identify with Europe.

For instance, an exercise used in one of the workshops at Hambach Castle invites the schoolchildren to draw "the house of Europe" holding a big pen together with the other participants without talking. The next step is to "fill the house". As the practitioner in charge of the exercise explained, each of the participants writes inside a window what Europe means to him or her personally. Then they look for similarities across Europe and write them as the foundation of the house. On the roof they write visions about their ideal, imagined Europe and in a shed their criticism about the disadvantages of Europe. The exercise continues with a discussion about these meanings, similarities, visions, and criticism attached to Europe. The value of this exercise is precisely that it offers an arena for debate and dispute, according to the practitioner.

This example of participatory pedagogic activity aiming to build community encourages participants' own meaning-making and critical debate about Europe and belonging to it. Simultaneously, it illustrates the concrete attempts to "construct Europe" through the activities of an EHL site. In a similar vein, a project called Visions of Europe 2.0 at the Alcide De Gasperi House invites young people to reflect their ideas of Europe. In an exercise in this project, participants are asked to imagine which animal, food, or cartoon character the EU would be.

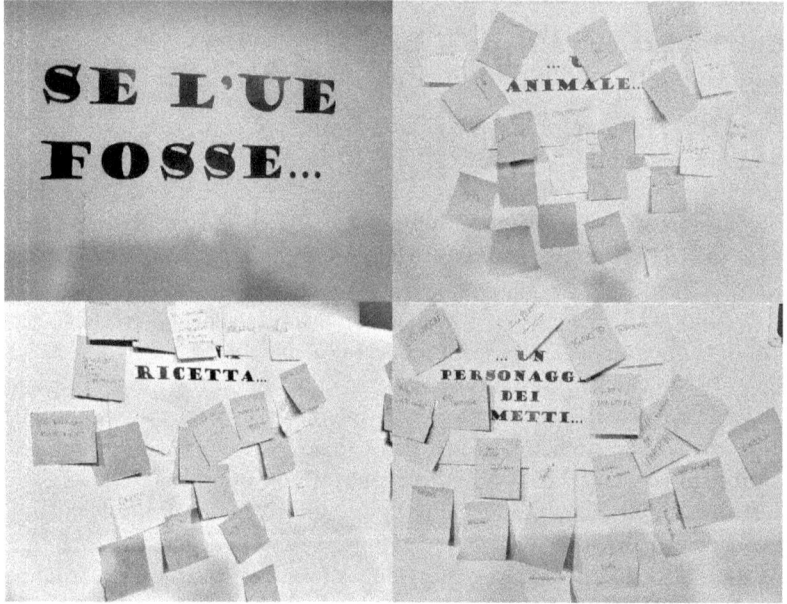

Figure 6.1 A warm-up exercise related to the Visions of Europe 2.0 project, organized by the Alcide De Gasperi House, prompted the participants to think which animal, food, or cartoon character the EU could be. Photo: EUROHERIT

Building affective communities

Engaging with heritage in affective ways (see Chapter 7) may be a step towards a more intimate and personally meaningful visit experience that evokes visitors to participate more actively in or beyond the heritage site. Based on the interviews with both practitioners and visitors, heritage experiences at the EHL sites consist of several affective and emotional elements: moving personal memories or autobiographical events, interactive practices engaging the visitors with heritage in depth, touching narratives, and the impressiveness of the place. These elements contribute to the emotional experience, creating deeper identification with the topics and the pasts addressed at the sites and empathy to people in different times and places. Together they can construct an affective community, which is not necessarily attached to any particular place or time. Indeed, affective means are often used in building communities and belonging, and further research on the connections between emotions and politics related to belonging has been called for (Guibernau 2013).

When the visitors emphasized their personal relation to heritage and their identification with the narratives told at the EHL sites, they attached to cultural heritage the potential to strengthen some sort of deeper experience of past events. Several visitors to different sites felt that the story told there was theirs and said that they could identify with the sites through their own biographies and memories. These memories did not need to be from the same time or place as the site narrative, but they could be about the same theme. For example, two visitors to Hambach Castle related to the site narratives about democracy and freedom of expression and speech and its feminist perspective to the Hambach Festival through their own experiences. One of them remembered that in the 1970s, she personally experienced hot debates about feminism and democracy (VS7/1). Similarly, the other connected the visit to Hambach Castle to memories from his youth.

> Yes, it's absolutely part of my story, I mean, in my youth we strongly discussed basic democratic structures and tried to advance them […] they were fundamental values, which certainly had their origin here.
>
> (VS7/2)

These visitors identified with the struggle for democracy in the Hambach Festival in 1832, represented in the narrative of the Hambach Castle, based on their own experiences in the 1970s. The next quote manifests how identification with the narrative of the site and the past it addresses can be immersive and affective. The visitor to the Alcide De Gasperi House explained that when he was in the museum,

> I completely felt myself in the life of De Gasperi, so I was like De Gasperi. And during the entire museum I felt like … because it's my history, the history of my father, my mother …
>
> (VS1/11)

This underlining of one's ownership of and identification with the narratives displayed at the sites discursively create a community of 'us'. "[The site is] about who we are as a people" (VS3/29), as one visitor summarized. Another visitor agreed: "to me it's about my history. It's the history of our people. It happened in the lifetime of my parents and my grandparents" (VS3/21). Visitors frequently referred to their grandparents, grandchildren, and other family members in their accounts, which indicates that they included several generations in the past, present, and future in this community. In brief, cultural heritage is understood as a building block of a community and its identity: "if you forget it, the community disintegrates", as one visitor noted (VS1/9).

The visitors commonly explained how particular elements and more or less interactive practices at the sites made their experience emotional, touching, and moving, helping them to identify with the narrative displayed at the site concerned. For example, a song could help the visitors to "put [herself] in the situation" of the past, as a visitor from Hambach Castle explained (VS7/6). Similarly, the photos, videos and the room where Alcide De Gasperi was born were experienced as powerful symbols of the past at his home museum. Such elements not only make the experience more emotional but also make the narrative of the site more concrete, as the visitors frequently highlighted. In reverse, a lack of emotional elements at the EHL sites might lead to a lack of emotions and weak identification with the site narrative, as described by a visitor of the European District of Strasbourg. She stated:

> it does not necessarily trigger emotions, [for] me it is not big enough, or I don't know, colourful enough. You just have black and white pictures of people's movements, it doesn't speak to me emotionally […] in order to trigger me emotionally. It would either need more colour [or] more explanation.
>
> (VS4/17)

Similar to the visitors, the practitioners also thought that emotions and affectivity can foster visitors' empathy and identification with the narratives told by the sites, so they aimed at creating affective experiences in the exhibitions and other activities. According to one practitioner at Camp Westerbork, the aim of the site is to touch visitors emotionally, to prepare them to interact with the theme and learn: "if you want to give them information and want them to learn something, the first step is that they are touched by the subject. Then they are more prepared to interact with the subject" (P14). The site seeks "to really engage people on the spot", for example through stories told by a survivor via interactive elements (P14). Thus, the stated purpose is not only to create an emotion but to prompt visitors' curiosity for knowing more.

A further way to bring sites closer to visitors is to connect them to topical issues, such as migration. According to the practitioners, the sites try to make the visitors ask themselves: what would I have done in that situation? More than that, the sites seek to make the visitors reflect their choices in their current life. This bridging between past and present may be interpreted as a way of building a cross-temporal community around the topic of the site, including the visitors from different places, the site, and the people whose life it describes. The glue in this community is empathy.

Several of the interviewed visitors talked about the empathy created by reflecting on the past in the present situation. Some visitors emphasized that the site itself feels impressive: just being in the place gave them an experience of authenticity that helps to make the past come alive. For example, a visitor "found it very moving and touching" to visit Robert Schuman House and she emphasized how she really imagined Schuman to be walking, thinking, and working on the very same spot: "I find it moving, to imagine all of this" (VS10/1; see also Chapter 8). The experience of authenticity – "seeing with my own eyes" (VS1/2) – can arouse both emotions and empathy. A visitor to Alcide De Gasperi House reported that the visit "touched me very much in the sense that [...] I love putting myself in the reality [of how] someone else lived". She felt that "seeing with my own eyes something so personal [is] involving me very much" (VS1/2).

Thinking about past difficulties and suffering touched visitors, making them feel sad but also connected to the people of the past. Positive emotions such as admiration and courage roused by cultural heritage can be building blocks of heritage community: the visitors at Alcide De Gasperi House report receiving from their visit inspiration and motivation to contribute to the today's society. The visitors commonly imagine themselves in the past time and compare it to their present, with its rights and freedoms that did not exist in the past. The heritage experience enables them to reflect on the present and in several cases to feel compassion to people in trouble today, such as refugees.

Moreover, the visitors commonly expressed thankfulness and respect towards those who had suffered through hard times or fought for a better future. One visitor to Hambach Castle explained how he felt grateful for democracy: "big respect for this achievement. This surely is an emotional thing" (VS7/4). As the quote below from an interview with a visitor to the Historic Gdańsk Shipyard indicates, reflecting on the suffering of earlier generations and the subsequent improvement of living conditions can be experienced as emotional.

> This is a very emotional place. I am quite young still, and I think for older people, who remember these times, it is must be very difficult to pass through it. In this big blue car, where you can sit and watch these videos, how they treated people. This is terrible for me, because I do not know

how it is possible. ... I live in a country where if I want to go to a shop, I go, if I want to go abroad, I go, and no one forbids me, and no one will tell me that I cannot go out on the street at 8 pm [...] sometimes my heart aches, and tears, the tears roll from my eyes because I know that my grandparents and parents have lived through this. They were here and they were fighting, and they could lose their lives, and many people lost their lives. So, it is very emotional.

(VS8/23)

Based on our interview data, experiencing heritage and sharing the narratives in the exhibitions and activities at the EHL sites generates emotions and empathy in the visitors. These sentiments can be seen as elements in an affective community, constructed in the interviews. This heritage community can be interpreted as a community of meaning, since it is based on identification with the topics addressed at the sites and on recognition of their relevance for the present and the future, rather than on concrete spaces or practices. It is cross-generational and constitutes links between places and times (see Kaasik-Krogerus 2019). Anyone who acknowledges the relevance of heritage and shares the meanings given to the themes addressed at the sites can be members of this community. Thus, it can be seen as a community of memory, in which tradition is important and stories about the past are retold in order not to forget the past; the explicit orientation to the future and future generations makes it simultaneously a community of hope (Bellah et al. 2008, 153). Such a community construction can be relatively inclusive, although it is debatable whether people who give very different meanings to one site still belong to the same heritage community.

Community building in the EHL

Our ethnographic research confirms that the relations between heritage, community, and participation are extremely complex (see Tauschek 2015, 292). Based on our investigation of the interviews with the practitioners and visitors of the EHL sites, we constructed three types of heritage communities through the notion of participation in heritage. First, the locals around the EHL sites build their relations to them through the place itself and through the topics addressed there. Communities around the sites are built from locals living in the close surroundings and their everyday practices but also their memories, meanings, and complex relations to the narratives of the sites.

Second, Europe in the interviews is a community under construction. While this European community, particularly when understood as the EU, is experienced as distant, both the practitioners and visitors also conceptualize it as a building process in which everyone can participate. Moreover, the EHL action and sites are seen as capable of creating opportunities to participate in this construction. Since the European dimension of heritage is commonly emphasized at the EHL sites, heritage is acknowledged in the interviews as one element in this community in the making, pointing to the idea of a shared past as its building block. Rather than only an economic or administrative community, Europe is produced as a cultural, symbolic, political, or value community in the interviews.

Third, through the discussions on affective elements and experiences in the sites, an affective community is constructed in the interviews. This community is not necessarily attached to any particular place or time, but consists of visitors' memories, engagement, and experiences related to the site and their identification with its narratives. In the style of the Faro Convention (Council of Europe 2005), the members of this sort of heritage community are all those who consider this heritage important. This community of meaning is based on shared meanings given to heritage, rather than on a concrete bond to the site itself or existing personal relations between different community members. It enables feeling empathy towards people in the past, present, and future. All three types of community constructions are "imagined communities" (Anderson 1999), constructed through identifying with heritage and 'mentally' sharing it, without necessarily knowing the other members personally or concretely acting upon this heritage. They indicate that the EHL goal of creating transnational networks and a sense of belonging is acknowledged by both practitioners and visitors at the EHL sites.

The intangible aspect of cultural heritage prominent in the EHL together with its transnational perspective open potential for new types of heritage communities to emerge, if the Faro Convention's emphasis on inclusiveness and democratic participation as well as heritage dissonance are taken seriously. Because of the complex relation between heritage and community, particularly in the context of participatory governance, it is important to ask whether, at the EHL sites, "jointly-run projects tend to involve things that are done *for* communities, rather than *with* them" (Waterton and Smith 2010, 7; emphasis original). Although participatory practices have their origins in ideas of social justice and the empowerment of marginalized groups (Adell et al. 2015, 11), they can result in domesticating the very people they seek to engage and empower. Based on our interview data, the EHL sites explicitly attempt to engage visitors in heritage and support their community construction processes, but at the same time their activities may take a top-down approach to visitors and communities, thus exemplifying governmental communitarianism (Rose 1999a, 1999b; Delanty 2006; Miller and Rose 2008).

We interpret the EHL sites as poly-spaces, since a variety of different meanings and temporal layers are attached to each of them in the interviews. We have developed the concept of poly-space to make sense of heritage sites that always simultaneously involve multiple spatial, temporal, and affective experiences in one physical space (see Chapter 7). Consequently, we recognize aspects of poly-space in all the three community constructions discussed in this chapter. Since the EHL sites have gone through several phases over time, the locals' relationship with them also includes several temporal layers, constructed through personal memories, ways of engagement, family ties, and so on, as the interviews indicate. The European community is formed by the interviewees with their own unexpected assemblages of various elements that are not tied to geography, such as values and citizens' participation, and that cover both past, present, and future. According to the interviewees, this European community inherently includes the local communities around the individual EHL sites: "local" is presented as "European", following the core aim of the EHL to create the idea of European heritage and thereby European belonging through the labelled sites. The affective community, finally, is constructed through empathy and emotions, which are key aspects of our concept of poly-space. Even though these experiences are site-specific, they refer beyond the sites and beyond the present time, to a poly-spatial belonging.

References

Adell, N., R. F. Bendix, C. Bortolotto, and T. Markus, eds. 2015. *Between Imagined Communities and Communities of Practice: Participation, Territory and the Making of Heritage*. Göttingen: Universitätsverlag Göttingen.

Adell, N., R. F. Bendix, C. Bortolotto, and T. Markus. 2015. "Introduction". In *Between Imagined Communities and Communities of Practice: Participation, Territory and the Making of Heritage*, edited by N. Adell, R. F. Bendix, C. Bortolotto, and T. Markus, 7–21. Göttingen: Universitätsverlag Göttingen.

Anderson, B. (1983) 1999. *Imagined Communities: Reflections on the Origin and Spread of Nationalism*. Reprint. London: Verso.

Anthias, F. 2013. *Identity and Belonging: Conceptualisations and Political Framings*. öln: Research Network for Latin America. www.kompetenzla.uni-koeln.de/sites/fileadmin2/WP_Anthias.pdf.

Antonsich, M. 2010. "Searching for Belonging: An Analytical Framework." *Geography Compass* 4 (6): 644–659.

Beck, U. and Grande, E. 2007. *Cosmopolitan Europe*. Cambridge, UK: Polity Press.

Bellah, R. N., R. Madsen, W. M. Sullivan, A. Swidler and S. M. Tipton. (1985) 2008. *Habits of the Heart: Individualism and Commitment in American Life*. Reprint, Berkeley: University of California Press.

Bruter, M. 2003. "Winning Hearts and Minds for Europe: The Impact of News and Symbols on Civic and Cultural European Identity." *Comparative Political Studies*, 36 (10): 1148–1179. https://doi.org/10.1177/0010414003257609.

Bruter, M. 2004. "Civic and Cultural Components of a European Identity: A Pilot Model of Measurement of Citizens' Levels of European Identity." In *Transnational Identities: Becoming European in the EU*, edited by R. K. Herrman, T. Risse and M. B. Brewer, 186–213. Lanham, MD: Rowman & Littlefield.

Bruter, M. 2005. *Citizens of Europe? The Emergence of a Mass European Identity*. New York: Palgrave Macmillan.

Committee on a People's Europe. 1985. A People's Europe: Reports from the Ad Hoc Committee. Bulletin of the European Communities, Supplement 7/85.

Council of Europe. 2005. Framework Convention on the Value of Cultural Heritage for Society. Faro, 27.10.2005. *Council of Europe Treaty Series – No. 199.* www.coe.int/en/web/conventions/full-list/-/conventions/rms/0900001680083746.

Crooke, E. 2015. "Museums and Community." In *Companion to Museum Studies*, edited by S. Macdonald, 168–185. New York: Blackwell.

Delanty, G. 1995. *Inventing Europe: Idea, Identity, Reality.* Basingstoke: Macmillan.

Delanty, G. 2005. "The Idea of a Cosmopolitan Europe: On the Cultural Significance of Europeanization." *International Review of Sociology* 15 (3): 405–21.

Delanty, G. (2003) 2006. *Community.* Reprint. London: Routledge.

EC (European Commission). 2017. *"European Heritage Label: 2017 Panel Report."* Brussels: European Commission.

EP&C (European Parliament and the Council). 2011. "Decision no. 1194/2011/EU Establishing a European Union Action for the European Heritage Label." *Official Journal of the European Union* L 303: 1–9.

The Faro Way (2018) Enhanced Participation in Cultural Heritage. https://europa.eu/cultural-heritage/news/faro-way-enhanced-participation-cultural-heritage_en.

Herrmann, R. and M. B. Brewer. 2004. "Identities and Institutions: Becoming European in the EU." In *Transnational Identities: Becoming European in the EU*, edited by R. K. Herrman, T. Risse, and M. B. Brewer, 186–213. Lanham, MD: Rowman & Littlefield.

Hertz, E. 2015. "Bottoms, Genuine and Spurious". In *Between Imagined Communities and Communities of Practice: Participation, Territory and the Making of Heritage*, edited by N. Adell, R. F. Bendix, C. Bortolotto, and T. Markus, 25–27. Göttingen: Universitätsverlag Göttingen.

Guibernau, M. 2013. *Belonging: Solidarity and Division in Modern Societies.* Cambridge, UK: Polity Press.

Kaasik-Krogerus, S. 2019. "Identity Politics of the Promotional Videos of the European Heritage Label" *Contemporary Politics.* doi: 10.1080/13569775.2019.1611207.

Kirshenblatt-Gimblett, B. 2006. "World Heritage and Cultural Economics." In *Museum Frictions: Public Cultures/Global Transformations*, edited by I. Karp, C. Kratz, L. Szwaja, and T. Ybarra-Frausto, 161–202. Durham, NC: Duke University Press.

Lappalainen, P. 2017. "Hallinto- ja kansalaisaloitteinen osallistaminen, demokratia ja politiikka." In *Poliittinen osallistuminen: Vanhan ja uuden osallistumisen jännitteitä*, edited by E. Kestilä-Kekkonen and P-E. Korvela, 110–133. Jyväskylä: SoPhi.

Lefebvre, H. (1974) 2002. *The Production of Space.* Translated by D. Nicholson-Smith. Reprint, Oxford: Blackwell Publishing.

Lisbon Treaty. 2007. "Treaty of Lisbon Amending the Treaty on European Union and the Treaty Establishing the European Community, Signed at Lisbon, 13 December 2007 (2007/C 306/01)." *Official Journal of the European Union* C 306.

Lähdesmäki, T., T. Saresma, K. Hiltunen, S. Jäntti, N. Sääskilahti, A. Vallius, and K. Ahvenjärvi. 2016. "Fluidity and Flexibility of 'Belonging': Uses of the Concept in Contemporary Research". *Acta Sociologica* 59 (3): 233–247.

Mayer, F. C. & Palmowski, J. 2004. "European Identities and the EU: The Ties That Bind the People of Europe." *Journal of Common Market Studies* 42 (3): 573–598.

Miller, P. and Rose, N. 2008. *Governing the Present: Administering Economic, Social and Personal Life.* Oxford: Polity.

Murawska-Muthesius, K. and P. Piotrowski. 2015. *From Museum Critique to the Critical Museum.* London: Routledge.

Newman, A., F. McLean and G. Urquhart. 2005. "Museums and the Active Citizen: Tackling the Problems of Social Exclusion." *Citizenship Studies* 9 (1): 41–57.

Nousiainen, M. 2016. "Osallistavan käänteen lyhyt historia." In *Hallinnan ja osallistamisen politiikat*, edited by M. Nousiainen & K. Kulovaara, 158–189. Jyväskylä: Sophi.

Patel, K. K. 2013. "Introduction." In *The Cultural Politics of Europe: European Capitals of Culture and the European Union Since the 1980s,* edited by K. K. Patel, 1–15. London: Routledge.

Patel, K. K. ed. 2013. *The Cultural Politics of Europe. European Capitals of Culture and European Union Since the 1980s.* London: Routledge.

Poria, Y., A. Reichel, and R. Cohen. 2011. "World Heritage Site – Is It an Effective Brand Name? A Case Study of a Religious Heritage Site." *Journal of Travel Research* 50 (5): 482–495. doi: 10.1177/0047287510379158

Patuelli, R., M. Mussoni and G. Candela. 2012. "The Effects of World Heritage Sites on Domestic Tourism: A Spatial Interaction Model for Italy." http://dx.doi.org/10.2139/ssrn.2084192.

Pichler, F. 2008. "European Identities from Below: Meanings of Identification with Europe." *Perspectives on European Politics and Society* 9 (4): 411–430.

Pichler, F. 2009. "Cosmopolitan Europe: Views and Identity." *European Societies* 11 (1): 3–24.

Risse, T. 2003. "European Identity and the Heritage of National Culture." In *Rethinking Heritage. Cultures and Politics in Europe*, edited by R. S. Peckham, 74–89. London: I.B.Tauris.

Risse, T. 2006. "Neofunctionalism, European Identity, and the Puzzles of European Integration." *Journal of European Public Policy* 12 (2): 291–309.

Rose N. 1999a. *Powers of Freedom. Reframing Political Thought.* Cambridge: Cambridge University Press.

Rose N. 1999b. Inventiveness in Politics. *Economy and Society* 28 (3): 467–493.

Sassatelli, M. 2009. *Becoming Europeans: Cultural Identity and Cultural Policies.* Basingstoke: Palgrave Macmillan.

Shore, C. 1993. "Inventing the 'People's Europe': Critical Approaches to European Community "Cultural Policy."" *Man* 28 (4): 779–800.

Shore, C. 2000. *Building Europe: The Cultural Politics of European Integration.* London: Routledge.

Shore, C. and A. Black. (1994) 1996. "Citizens' Europe and the Construction of European Identity." In *The Anthropology of Europe: Identities and Boundaries in Conflict*, edited by V. A. Goddard, J. R. Llobera and C. Shore, 275–298. Reprint, Oxford: Berg.

Smith, L. 2006. *Uses of Heritage.* London: Routledge.

Tauschek, M. 2015. "Imaginations, Constructions and Constraints: Some Concluding Remarks on Heritage, Community and Participation." In *Between Imagined Communities and Communities of Practice: Participation, Territory and the Making of Heritage*, edited by N. Adell, R. F. Bendix, C. Bortolotto and T. Markus, 291–306. Göttingen: Universitätsverlag Göttingen.

Walters, W. and J. H. Haahr. 2005. *Governing Europe. Discourse, Governmentality and European Integration.* London: Routledge.

Waterton, E. and L. Smith. 2010. "The Recognition and Misrecognition of Community Heritage." *International Journal of Heritage Studies* 16 (1–2): 4–15.

Watson, S. and E. Waterton, eds. 2010a. Special Issue on Heritage and Community Engagement. *International Journal of Heritage Studies* 16 (1–2): 1–159.

Watson, S. and E. Waterton. 2010b. "Heritage and Community Engagement: Editorial." *International Journal of Heritage Studies* 16 (1–2): 1–3.

Young, L. (2002) 2003. "Rethinking Heritage: Cultural Policy and Inclusion." In *Museums, Society, Inequality*, edited by R. Sandell, 203–212. Reprint, London: Routledge.

Yuval-Davis, N. 2006. "Belonging and the Politics of Belonging." *Patterns of Prejudice* 40 (3): 197–214.

Zagato, L. 2015. "The Notion of 'Heritage Community' in the Council of Europe's Faro Convention: Its Impact on the European Legal Framework." In *Between Imagined Communities and Communities of Practice. Participation, Territory and the Making of Heritage*, edited by N. Adell, R. F. Bendix, C. Bortolotto and T. Markus, 141–168. Göttingen: Universitätsverlag Göttingen.

Part IV

Embodying Europe

Chapter 7

Heritage sites as poly-space

It only has its impact on a later age. Then you become conscious that you have lived in the barracks, where the Jews also lived. [...] When you are a child, you just experience the four seasons as a child experiences them. So: freedom and happiness ... we would play in the forest all day. We had not become aware yet that we were living in the barracks. [...] I never realized it. It is a beautiful place to live but, yeah, all that had happened, happened. The large barracks were all there, the places where they called them up, they were still there.

(VS3/20)

This is a quote from a visitor interview we conducted at Camp Westerbork. Our interviewee arrived in the Netherlands with his family in 1951. He belongs to the group of Moluccans who left Indonesia at the end of the Dutch colonial reign and were housed by the Dutch government in the barracks of the former Camp Westerbork, then renamed Schattenberg, where he spent his youth. This vignette aims to highlight the experience of bizarreness related to the place, which this man encountered when re-visiting the site of Camp Westerbork/Schattenberg. His experience referred to the changed function of the site, its multi-layered past, the reception of space and time, and the conflicting and surprising emotional experiences it can produce. As he reflected in his interview, the same site was his home for many years, but a place of suffering for the former detainees during World War II.

For two project researchers who visited the site, the bizarreness of Camp Westerbork was primarily connected to its materiality and atmosphere. It was partly evoked by the 'look' of the site, for instance, the view of the radio telescopes surrounded by a barbed wire fence to keep out intruders or the glass construction around the house of the former Camp Commander. The notion of bizarreness included elements of unexpectedness and surprise that manifested in the chance encounter one of the researchers had on her way to Camp Westerbork with a man who, like the interviewee quoted above, had lived on the premises after World War II. His vivid and fond memories of his childhood intersected with her impressions of her visit, giving her an alternative insight into and encounter with the multi-layered heritages of the site.

Each member of our research team had similar 'bizarre' experiences during their fieldwork. These surprising encounters were often unexpected and unplanned. They were spurred by moments when our attention shifted to some minor details or trivial events during our engagement with the site or inter-action with the visitors. These led to a brief disconnection from the present experience of the heritage site, which, paradoxically, facilitated a closer affective and cognitive connection with the past, place, people, and contexts across tem-poral and spatial boundaries. In retrospect, these experiences became very sig-nificant for comprehending the world(s), people, and life entangled with our fieldwork sites, giving us new understandings about heritage sites and the idea of cultural heritage itself. As we have come to realize, these experiences may have changed how we relate to heritage and perceive its meanings.

To make sense of our fieldwork experiences, we introduce the concept of poly-space. It helps us to see how heritage sites enable the simultaneous exist-ence of multiple moments and overlapping spatial, temporal, affective, sensory, and cognitive experiences in one physical place (see Turunen et al. forth-coming). Although we became aware of it while reflecting on our fieldwork, we would like to emphasize that poly-space is not necessarily a phenomenon only connected with heritage sites. Our intention in this chapter is not to explore poly-space *per se*, but to show that the experience of poly-space is inherent in spaces, such as heritage sites. As such, visitors to heritage sites can be perceived as participants in the processes and flows of experiences, imagin-ations, reflections and knowledge production that goes on in these spaces, and that can produce changes in their experience and interpretation of the past. We do not understand poly-space as a 'finished product' but as continuously generated in the encounter with different qualities and configurations that form, and are part of, heritage spaces. This means that poly-space may vary in intensity depending on individual affective capacity and the context in which it is experienced.

On the basis of our fieldwork, we define poly-space as simultaneously consisting of and generating the following elements and experiences: (1) a notion of suddenness and surprise, (2) an experience of bizarreness, (3) social agency and interaction, and (4) affect, emotion, and empathy. All of these aspects are fundamentally entangled with spatiality and temporality. As our concept of poly-space is closely related to our experiential encounters "in, of and within heritage sites" (see Waterton and Watson 2013, 547) and our pro-duction of knowledge "in, about and through atmospheres" (see Sumartojo and Pink 2019, 11), it enables us to discuss affects, experiences, and reflections as well as to share, dissolve, and transform different aspects of spatiality, tempor-ality, and movement in spaces. Indeed, poly-space is characterized by a moment of flux that blurs the boundaries between space, place, and time, and thereby challenges our preconceived notions of the relationships between spatiality, temporality, and heritage. As heritage sites engage with multiple temporal layers and narratives, they can produce experiences of poly-space.

Poly-space helps us to make sense of the temporal and spatial dimensions of heritage narratives and practices. We experienced the sites as poly-space, as both researchers and visitors, but we learned more about poly-space through our collective approach to this project. Discussing our specific and shared experiences helped to develop our thoughts related to our experience of various temporal and spatial dimensions in the field. Poly-space therefore encouraged us to (self-) reflection and helped to illuminate individual experiences felt at the heritage site, thus making visible the dissonance always inherent in cultural heritage (see the Introduction and Chapter 5). The concept of poly-space sheds light on what heritage does, thereby connecting to its transformative potential (see Crang and Tolia-Kelly 2010; Waterton 2014; Kisić 2017). This understanding can potentially change the experience and perception of temporal and spatial dimensions in heritage and bring about empathic connection to other people.

We begin this chapter by explaining how we perceive the relationships between time, space, and heritage. We then discuss the four core dimensions of poly-space and how they work together in influencing and possibly changing our perceptions of space and time. While these elements are introduced separately, they cannot be viewed alone or apart from space, time, or movement between different dimensions. Rather, the concept of poly-space enables us to combine diverse elements, phenomena, and processes, also with other concepts. We particularly draw on the personal (and auto-ethnographic) observations and experiences of our team members during and after our fieldwork at the EHL sites. As we did not know beforehand that our fieldwork would produce experiences that forced us to re-conceptualize time and space, we did not include questions on this in our field interviews. However, whenever possible we also draw from the interviews and exhibitions at the sites, as 'seeds' of poly-space can be identified throughout our broader ethnographic data. We conclude by contemplating what makes heritage sites particularly potent poly-spaces.

Space, time, and heritage from a poly-space perspective

Our concept of poly-space connects to the much-discussed 'spatial turn' in human sciences that has influenced the scholarly understanding of reality as constructed and determined by complex spatial relations (e.g. Lefebvre 1991; Massey 2005; Lähdesmäki 2018). For debating heritage, the division between space and place is an important starting point. Traditionally, space has been conceptualized as an abstract and 'neutral' spatial entity, whereas place is often perceived as linked to a more specific, concrete, and subjective spatial experience. In the study of heritage and culture, the emphasis is often on place, which is perceived as the physical point "to which subjects relate their own stories, memories, emotions, and notions" (Lähdesmäki 2014, 196; see also Giddens 1990, 18–19; Hall 1992; Paasi 1996, 207–208; Casey 1997, 334–339). Focusing on place emphasizes how heritage works as a process that connects or marks particular memories to specific historical sites or cultural landscapes, which is also called "placing heritage" (Lähdesmäki 2016).

During past decades, various scholars have contributed to developing a relational approach to space, seeing places and spaces as entangled heterogenous entities (Massey 1991, 2007, 22, 2005, 9; Harvey 1996; Soja 1996; Thrift 1996). When discussing our experiences during fieldwork, we noticed a conceptual shift in our understanding of heritage sites: from the idea of a concrete place to the more abstract concept of space, which can contain multiple overlapping and temporal layers. In this context, we find Foucault's (1986, 25) concept of heterotopias particularly interesting: he defines these as mirrored utopias that are essentially "unlike ordinary cultural spaces". Heterotopias exist in all cultures and are guided by certain principles. They are places of crisis, transformation, and deviation, both existing and "place[s] without a place" at the same time (Foucault 1986, 27). Foucault cites the ship as "the heterotopia par excellence" (Foucault 1986, 27) but also gives other examples of heterotopias, such as boarding schools, prisons, theatres, gardens, graveyards, and museums. Put together, these heterotopias can form an abstract space of alterity, but alone they exist as actual places. Although heritage sites and museums are often perceived as concrete places, they can also be seen as heterotopias.

While the spatial turn has been interpreted as a response to the previously privileged position of time in scholarly discussions in human sciences (Soja 2008), we draw on discussion that see these two dimensions as inseparably intertwined. To stress the temporality of space, Massey (2005) has used the concept of time-space. According to her, spaces are not static entities but continuous processes that are influences by their past. This Masseyan reading of space, as constituted by its past, present, and future layers, facilitates conceptualising heritage sites as multi-temporal and multi-spatial, capable of producing a hybridized experience of time and space. Emphasizing this experiential aspect, Crouch likens heritage to a journey that is intersubjective, occurs in and among instants and moments, but acts relationally with time, referring to the complex intermingling of time and space inflected with affect and feeling about "ourselves and our relationships in the world" (Crouch 2015, 76). This view emphasizes both the movement in space and the multiple and diverse moments and temporalities embedded and experienced in heritage.

Although previous research is helpful in understanding heritage sites as poly-space, it does not satisfactorily capture the temporal and spatial hybridity that is present in our data. We developed our concept of poly-space in response to a conceptual problem: defining a place often requires distinguishing it from other places and spaces. This clear demarcation contrasts with what we perceived and experienced in our field research: a crossing, overcoming, or mixing of various spatial, temporal, and social boundaries.

We wanted our idea of poly-space to reflect the bizarreness and ambiguity associated with our temporal and spatial experiences during the fieldwork.

When arguing for a *poly*sensory understanding of heritage, Sather-Wagstaff (2017, 17) comments that:

> while it is normative to employ prefixes for words from the same language of origin, the employment of a non-isomorphic prefix does occur as a means to expand or disrupt normative, long-standing definitions for a term.

Accordingly, poly-space (Greek prefix and Latin root) seeks to "understand (if not encourage) ambiguity and slippage in meaning-making" (Sather-Wagstaff 2017, 17), that point to a fluid and processual understanding of the phenomenon. This kind of understanding of poly-space has similarities with Soja's (1996, 56) concept of third space that binds together

> the abstract and the concrete, the real and the imagined, the knowable and the unimaginable, the repetitive and the differential, structure and agency, mind and body, consciousness and the unconscious, the disciplined and the transdisciplinary, everyday life and unending history.

The concept of poly-space, however, helps us to highlight the disruption and movement between multiple experiential spaces and temporal layers tied to the physical place and subjective experience of the heritage site. This mobility through different layers of meanings comes close to what Crouch (2015, 185) describes as "flirt[ing] with space". It entails engaging with varying trajectories of time and the movement of things, referring to the openness with which heritage sites are encountered, participated in, and given value and meaning in relation to our lives (Crouch 2015, 187). A crucial aspect of this flirting is the emphasis on the experiential world, and the different affective and sensory capacities individuals have in deciphering their environments. Our bodies do not make sense of and attune to their surroundings in a neutral way (e.g. Tolia-Kelly 2006; Ahmed 2010) but our experiences and their decoding are deeply subjective, conditioned by our own capacities and earlier experiences. Poly-space acknowledges this subjectivity in our engagements with heritage sites.

This experiential dimension is precisely what sets poly-space apart from Foucault's heterotopia. Poly-space is not a particular place within heritage sites waiting to be discovered and to which entrance can be negotiated. Rather, it is a potentiality, or an abstract affective moment. It links the different, yet simultaneous, aspects of space – the perceived, the conceived, and the lived, as theorized by Lefebvre (1991, 38–41) – with the narrative temporal layers of the site, and with the affective, imaginative, and reflective disposition of the visitor. As it is conditioned by the affective capacities of people who enter and become part of poly-space by engaging with the materiality and narratives of the site, it fails to actualize as a concrete place. Rather, poly-space is an individualized experience of flux on the space-time horizon that is entangled with the broader stories and meanings of the particular heritage site.

Due to its processual and relativist nature, poly-space questions not only the categorical separation between space and place, but also between space and time (Massey 2005). The different temporal layers essentially 'feed into' each other, producing a sense of hybrid time that is simultaneously embedded in several temporal layers. Furthermore, according to Crouch (2015), the notion of space enables us to understand that cultural heritage is not isolated from our present 'living' but connected to the experiential and atmospheric aspects of space and time. Sumartojo and Pink (2019, 15) see atmospheres as "ongoing sensory and affective engagement with our lives and their impressions, sensations, and feelings and the environments through and as part of which they play out". This atmospheric element that connects sensory and affective dimensions of our experience with their physical surroundings is a crucial element to the sense of bizarreness that is a key aspect of poly-space. It enables people to feel a connection and empathy with other people in different spaces and times.

Four elements of poly-space

Suddenness and surprise

> After walking around the remains of the Roman settlements in Carnuntum [Austria], I went alone to visit again the kitchen of the Villa Urbana [in the late afternoon]. I surprised two small birds in the kitchen picking on bread, which is part of the fresh props. It then suddenly occurred to me that such situations had happened at precisely the same spot but some 1,700 years ago, when birds flew into the kitchen to pick food leftovers on the bare ground or the table, and were startled by the entrance of a slave, a servant, or the mistress of the house. It helped me to reimagine, or actually see the past with different 'eyes', making it also part of a personal experience for me and imagining it as a personal experience for people unknown to me who had lived almost 2,000 years ago.

In her account, which is part of a report on field research in Carnuntum written for other members of the project, the researcher addresses one important element of poly-space, namely suddenness and surprise. The incident surprised the researcher in two ways: first, she had not expected to meet the birds in the kitchen. During her previous visit to the kitchen as part of a guided tour and later while doing observations she had not given any thought to birds (or other animals) entering the villa and attacking the fresh props. Second, she was surprised by what impact this chance encounter had on her ways of relating to the site. She knew from the tour and publications that the kitchen had been reconstructed in its former location. Based on this knowledge, the encounter made a new impression on her and produced a notion of experiencing multiple temporal layers intersecting with each other. The researcher's discussion of her experience of multi-layered temporality in the material representation of the site reminded us that multiple senses are at work during our engagements with heritage and space.

The fact that the open-air site was surrounded by a wall produced the notion of an enclosed heritage site, similar to a museum, that made the researcher perhaps unconsciously focus on the material representation of the site and observe what affective and polysensory experiences were connected with it. However, the presence of the birds transgressed the idea that the space was frozen in time, forcing her to acknowledge it in a different way. Paying attention to the previously neglected role of animals and vegetation turned the visit into an experience of an enlivened and "lived" space (see Lefebvre 1991). Furthermore, the chance event raised the idea of sharing similar experiences with others, who were more likely to be people from the past than present visitors. This made the brief encounter with the birds a serendipitous and special experience that provoked new reflections on the spatial and temporal dimensions at a heritage site and how they interrelate at a visit.

Coined by Horace Walpole in the late eighteenth century, the term serendipity is usually understood as an unanticipated, beneficial discovery that was not made on purpose (Foster and Ford 2003, 321) but rather suggests an "accidental wisdom" (Calhoun 2004). However, as Ingraham (2019, 112) argues, serendipity is "first about the encounter and possibility of entering into a new relation, and only thereafter about discovery and fortuity". Ingraham (2019, 107, 117) further describes serendipity as "a mode of affective encounter influenced by the infrastructures that mediate their expectable force" and as a "cultural technique of discovery" based on different techniques. Visiting creates opportunities for serendipity and allows for a more-than-representational and affective engagement with heritage sites, based on embodied practices and performances (see Waterton and Watson 2013; Waterton 2014; Crouch 2015; Dittmer and Waterton 2017).

Drawing on Bagnall (2003), we understand visitors to heritage sites as actively engaging with heritage in complex and diverse ways, as much in emotion and imagination as in cognition (Bagnall 2003, 87). The felt experience of a site and (unconscious) engagement with the affective atmosphere is important in poly-space. It facilitates a certain openness to serendipitous experiences through increased but unconscious attention to the "replication of the affective atmospheres" (Dittmer and Waterton 2017, 58) that are present in heritage sites and museums. While the encounter with the birds was serendipitous, the earlier immersion in haptic and visceral experiences at Carnuntum might have made the researcher more open to such unanticipated encounters. This readiness is constructed in the interaction between the site and the visitor and does not necessarily amount to anticipation (on the relationship between anticipation and atmospheres, see Sumartojo and Pink 2019). It remains more elusive and thereby contributes to the unexpectedness embedded in the experience of poly-space.

Encounters can activate different types of attention, not all of which will lead to cognitive breakthroughs or relevant discoveries (see Ingraham 2019, 115). For instance, the above-described encounter with the birds made deeper cognitive understanding possible only when the researcher shared this experience with other team members. This act of sharing unintentionally initiated a broader discussion about 'what heritage does' when visitors become affectively engaged with it. Diverse encounters within the spaces of heritage sites (e.g. engagement with technologies, the narrative, or with other bodies/museum-goers) may prepare visitors to engage with experiences of poly-space. While serendipity and chance can set in motion different processes of reflection, poly-space is attuned to both affect and the discursive aspects of heritage, and thereby refers to and expands into various processes of meaning-making.

Poly-space is a result of the intersection and simultaneousness of various temporal, spatial, discursive, and affective dimensions that encourage bodily and cognitive engagements at a specific time and location. Thus, poly-space is not purposefully evoked: it happens to us, our body and mind, in a split second, and may impact on our interpretation of the past. Serendipity, surprise, and suddenness are affective elements of experiencing poly-space and explain the temporal and spatial tensions we sometimes experience during heritage visits.

Experience of bizarreness

> The former camp site of Westerbork is roughly 2.5 kilometers away from the heritage centre. Before arriving at the site, you walk past a giant field with radio telescopes. Due to the telescopes, the use of mobile phones was forbidden throughout the camp site and the nature paths leading to it. I found it really strange that the field with the radio telescopes was surrounded by a fence of barbed wire. I understand the need to put a fence around them, but the barbed wire seemed unnecessary and out of place considering the history of the camp. They also used barbed wire at the former camp site but for a different purpose: it was not to keep people out, but to bring out the historical reality of the camp, to remind us of the violent attempts to keep people in.

The primary field researcher at Camp Westerbork described the bizarreness she encountered during her visit, particularly in relation to the materiality and experience of the space. The bizarreness of the space is highlighted by the view of radio telescopes, which cuts through the natural and historical landscape of the site. The sight of the telescopes also disconnects from the narrative one would expect to find at this site and therefore enable a different encounter with its heritage. At the same time, the barbed wire around the telescopes become associated with the historical context.

Figure 7.1 The radio telescopes, Camp Westerbork, Netherlands. An example of bizarreness. Photo: EUROHERIT

Bizarreness does not need to be negative; it can simply intensify another approach to the heritage site. Other visitors noticed the bizarreness of Camp Westerbork as well. In particular, one young student among our interviewed visitors emphasized her emotive impressions of the radio telescopes during her visit, but for other reasons than expected.

> By coincidence, I had just read *De Ontdekking van de Hemel* [The Discovery of Heaven] by Harry Mulish. [...] When I passed the telescopes, I thought, 'I have to see them'. It was such a coincidence that we came here. [...] It is really strange, because if I had come here a year ago, then I would have gone to Westerbork, and I would have found it strange to hear about all the later purposes of the place. But because I had read this book, I already knew a bit about the later purposes of the terrain.
>
> (VS3/6)

Her association with something that was not part of the site narrative but sparked personal memories shows that different layers of affect experience may become mixed while visiting heritage sites. This links to another important element of the bizarre: atmosphere. Atmospheres can be understood with Anderson (2009, 80) as "impersonal in that they belong to collective situations and yet can be felt as intensely personal". As he explains, an atmosphere "discloses the space-time of an 'expressed world' – it does not re-present objective space-time or lived space-time" (Anderson 2009, 79). At the same time, as Mains (2017, 180) points out, cultural heritage is an "inherently spatial and temporal concept. It is also rooted in the notion of meaningful ties to specific landscapes and events – a connection to place that has emotional resonance". As such, heritage sites may produce complex associations, and the sense of place is connected to the degree of value we give it (Mains 2017, 181). While a site may be regarded as an interesting place to visit because of its association with a known historical event, it does not necessarily have the same impact as a location that manages to raise a more personally meaningful response. Heritage sites are bizarre spaces in terms of both their materiality and atmospheres and allow for a subjective understanding of heritage. Places alone do not signify anything (Assman 1999, 76) but cultural mnemonics keep memories bound to a place and allow them to signify beyond it as a space. Thus, recognition of the bizarreness of a heritage site has the potential to touch and affect through a shared cultural and social disposition (see Muntéan 2017).

We understand the bizarreness of a heritage site in relation to its possible multiple narratives and complex past, which emphasize "the everydayness of political and politicized identities and places" (Mains 2017, 181). For instance, the multiple past uses of Camp Westerbork makes the space of this heritage site a bizarre experience. While the focus of the heritage centre is on the transit camp for detaining and transporting Jews, Roma, and Sinti to concentration and extinction camps in the East, it also refers to the use of space that intersects with other histories and understandings at the site. In the late 1930s, the camp was built as a refugee camp for European Jews but after the Second World War it was used as an internment camp for Nazi collaborators until 1948. For a short time, the barracks were used as a repatriation camp for Dutch colonial officers before the site, now renamed Schattenberg, housed Moluccan soldiers and their families from the former Dutch colonies in Indonesia for another 20 years. In 1969, part of the camp space was transformed by installing big radio telescopes used for astronomy research, and the Camp Westerbork Museum opened only in 1983. Thus, Camp Westerbork is an example of how heritage is a relative concept that may shift over time and vary for different social groups visiting, or living at, the same site. The dissonance and variation in views of history make it a highly complex and political phenomenon (Timothy and Boyd 2006, 3; Mains 2017, 181). While its geographical location remains unchanged, the meaning of the site changes over the course of time.

Social agency and interaction

On my very first fieldwork day, I experienced how this ambivalent relationship was performed there in the neighbourhood [of the Great Guild Hall]. On Wednesday afternoon, I heard shouts and noise from outside until the museum staff closed the large front door. I asked about this noise the next day during one of my interviews. It turned out that it was a protest in front of the Russian embassy [located just next to the museum], as my interviewee captured it, "against Russia, for Ukraine". This weekly protest is repeated every Wednesday afternoon, so according to the museum practitioner, it helps them to recall that, 'oh, it is Wednesday again'. This experience made me feel that the past, present and the future are indeed entangled and also very much 'alive' and 'in action' in heritage sites, sometimes in a rather surprising way.

Social agency and interaction are other important elements of poly-space, as this report by one of our project researchers shows. We understand agency as a process of social engagement, in which actors can both habitually reproduce and critically reflect on the past and present, imagine alternative possibilities, and contextualize past habits and future projects within the contingencies of the moment (see Emirbayer and Mische 1998). The spatial turn has guided scholars to explore various social dimensions of space that inform individual and collective experiences and participation. In these views, space is not only seen as a physical frame for human interaction but also as a performative catalyst of interaction and social relations (Massey 2005; Crouch 2015). The researcher's account above reveals the sudden collusion between the museum/heritage site and 'street life' she experienced in the lobby of the Great Guild Hall. The past can become repeated and the same interactions and antagonism of the past may continue in the present, albeit in different ways. The concept of poly-space allows us to emphasize and recognize discontinuities intrinsic to heritage and experienced by us at the EHL sites, as the next account, from the researcher's visit at Franz Liszt Memorial Museum, highlights.

> I felt it was a big contrast to stand in Liszt's living room surrounded by his pianos, paintings of him made by famous Hungarian painters, marvellous old furniture, decorative wallpaper, chandeliers, and so forth, to listen to his music through the audio guide, and to look from the balcony window to the Vörösmarty utca metro station and see today's people walking and hanging around it. For example, two young black men wearing trendy street clothes and headphones passed the windows while I looked out. They seemed to be so far from the reality of the room, although just some metres away. It felt that the past and today's world were there in this quarter at the same time, but without any connection to each other.

The connection of the same space to a simultaneous experience of different space dimensions and temporalities can produce a momentarily confusing experience, which breaks with normality and renders the heritage site bizarre. In retrospect, however, this experience helped the researcher to better understand the heritage site and what heritage was about: selected pieces from the past obviously lose their original contexts when they are transmitted in time, which allows new contexts to replace the old ones. She simultaneously felt

Figure 7.2 The view from the living room in the Franz Liszt Memorial Museum in Budapest, Hungary. Photo: EUROHERIT

distance and connection to other people, in the past and present, and in spaces that are separated but located in the very same place. She recalled that it was

> a moment of a personal feeling or emotion that made me think that this really is a bizarre place. I think this insight even amused me. I first thought that 'they have to do something with this site' to update it and to connect it better to the changing time and space around it and later: 'no, they should not do anything to this place' as it has its own time and space.

As evident in this example, poly-space includes literal experience of different temporal and spatial dimensions. The interaction and hybridity of the different layers of time encountered in the space of heritage may generate social agency. In this understanding, heritage sites help visitors to actively negotiate with them (see Witcomb 2015). Our field research produced this experience, as the following account shows.

> When I entered the last room of the Alcide De Gasperi House, I looked down from the gallery into the room below, in which there was an empty cradle. I was alone and struck by the darkness and peacefulness of the

room, the only light emerging from the projection of random pictures showing children from past times. While standing there and listening to the soft lullaby sung in the regional dialect of De Gasperi's home region, I experienced that several times were merging in that tiny spot. I thought about the young students I had interviewed. Their enthusiastic words echoed in my ears: they deeply felt the need to continue and protect the European dream De Gasperi had pursued and that had taken its starting point here, in this house, where he was born. I felt like I was concretely standing simultaneously both in the past and future.

For this researcher, distinct layers of knowledge and affective experiences intermingled with the experience of multiple spatial and temporal dimensions. In addition to 'hybridizing' experiences of time creating overlapping and intersecting notions between the past, present, and future, multiple spaces are also entangled in poly-space. On the one hand, Alcide De Gasperi worked in many different places during his lifetime, so the site narrative connects to multiple contexts. On the other hand, the researcher's experience of multiple spaces was constructed in interaction with the other visitors and became directly linked with their personal (present and future) agency. The researcher later reported that her interviews with young students at Alcide De Gasperi House made a lasting impression on her. These visitors expressed an interest in moving between several places in their lives, but already viewed and understood Europe as going beyond the narrative of the heritage site and their current living environment. While the subjective and affective experiences or atmospheres the visitor might encounter help to create poly-space, meaning-making is equally important for facilitating understanding across the limitations of interpretation at particular heritage sites (see Schorch, Waterton, and Watson 2017, 96).

Affect, emotion, and empathy

Arriving at Camp Westerbork, our taxi driver revealed he had been born in the camp and lived his whole childhood happily playing in the forest and living with his Moluccan community in the former camp buildings after the war. Later when walking around the site, I kept hearing the laughter of the Moluccan children in the back of my mind. Although surrounded by sad stories of the Jews, Roma, and Sinti, the memories of his happy, innocent childhood lingered and almost haunted me throughout my visit. Reminding me of hope. Without my chance encounter in the taxi, my visit would have been very different.

This project researcher's fieldwork account emphasizes the crucial role of personal narratives and biographies for engaging with cultural heritage, which can have a strong impact on how we understand and engage with it. In addition to the taxi driver, the researcher also happened to interview two other

Moluccan former inhabitants of Schattenberg and by chance spoke with a Jewish survivor of Camp Westerbork who had come to commemorate his perished family members. The biographical element was further emphasized by the strongly affective experience evoked in the temporary exhibition, "De Namen" by the Dutch artist Bart Domburg, which showed the names and ages of the 102,000 perished Jews, Roma, and Sinti of Camp Westerbork, written by hand on 29 walls measuring 1.5 x 3 metres. Each of these encounters produced different emotional, tangible, and/or visually powerful experiences in relation to the same heritage site during the same period.

The ways in which visitors react to different narrations and exhibitions is deeply conditioned by their personal histories and affective capabilities. Visitors have their own "assemblages of personal and cultural subjectivities", such as past experiences, educational knowledge, cultural beliefs, and family background, "all of which operate in tandem with our temperaments and dispositions" (Schorch, Waterton, and Watson 2017, 96). This personal 'baggage' enables us to engage with the past in various ways. Visitors can experience the same site in manifold ways during the same visit, and the same person can experience the same space in different ways, partly due to their awareness of how the heritage site resonates with their own beliefs and emotional connections (Mains 2017). Such encounters help to 'colour' the story, memory, and heritage, influencing how we understand and make meaning of the past. The experience of poly-space in heritage sites is therefore very individual, as it connects to personal associations and experiences. At the same time, only our personal associations and experiences enable the experience of poly-space.

Poly-space in heritage sites can also increase empathy across temporal and spatial boundaries, which circulates between people and contexts in the present, past, and future (see Ahmed 2004), but which is not bound to an object or its present materiality at the sites. Crouch (2015, 186, 187) argues in this context that "multi-sensual experiences and their immanence and possibility" in performed and embodied encounters with a site have the capacity to affect encounter with the present, marking "what constitutes and may be constituted by heritage remains full of potential". The researcher's encounter with the Moluccan taxi driver blurred and extended her experience of space and time beyond a 'fixed' European representation of cultures and history, and intersects with other spaces, histories, and encounters outside Europe (see Crouch 2010). Heritage experiences are constituted through social and spatial practices that are inherently contradictory. They are strengthened and challenged through ongoing activities that may not be particularly striking, but which nonetheless reinforce notions of place and identity. As Mains (2017, 183) suggests, emotion interweaves complicated visceral narratives with different aspects, such as tourism, politics, and ongoing negotiation of identities. Thus, heritage sites are part of larger representations of power and space.

When visitors engage with heritage sites, they may experience the other, and what it is like to be the other. As Witcomb (2013, 267) explains, "this requires imagination and the ability to empathize, an ability that is encouraged by affective encounters". She argues that objects can trigger an emotional response based on the visitor's partial knowledge of the past, creating an opportunity to engage the viewer directly and fostering a dialogue with those who experienced the past. The same applies to heritage sites as poly-spaces – in this case, the engagement may be more intense, as diverse spatial and temporal dimensions partly overlap and contradict each other. Poly-space is essentially about affective atmospheres and emotive experiences contributing to develop empathy, as a final account by our team member shows.

> We visited the "Voice from the Sea" installation, a.k.a. the dragon's breath [in Sagres Promontory]. It was a spiral shaped echo chamber, built on the top of the caves, which connect the promontory to the sea below. In the chamber, a surge of warm air rushes through the caves in the rhythm of the waves and surrounds you with an explosive wind that shoots your hair up and roars around you. Suddenly I was overwhelmed with the stories we had heard the day before, like the ones about Prince Henry the Navigator. Henry's emblem was the black dragon and as I sat and listened to the 'dragon breathing', my mind travelled to the past, to people who came to the promontory, under the dark sky, with wooden torches in their hands and fear in their hearts to meet the dragon the fortress owner had locked up in the caves below.

Experiences and meaning-making in and through poly-space

Our concept of poly-space is not theory-driven but inspired by what we found in the field. Poly-space refers to the multiple realities and spaces that are part of every heritage site. We found that classical or traditional conceptualization of cultural heritage and its space-relationship did not adequately describe what we experienced at the sites. The conceptual divisions between atmospheres and representations (or between affect and emotion) may help to highlight specific aspects of heritage experiences but they do not necessarily help us understand how these dynamics are entangled and how visitors perceive this entanglement. Together, by sharing our experiences and reflections, we came to understand that poly-space is plural and diverse, and contains multiple, equally important realities, times and spaces. Our research showed that everyone had different ways of experiencing and perceiving how sites can break with 'normality'. While we refer to poly-space in relation to heritage sites, we would like to emphasize that poly-space can be experienced outside a specific heritage context.

Our understanding of poly-space contributes to the discussion of bodily, emotional, and intellectual engagement with heritage that are crucial in constituting a feeling for a place, event, and individual, or group of people. Poly-space connects to recent discussions of atmospheres (e.g. Anderson 2009; Crouch

2010; Edensor and Sumartojo 2015; Sumartojo and Pink 2019). Sumartojo and Pink (2019, 13) point out that

> atmospheres might not just be something that are passively apprehended, but actively shape how we understand our worlds, because they carry implications for what feels "right" (or "wrong"), with the capacity to shape our ongoing ways of understanding the world.

We suggest poly-space is a similar and related phenomenon to that of atmosphere. Both give evidence that we feel "something" (Anderson 2009) in the field that is non-verbal but nevertheless meaningful, and therefore crucial in constituting a feeling for a place or event. The experience of atmospheres produces poly-space. Thus, poly-space is not a factual space or place but an experience that helps us to reflect on things we did not necessarily anticipate or have in mind before visiting a site. Rather, the sudden, subjective experience of the temporal and spatial dimensions collapsing (or widening) facilitated diverse insights. Poly-space positions people, events and places simultaneously on many axes and helps us to understand how people experience the world and how these experiences mutually reinforce and influence each other. Thus, poly-space is a complex interplay of multiple elements and contexts. This interplay can set in motion a process of reflection that can create new insights. More than the concept of atmospheres, poly-space emphasizes the dialogic nature of and engagement with spaces.

Spaces are expressions and concrete places of human interaction. Heritage sites bring different people together in a dialogue across cultural boundaries (Macdonald 2013; Witcomb 2015), which enables the transformative potential of heritage to be articulated and understood. As spaces are an expression of social and cultural change, they may refer to notions of otherness that challenge power relations and exclusionary senses of belonging (see Hall 1997). Similar to the imaginative dimension of sharing roots, routes, and cultural symbolic representation (Clifford 1997), poly-space encourages encounters across spatial and temporal boundaries and allows for the imaginative integration of separate time dimensions, places, groups, and individuals. Poly-space also incorporates multiple understandings of what signifies spatiality or temporality and may thus alter the meaning of space and time for the individual. As a poly-space, a heritage site is shaped and perceived by individual agency and imagination, which goes beyond its affective or material quality.

The concept of poly-space helps us to understand what heritage does, that is, its transformative potential (see Crang and Tolia-Kelly 2010; Waterton 2014). Similar to space, poly-space means "different things to different people at different times" (Taheri et al. 2016, 21; see also Cohen 2002, 262; Pritchard and Morgan 2006). It becomes invested with symbolic significance and is characterized by the dynamic and complex interplay of various sensory, affective and intellectual responses, engagements, and meaning-making processes. Likewise, we see time in heritage as neither simply linear nor a process resulting in a changed status quo, but as an ongoing transformative process in which (self-)reflection is inherent.

Associating bizarreness with a concrete heritage site increases reflection on space and forms a different relationship with it (see Mains 2017, 181). The multiple, affective, and subjectively experienced layers surrounding heritage help to give it a certain meaning. The unexpected experience of moving between and across the layers may help to reveal the dissonance always inherent in heritage. Moreover, serendipity in encounters at heritage sites may trigger or enable new, creative reflection on the political and social impact of heritage, in the past and present. Thus, poly-space may increase the ability to reflect on otherness, making it easier to construct relationships with other individuals and contexts across temporal and spatial boundaries, and potentially promoting empathy.

Another aspect of poly-space is its ability to create experiences that connect particular places into broader spaces in which the narratives of the heritage site take on multiple meanings. Different groups react to and interpret the story being told differently, so local, regional, national, *and* European cultural heritage needs to be interpreted from multiple points of view. As a result of increased mobility and migration, within and beyond Europe, heritage is being reinterpreted through manifold perspectives, including those of 'outsiders'. Our interviews show that the notion of a European community is not tied to geography but contains multiple temporal and spatial aspects, such as values or citizens' participation (see Chapter 6). The notion of community is constructed through affect and emotive experiences, which are key aspects of our concept of poly-space. Although we have discussed these experiences in relation to specific sites at specific times, they refer to a poly-spatial belonging that can help to produce the idea of a transnational heritage and belonging to Europe in future.

The multitude of reactions and experiences "of, at, within, and towards" a specific heritage site turn it into a space that is characterized by multiple and partly conflicting experiences, or poly-space. Poly-space may elicit many overlapping and intersecting responses to the different dimensions in which it is situated. Heritage and the narrativization of heritage connect a particular place and its space across diverse temporal layers and through different experiential encounters. A heritage site has the potential to be experienced differently, as it refers simultaneously to many places and times. This multiplicity of experiences may turn the site into a space where the values and meanings of its heritage can be discussed and intersected with different histories, spaces, and ideas that open up manifold interpretations across seemingly fixed periods and cultural perspectives. In this way, poly-space also contributes to emphasizing the processual and constructivist aspect of heritage.

References

Ahmed, S. 2004. "Affective Economies." *Social Text* 22 (2): 114–139. Project MUSE, muse.jhu.edu/article/55780.

Ahmed, S. 2010. "Happy Objects." In *The Affect Theory Reader*, edited by M. Gregg, and G. J. Seigworth, 29–51. Durham, NC: Duke University Press.

Anderson, B. 2009. "Affective Atmospheres." *Emotion, Space and Society* 2: 77–81. doi: 10.1016/j.emospa.2009.08.005.

Assman, A. 1999. "Das Gedächtnis der Orte." In *Orte der Erinnerung. Denkmal, Gedenkstätte, Museum*, edited by U. Borsdorf, and H. T. Grütter, 59–75. Frankfurt a. M.: Campus.

Bagnall, G. 2003. "Performance and Performativity at Heritage Sites". *Museum and Society* 1 (2): 87–103. doi: 10.29311/mas.v1i2.17.

Calhoun, C. 2004. "Accidental Wisdom: Robert Merton's Serendipitous Findings.", Book Forum, Summer. ISSN 1098–3376.

Casey, E. S. 1997. *The Fate of Place: A Philosophical History*. Berkeley: University of California Press.

Clifford, J. 1997. *Routes: Travel and Translation in the Late Twentieth Century*. Cambridge, MA: Harvard University Press.

Cohen, S. 2002. "Sounding Out the City: Music and the Sensuous Production of Place." In *In Spaces of Post-Modernity: Readings in Human Geography*, edited by M. J. Dear, and S. Flusty, 162–188. Oxford: Blackwell.

Crang, M., and D. P. Tolia-Kelly. 2010. "Nation, Race, and Affect: Senses and Sensibilities at National Heritage Sites." *Environment and Planning A* 42: 2315–2331. doi: 10.1068/a4346.

Crouch, D. 2010. "The Perpetual Performance and Emergence of Heritage.", in *Culture, Heritage and Representation: Perspectives on Visuality and the Past*, edited by S. Watson, and E. Waterton, 57–71. Farnham: Ashgate.

Crouch, D. 2015. "Affect, Heritage, Feeling." In *The Palgrave Handbook of Contemporary Heritage Research*, edited by E. Waterton, and S. Watson, 177–190. London: Palgrave Macmillan.

Dittmer, J., and E. Waterton. 2017. "Affecting the Body: Cultures of Militarism at the Australian War Memorial." In *Heritage, Affect and Emotion. Politics, Practices and Infrastructures*, edited by D. P. Tolia-Kelly, E. Waterton, and S. Watson, 47–74. London: Routledge.

Edensor, T., and S. Sumartojo. 2015. "Designing Atmospheres: Introduction to Special Issue." *Visual Communication* 14 (3): 251–265. doi: 10.1177/1470357215582305.

Emirbayer, M., and A. Mische. 1998. "What Is Agency?" *American Journal of Sociology* 103 (4): 962–1023. doi: 10.1086/231294.

Foster, A., and N. Ford. 2003. "Serendipity and Information Seeking: An Empirical Study." *Journal of Documentation* 59 (3): 321–340. doi: 10.1108/00220410310472518.

Foucault, M., and J. Miskowiec 1986. "Of Other Spaces." *Diacritics* 16 (1): 22–27. doi: 10.2307/464648.

Giddens, A. 1990. *The Consequences of Modernity*. Cambridge, UK: Polity Press.

Hall, S. 1992. The Question of Cultural Identity. In: *Modernity and its Futures*, edited by S. Hall, T. McGrew, and D. Held, 273–327. Cambridge, UK: Polity Press and Open University.

Hall, S. 1997. *Representation: Cultural Representation and Signifying Practices*. London: Sage and Open University.

Harvey, D. 1996. *Justice, Nature and the Geography of Difference*. Oxford: Blackwell.

Ingraham, C. 2019. "Serendipity as Cultural Technique." *Culture, Theory and Critique*, 60 (2): 107–122. doi: 10.1080/14735784.2019.1579657.

Kisić, V. 2017. *Governing Heritage Dissonance: Promises and Realities of Selected Cultural Policies*. The Hague: European Cultural Foundation.

Lähdesmäki, T. 2014. "Discourses of Europeanness in the Reception of the European Capital of Culture Events: The Case of Pécs 2010." *European Urban and Regional Studies* 21 (2): 191–205. doi:10.1177/0969776412448092.

Lähdesmäki, T. 2016. "Politics of Tangibility, Intangibility, and Place in the Making of a European Cultural Heritage in EU Heritage Policy." *International Journal of Heritage Studies* 22 (10): 766–780. doi:10.1080/13527258.2016.1212386.

Lähdesmäki, T. 2018. "Introduction: Time and Spatial and Social Turns in Architectural Research." In *Time and Transformation in Architecture*, edited by T. Lähdesmäki, 1–16. Leiden: Brill.

Lefebvre, H. 1991. *The Production of Space.* Translated by D. Nicholson-Smith. Oxford: Blackwell.

Macdonald, S. 2013. *Memorylands: Heritage and Identity in Europe Today.* London: Routledge.

Mains, S. P. 2017. "From Menie to Montego Bay: Documenting, Representing and Mobilising Emotion in Coastal Heritage Landscapes." In *Heritage, Affect and Emotion. Politics, Practices and Infrastructures*, edited by D. P. Tolia-Kelly, E. Waterton, and S. Watson, 179–200. London: Routledge.

Massey, D. 1991. "A Global Sense of Place." *Marxism Today* 38: 24–29.

Massey, D. 2005. *For Space.* London: Sage.

Massey, D. 2007. *The World City.* Cambridge, UK: Polity Press.

Muntéan, L. 2017. "Touching Time. Photography, Affect and the Digital Archive." In *Heritage, Affect and Emotion. Politics, Practices and Infrastructures*, edited by D. P. Tolia-Kelly, E. Waterton, and S. Watson, 201–218. London and New York: Routledge.

Paasi, A. 1996. *Territories, Boundaries and Consciousness: The Changing Geographies of the Finnish-Russian Border.* Chichester: John Wiley.

Pritchard, A., and N. Morgan. 2006. "Hotel Babylon? Exploring Hotels as Liminal Sites of Transition and Transgression." *Tourism Management* 27 (5): 762–772. doi: 10.1016/j.tourman.2005.05.015.

Sather-Wagstaff, J. 2017. "Making Polysense of the World: Affect, Memory, Heritage." In *Heritage, Affect and Emotion: Politics, Practices and Infrastructures*, edited by D. P. Tolia-Kelly, E. Waterton, and S. Watson, 12–29. London and New York: Routledge.

Schorch, P., E. Waterton, and S. Watson. 2017. "Museum Canopies and Affective Cosmopolitanism: Cultivating Cross-cultural Landscapes for Ethical Embodied Responses." In *Heritage, Affect and Emotion. Politics, Practices and Infrastructures*, edited by D. P. Tolia-Kelly, E. Waterton, and S. Watson, 93–113. London and New York: Routledge.

Soja, E. 1996. *Thirdspace: Journeys to Los Angeles and Other Real-and-Imagined Places.* Oxford: Blackwell.

Soja, E. W. 2008. "Taking Space Personally". In *The Spatial Turn: Interdisciplinary Perspectives*, edited by S. Arias, and B. Warf, 11–35. London: Routledge.

Sumartojo, S., and S. Pink. 2019. *Atmospheres and the Experiential World. Theory and Methods.* London and New York: Routledge.

Taheri, B., K. Gori, K. O'Gorman, G. Hogg, and T. Farrington. 2016. "Experiential Liminoid Consumption: The Case of Nightclubbing." *Journal of Marketing Management* 32 (1–2): 19–43. doi: 10.1080/0267257X.2015.1089309.

Timothy, D. J., and S. W. Boyd. 2006. "Heritage Tourism in the 21st Century: Valued Traditions and New Perspectives." *Journal of Heritage Tourism* 1 (1): 1–16. doi: 10.1080/17438730608668462.

Thrift, N. 1996. *Spatial Formations*. London: SAGE.

Tolia-Kelly, D. P. 2006. "Affect: An Ethnocentric Encounter?" *Area 38* (2): 213–217. doi: 10.1111/j.1475-4762.2006.00682.x.

Turunen, J., V. L. A. Čeginskas, S. Kaasik-Krogerus, T. Lähdesmäki, and K. Mäkinen. Forthcoming. "Poly-Space: Creating New Concepts through Reflexive Team Ethnography." In *Challenges and Solutions in Ethnographic Research. Ethnography with a Twist*, edited by T. Lähdesmäki, E. Koskinen-Koivisto, V. L. A. Čeginskas, and A.-K. Koistinen. Routledge.

Waterton, E. 2014. "A More-Than-Representational Understanding of Heritage? The 'Past' and the Politics of Affect." *Geography Compass* 8 (11): 823–833. doi: 10.1111/gec3.12182.

Waterton, E., and S. Watson. 2013. "Framing Theory: Towards a Critical Imagination in Heritage Studies." *International Journal of Heritage Studies* 19 (6): 546–561. doi: 10.1080/13527258.2013.779295.

Witcomb, A. 2013. "Understanding the Role of Affect in Producing a Critical Pedagogy for History Museums." *Museum, Management and Curatorship* 28 (3): 255–71. doi: 10.1080/09647775.2013.807998.

Witcomb, A. 2015. "Thinking about Others through Museums and Heritage." In *The Palgrave Handbook of Contemporary Heritage Research*, edited by E. Waterton, and S. Watson, 130–143. Houndsmill: Palgrave Macmillan.

Chapter 8

Bodies in European cultural heritage

Heritage sites are important actors in diverse processes of generating and transmitting affect in relation to memory, representation, and formation of identities by offering a place for "doing and feeling" (Crang and Tolia-Kelly 2010, 2136; see also Ahmed 2004; Thrift 2004; Lähdesmäki 2017). As part of the 'affective turn', scholars in heritage studies have become increasingly interested in exploring how we encounter, interact, and communicate with the social and physical world through our senses and bodies. Embodied practices and performativity give narratives meaning, contributing to understandings of history and future visions. But as Macdonald (2013, 80) writes, while "the discursive and the embodied/material [of the heritage sites] do not necessarily 'say' the same things" or necessarily "work in the same ways or produce the same effects", the politics of affect and senses are intertwined with processual constructions of memory and knowledge. Scholars therefore argue for bringing together affect and discourse in heritage analysis (Munroe 2017; Sather-Wagstaff 2017, 13).

In this chapter, we draw on representational and more-than-representational theories, as well as the concepts of performativity, affective practices, and polyspace, to analyze the relation between heritage, affective experiences, and bodies. In our view, visits to heritage sites are always accompanied by an act of interpretation and a process of affective-discursive meaning-making (Munroe 2017, 117). We follow recent heritage scholars' criticism of attempts to create a division between the body, cognitive processes, and socio-historical context (Macdonald 2013, 81; see also Sather-Wagstaff, 2017, 13; Tolia-Kelly et al. 2017). Instead, we connect heritage experiences with the discursive construction of power politics, human agency, and memory-making (Munroe 2017, 117; Sather-Wagstaff 2017, 15, 24).

First, we analyze how human bodies and their manifold representations featuring in the exhibitions of the EHL sites can be understood as emotionally charged, or "sticky", elements (see Lähdesmäki 2017). We draw here on the work of Ahmed (2004, 2014) to scrutinize the ways, in which these representations materialize as 'body-objects' in the process of narrative constructions at heritage sites and become "sticky objects", that is, infused with affect and emotion in the interpretation and understanding of heritage. We argue that human bodies are particularly sticky due to their ability of invoking a sense of empathy in the viewer. According to Ahmed (2014, 2004), such objects play a crucial role in the cultural process of collective memory construction.

Affect itself is about more than bodies, bodily processes, and embodiment: it is about the circulation between people, objects, and signs that can be understood as "a matter of how we come into contact with objects and others" (Ahmed 2014, 208, 45). As Ahmed (2014, 45) points out, the circulation of affect arises through specific cultural processes, often accumulated across a sign or figure, which become "sticky surfaces", in which affect nestles. The objects do not have an independent "affective charge" but are embedded in historically contextualized experiences, memory, and meaningful, affectively loaded practices in interaction with bodies and places (Waterton 2014; Frykman and Povrazanović Frykman 2015, 20; Wetherell 2015; see also our Chapter 7). Hence, understanding bodies as "beholders of affect" (Frykman and Povrazanović Frykman 2015, 24) makes it possible to explore how subjects become invested in particular social structures and make sense of the world around them.

Second, we focus on the visitors' bodies as vehicles of embodied knowledge and containers and conductors of affective experiences. We understand the visitor's body as a recipient, store, and creator of knowledge, emotions, and affective experiences that plays an active role in processes of meaning-making. We explore the transmission and experience of affective atmospheres at heritage sites and, particularly, how visitors' affective experiences are articulated and circulated within the heritage sites. This raises the question as to how visitors notice, translate, and capture such experiences of heritage. We focus on their photographs, which we see as a creative way in which visitors try to engage with the affective atmosphere at a specific heritage site and at a specific time. We discuss how the visitor's body can be understood as a 'resonating membrane', making contact with affective experiences and processing them at the same time. Central to this is an understanding of the body as a "space of visceral processing" (Papoulias and Callard 2010, 34) that constructs meaning of heritage as a cultural experience outside of representations and as subjective, emergent *in situ*, and creating a feeling of affinity (Waterton 2014).

The examination of bodies, embodiment, and affect in this chapter is based on multiple modes of engagement and methodological approaches. We draw on our field research notes dealing with our personal experiences of the EHL sites as well as our observation of exhibitions, guided tours, and visitors' movement and participation in various activities at the sites. We also utilize our interviews with heritage practitioners and visitors, and the photographs taken by the visitors during their visits. In order to gain deeper knowledge of the visitors' experiences and the ways in which they creatively and performatively captured their affective experiences during their visit, we explored these photographs in the context of the visitor interviews, our fieldnotes, exhibition information, and other photographs of the same site.

It is a methodological challenge to analyze affect, affective experiences, and the potential of affective atmospheres at heritage sites at which the researcher has not physically been present (see Povrzanović Frykman 2015). As we had divided our fieldwork between the 11 EHL sites, our analysis draws strongly on numerous discussions and email exchanges between members of the research team during and after the fieldwork period. These discussions sparked new insights and made it possible for us to develop our individual observations, experiences, and interpretations together, and to extend these discussions to explore the sites' affective atmospheres and the visitors' experiences (for details of our team ethnography see Turunen et al. forthcoming). Furthermore, these discussions made us realize that while affective experiences can be represented, they may also trigger new affective experiences in those who try to remember them. Researchers need to use a combination of different approaches in order to contextualize and write about such experiences.

Bodies as sticky objects

Bodies are "sticky objects" (Ahmed 2004, 2014) in two ways: their representation and the affective experiences of and with(in) them. The stickiness of bodies can be understood in relation to the reconstruction and transmission of normative discourses about Europe's past that are often taken for granted and repeated in various contexts. However, both the representation and absence of bodies elicit an effect on visitors to EHL sites. Next, we attempt to engage with both the representation of bodies and affective experiences they evoke in the visitors. Our analysis is inspired by Kaasik-Krogerus's (2018) discussion of the stickiness of bodies in relation to the exhibition in the European Solidarity Centre at the Historic Gdańsk Shipyard but broadens here to include the other fieldwork sites.

The EHL sites try to show a broad scope and plurality of bodies in their exhibitions and narratives by situating them in different geographical, temporal, and situational contexts (however, see Box 9.1). They often represent bodies as either heroes or victims, or as absent or present bodies. In the context of European cultural heritage, heroes include extraordinary European individuals (e.g. in Robert Schuman House, Alcide De Gasperi House, Mundaneum, or Sagres Promontory) and a nameless mass of bodies at different times and locations in Europe's past (e.g. Sagres Promontory, Hambach Castle, Great Guild Hall, or Carnuntum). The boundaries in the representation of bodies are often overlapping and fluid at many EHL sites (e.g. European Solidarity Centre, Great Guild Hall, Hambach Castle, and Camp Westerbork). While we elaborate bodies in terms of clear-cut categories of individual heroes versus (heroic) masses, victims versus perpetrators, and absent/present bodies, we understand that their meanings are in flux and all categories entangled. However, the use of binaries helps to contrast different perceptions of heritage. Heroes and victims produce a sticky and positive notion, while perpetrators, but also masses, evoke empathy to a much lesser degree. Engagement with heritage can both destabilize and consolidate our preconceived ideas of these categories. In what follows, we first discuss how the representation of bodies as heroes or anonymous masses at the EHL sites embody narratives and values related to the past. Then we move on to explore how the sticky representations of bodies address difference, both by producing and dissolving boundaries and dichotomies. Finally, we investigate the role, which absent bodies in the representation of the EHL sites play in strengthening affective experiences during the visit.

Sticky heroes

The bodies and personalities of 'heroic' individuals are evoked in various ways, such as in photographs, portraits, busts, caricatures, narratives, or through personal belongings and objects at the EHL sites. The representation of their bodies in the exhibitions serve as illustrations of their specific achievements and commitment and help to highlight how they contributed to the making of Europe in its present form, thus also meeting the requirements of the EHL criteria. At the same time, the bodies (and their representations) become personalized as specific attributes are bestowed on them, such as 'Europe's Founding Fathers' (e.g. Robert Schuman or Alcide De Gasperi), 'pacifist' (Otelet and La Fontaine at Mundaneum), 'leader of the Solidarity Movement' (Lech Wałęsa at the European Solidarity Centre), 'first President of the European Parliament' (Simone Veil at Lieu d'Europe), or 'outstanding composer and musician' (Franz Liszt at the Liszt Academy of Music). The attributes highlight their merits and help to elevate the individuals to notable and memorable persons of Europe's past. At the same time, the association of these individuals with certain attributes may become sticky for the visitors and affect the way, in which they relate to these individuals in the future, thereby helping to affirm the AHD.

In contrast, the masses of individuals and European people(s) remain anonymous but they are often pictured in movement (e.g. demonstrating, marching, fighting, or celebrating) and their agency relates to political and social change. For instance, one section of the Lieu d'Europe is dedicated to "Europe: Men and Women" and highlights the shared commitment of different people across Europe – men, women, children, old, and young – to the creation of civil society. The exhibition shows pictures of people participating in the *Solidarność* movement (Gdańsk, 1980), in the Baltic Chain (23 August 1989), the launch of the *Indignados* movement in Madrid (February 2011), or in the demonstrations against the Iraq War in Budapest (March 2006) and London (October 2006), against the death penalty (Paris, November 1976), or against domestic violence (Madrid, November 2008). As each of these images is accompanied by quotes from famous people about the importance of civil participation and agency, the pictures interconnect agency with everyday life and suggest that all of 'us' can make a difference as 'ordinary', or 'banal heroes'.

At the same time, the represented masses of anonymous people also serve to address the diversity of European societies. For instance, one section of the exhibition at Camp Westerbork deals with Moluccan refugees who arrived there from the former Dutch colonies in the late 1940s and 1950s and lived on the Camp's premises for over 20 years. The section attempts to highlight the historical diversity of Dutch society and show how people arriving from outside Europe constitute an integral component of it (cf. Turunen n.d.). Similarly, the exhibition at the Great Guild Hall highlights the fact that people from different parts of Europe cohabited in the same geographical space over centuries and all participated in cultural and social processes.

The representation of bodies also has a didactic mission and guides our understanding of what to remember (see Dittmer and Watson 2017). For instance, the films and pictures showing the inmates of Camp Westerbork during World War II vividly remind the viewer of the need to learn from the past. The representation of bodies in the exhibition directly links to the horror faced by the victims. Visitor interviews reveal that they regard the detainees of Westerbork as victims, feel with them, express their empathy with their fate and their incomprehension about the historical events. One Dutch woman in her late 60s wondered how "people can do this to each other. That really touches me. I think it is so, so bad. This total lack of respect for another human being" (VS3/3). In the face of the victims of the Holocaust, the value of peace and forgiveness is emphasized and connected to narratives about the role which historical events and people, known and unknown, played in developing EUrope today.

The visits to the EHL sites work on the visitors simultaneously at multiple levels: thus, the narrative construction of Europe's past becomes consolidated through affects. The past and heritage materializes, is felt, and expressed in bodies, objects, and places, and is accompanied by embodied sensory and affective experiences that are constructed and performed over time and space (Macdonald 2013, 79). Bodies, texts, objects, artefacts, the landscape, and environment of the heritage site all participate in creating an affective atmosphere that is "produced, performed and emerging in the embodied and creative uses of heritage generated by people" (Haldrup and Bærenholdt 2015, 53). Narrative constructions are never emotionally neutral but need to be conceived of as "a series of powerfully emotive, affective connections", which "hold us in place in the world, tell us who 'we' are and where 'we' come from and quite literally 'mean' something" (Munroe 2017, 155; see also Macdonald 2013, 223). As Watson, Waterton, and Smith (2012, 6) argue, "embodied and multi-sensuous processes" pose "concrete social and cultural consequences, not only for those experiencing the moment but also for those who are represented and 'understood' by this process". Wetherell (2012, 22) proposes locating affect and emotion in social practice. Her concept of affective practice then relates to how routine ways of meaning-making and reflection are embedded within certain emotional regimes that constrain how we act, feel, and think.

The representations of bodies in the context of the EHL sites certainly contribute to generating a normative discourse (Smith 2006) of who is (worth being) remembered in Europe's present and future and what counts as 'European bodies'. This mediates specific ideological positions and societal values, and connects to issues of belonging, power relationships, equity, and recognition (see also Box 9.1). It affects the understanding that Europe shares much the same civilizational heritage in liberal democracy, capitalism, Christianity, cultural values, and political authority (Delanty 2017, 126, 128), and highlights the relevance of heritage in contemporary processes of inclusion and exclusion in Europe. In this respect, the representation of bodies at the EHL sites contributes to the canonization of the EU founding myth and a saga of Europeanization based on Europe's extraordinary past (Trenz 2014; Lähdesmäki 2018). The dominance of the representation of white, male, privileged, and aged individuals and their achievements co-produce a gendered and class-specific heritage discourse (see Chapter 9).

In contrast, the masses are more diverse and often pictured in the act of protesting for social justice and equality, human rights, peace, and democracy – which correspond to the values that the EU uses in its identity and legitimacy building. While these issues connect to the agency and movement of people across Europe in their historical pursuit of individual and collective autonomy and rights, they intertwine a specific value discourse with power struggles and certain expectations. The normative representations of bodies become sticky as the visitors accommodate certain regimes and modes of thinking and behaving with Europe's past, which influence the imagination, visualization, and understanding of the past. This may result in a repetitive reconstruction and transmission of normative discourses as taken for granted in various contexts. For instance, the specific emotions conveyed in photographs, such as joy at the fall of the Berlin Wall (Lieu d'Europe) or helplessness and despair when facing tanks, police, and soldiers during martial law in Poland in the 1980s (European Solidarity Centre) show how bodies embody specific values, such as solidarity, democracy, human rights and peace. By extension, the display of bodies can thus assist in forming the ideal of a 'good' European citizen who is motivated to seek political, social, and cultural transformations for the good of society.

Sticky representations

The representation of bodies at museums and heritage sites often help to establish a sticky conception of biased categories based on differentiation and difference (Ahmed 2014, 191), such as 'sophisticated' and 'uncivilized', 'normal' and 'abnormal', or 'able' and 'disabled' bodies. The representation of social and cultural conceptualizations of bodies in Europe's heritage can contribute to bias based on looks, skin colour, origin, and ability, and thereby raise questions about the conception and absorbance of diversity in European societies.

Visitors to EHL sites encounter normative categories of emotions and affect, often evoked in dichotomous terms such as empathy or dislike (with individuals and groups of people alike), which inform socially and culturally acceptable ways of relating to the past. For instance, the discursive and material representation at Camp Westerbork and the European Solidarity Centre familiarize visitors with the past through the bodies of victims and perpetrators. The affective experiences transported by the sight of the victims' bodies and the materiality of the site connect to the understanding of heritage sites as places of collective remembrance (Tolia-Kelly 2004; Macdonald 2013; Dittmer and Watson 2017; see also Nora 1998). In this case, empathy with the victims also produces a form of stickiness that emphasizes the need to learn from the past.

At the same time, the EHL sites skilfully manage to dissolve the perception of 'fixed' boundaries they have helped to create. While the focus in Camp Westerbork is on the detainees and victims of the Nazi dictatorship, big canvases in the part of the open-air museum show images and biographical information of the camp's German staff and Dutch Nazi collaborators, including descriptions of their demeanour by former camp prisoners (Figure 8.1). The exhibition also provides information about the ambiguous role of some prisoners in camp life, which destabilizes the clear boundaries between perpetrators and victims. Similarly, the European Solidarity Centre gives evidence of violence committed

Figure 8.1   One of the canvases showing both perpetrator and victim. Camp Westerbork, the Netherlands. Photo: EUROHERIT

Figure 8.2 Braziers used during martial law in 1980 (bottom left). European Solidarity Centre, Poland. Photo: EUROHERIT

by the military and police forces during the martial law period in Poland, but the display of braziers used by military patrols to keep warm shows that they were also 'just' people who could feel the cold (Figure 8.2).

With such representations, the EHL sites help to challenge preconceived perceptions about victimhood, heroism, and perpetrators as implied in the representation of bodies and contribute to 'humanizing' them, which challenges the view of the past in simplified categories of 'good' and 'bad'. This is no longer a question of who is innocent or guilty in the historical context, but the representation of the bodies and material objects connected to bodies enable visitors to regard victims *and* perpetrators as humans. This does not diminish the horror of the Holocaust, of which the visitor gets a sense at Camp Westerbork, but rather contributes to intensifying it and contextualizing the actions intended to dehumanize millions of people. As some visitors stated in the interviews, this makes them think about their own role in the present European crises dealing with the causes, the reception, and (de)humanization of refugees. The same goes for the example in the European Solidarity Centre; it makes some visitors reflect more about people's concerns in the past but also about topical political issues and social injustice today. The representation of bodies at heritage sites and museums may create differentiation and establish biased categories, but affective experience connected with the representation of bodies may dissolve such boundaries. Such sites create opportunities for encounter across temporal boundaries and cultural differences by offering a way of negotiating the limitations of interpretation (see Staiff 2014, 157; Schorch, Waterton, and Watson 2017, 94) and thereby humanizing our experience with heritage.

The ambiguous representation of bodies breaks usual patterns of perceiving and categorizing groups of people and situations, as is the case at Camp Westerbork and the European Solidarity Centre. Affective experiences are crucial for heritage experiences and can trigger cognitive processes of reflection and interpretation in the visitors, which may produce new insights and challenge taken-for-granted positions (Witcomb 2013, 246, 257). The EHL sites play an important role in deepening the understanding of historical and present contexts and inspiring public debate about who has a place in Europe's past and present. In this, they help to address the drawing of social and political boundaries between various groups and sharpen our awareness of discriminative mechanisms underlying biased perceptions of who belongs to Europe's contemporary societies, thereby making an important contribution to dealing with diversity in the present.

Sticky absent bodies

As representation at heritage sites and museums is commonly arranged around aspects of memory, place, and practice, they need to engage their visitors through embodied practices and emotional-cognitive experiences. Affective experiences play an important role in the production of embodied heritage, knowledge, imagination, and memory (Staiff 2014, 47; Waterton and Watson 2014, 76; Dittmer and Waterton 2017, 53), which raises the question of how visitors experience heritage sites that are defined by absent bodies, or no bodies. This question connects to the aforementioned aspect of 'humanizing bodies'. The visitors' affective engagement with the exhibition enable to think across the representation of bodies and body-objects. As the focus shifts towards the people who are presented and represented in the exhibition and no longer stays on the material objects and representations of bodies, the people and their stories become real by virtue of the visitor's imagination and affective experiences.

While physical absence is often associated with passive, silenced, and powerless people, the absence of actual bodies at heritage sites can work in the opposite direction and elicit powerful affective experiences in the visitors. When physical bodies are not present, the feeling of their absence may be intensified, thus, paradoxically contributing to recreating a sensation of their presence, as we observed at the EHL sites. For instance, Camp Westerbork provides several examples of how (physically) absent bodies become charged with affect and manage to express knowledge of the historical contexts. This is done through displaying the material evidence of the absent bodies, such as letters and postcards from the deported. The memory embedded in the encounter with the objects may evoke an affective atmosphere and result in a "felt presence" at heritage sites (Tolia-Kelly 2017, 35) that can strengthen affective experiences for the visitor. Another example from the exhibition at Camp Westerbork is the display of a curved wall filled with photographs and film excerpts of Jewish families and framed by two maps of the Netherlands. The one on the left marks with red spots the Jewish settlements in 1940, while the one on the right, dated 1945, is empty (Figure 8.3).

The interplay between absent and present bodies in this example raises two equally important aspects. First, the maps are a powerful symbol and visualization for the transformation of the Netherlands from a place that was filled with a vivid Jewish life before World War II to a place almost void of Jewish life, with only a small number of survivors in 1945, which makes the scale of the destruction quite visible and easy to grasp. The absent bodies become sticky as they create empathy, but at the same time their role as victims is emphasized. As Schorch, Waterton, and Watson (2017, 107) put it, a "culture itself cannot speak or engage in an encounter and dialogue: it depends on the face and story of a cultural actor". Heritage depends on dialogue between cultural human beings. Objects cannot stand for themselves: they have to be interpreted (Ahmed 2014, 45) and the interpretations depend on interpersonal dialogue and circulation of affect between bodies.

Second, the wall contributes to intensifying the presence of people from the past despite their physical and bodily absence as, in the pictures, they are

Figure 8.3 Pictures of the past. Camp Westerbork, the Netherlands. Photo: EUROHERIT

gazing directly at the visitor. The photographs give a face to the absent bodies, thereby evoking affective experiences – or faciality, in the sense of Deleuze and Guatteri's (1987) concept – that makes a face signify and subjectify an individual. The face connects to the understanding of becoming as a constant process of change and is part of the "lived body" that is not perceived as only an object but alludes to our experience of the world (Merleau-Ponty 2006, 239). Hence, the pictures emphasize that the bodies were living persons, disconnected from the victimhood and horror with which the camp is usually associated.

Camp Westerbork is a "space of cross-cultural encounter" (Waterton and Watson 2014, 76; Schorch, Waterton, and Watson 2017, 94) between the absent bodies and the visitor, which also empowers the subject of perception. Like the curved wall, both the temporary exhibition that visualizes the absent bodies of the dead by listing the names of all the 102,000 perished people and the audio recital of their names restore their humanity and create a strong affective experience for the visitors. They turn the mass of victims encountered during the visit and in history lessons into humans again, and by giving people a face and name, these persons become more than 'just' anonymous victims. Affective experiences felt in the context of representation of bodies facilitate the recreation of bodily presence at heritage sites. This results in dissolving the temporal distance between their absence and our present lives. The eyewitness project at Camp Westerbork produces a similar effect as former victims receive a face, a body, a voice, and a name, and thereby empower individuals, which enables them to exit the anonymity and the victimhood into which they were forced by historical circumstances. This particular project creates the opportunity for visitors to see, hear, come into close contact with, and speak to people who represent the past.

The visit to a heritage site intertwines complex cognitive processes with the experience of manifold senses, including the visual, sensory, haptic, imaginative, unconscious, subjective, interpersonal, or affective, which make it possible for visitors to connect and at the same to disconnect from time and space. Bodies are "sticky surfaces", where affect accumulates and surfaces (Ahmed 2014, 191), shaping the subject who feels and experiences, and giving her, or him, a performative identity and subject position (see Wetherell 2015). At the same time, affect as an "in-between" and "relational" phenomenon (Wetherell 2015, 158) can help (representations of) bodies to elicit affectively charged attachments in the audiences and articulate culturally embedded practices and acts of interpretations (see Wetherell 2015, 160, 2012, 53, 76; Schorch, Waterton, and Watson 2017, 94, 96). This powerfully connects the bodies as sticky objects to the embodied reactions of the visitors' own bodies. While heritage sites facilitate and capture the "circulation of objects, people, emotions, and ideas" within and between bodies (Crang and Tolia-Kelly 2010, 2316), affective experiences, and complex cognitive processes of knowledge production mutually reinforce each other, during and after the visit. The representation of bodies enables the visitor to sense "something" by being touched and affected, as well as to process "something" (Anderson 2009, 78) involving numerous other sensations than the verbal, and can generate empathy. This experience of empathy based on the stickiness of bodies is closely tied with the experience of poly-space, which can both produce powerful affective experiences in the visitor and imbue the heritage site with a specific affective atmosphere, as outlined in Chapter 7.

Bodies as resonating membranes

Bodies can also be seen as 'resonating membranes' through which affective experiences at heritage sites penetrate visitors' bodies, resonate in them, and become creatively transformed and expressed. Visitor bodies include not only the physical experience of engaging with artefacts, installations, and interactive modes of engagement at heritage sites, but more importantly refer to the visitors' capacity of being touched, affected, and experiencing feelings during their visits. The body remembers and stores affective and polysensory experiences; such experiences captured in objects may re-stimulate memory (see various contributions in Tolia-Kelly et al. 2017). For instance, the nascence of empathy in the context of heritage visits emphasizes the importance of a "felt presence" (Tolia-Kelly 2017, 104) over factual information for engaging with others, developing a notion of solidarity, or making sense of the world. As Merleau-Ponty (2006, 275) writes, the body is not only an object among all other objects, a nexus of sensible qualities among others, but an object which is sensitive to all the rest, which reverberates to all sounds, vibrates to all colours, and provides words with their primordial significance through the way in which it receives them. He points out that without reducing the significance of the word, the body is a "constituted and constituting object in relation to other objects", which "uses its own parts as a general system of symbol for the world, through which we can consequently 'be at home in' the world, 'understand' it and find significance in it" (Merleau-Ponty 2006, 275). Bodies share the ability to amplify and circulate affects, as well as to resonate with or disrupt affects, in this bodies are "embodied performativities" (Schorch, Waterton, and Watson 2017, 94).

However, the emphasis of the "incorporeal potential" (Clough 2009, 48) of affective experiences over the discursive engagement ignores the fact that visits to heritage sites are never only either affective experiences or discursive engagements but combine both approaches. In this context, visitor photographs can be seen as part of embodied practices and performances related to memory and meaning-making (Scarles 2009; Haldrup and Bærenholt 2015). Photographs can be used as a medium to explore how people articulate, co-create, produce, and capture affective experiences during their visit to a heritage site, and how the act of photography connects to interpretive and cognitive processes.

Photography is usually discussed in relation to memory, encounter, and embodied practices or as part of touristic engagement (Scarles 2009, 471) but photographs can also help in exploring how the experience of affect and representation impacts on visitors at heritage sites, and show how the visitors' bodies can resonate in the poly-space there. During our fieldwork, we asked visitors whether they would be willing to show us photographs, which they deemed the most meaningful in the context of their visit. Our analysis of these images shows that visitors engaged in different ways with the heritage of, at, and within heritage sites (see Waterton and Watson 2013, 547). Analyzing visitors' photographs can thus provide valuable resources for understanding the relation between affect, emotion, senses, materiality, and discourses as inherently central aspects of the heritage context (see Bagnall 2003; Smith 2006; Crouch 2010, 2015). In the following, we will examine how the visitors' photographs reflect different forms of embodied and affective engagement with the past. Based on our understanding of the visitor's body as resonating through and with affective experiences, we discuss how the photographs relate to the visitors' engagement with the heritage sites and produce symbolic understandings of heritage, filter heritage and blur spatial and temporal boundaries. We approach photographs as creative and performative examples of the visitors' affective practices that can be both text-based and polysensory and also generate empathy.

Reverberation and absorption of symbolic representations

Visitors took photographs at the EHL sites for different purposes and connected the images to different affective experiences. There are examples of 'typical' touristic engagement that aim to capture key icons of the heritage site, be they objects, bodies, or the materiality of the site. This category includes photographs of well-known places and objects at the EHL sites, such as Gate No. 2 of the Shipyard in Gdańsk (Figure 8.4), renowned personalities, such as the European 'Founding Fathers' at Robert Schuman House, or pictures taken for their aesthetic value, such as Liszt's living room at his home museum. This kind of photographing is not necessarily about reproducing famous pictures, although the gate, for instance, is frequently pictured in reports about the Shipyard or Solidarity movement. It rather speaks of the visitors' personal engagement with the site that anticipates certain experiences of the visit and confirms well-known images or place characteristics of a heritage site based on its symbolic representation (Scarles 2009, 480). Visitors aim to capture objects and motifs that are "filled with their own piece of history", as a Dutch visitor to Camp Westerbork explained, as they allow for immersion in the past. She said that her photograph of the staged interior of a former barrack represents a "piece of memory" of the site that enables her to engage with "the people who have lived in Camp Westerbork" (VS3/8).

The photographs document what visitors register as heritage and in what ways they become attuned to the meaning of a heritage site. Symbolic understandings of heritage unconsciously reverberate in the body during the visit and the visitor absorbs them as part of their meaning-making processes. For instance, a Polish visitor to the European Solidarity Centre who chose to

Figure 8.4 The visitor's perspective on the Gate No. 2. The Historic Gdańsk Shipyard, European Solidarity Centre, Poland. Photo: EUROHERIT

photograph the famous Gate No. 2 referred to it as "the most important place [...] because it is a very symbolic place. [...] Well, everyone in Poland knows this" (VS8/9). Such photographs, then, are part of both memory work and of proving that one was at an established historical and symbolic place. The visitor's prior knowledge of the role of the site and familiarity with its dominant narrative are paramount for the choice of the motifs, which become meaningful in relation to the accepted and incorporated canon of the heritage site (see Scarles 2009, 468).

Filtering heritage experiences

The visitor photographs can be understood as a creative and playful approach to the past, spurred by the moment of the visit. Some of the photographs refer to a specific moment entangled with various emotions, such as surprise, amusement, or fleeting fascination, which conveys one of the visitors' ways of accessing the poly-space of heritage sites. Again, visitors' bodies act as membranes, which allow for the permeability of manifold experiences and cognitive processes. In this respect, the visitor's body can also be understood as a filter that refines the heritage visit by concentrating on specific moments and experiences. In several photographs, visitors chose to capture practices of playfulness, discovery, and imagination, or the observation of bizarreness in relation to their visit.

An example of a playful engagement with heritage is the diorama of the Hambach Festival, constructed with Playmobil figures, which was photographed at different occasions by the interviewed visitors. In the interviews, they usually stated that the picture was meant for their grandchildren who were not present during the visit. However, it became clear that the visitors were equally amused and impressed by the sight of how such a complex historical event as the Hambach Festival could be represented and made tangible with objects that commonly are regarded as children's toys. Similarly, the photograph of the re-enactment at the Great Guild Hall, in which one visitor portrayed her husband posing with a helmet and holding a sword and shield, is not just about creating a joyful memory of the visit. It also served as an attempt of momentary iden-tification with the past and as a playful way to gain access to it. As the husband explained during the interview, enacting a medieval knight was part of "putting yourself in their shoes, just to feel that heavy thing [helmet] on your head. You'd have to fight in that" (VS6/8).

One visitor shared with us an image of a fish in Carnuntum, which could have been easily overlooked during the visit as it was partly hidden. However, while for us the picture might represent a detail and maybe even an insignifi-cant part of the visit, the discovery of the fish was a very special and affectively charged experience for the visitor. Having watched the film *Quo Vadis* just before her visit to the Archaeological Park Carnuntum, the visitor interpreted the fish as a secret symbol of Christianity in Roman times. Judging from the hidden position of the image, the woman was persuaded that the house owner must have secretly been a Christian, thus mixing the material representation of Roman times at the site with her personal imagination of the past. However, this discovery opened up new ways of engaging affectively and cognitively with the past and present, based on the role of Christianity in modern European societies.

As Dicks (2015, 376) puts it, "visitors come to the museum trailing a largely unconscious history of thought, schemes, and memories which provide the immediate standpoint from which they relate to the history presented to them". The above-mentioned visitor actively engaged with the construction and cre-ation of the subject and context in her photograph, and she negotiated heritage through the combination of imagined and experienced encounters. The photo-graph of the fish can be seen as an attempt to capture the moment and context when the visitor encounters the sensation and excitement of discovering a part of the past and connecting it to a broader story. Thus, the act of photographing enables visitors to express the range of their experiences, feelings, and moods bound up in concrete bodily performances and tangible engagements with the past (Haldrup and Larsen 2003). However, while in the act of photography the visitor attempts to express the meaning she attributes to the site, the photo-graph can later become a less meaningful object and experience when the memory of the discovery and its affect has faded (Dicks 2015, 375).

The way in which visitors filter heritage becomes visible in enhanced and embodied engagement with the past. A visitor to Robert Schuman House photographed part of Schuman's garden, his home, including the window of his study on the first floor and the window of the room on the ground floor where he died. In the background, the image also shows the tower of the church in which Schuman, a practising Catholic, prayed during his lifetime, and where he was buried. The affective experiences connected with the visit only unfolded when the visitor explained that by photographing, she

> imagined, how he [Robert Schuman] walked through the garden and thought after having read documents, while working on proposals or when reading Monnet. Or how he considered how to react to certain things, or how to draft a concept. I find it moving to imagine all of this.
>
> (VS10/1)

As Scarles (2009, 484) suggests, photographs can be understood as imaginations of space that are "produced and consumed as active, lived encounters with place, instilling life and mobilizing deeper affiliations between self and other through a series of both imagined and experiential encounters". This emphasizes the intersubjective nature of photographs, which participate in the circulation of affect and become infused with the visitor's discursive meaning-making of heritage at and within heritage sites (see Haldrup and Bærenholdt 2015, 53). The photograph attempts to capture the visitor's imagination of the space that combines her affective experiences and a discursive engagement with the historical past. The composition of the photograph is both a staged and imminent performance of Robert Schuman House (Scarles 2009, 485), in which the visitor's act of walking on Schuman's path, literally and metaphorically, intersect. For the visitor, the photograph provides an opportunity for exploration, adjustment, and understanding via her intersubjective experiences: it becomes a vehicle through which the performative spaces of heritage are activated and enlivened (Scarles 2009, 485).

Photography is one of many ways, in which visitors actively and creatively engage with heritage experiences inherent and prompted by poly-space. When entering the former camp of Westerbork, visitors face the former house of the camp commander, which is surrounded by a glass structure. We are used to finding objects under glass when visiting museums, but the view of a house under glass provokes a sudden realization of the bizarreness of the heritage site (Figure 8.5). While visitors encountering objects in showcases in a museum have the choice whether to pass and ignore them or not, this time they are forced to notice a whole house under a glass construction. The view simultaneously requires and provokes some sort of response, which sets in motion different processes of reflection and interpretation regarding the current and past uses of the site, and their spatial qualities. Visitors are forced to rethink their own position, including whether they are inside or already outside the

Figure 8.5 The Commander's House re-photographed from a visitor's photograph. Camp Westerbork, the Netherlands. Photo: EUROHERIT

heritage site. This photograph captures the visitor's processes of interpretation that link her subjective experiences of the space and her cognitive knowledge of the past, which become equally important for conceiving the heritage site as embedded within poly-space, as the following quote shows:

> just the idea: that it is a normal house now when you walk around it, but in that time it must have had a whole different association. When you passed that house, someone who had a lot of power over your life was living there. And such a building loses this emotional value over the years.
>
> (VS3/6)

Affective experiences can become interwoven with broader discussions, such as the emotional values ascribed to an object and the past. Similarly, the photograph of the house under glass manages to transmit the significant recognition, sensation, or feeling that something is out of place or provoke intensive affective experiences, which do not need to have the same effect when narrated. In this, the visitor's photograph can be seen as "a felt, subjective and embodied positioning", subject to particular historical contexts and conditions (see Sather-Wagstaff 2015, 191) that helps us to understand the meaning of heritage sites, history, and objects that only arises in the interaction between bodies or people and their material and natural environment (Staiff 2012, 42).

This photograph also shows how the visitor's body resonates in and becomes permeable for experiences and observations of poly-space.

The visitors' photographs also connect to the question of the 'authenticity' of heritage. For instance, a Dutch couple in their late 60s took photographs of the train and rails at the Camp Westerbork. Partly, these pictures acted as a reminder of the past, "the idea that people can do this to each other", as the woman put it, but they also confirmed personal stories they had been told by their parents about World War II. As she explained:

> the combination really makes an impression on me. My mother also had a number of classmates who all of a sudden disappeared from school. And they found the letters that people threw out of the train, next to the tracks. That's what my mother said.
>
> (VS3/3)

While the photograph is a creation, it also serves as a "trace of reality" (Muntéan 2017, 205). The letters and other objects in the exhibition at the heritage site confirmed the visitor's mother's stories and added another layer of 'authenticity' to her visit. Authenticity in this context must be understood as "dynamic, performative, culturally and historically contingent, relative" (Silverman 2015, 69), and strategically enhancing affective experiences for the visitor. The photographs, then, are a performance that combines affective experiences evoked by the knowledge the visitor (believes they) have about history, and confirmed by the knowledge and affective experiences imparted by the heritage site, thus "enacting and mixing multiple levels of heritage, stories and experiences together" (Halderup and Bærenholdt 2015, 65; see Lean 2012, 278).

Blurred boundaries

As discussed in Chapter 7, affective experiences and atmospheres are very powerful elements in heritage visits that can create very strong visceral experiences in the visitors. Many of their photographs are attempts to engage with precisely this sensation of poly-space. EHL sites become infused with "affective atmospheres" (Tolia-Kelly 2017, 36) and contribute to attuning us to the dynamics and pluralities of particular narrative constructions across time and space. While membranes can act as boundaries between different layers, visitors also engage with the transcendence of these boundaries, as testified in their photographs.

For instance, one visitor to Carnuntum photographed his partner lying on a sofa in the hall of the thermal bath, re-enacting the role of a Roman visitor (Figure 8.6). However, in the interview the photographer explained that he had taken the picture because of its ambiguity. On the one hand, the photograph represented a memory of the fun of acting out Roman times and conveyed the beautiful design and decoration of the site, which partly raised doubt about how 'truthful' this reconstruction was of the Roman original. On the other hand, for others unfamiliar with this heritage site, this photograph could just be a holiday snap from a stay in a modern spa, as everything looked new and in perfect shape. Thus, the photographer tried to convey with the photograph the blurred boundaries between the present and past and express what he had experienced in this moment. The photograph attempted to capture affective experiences and interpretations, and thereby it embodied visualities that enabled the encounter between materiality and corporeality inspired by what the visitors had seen, heard, felt, and sensed (see Scarles 2009, 474). As the photographer put it:

> we had lots of fun, because we thought about how life must have been in those days and, and that it's not so much different than today, you know, because it's really a, quite a, luxurious place. And I also wondered to what extent this room – to what extent that room was faithful to the actual state of things in those times. Because it was so luxurious, so nice, that it almost, it can almost be a nice stay in a hotel or a villa in Tuscany, you know.
>
> (VS2/2)

The picture taken by another visitor to Carnuntum similarly expresses the blurred boundaries of the spatial and temporal dimensions of heritage sites. She shared a photograph that she had sent to her mother as a greeting from Carnuntum, and which showed a glass of *Eiskaffee* (cold coffee with ice cream) in the foreground and the reconstructed Roman thermal bath in the background. The visitor herself referred to the photograph during the interview as representing "the modern pleasure in ancient Rome", thus playfully combining different influences that guided her visit (VS2/12). Her photograph attempted to capture the affective experience of time travel during the visit that, on the one hand, reconciled the distance between past and present, and, on the other, could still evoke happy and pleasant memories and feelings in the future.

Some visitor photographs, like the picture of Robert Schuman's car, a dark Simca Aronda, or the photograph showing a (staged) shop and fridge from communist Poland in the 1980s, show items that seem to play only an inferior role in the narratives of the respective site. However, they may be meaningful in relation to the experience of poly-space. While such photographed objects may reflect the visitors' temporary interests in certain objects during their visit to the heritage site, they also refer to personal memories related to these objects or to stories from the past (Lean 2012, 275). The visitor photographs play a role in stimulating embodied memories of encounters, places, relationships, performances, and moments that act as "symbols of our past experiences" and at the same time "evoke and animate memories, which inform our present self" (see Bærenholdt et al. 2004, 117; Morgan and Pritchard 2005, 41). Equally, these photographs give evidence of how the visitor attributes more than symbolic

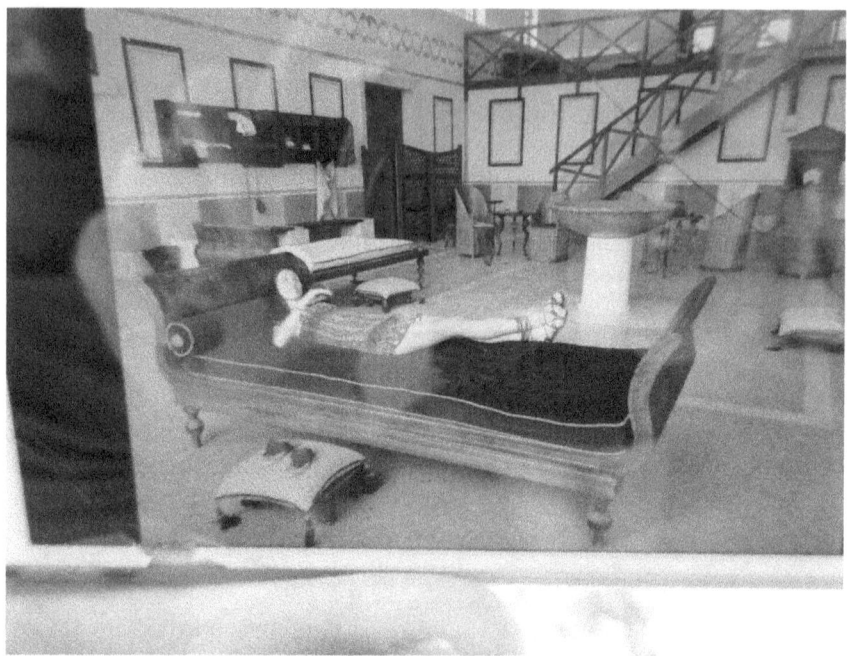

Figure 8.6 The re-enactment of Roman times. Archaeological Park Carnuntum, Austria.
        Photo: EUROHERIT

understandings to a specific heritage site, which can also facilitate processes of identification.

While the car at Robert Schuman House reminded the photographer of his childhood and of a relative who used to own such a car, it also referred to the visitor's impression of Schuman still lingering in his home. The displayed objects and furniture in the house seemed to be preserved in the late 1950s or early 1960s, and this allowed the visitor to travel back to a time with which he could identify. Following the logic of the staged house, Schuman's car in the garage created the notion that he was only temporally absent. While the practice of staging at heritage sites certainly guides the visitor's gaze and inter-pretation, the photographs are not just "static, distanced and disembodied" encounters or representations (Bærenholdt et al. 2004, 101) but can capture emotive and affective experiences. Similarly, the picture of the empty shop was taken by a young Polish couple, born years after the events of the Solidarity Movement, who had no personal recollection of communist Poland. However, seeing the shop and fridge during their visit, they were reminded of their parents' stories about food shortages and empty shelves in the shops. Time often acts as boundary between then and now and complicates notions of identifi-cation. However, the photograph of the young couple expresses a notion of identification with the stories of their parents and thereby helps to reconcile and mutually reinforce narratives of the past with the present self.

The same can be said about the visitor photographs of Liszt Academy of Music, which give evidence of how visitors try to make sense of the past and thereby blur boundaries. Many visitors stated in the interviews that they were impressed by the size of Liszt's hands, made visible in the exhibition by the display of different casts. These casts of his hands also figure in several photographs, in which the visitors compared Liszt's hands with their own. Photographing Liszt's hand casts helped the visitors to validate their ideas about Liszt's musical genius and to get a feeling for his musical skills. The physical act of touching helps to create a felt experience that includes reflection and positions the visitors in "webs of affects and other cultural frames and occurrences, in atmospheres" (Crouch 2015, 179). The visitor bodies facilitate the transportation of meanings and ideas connected with the heritage visit.

Empathy and creative performance

Photographs are performative acts that can give evidence of how visitors engage empathetically, creatively, and in some cases with artistic skill, with the past and memory at the heritage sites. For instance, the memory of the Holocaust is strongly associated with the images of rails and train wagons, and likewise images of these at Camp Westerbork symbolize the detention and deportation that led most detainees to death. An EHL Panel Report on Monitoring (EC 2016) also uses a picture of the memorial made of bent rails next to a former watchtower to illustrate Camp Westerbork. Visitors can freely walk around these objects and several visitors seized upon these leitmotifs and took pictures of the train wagon, the rails and the watchtower.

One young student visiting Camp Westerbork engaged very aesthetically with the site but at the same time managed to produce a valuable experience of trying to capture a feeling and understanding of the past. Compared to other visitors, she chose a different perspective on the objects. In one of her photographs (Figure 8.7), she focused on the underside of the train wagon, creating the impression of a moving train. This photograph recalled the role trains had played in the Holocaust and alluded to specific stories of people throwing letters and postcards from the trains as their last greeting to friends and relatives. Some of these messages are displayed in the exhibition of Camp Westerbork, and the stories of transportation is further highlighted by pictures and films showing people arriving and leaving the camp by train. These stories and pictures are strongly charged with emotions such as sadness, fear, and despair, to which visitors also referred in the interviews. The student's photograph manages to transmit such emotions, but the full potential of the affective experience would not be possible to grasp without prior knowledge of the Holocaust. Her photograph directly interacts with the discursive and visual representation of the past at the site. As she explained, she attempted with her

Figure 8.7 The train on the rails. Camp Westerbork, the Netherlands. Photo: EUROHERIT

photographs to capture the "history that is behind an object" (VS3/6). While her choice of motif reinforces a "collective gaze" on the past, such photographs are never just representations but constructed as mediated discursive spaces and infused with subjective, reflexive engagements (Scarles 2009, 269). The photograph attempts to embody the visual, polysensory, and manifold ways in which the visitor encounters heritage, imaginatively, cognitively, and experientially (see Scarles 2009, 466–468; Crouch 2015).

Her photograph creatively catches the narrative of the site, and a viewer equipped with knowledge of its history is hit by the powerful expression of what this object intends to convey. Photographs can be seen as an affective way of engaging with the past, in which knowing about it plays an important role in conveying affects. Similar to a 'resonating membrane', the visitor's body reacts to multiple stimulations during the visit to a heritage site, processes these experiences, and encourages reflection on the representation of heritage. Performative practices transform the visitor from a passive recipient into a social actor who produces their own meanings with the spaces and facilitates diverse processes of meaning-making (see Bagnall 2003, 87; Schorch, Waterton, and Watson 2017, 97).

The act of photographing actively involves the visitor in reflection on the past and in creative interpretation of their affective experiences and sensations provoked by the visit to the heritage site. Memory is not only reified and contained in artefacts, buildings, or places, but constructed through engagement with material objects in space and over time, making it more than just a thing (Sather-Wagstaff 2015, 195). Camp Westerbork is an EHL site that deals with memory work related to difficult history (Macdonald 2009), dissonant heritage (Tunbridge and Ashworth 1996), or heritage that hurts (Sather-Wagstaff 2011), and photographs are an embodied way of engaging with this heritage.

Diverging heritage interpretations

During the analysis, we became interested in what the visitors' photographs could tell us about their affective and interpretive engagement with those EHL sites that lack a coherent or affective narrative. For instance, the exhibition at Lieu d'Europe, commissioned by the City of Strasbourg, mediates the shared history of the city and Europe by introducing the functions and values of the European institutions located in Strasbourg and by referring to important women and men of Europe's recent history. In the interviews, visitors describe the exhibition as informative but also as very sober and "graphically poorly done" (VS4/14), without eliciting any affective or emotional response. Similarly, the Mundaneum is not an easy heritage site for visitors. It received the EHL for the archive and the ideas embodied by its founders, Paul Otlet and Henri La Fontaine, but access to the archive is limited to research visits by scholars and artists. It is difficult for visitors to establish a connection between the content of the exhibition and the Mundaneum as an EHL site. Also access to facts about the history and heritage of the Sagres Promontory was limited as a storm had recently destroyed its exhibition halls, which were undergoing reconstruction during our fieldwork. Without either an exhibition or a well-functioning information centre, the visit to the promontory was dominated by the view of the fort and the surrounding landscape.

Left to imagine what the site was about for themselves, most of the visitors simply let the atmospheric experiences of the promontory work on them, which often evoked affective experiences. As one visitor explained:

> I took a panorama that included the, you know, basically the cliff edges, like the edge of the world. And I mean, you can understand that [...] a few hundred years ago, they believed that the world ends on a cliff. Maybe the latter ends in a cliff and the world is flat.
>
> (VS11/33)

The interviews show that the visitors' interpretation of the site is largely subjective and bodily, related to the combined polysensory engagements and spatial quality of the visit (Haldrup and Bærenholdt 2015, 63; Sather-Wagstaff 2017, 15). Their photographs represent attempts to capture the beauty and power of nature, such as the landscape, cliffs, wind, sun, the waves, and birds.

Inspired by the natural limitation of the space, several visitors claimed during the interview that they felt as if they were "at the end of the known world" (VS11/10). However, visitors process their experiences in individual ways in relation to context and location and can feel differently affected by what they see and feel. As Dudley (2010, 10) states:

> [o]ur senses, spatial locations and movements determine how we experience and interpret the world of which we are a part, and in turn those spatial aspects and our senses themselves are culturally constituted: rather than simply biologically determined givens, they fluctuate not just within our individual mental realms but across time, places and culture.

Limited to the affective engagement, visitors can nevertheless gain an insight into the contextual significance, time, and place of the heritage site, experiencing conflicting feelings (Edwards 2010, 26). As a young woman explained, while "the ocean was very peaceful", she got the opposite feeling when she saw the fort's gun turrets and cannons:

> so it's kind of this contradictory between, you know, it's very peaceful and everything right now, and I'm very glad I can enjoy it right now, and I don't have to be here when it was, if it was ever having to protect against intruders or something like that.
>
> (VS11/9)

At Sagres Promontory, language is not the central means of experiencing, interpreting, and making meaning of the heritage but the visitors predominantly rely on affective, polysensory, and embodied practices, taking numerous photographs. In comparison, significantly fewer pictures were taken at the Mundaneum and Lieu d'Europe. However, even at these two sites, we could observe in the visitor photographs and interviews that intellectual and text-based engagements with the exhibition can produce some affect and enable visitors to gain control over their heritage experience, which may in turn produce affective interpretations.

In the photographs, the visitors to Lieu d'Europe and Mundaneum intuitively picked up something from the exhibition that amplified their affective experiences. For instance, a young woman at Mundaneum took a picture of a quote by Alan Turing, who with his team managed to break the enigma code during World War II, which read: "[f]inding your way is a personal matter, a matter of readings, meetings, family sometimes, friendship most often". Although she claimed in the interview that the exhibition, entitled "TOP SECRET. A World of Codes and Ciphers", dealt with "things you couldn't take pictures of" (VS9/10), this message captured the idea of empowerment and interaction, which she found important. Similarly, a Swiss visitor photographed a German proverb on the upper floor of the Lieu d'Europe (hosting the Information Centre on

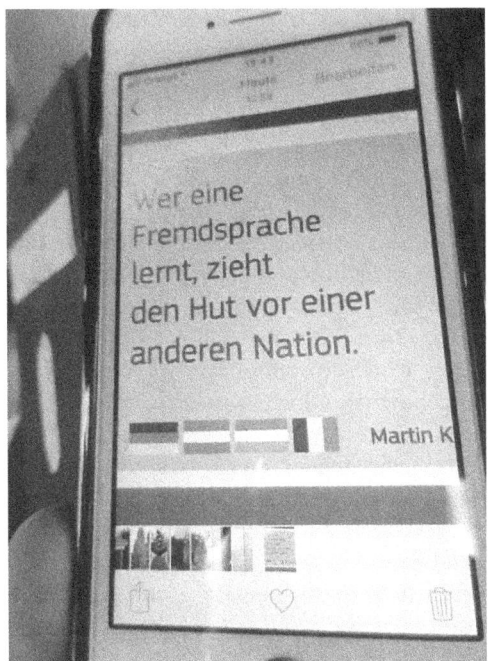

Figure 8.8 The proverb. Lieu d'Europe in Strasbourg, France. Photo: EUROHERIT

European Institutions, CIIE), which read "[a]nyone who learns a foreign language, honours another nation" (Figure 8.8). The choice of motif supported the visitor's personal interpretation of the most important message of her visit, which she wanted to take back home. Photographs can stimulate memories and emotions inherent in the objects and spaces of a visit (Scarles 2009) but can also capture and make tangible memories and emotions beyond those represented at the sites, thus containing very nuanced and deep personal meanings.

In all three cases, the visitors' interpretation differed more from the intended messages at these sites than at those other EHL sites that provided a more balanced access to the heritage narrative and opportunity for affective engagement. Nevertheless, visitors were still able to form personally meaningful interpretations of these heritage sites. The knowledge production and interpretation of history resulted from the visitors' embodied practices and polysensory engagements with Sagres Promontory, while at Lieu d'Europe and Mundaneum, affective experiences were entangled with intellectual approaches and interpretative processes.

Embodied heritage

Bodies in heritage can be understood as both sticky objects and resonating membranes. The interplay between sticky and resonating bodies is at work

during a visit to a heritage site, and they are of equal importance for producing and absorbing affect and knowledge. Bodies as sticky objects are able to
evoke empathy and initiate processes of reflection and interpretation. At the
same time, the emotive quality of an object or body can create lasting stickiness
and influence future interpretations and understandings. Bodies as resonating
membranes function as a filter that helps to select, absorb, and transform certain ideas and affective experiences. This resonating self reverberates within a
wide range of experiences, practices, and activities encountered at heritage sites.
While discursive representations may reinforce affective experiences, lack of
affective engagement and narrative can limit the intensity and extent of a heritage experience for visitors (see Macdonald 2013).

The stickiness of representation articulates culturally embedded interpretations as affectively charged attachments, which support the promotion of
Europe's "heroic and extraordinary" past. At the same time, such representation favours the transmission of specific gender, racial, and social stereotypes,
which has an impact on our understanding of Europe's heritage and of who
belongs to Europe. However, our research shows that heritage representations
can contribute to stirring up and breaking with preconceived images, ideas,
and ideologies. The EHL sites can help to challenge the unilateral representation of diversity, and the visitor's affective practices and activities encourage
linking between the past and present across diverse backgrounds and histories.
Affective understanding creates the opportunity to broaden traded perceptions
and understandings of Europe and thereby directly influence processes of
constructing belonging to Europe.

Bodies are resonating membranes that respond and form polysensory and
cognitive processes of meaning-making. In this context, photographs have the
capacity to capture and preserve the embodied intensities of such encounter and
re-evoke the polysensory experiences that were felt at a specific place and time
and in a specific context, which can produce new and potentially conflicting
insights for the visitor (Scarles 2009, 482; Edwards 2010, 25). As heritage is not
a "thing but, rather, a process" (Schramm 2015, 442), heritage sites must therefore be understood as spaces in which "transformative experiences are possible
because of the ability of objects to reach out and literally touch someone"
(Witcomb 2010, 40).

In their photographs, visitors attempt to reconcile the different ways and
cues, which form their understanding and experience of the site. While
photographs do not always reflect the narrative of the site, they often show that
heritage visits stimulate visitors to creatively merge what they feel there and
what thoughts and associations a site provokes in them into a creative meaning-
making. The visitor photographs may generate empathy with the historical
experiences of others, thereby meeting the educative objective to learn from
the past. At the same time, they also present a form of affective practice that
activates processes of reflection during and after the visit. The photograph itself

can be seen as co-performing affective experiences that produce and highlight 'authentic' notions of heritage at the time when the picture is taken, and again later when reviewing the picture. The photograph not only creates visual memories but it transmits the affective experiences at the site and thus helps people establish realities and produce tangible memory through concrete bodily performance (Haldrup and Larsen 2003, 27; Scarles 2009, 471). The photograph helps to embody memories, emotions, and moments, which can still later elicit corporeal and multisensory reactions (see Lean 2012, 277).

The representation and affective experiences of bodies intersect with the generation of empathy. Empathy is profoundly affective in that it triggers and sets in motion embodied practices and acts of meaning-making that shape the ways in which heritage is experienced and imagined (Wetherell 2012; Schorch; Waterton, and Watson 2017, 94). Similarly, empathy can help to produce notions of solidarity and acceptance in a heterogeneous society or polity such as the contemporary EU. As a side-effect, empathy simultaneously contributes to consolidating ideas and categories of people, and thus can also participate in the strengthening of AHD, instead of promoting alternative and more inclusive narratives. Hence, empathy can prompt new social and political processes of interpretation of what Europe is now and can be in future, based on the understanding of the past and become thus relevant in relation to the transformative potential of heritage (see Delanty 2017, 186).

References

Ahmed, S. 2004 "Affective Economies." *Social Text* 22 (2): 114–139. Project MUSE, muse.jhu.edu/article/55780.

Ahmed, S. 2014. *The Cultural Politics of Emotion.* Edinburgh: Edinburgh University Press.

Anderson, B. 2009. "Affective Atmospheres." *Emotion, Space and Society* 2(2): 77–81. doi: 10.1016/j.emospa.2009.08.005

Bærenholdt, J. O., M. H. Pedersen, J. Larsen, and J. Urry. 2004. *Performing Tourist Places.* Aldershot: Ashgate.

Bagnall, G. 2003. "Performance and Performativity at Heritage Sites." *Museum and Society* 1 (2): 87–103. doi: 10.29311/mas.v1i2.17.

Clough, P. T. 2009. "The New Empiricism: Affect and Sociological Method." *European Journal of Social Theory* 12 (1): 43–61. doi: 10.1177/1368431008099643.

Crang, M., and D. P. Tolia-Kelly. 2010. "Nation, Race and Affect: Sense and Sensibilities at National Heritage Sites." *Environment and Planning A* 42 (10): 2315–2331. doi: 10.1068/a4346.

Crouch, D. 2010. "The Perpetual Performance and Emergence of Heritage." In *Culture, Heritage and Representation: Perspectives on Visuality and the Past*, edited by S. Watson, and E. Waterton, 57–71. Farnham: Ashgate.

Crouch, D. 2015. "Affect, Heritage, Feeling." In *The Palgrave Handbook of Contemporary Heritage Research*, edited by E. Waterton, and S. Watson, 177–190. London: Palgrave Macmillan.

Delanty, G. 2017. *The European Heritage: A Critical Re-Interpretation*. London: Routledge.

Deleuze, G., and F, Guatteri. 1987. *A Thousand Plateaus*. London: Continuum.

Dicks, B. 2015. "Heritage and Social Class." In *The Palgrave Handbook of Contemporary Heritage Research*, edited by E. Waterton, and S. Watson, 366–381. London: Palgrave Macmillan.

Dittmer, J., and E. Waterton. 2017. "Affecting the Body: Cultures of Militarism at the Australian War Memorial." In *Heritage, Affect and Emotion: Politics, Practices and Infrastructures*, edited by D. P. Tolia-Kelly, E. Waterton, and S. Watson, 47–74. London: Routledge.

Dudley, S. H. 2010. "Museum Materialities: Objects, Sense and Feeling." In *Museum Materialities. Objects, Engagements, Interpretations*, edited by S. H. Dudley, 1–17. London: Routledge.

Edwards, E. 2010. "Photographs and History: Emotion and Materiality." In *Museum Materialities. Objects, Engagements, Interpretations*, edited by S. H. Dudley, 21–38. London: Routledge.

Frykman, J., and M. Povrzanović Frykman. 2015. "Affect and Material Culture: Perspectives and Strategies." In *Sensitive Objects: Affect and Material Culture*, edited by J. Frykman, and M. Povrzanović Frykman, 9–28. Lund: Nordic Academic Press.

Haldrup, M. and J. Larsen. 2003. "The Family Gaze." Tourist Studies 3 (1): 23–45. doi: 10.1177/1468797603040529.

Haldrup, M., and J. O. Bærenholdt. 2015. "Heritage as Performance." In *The Palgrave Handbook of Contemporary Heritage Research*, edited by Waterton, E., and S. Watson, 52–68. London: Palgrave Macmillan.

Kaasik-Krogerus, S. 2018. "Mediating 'Eastern' Bodies: A Case Study of the Solidarity Center." Paper presented at *Sovereign Bodies and Bodily Sovereignty: Mediation of Body in Semi-Authoritarian Countries*, Leeds, April 11–12.

Lähdesmäki, T. 2017. "Politics of Affect in the EU Heritage Policy Discourse: An Analysis of Promotional Videos of Sites Awarded with the European Heritage Label." *International Journal of Heritage Studies* 23 (8): 709–722. doi: 10.1080/13527258.2017.1317649.

Lähdesmäki, T. 2018. "Founding Myths of European Union Europe and the Workings of Power in the European Union Heritage and History Initiatives." *European Journal of Cultural Studies*. doi: 10.1177/1367549418755921.

Lean, G. 2012. "The Lingering Moment." In *The Cultural Moment in Tourism*, edited by L. Smith, E. Waterton, and S. Watson, 274–291. London: Routledge.

Macdonald, S. 2009. *Difficult Heritage*. Oxford and New York: Routledge.

Macdonald, S. 2013. *Memorylands: Heritage and Identity in Europe Today*. London: Routledge.

Merleau-Ponty, M. (1945) 2006. *Phenomenology of Perception*. Translated by Colin Smith. Reprint, London: Routledge.

Morgan, N., and A. Pritchard. 2005. "On Souvenirs and Metonymy: Narratives of Memory, Metaphor and Materiality." *Tourist Studies* 5 (1): 29–53. doi: 10.1177/1468797605062714.

Munroe, L. 2017. "Constructing Affective Narratives in Transatlantic Slavery Museums in the UK." In *Heritage, Affect and Emotion. Politics, Practices and Infrastructures*, edited by D. P. Tolia-Kelly, E. Waterton, and S. Watson, 114–132. London: Routledge.

Muntéan, L. 2017. "Touching Time: Photography, Affect and the Digital Archive." In *Heritage, Affect and Emotion. Politics, Practices and Infrastructures*, edited by D. P. Tolia-Kelly, E. Waterton, and S. Watson, 201–218. London: Routledge.

Nora, P. 1998. "The Era of Commemoration." In *Realms of Memory. The Construction of the French Past, Volume III: Symbols*, edited by P. Nora, 609–637. New York: Columbia University Press.

Papoulias, C., and F. Callard. 2010. "Biology's Gift: Interrogating the Turn to Affect." *Body and Society* 16 (1): 29–56. doi: 10.1177/1357034X09355231.

Sather-Wagstaff, J. 2011. *Heritage that Hurts: Tourists in the Memoryscapes of September 11*. London: Routledge.

Sather-Wagstaff, J. 2015. "Heritage and Memory." In *The Palgrave Handbook of Contemporary Heritage Research*, edited by E. Waterton, and S. Watson, 191–204. London: Palgrave Macmillan.

Sather-Wagstaff, J. 2017. "Making Polysense of the World: Affect, Memory, Heritage." In *Heritage, Affect and Emotion: Politics, Practices and Infrastructures*, edited by D. P. Tolia-Kelly, E. Waterton, and S. Watson, 12–29. London: Routledge.

Scarles, C. 2009. "Becoming Tourist: Renegotiating the Visual in the Tourist Experience." *Environment and Planning D: Society and Space* 27 (3): 465–488. doi: 10.1068/d1707.

Schorch, P., E. Waterton, and S. Watson. 2017. "Museum Canopies and Affective Cosmopolitanism: Cultivating Cross-cultural Landscapes for Ethical Embodied Responses." In *Heritage, Affect and Emotion. Politics, Practices and Infrastructures*, edited by D. P. Tolia-Kelly, E. Waterton, and S. Watson, 93–113. London: Routledge.

Schramm, K. 2015. "Heritage, Power, Ideology." In *The Palgrave Handbook of Contemporary Heritage Research*, edited by E. Waterton, and S. Watson, 442–457. London: Palgrave Macmillan.

Silverman, H. 2015. "Heritage and Authenticity." In *The Palgrave Handbook of Contemporary Heritage Research*, edited by E. Waterton, and S. Watson, 69–90. London: Palgrave Macmillan.

Smith, L. 2006. *Uses of Heritage*. London: Routledge.

Staiff, R. 2012. "The Somatic and the Aesthetic: Embodied Heritage Tourism Experiences of Luang Prabang, Laos." In *The Cultural Moment in Tourism*, edited by L. Smith, E. Waterton, and S. Watson, 38–55. London: Routledge.

Staiff, R. 2014. *Re-imagining Heritage Interpretation: Enchanting the Past-future*. Aldershot: Ashgate.

Thrift, N. 2004. "Intensities of Feeling: Towards a Spatial Politics of Affect." *Geografiska Annaler, Series B: Human Geography* 86B (1): 57–78. doi: 10.1111/j.0435-3684.2004.00154.x.

Tolia-Kelly, D. P. 2017. "Race and Affect at the Museum: The Museum as a Theatre of Pain." In *Heritage, Affect and Emotion: Politics, Practices and Infrastructures*, edited by D. P. Tolia-Kelly, E. Waterton, and S. Watson, 33–46. London: Routledge.

Tolia-Kelly, D. P., E. Waterton, and S. Watson. 2017. *Heritage, Affect and Emotion: Politics, Practices and Infrastructures*. London: Routledge.

Trenz, H.-J. 2014. *The Saga of Europeanisation: On the Narrative Construction of a European Society*. (ARENA Working Paper 7 July 2014). Oslo: Arena. www.sv.uio.no/arena/english/research/publications/arena-working-papers/2014/wp7-14.pdf.

Tunbridge, J. E., and G. J. Ashworth. 1996. *Dissonant Heritage: The Management of the Past as a Resource in Conflict*. Chichester: J. Wiley.

Turunen, J. n.d. Borderscapes of Europe: Cultural Production of Border Imaginaries through European Heritage." Unpublished manuscript.

Turunen, J., V. L. A. Čeginskas, S. Kaasik-Krogerus, T. Lähdesmäki, and K. Mäkinen. Forthcoming. "Poly-Space: Creating New Concepts Through Reflexive Team

Ethnography." In *Challenges and Solutions in Ethnographic Research: Ethnography with a Twist*, edited by T. Lähdesmäki, E. Koskinen-Koivisto, V. L. A. Čeginskas, and A.-K. Koistinen. London: Routledge.

Waterton, E. 2014. "A More-Than-Representational Understanding of Heritage? The 'Past' and the Politics of Affect." *Geography Compass* 8 (11): 823–833. doi: 10.1111/gec3.12182.

Waterton, E., and S. Watson. 2013. "Framing Theory: Towards a Critical Imagination in Heritage Studies." *International Journal of Heritage Studies* 19 (6): 546–561. doi: 10.1080/13527258.2013.779295.

Waterton, E., and S. Watson. 2014. *The Semiotics of Heritage Tourism*. Bristol: Channel View Publication.

Watson, S., E. Waterton, and L. Smith. 2012. "Moments, Instances and Experiences." In *The Cultural Moment in Tourism*, edited by L. Smith, E. Waterton, and S. Watson. New York: Routledge.

Wetherell, M. 2012. *Affect and Emotion: A New Social Science Understanding*. London: Sage.

Wetherell, M. 2015. "Trends in the Turn to Affect: A Social Psychological Critique." *Body & Society* 21 (2): 139–166. doi: 10.1177/1357034X14539020.

Witcomb, A. 2010. "Using Objects to Remember the Dead and Affect the Living: The Case of a Miniature Model of Treblinka." In *Museum Materialities: Objects, Engagements, Interpretations*, edited by S. H. Dudley, 39–52. London: Routledge.

Witcomb, A. 2013. "Understanding the Role of Affect in Producing A critical Pedagogy for History Museums." *Museum Management and Curatorship* 28 (3): 255–271. doi: 10.1080/09647775.2013.807998.

Chapter 9

Europe's gendered heritage

Gender can be used as an analytical category to explore how societies and their structures are perceived in the everyday. Previous work on gender in heritage studies has focused on representation, and on how gender performances and roles interact and are articulated within museums, heritage sites, monuments, and heritage collections (e.g. Nenadic 1994; Porter 1996; Sørensen 1999; Sørensen 2000). While gender can inform the understanding of material culture, cultural practices, space, and identity, newer research is informed by critical gender studies that consider whose identities are being represented and reinforced, and what consequences a gendered perspective has on contemporary culture and society (Smith 2008, 159, 2006; Waterton and Watson 2015; Grahn and Wilson 2018).

Over the past 20 years, intersectionality, connected to feminist standpoint theory, has become more important in the critical analysis of gender in heritage and curatorial practices (Crenshaw 1991; Porter 1996; Summers 2000; Lykke 2003, 2010; de los Reyes and Mulinari 2005; Grahn 2011; Robert 2014). These studies contribute to understanding the effects of mutually reinforced hierarchical power relations in society that are often intertwined with structures of oppression and taken-for-granted processes of identity construction. Discussions about the connections between heritage and gender, both in history and in present representations and discourses of complex power relations in society, can alter hegemonic discourses of power and social, political, and cultural norms. The theory of intersectionality emphasizes the conceptual category of gender and how it acts and intersects with other social categories, such as class, race, ethnicity, nationality, sexual preference, or dis/ability. In intersectionality theory, gender can be used to critique modern society through addressing social, political, and cultural inequalities (Reading 2015; Grahn 2018, 266). As Smith (2008, 159) points out, gender constructions have a range of implications for the perception, value, and argumentation of women, men, and their social roles, as politically or culturally neutral construction, commemoration, and expression of gender identities is impossible, also in heritage.

In a recent edited volume on gender and heritage, Grahn and Wilson (2018) seek to combine the approaches of critical gender and heritage studies to recognize the increasingly central role of gender in heritage. Critical gender heritage studies aim to draw attention to the role of gender in the consumption of heritage in society that goes beyond the construction of identity, and explore the impact of gender constructions on society (see Reading 2015, 401). The combined field of critical gender heritage studies challenges the lack of intersectionality, peripheral location, or absence of critical gendered perspectives, and the stereotypical depictions of gender in dominant heritage discourses, representations, and performances (Wilson 2018, 6). The aim of this critical gendered viewpoint is to look beyond gender and to assess "the policy, practice, economics and ethics of cultural heritage to ensure a movement towards social justice" (Wilson 2018, 10), highlighting the political, intersectional motivations that are at the core of critical gender heritage studies and shape cultural heritage.

Gender equality has been a defining characteristic of European equality policy since the Treaty of Rome (1957), which introduced the regulation on equality between women and men in the labour market as part of the principle of non-discrimination (1957, Art. 119). The non-discrimination policy has had a major influence on the European economic and social integration process and on advancing new non-discrimination rights in the member states. However, the European Community's public actions regarding gender equality were limited until the early 1990s (Jacquot 2015, 24). The idea of equality between women and men is a pillar of EU social policy and an essential value and fundamental right that has both a social and economic function in the framework of the common European economic and labour market (Jacquot 2015, 35). Since the 1980s, the European Community and later the EU has strengthened measures to promote the equal treatment of women and men in access to employment, societal participation, child care, and social security. With the Treaty of Amsterdam (1997, articles 3 and 13), the EU extended the advancement of equal treatment and gender equality between women and men as a political goal, as well as the promotion of non-discrimination legislation and developments, beyond the member states. The repetitive references to "equality between women and men" as opposed "between genders" reinforces the binary norm of gender representations in EU documents.

As a fundamental value of the EU, strengthening and promoting equality between women and men is included in the objectives and criteria of the EHL. Although the decision on the EHL action (EP&C 2011, 1, 3) does not explicitly ask the sites to promote gender equality, it underlines shared values as the bases for strengthening a sense of belonging to the EU and support for European integration. For instance, applicants have been asked to describe in the application form "to what extent [has] your site significantly contributed to the development and/or promotion of one or more of these values" (EC 2014, 7). Through direct references to official EU treaties, the EHL application form during the first three selection rounds explicitly refers to equality between women and men as one of the EU's fundamental values that the sites are expected to demonstrate, thereby reproducing the treaties' exclusionary rhetoric as discussed earlier.

While we understand that gender includes positions outside of the perceived categories of women and men, the EHL sites in our data maintain and transmit a normative binary understanding of gender. As a result of our field research, we have roughly classified the 11 EHL sites into two groups. Some sites accentuate the male perspective and contribution to Europe's societies and political, social, and cultural life in the past and present, whereas other sites attempt to include a more balanced, but still binary, perspective on gender in their narratives. In this chapter, we first discuss the EHL sites that present a strong male bias, before turning to the other sites that attempt to include women in their narratives and highlight a female view of heritage. The data used encompasses the site exhibitions and documentation materials, our field research notes, and photographs taken at the sites. In addition, we draw on the analysis of interviews that were conducted with visitors and heritage practitioners at the sites and with officials at the European Commission. Our close reading of the data was guided by our interest in the representation of gender and gendered narratives at the EHL sites, and how these representations and narratives were produced and naturalized. In our reading, we also utilize the affect and embodiment theories discussed in Chapters 7 and 8.

Male biased and gender-blind narratives

The European Commission has awarded the EHL to two sites that focus on the EU's 'Founding Fathers', Robert Schuman and Alcide De Gasperi. The founding myth of the EU incorporates a strong white, male, Western-European bias into heritage (see Smith 2006, 2008) that stands in the tradition of framing the past by emphasizing important historical men and prioritizes their political and military activities (see Joyce 1996; Warner 2000). Besides the home museums of these two men, the Franz Liszt Memorial Museum and Sagres Promontory can be seen as reflecting "gender-blindness" (Grahn 2018, 263) in their exhibitions by constructing a dominating male narrative, without addressing unequal power relations. Moreover, the gendered narratives and naturalized male positions at these sites are affectively – and, thus effectively – transmitted through drawing on 'authentic' and intimate views of the lives of 'Europe's Great Men'.

By personalizing the exhibitions with pictures, staged props, (replicas of) personal objects, letters, and documents, the exhibitions at the former homes of Robert Schuman and Alcide De Gasperi convey an intimate and empathetic view into the political and private lives of these two men. The displays and objects instil a notion of connection in the visitors and seemingly offer an 'authentic' and intimate glimpse in the lives of the two men. In our interviews, visitors to Robert Schuman House frequently claimed that the site managed to convey the impression that Schuman was still present in the house. One of the heritage practitioners (P32) working at this site explained that after Schuman's death there was a desire to preserve the house to enable a deep immersion in his life that emphasized the contrast between the simplicity of his lifestyle and his extraordinary work and writings. There are no signs or information boards in the building in order to make the house look 'natural'. The furnishing, with his worn-out armchair and the display of intimate objects, such as a toothbrush, toothpaste or a razor, create the impression that Schuman only recently left the house.

Similarly, the exhibition of the Franz Liszt Memorial Museum tries to create a 'true' representation of Liszt and his lifetime by displaying original objects, books, and instruments that belonged to him. The staging of furniture from the period in which he lived furthermore suggests that they were his own. Moreover, the recordings of his compositions, which are available across the exhibition, enable visitors to immerse themselves in different phases of his lifework. The 'authenticity' of Liszt's personal objects and the cast of his hands particularly fascinated the interviewed visitors. Some of them even sought a more personal connection with him by photographing their own hand next to the cast. Although the main exhibition at Sagres Promontory was under construction during our fieldwork, the site aims to narrate a heroic European story by highlighting the role of Prince Henry the Navigator and, by extension, the role of men as explorers, adventurers, inventors, creators, and achievers. These narratives distinguish men as the core actors in what is framed as Europe's development and expansion, and this view is also reproduced in the interviews with both visitors and practitioners.

By telling a story of a male hero, the heritage sites easily naturalize a gendered view of the past. Our field research indicated that the heritage practitioners do not understand themselves as promoting an exclusively male perspective on heritage. As one heritage practitioner at Robert Schuman House (P33) pointed out, the site narrative is not limited only to "the place of a European [Founding] Father" but rather represents European cultural heritage, which "can unify men and women of Europe and can explain the culture of every [all] countries that are composing the European Union". However, precisely such a view naturalizes the link between the past male heroes – the EU's 'founding figures' – and culture and society in today's Europe, and thereby contributes to cementing the narrative of extraordinary men and their role in Europe's history. The binary view of gender with a male bias becomes embedded in European social structures and thereby sidelines debates on the multiplicity of gender (e.g. Linstead and Pullen 2006). The analysis of visitor interviews shows how effectively the sites succeed in transmitting this kind of narrative, including its gendered view, to their audiences.

The gendered view on heritage can even be seen in the various attempts by heritage practitioners to overcome it. One of the interviewed practitioners at Robert Schuman House (P33) emphasized the importance of mediating European cultural heritage in terms of "the history of different men and women on the continent", thereby reproducing an idea of heritages being inherently gendered. As the same practitioner continues, it is important to make "Europe really interesting for people, for showing that they are real members of the European Union". This suggests that the male and female perspectives would be equally rendered visible in Europe's cultural heritage, and at the same time representative of gender diversity. However, this kind of rendition reinforces the binary gender norm and excludes all other gender identities.

The narratives at the four aforementioned EHL sites emphasize the men's personalities and the importance of their work, while the women in their lives or women's role in society in general are marginalized. When references to women are included in the exhibitions, they are displayed through traditional female roles of loving mother, carer, or supporter who gives nurturing and emotional comfort to men. In relation to male heroes, women are positioned in subordinate roles representing the personal and affective aspects of life, while men appear as detached, active, thoughtful, and reasoned doers. For instance, Robert Schuman House introduces two women who played an important role in Schuman's life, namely, his mother and, in later life, his housekeeper. His mother Eugénie Duren instilled a strong Catholic social, intellectual, and moral basis, from which he drew great inspiration for his thoughts and political work. Schuman's housekeeper Marie Kelle is described having created the necessary peace and security of an ordered and well-run house for him to devote his energies to his work. Robert Schuman House displays material evidence of the housekeeper that enable visitors to visualize her: her room, a scarf, and a picture. Despite her material presence, Marie Kelle does not become visible at the site, but she remains absent.

In a similar vein, the exhibition about De Gasperi emphasizes that he drew energy and support from his family life with his wife and three daughters. The biography of Liszt in his memorial museum also suggests that the women in his life and his children shaped his musical life in important ways. The role of women in society at the times of Henry the Navigator are not further explored or made visible at Sagres, although one heritage practitioner (P34) at the site clearly linked women to the narrative of the value, commitment, and importance of the sea travels and discoveries for Europe's development and heritage. However, the exhibitions at these EHL sites do not further sensitize the visitor to the role of women in society beyond the domestic field or offering moral encouragement and practical support to men. For instance, the exhibition at Alcide De Gasperi House Museum strongly mobilizes social inequality as an important topic of broad societal concern, as the visitor interviews show. For example, a young Italian student visiting the house explained that she felt:

> the same inequality that he [Alcide De Gasperi] felt and that made him to have and to develop this vision. I saw it, too. I saw inequality and I felt inequality, even if I'm in 2017, I've felt it.
>
> (VS1/1)

However, our interviewed visitors did not address gender when discussing issues of inequality or solidarity. While the exhibitions in the former homes of Robert Schuman and Alcide De Gasperi alert the visitors to societal inequality in and beyond Europe, the issue of gender inequality is often erased by the male-centred perspective of the displays. Wilson (2018, 9) claims that critical gender perspectives constitute a key means of disrupting and altering the authorized heritage discourse (Smith 2006). Indeed, a number of scholars have criticized the fact that gender is either ignored in heritage discourse, or taken for granted alongside concepts of ethnicity and class, which reduces gender in heritage to "a women's problem" and "what women do" (Smith 2008; Reading 2015, 401; Setlhabi 2018; Blake 2018). These EHL sites focus on either the political contribution the 'Founding Fathers' made to the European project, or cultural or historical achievements of canonized 'Great Men' for Europe's heritage. Thus, these narratives remain frozen in a time when there was a lack of broader awareness for the issue of gender equality in European societies.

Attempts at including women in the narrative of the European project

From the so-called sexual revolution and the women's movement of the 1960s and 1970s, to the #MeToo debates in the 2010s, the topical issue of gender (in)equality has extended to various areas of social, economic, political, and cultural life. Some of our interviewed EU officials raised the issue of gender and a need for change in EU policy and related discourses. These views suggest an increasing insight into the importance of gender equality as an "uncompleted process" (E4), which requires ongoing political and social effort. This shift is combined with an understanding that the EU needs to respond to new societal challenges by embracing a less monolithic and normative cultural narrative than the current one. As another EU official (E6) put it, a new narrative is needed to increase the understanding that:

> there is also an important generational turn, so the only overwhelming cultural narrative, which was 'we can create peace', compared to the past, it is less appealing for new generations. So, another type of cultural narrative is probably needed, and I hope that it will be something based on cultural heritage, and non-normative interpretation of cultural heritage. Giving opportunities to work with different European cultures; interpretations of the past that can give voice to communities that really struggle to find themselves, whether they are migrants, whether they are minorities, whether they are women.

This interviewee stresses the importance of hearing women's voices and including them in a new, non-normative narrative of Europe, in which different subordinated voices are intersectionally acknowledged. At the same time, the quotation indicates how women are still categorized as a group on the margins, clustered together with migrants and minorities who are all seen as struggling to 'find themselves' or their position in society.

Despite the growing awareness of gender (in)equality, the female absence in the European project becomes piercingly noticeable at Lieu d'Europe. Its exhibition focuses on explaining the historical reasons and origins of the EU, its diverse institutions, and their tasks. An effort is made to give a 'human face' to the abstract European project, as one visitor in her mid-20s explained:

> I think sometimes for many people, including myself – I guess for everyone – it's hard to really grasp what Europe is. Especially if you're not physically in Strasbourg or in Brussels where the people are actually working. It's very easy to be like 'yeah, it's people meeting in far-out [sic!] places, doing far [sic!] things that don't concern me at all', and I think here [at Lieu d'Europe], it sort of shows that there actually is a sort of human dimension behind it.
>
> (VS4/17)

The exhibition at Lieu d'Europe seeks to include women in the narrative of the European project. The attempt, however, dries up in repetition of the common EU story, as discussed above, without any serious efforts to change or critique either the inherent male perspective or the exclusion of women. The section "Europe: Men and Women" of the exhibition shows several great and important people who have made an outstanding contribution to the European project: all men, with the exception of Simone Veil. The quotes and the portraits of the core politicians behind European integration – Robert Schuman, Paul-Henri Spaak, René Cassin, Willy Brandt, and Simone Veil – are intended to create a human touch by emphasizing the personal struggles of a few individuals for peace, justice, tolerance, and freedom in Europe. The section continues to highlight the role and achievement of European civil society, the "Europe of citizens", linking it through photographs to more recent events and movements fighting for political change at the end of the Cold War (e.g. *Solidarność*, the Baltic Chain), or the Europe-wide anti-austerity movements (e.g. the 2011 launch of the *Indignados* in Madrid).

The message about the importance of active citizen engagement in bringing about change for the public good is supported by other pictures taken between 1976 and 2008, which show people's political participation in protests against the Iraq War, death penalty, or domestic violence. All displayed pictures in the section show women, men, and children united in their collective struggles. Simone Veil, as the only representative of the women of Europe, stands out alone among the men and the masses in the exhibition, which stresses even more poignantly the lack of female perspective on Europe's history and heritage. The women are there, and yet not there: they become a "materialised absence" (Bergsdóttir and Hafsteinsson 2018, 109). Viewing the absence of

Figure 9.1 Europe's Great Men and one Woman. Lieu d'Europe, France. Photo:
EUROHERIT

women as part of causal relationships or as a pre-existing entity generates its
own dynamics and can critically affect the social world around (Bergsdóttir
and Hafsteinsson 2018, 101). This presence of men and absence of women (in
terms of untold stories and forgotten experiences) create a specific and exclusionary understanding of gender roles and the past that cements a bias about
who participates in making heritage (Bergsdóttir and Hafsteinsson 2018, 99).

The narratives of the EU's founding figures highlight the story of the 'Great
Men' in the struggle for peace, economic prosperity, and civil rights but neg-
lect the narrative of the 'Great Women' of Europe, past and present. Powerful
women in history and politics are usually treated as exceptions to the rule
instead of as inspiring and engaging examples. Despite the important role of
women in Europe's history and contemporary societies, the exhibition at the
Lieu d'Europe creates no awareness of the 'Great Women' who have participated
in the European project's political developments, debates, and cultural transformations. In the last 70 years, women have been elected and served as prime
ministers, presidents, parliamentarians, or high court judges in a number of
EU states. At the time of writing, there are five female presidents of European
Union member states: Marie-Louise Coleiro-Preca (Malta), Kolinda Grabar-
Kitarović (Croatia), Dalia Grybauskaitė (Lithuania), Kersti Kaljulaid (Estonia),

and Zuzana Čaputová (Slovakia), and two queens as head of state (Denmark, UK). Recent European politics have been strongly shaped by German chancellor Angela Merkel (also elected as the most influential and powerful woman in the world), and UK's Prime Minister Theresa May, despite her being less in control than Margaret Thatcher, who was known as the Iron Lady. Two new women follow in the footsteps of Foreign Policy Chief Federica Mogherini at EU level: Christine Lagarde, the incoming President of the European Central Bank, and Ursula von der Leyen, who was elected as the first female President of the European Commission. Even anti-European movements in the various member states are strongly shaped by women, such as Marine Le Pen (Rassemblement National, France), Georgia Meloni (Fratelli d'Italia, Italy), or Laura Huhtasaari (Perussuomalaiset, Finland).

As stated before, gender equality has been a defining characteristic of European equality policy since the 1970s. In fighting sex-based discrimination, the EU has moved beyond a market-oriented regulatory approach and imposed a number of norms and values on its member states (Jacquot 2015, 175). The European policy of gender equality is based on an egalitarian social order, which is essential for the way the EU presents itself both to its citizens and to the outside world (Jacquot 2015, 182). However, the omission of women from the EU's founding history affects the understanding of social and gender equality in European societies and influences public recognition of gender roles in them.

While heritage can address the gap between norms, values, ideals, and reality, women are frequently portrayed in submissive or insignificant roles in heritage narratives, with a focus on domesticity and child-rearing, or as an appendage to men and their political, social, cultural, and intellectual achievements (Scott 2018). The absence of women in Europe's heritage and history raises several important questions: How can gender equality progress if no public attention is given to powerful and inspirational models of female empowerment, or if the issue of societal gender inequality is not addressed? Who is included, and who decides which person or event is worth being remembered in the EU's canon of heritage? Failing to reflect on the role women played in the fight for social rights and peace, or in political movements or crucial developments in European society runs the risk of representing a "monolithic" structure of society (Blake 2018). This is a crucial aspect at a time when populist movements across Europe are reducing women's roles and perspectives to conservative images that prioritize child-bearing and family care (see Meiler 2019).

Developing critical perspectives to gender at the EHL sites

Grahn (2018, 255) argues that heritage institutions have a great responsibility to be aware of how to integrate gender and other social categories into museums and heritage management work, and to alert visitors to the complexity of gender when narrating the past. Some EHL sites, such as the Great

Guild Hall, Camp Westerbork, Carnuntum Archaeological Park, Mundaneum, and Hambach Castle, try to include a female perspective in their narratives. However, their exhibitions do not necessarily present this as equally strong as the male perspective. While some aspects of the role of women in society are emphasized at the Great Guild Hall, Carnuntum, and Camp Westerbork, for instance, by highlighting their economic power (Carnuntum and Great Guild Hall) or active role as carers and nurses (Camp Westerbork), women's perspective often remains underrepresented. Both Carnuntum and Camp Westerbork try to treat men and women equally, but the historical accounts show that women and men were not equally treated in the past, as victims, slaves, or members of society. Women throughout history have been more frequently subjected to sexual violence, abuse, humiliation, and institutionalized violence than men. Moreover, some scholars even argue that the erasure of gender was a constituent element of the Holocaust (Reading 2002, 2015, 401; Jacobs 2008). It is therefore necessary to understand how heritage sites can contribute to overcoming historical imbalances in terms of gender and in intersection with other factors, such as ethnicity or race (see Box 9.1).

Box 9.1 The Whiteness of EUropean Heritage

Taking an intersectional approach to the biases embedded in heritage narratives enables a more profound analysis of differentiation beyond gender. Here we focus on two interrelated intersections – ethnicity and race.

Although the exhibitions explicitly differentiate between ethnic identities (the Europe of nation states) thereby actively engaging in identity work, for the most part these categorizations fail to include Europeans of colour in their representations, reinforcing the problematic connection between Europeanness and whiteness. The EHL is not alone: rather similar tendencies have been identified in other heritage and remembrance initiatives by the EU (e.g. de Jong 2011), as well as in other public and private museums across Europe (e.g. de Cesari 2017). These repeated representations of white EUropeans contribute to the social construction of both 'whiteness' and 'Europeanness' at the expense of Europeans of colour.

With the exception of extensive debates on the racialization of the Jews (and to lesser extent the Roma and Sinti) in connection to the Holocaust, debates on racism, racialization or 'racial' diversity are absent from EUropean heritage narratives. Based on our data, it seems that the only legitimate entry of Europeans of colour into the EUropean heritage narratives is through being depicted as migrants or refugees – as outsiders seeking entrance. Although the exhibitions at our fieldwork sites did include depictions of historical migrations of people of colour (for example the Moluccans in Camp Westerbork), they were primarily narrated only in a historical context, where their inclusion into society (or the failure of it) was left uncommented. As such, these migrant narratives produce a category of 'Europeans in waiting' (cf. Chackrabarty 2000), where certain migrant communities continue to be excluded, despite having decades if not centuries of European history of their own. This shows how pivotal topics of race, racialization, and whiteness are in contemporary Europe. Beyond addressing issues such as contemporary racism, they are central to the very notion of what Europe is and who Europeans are.

Although often represented as white, European heritage is not exclusively white. Rather, European history is full of examples that would enable breaking the white norm of Europeanness. These examples range from Roman emperors and soldiers of African descent to historical and vibrant black communities in cities like Lisbon and Paris, and from diverse historical and contemporary transnational Muslim influences to the cross-border heritages of the Roma and Jews in Europe, to name a few. Although attention was paid to the entangled histories of colonialism when choosing the sites for the fieldwork, only three fieldwork sites engaged with colonialism, trans-Atlantic slave trade, or decolonization in their exhibitions (Alcide De Gasperi House Museum, Camp Westerbork, and Sagres Promontory). Our analysis of applications for the EHL show that some candidate sites also discussed colonialism in their applications but were not awarded the Label. Out of the awarded sites, both Camp Westerbork (Moluccan refugees) and Sagres Promontory (the slave trade) engaged with the (often forced) mobilities that colonialism created, but neither positioned the people of colour who arrived in Europe as being European then or now. Moreover, EHL sites like the Archaeological Park Carnuntum could use their narratives of the historical ethnic and racial diversity of the Roman Empire to promote debates on contemporary culturally diverse societies in Europe.

Beyond the current EHL sites, there are also vast opportunities for engaging sites that would attempt to bring contemporary and historical minority and migrant cultural heritages, early Muslim influences throughout Europe and European indigenous heritages into European consciousness. Other sites could debate the continuing legacies of colonialism, trans-Atlantic slave trade, and the massive forced and free movement of people that they entailed. This would make contemporary European racism more visible and legitimize the historical existence of many European migrant communities. These critical engagements would challenge the whiteness of European heritage and enable a European heritage that would be more in line with contemporary, culturally diverse Europe.

The gender perspective constitutes an integral part of the narratives and guided tours of the European Solidarity Centre and Hambach Castle. For instance, the European Solidarity Centre offers a special guided tour that stresses the different labour conditions for women at the shipyard and their role in the *Solidarność* movement in the 1980s. As one heritage practitioner at the Centre (P26) put it, this special tour is also seen as a means of empowering women in the present with stories of strong women in the past. Empowerment also plays a role in audience engagement at Hambach Castle. The department of regional history at the University of Mainz was responsible for the final design of the site exhibition, and the interviewed heritage practitioners confirm that a female point of view is important to audience engagement and mediation of the narrative. While the exhibition is very text-heavy, it tries to visualize the Hambach Festival of 1832 through the eyes of five fictive characters, who represent the diverse social classes and status of those involved. The five fictive characters, three men, one woman, and one girl, are employed to enable visitors to understand how people back then experienced the Hambach Festival, and they accompany the visitor throughout the exhibition, predominantly at audio stations but occasionally also at reading stations. This is rounded up with interactive stations, which invite visitors to participate or to take home something self-made along from the exhibition and thereby aim to offer an affective experience of the heritage.

Other EHL sites also use personalized voices of the past in their exhibitions. For instance, at the Archaeological Park Carnuntum, visitors can select figures of a slave and a free Roman citizen on a screen, and read three alternative biographies of them, based on excavation data. Depending on the choice, various aspects of the Roman past are introduced through the eyes of a gardener, shoemaker, or teacher, or through the perspective of a rich patrician, the patron of a faithful slave, or a soldier of merit. Similarly, the new exhibition at Camp Westerbork, due to open in 2020, will let the visitors choose interactive guides, who, based on archival traces, embody a Jewish, Roma, or Sinti detainee, a German officer, a member of the Moluccan community who lived on the camp ground between 1951 and 1971, or a local inhabitant from the region. According to a heritage practitioner (P14), the exhibition will enable the visitor to choose the age, gender, and nationality of the guide in order to match their own details and interests.

The conceptualized female emphasis is more visible in Hambach Castle as a small part of the exhibition, entitled "Women and the Revolution". This section provides information on the role of women during the German revolution of 1848/49 and their active participation in the struggle for civic rights, national independence, women's political participation, and gender equality. By these means, the narrative tries to emphasize that women and families were among the 30,000 participants of the Hambach Festival in 1832, who met to discuss and call for national unity, freedom of opinion and religion, and the equality of men and women. The exhibition raises awareness that the organizers of the Hambach Festival explicitly expected the political involvement of women in the struggle for freedom and civil rights alongside men. One of the heritage practitioners (P22) at the site explained that the emphasis on women's role during the event in 1832 includes a challenge to women: "[h]ey, contribute! You must also fight for your own rights". The heritage site thus tries to encourage women to become active in their own lives. This idea of empowering women is particularly strong in the staged (and gendered) performances of the tours, as the same heritage practitioner described.

> Of the five guides involved in doing [the staged tours], in fact, four are women and one is a man. And exactly this aspect is exciting, when it is done by women, since the involvement of women was also absolutely new at the Hambach Festival. Actually, Siebenpfeiffer [one of the organizers in 1832] stressed in the invitations that not only men should come – and in the Biedermeier-period political events were only meant for men – but also women. They shouldn't be only decorative accessories anymore, but now they also should fight for their rights. And, indeed, a lot of women responded to the call [in 1832] and came, and many of them even smoked cigars. They sent a signal, a message with this. We have this one guide lady, who – only with the adult groups, with the children she doesn't do this, this would be a bad example for them – but with the adult groups she takes cigars along and even lights them up. She stands there in her costume and puffs a cigar in front of the people, like: 'what you men are able to do, I've been able to do all along, and for a long time'.
>
> (P22)

Hambach Castle attempts to explore the role of women in shaping society in Europe as well as their contribution to heritage-making by offering a more conscious and expanded representation of women as cultural producers and participants in political and social transformations. However, this female perspective remains to a certain degree separated from the grand narrative of the past, which continues to highlight the historical achievements of men. This raises a crucial problem with the representation of a female dimension of the past. Earlier concerns about the absence of women from representations of the past in museums led to the creation of special exhibitions with a focus on women (Reading 2015, 402). However, recently, there has been a shift in the theorizing of gender in heritage studies to the exploration of gendered power relations and the construction of gender in the representations of the past. Grundberg (2012) argues that while, compared to separate exhibitions about women, gender-integrated exhibitions make it easier to visualize the power relations and the structural oppression of women in society, they run the risk of rendering women invisible in history and thus confirming the traditional image of men as the sole agents of change.

It is a political choice whether to present a gendered perspective at the EHL sites. The sites are able to include different voices, approaches, and meanings in their narratives that can feed their visitors' feeling of belonging. One Portuguese practitioner argued that cultural heritage is "a symbol of identity" and a way of representing a "fractioned identity" in terms of "one element or two or three elements of that identity" (P35). She explained that:

> we choose what to preserve, what to safeguard, what to show to the others and talk to the others. Sometimes we are choosing a message that isn't the representation of all the identity. So, it's a political choice as well. And I think it should be also accompanied by scientific studies, historical studies. I think it's important to have a research team associated with this work. So, that it doesn't [turn into] only a political process. I think this is an important message to take. We should be able to create a research team dedicated to studying, researching these sites.
>
> (P35)

Scholars point out that critical academic research can make visible the intersectionality of socio-cultural categories of identity such as gender, class, and race in the reproduction of inequalities and experiences of belonging in social, political, and economic contexts (Grahn 2018, 258; Lariat 2018, 161). While the EHL steers the discussion on how to interpret European cultural heritage through certain narratives, it nevertheless gives much freedom to the respective sites to implement the European dimension in their exhibitions. The above example of Hambach Castle gives evidence to the importance of collaboration between heritage practitioners and scholars for opening up complex issues and mediating different perspectives on heritage.

The representation of women in workplace structures, curatorial practices, and management at heritage sites and museums has an important impact on the conceptualization of a gendered perspective in heritage mediation (Schwarzer 2010; Reading 2015, 388, 404). Similarly, unequal gender balance in the creation and decision-making of local, national, and international heritage policies and conventions may result in a cultural bias, influencing the identification, documentation, development, and safeguarding of heritage (see Moghadam and Bagheritari 2007). Although the representation of women in the institutional structures of heritage sites and museums does not guarantee the inclusion of a female perspective in their heritage narratives, it may challenge the male dominance of the authorized heritage discourse. This applies to some EHL sites, such as Camp Westerbork, Hambach Castle, and Mundaneum, where women dominate in the managerial and scientific positions. One heritage practitioner (P23) at the Hambach Castle expressed her concern for a female perspective as follows:

> [h]istory has often been written by men, historical research was predominantly done by men, and this actually affects the point of view in a different way. If we would start it all over, and women would write at least half of

it, history and many events would look totally different, I guess. So, in this sense it's a huge topic.

The insistence on a female perspective makes it possible to engage visitors not only cognitively but emotionally, and thereby helps to counter the authoritarian nature of stereotypical gender framings by drawing attention to more than one perspective and interpretation of the past (see Smith and Campbell 2015).

As each EHL site is different, collaboration between them may be challenging, in particular as regards the focus on heritage and the interpretations of its meanings. As one heritage practitioner (P31) in the Mundaneum pointed out,

> the reading that we can do in Belgium is not the same reading that we can do, for example, in Hungary. ... Or for example, between Belgium and France, we have […] not the same history. […] We can make some relations between what happened in Belgium before the twentieth century and how the democracy was developed or evolved. And perhaps to explain this and to compare [the] presentations.

The Mundaneum strongly focuses on narratives of pacifism, feminism, and knowledge transfer that reinforce the comprehension of cultural heritage and a value-based notion of European identity. The same practitioner as above referred to difficulties in the cooperation with another EHL site due to a different reading of the narrative of heritage. She tied the problems with the transfer of the exhibition about the biography of one of the founders of the Mundaneum, Henri La Fontaine, to the different societal context and valuing a female perspective of heritage:

> This exhibition was about Henri La Fontaine and his biography. And in the dialogue [conversation] that we had for the selection of this exhibition, the partner site said to me: "Is it necessary to speak about feminism? Is it necessary to speak about the freemason aspect of Henri La Fontaine? Is it necessary to speak about socialism, and so on?" So, because I'm a specialist for the question on feminism, for example, it was impossible to agree with [them]. And the person [Henri La Fontaine] is full of aspects, full of faces and facets, so it was impossible to select the aspects we are more [comfortable with]. So, I said: "it is impossible for the presentation in a critical and historical way" and it was very important to say that because I have another archivist in front of me. And so, it's important to say the truth, too, due to the documents also. And so, we have different ways to explain history and to say that socialism has given this and feminism that. And perhaps, it is not so easy to speak about this topic of feminism in [the other country]. It doesn't matter for me. But it's interesting to say and to present [this] in some [other] condition because it's difficult.
>
> (P31)

The need for a more inclusive perspective in European heritage

Heritage can both strengthen inclusion and diversity in society and, at the same time, serve as a barrier that excludes those whose heritage is not acknowledged (Waterton 2014, 830; Grahn 2018, 257). The EHL is still very strongly focused on the mediation of grand European narratives that prioritize a white, male perspective, but a stronger representation of a female perspective is necessary in order to constitute a more encompassing, inclusive, and diverse conception of Europe and the way in which European history is written. The idea of equality between people with different cultural, national, social, and linguistic backgrounds, and various religious, gender, and sexual orientations has been part of the EU integration since its inception. Alongside human rights, democracy, and peace, gender equality is an important aspect of the European Union that needs to be reflected in Europe's shared cultural heritage. A democratic, vernacular, and equal representation of heritage enables us to understand the past and the wider social and political context of belonging, identity, inclusion, or exclusion (see Crang and Tolia-Kelly 2010; Waterton 2014; Tolia-Kelly, Waterton, and Watson 2017). Heritage has a strong symbolic potential for constructing identities and shaping the images and narratives a society wants to preserve and remember (Dawson 1994, 48; Smith 2006, 87). As heritage is also about the relationship between the past, the present, and the future, the lack of female representation in the EHL and wider European heritage narratives has implications for the political and social representation of current and future generations of women, and the justified concern for gender equality.

Heritage institutions possess a high credibility in society for authentically (re)presenting the past and interpreting it according to modern patterns (Smith 2006; Grahn 2018, 256). Grahn argues that this credibility could be used to combat prejudice rather than reinforcing gender stereotypes and images of the past with regard to masculinity, femininity, class, ethnic belonging, or sexual orientation (Grahn 2018, 265; see also Sandell 2007). The EHL sites can contribute to developing public interest in the equal treatment of women in society on issues such as equal pay, and to their civil and human rights. Moreover, they can play an important role in constructing knowledge that helps make women's societal equality self-evident by addressing their participation in all areas of social, political, and cultural production, and in transformations in the past and present, both in Europe and beyond. This would be the first step towards trying to promote a broader, intersectional, and inclusive perspective in European cultural heritage.

References

Bergsdóttir, A., and S. B. Hafsteinsson. 2018. "The Fleshyness of Absence: The Matter of Absence in a Feminist Museology." In *Gender and Heritage. Performance, Place and Politics,* edited by W. Grahn, and R. J. Wilson, 99–112. Abingdon: Routledge.

Blake, J. 2018. "Gender and Intangible Heritage: Illustrating the Inter-disciplinary Character of International Law." In *Gender and Heritage. Performance, Place and Politics*, edited by W. Grahn, and R. J. Wilson, 207–222. Abingdon: Routledge.

De Cesari, C. 2017. Museums of Europe: Tangles of Memory, Borders, and Race. *Museum Anthropology*, 40(1), 18–35.

Chakrabarty, D. 2000. *Provincializing Europe: Postcolonial Thought and Historical Difference*. Princeton: Princeton University Press.

Crang, M., and D. P. Tolia-Kelly. 2010. "Nation, Race, and Affect: Senses and Sensibilities at National Heritage Sites." *Environment and Planning A* 42 (10): 2315–2331. doi: 10.1068/a4346.

Crenshaw, K. 1991. "Mapping the Margins: Intersectionality, Identity Politics and Violence Against Women of Color." *Stanford Law Review* 43 (6): 1241–1299. doi: 10.2307/1229039.

EC (European Commission). 2014. *European Heritage Label. Application Form 2014*. Brussels: European Commission.

EP & C (European Parliament and the Council). 2011. "Decision no. 1194/2011/EU of the European Parliament and of the Council of 16 November 2011 establishing a European Union action for the European Heritage Label." *Official Journal of the European Union* L 303: 1–9.

Dawson, G. 1994. *Soldier Heroes: British Adventure, Empire and the Imagining of Masculinities*. London: Routledge.

De los Reyes, P., and D. Mulinari. 2005. *Intersektionalitet: Kritiska reflektioner över (o) jämlikhetens landskap*. Liber: Stockholm.

Grahn, W. 2011. "Intersectionality and the Construction of Cultural Heritage Management." *Archaeologies: Journal of the World Archaeological Congress* 7 (1): 222–250. doi: 10.1007/s11759-011-9164-x.

Grahn, W. 2018. "The Politics of Heritage: How to Achieve Change." In *Gender and Heritage: Performance, Place and Politics*, edited by W. Grahn, and R. J. Wilson, 255–268. Abingdon: Routledge.

Grahn, W., and R. J. Wilson. 2018. *Gender and Heritage: Performance, Place and Politics*. Abingdon: Routledge.

Grundberg, M. 2012. *Theorising gender in heritage studies*. www.gu.se/digitalAssets/1367/1367109_p203-grundberg-women-history-or-gender-integration-.pdf.

Jacobs, J. 2008. "Gender and Collective Memory: Women and Representation at Auschwitz." *Memory Studies* 1 (2): 211–225.

Jacquot, S. 2015. *Transformation in EU Gender Equality: From Emergence to Dismantling*. (Gender and Politics Series). Houdsmills: Palgrave Macmillan.

De Jong, S. 2011. "Is This Us? The Construction of the European Man/Woman in the Exhibition It's Our History!" *Culture Unbound* 11: 369–383.

Joyce, R. A. 1996. "The Construction of Gender in Classic Maya Monuments." In *Gender and Archaeology: Essays in Research and Practice*, edited by Wright, R. P., 167–95. Philadelphia: University of Pennsylvania Press.

Lariat, J. 2018. "Impasse or Productive Intersection? Learning to 'Mess with Genies' in Collaborative Heritage Research Relationships." In *Gender and Heritage. Performance, Place and Politics*, edited by W. Grahn, and R. J. Wilson, 148–166. Abingdon: Routledge.

Linstead, S., and A. Pullen. 2006. "Gender as Multiplicity: Desire, Displacement, Difference and Dispersion." *Human Relations* 59 (9): 1287–1310. doi: 10.1177/0018726706069772.

Lykke, N. 2003. "Intersektionalitet – Ett Användbart Begrepp för Genusforksningen." *Kvinnovetenskaplig tidskrift* 1 (3): 47–56.

Lykke, N. 2010. *Feminist Studies: A Guide to Intersectional Theory, Methodology and Writing.* New York: Routledge.

Meiler, O. 2019. "Liebegrüße aus Verona" (– International Congress of Ultraconservative Rights and Their Family Image), *Süddeutsche Zeitung* (SZ, 1.4.2019), https://sz.de// 1.4390759, accessed 1.4.2019.

Moghadam, V., and M. Bagheritari. 2007. "Cultures, Conventions, and the Human Rights of Women: Examining the Convention for Safeguarding Intangible Cultural Heritage and the Declaration on Cultural Diversity." *Museum International* 59 (4): 9–18.

Nelson, S. M. 2004. *Gender in Archaeology: Analysing Power and Prestige.* Walnut Creek, CA: AltaMira Press.

Nenadic, S. 1994. "Museums, Gender and Cultural Identity in Scotland." *Gender & History* 6 (3): 426–434. doi: 10.1111/j.1468-0424.1994.tb00212.x.

Porter, G. 1996. "Seeing Through Solidity: A Feminist Perspective on Museums." In *Theorizing Museums*, edited by S. MacDonald, and G. Fyfe, 83–104. Oxford: Blackwell.

Reading, A. 2002. *The Social Inheritance of the Holocaust: Gender, Culture and Memory.* Basingstoke: Palgrave Macmillan.

Reading, A. 2015. "Making Feminist Heritage Work: Gender and Heritage." In *The Palgrave Handbook of Contemporary Heritage Research*, edited by E. Watson, and S. Watson, 397–413. Houndsmill: Palgrave Macmillan.

Robert, N. 2014. "Getting Intersectional in Museums." *Museums & Social Issues* 9 (1): 24–33. doi: DOI: 10.1179/1559689314Z.00000000017.

Sandell, R. 2007. *Museums, Prejudice and the Reframing of Difference.* London: Routledge.

Schwarzer, M. 2010. "Women in the Temple: Gender and Leadership in Museums". In *Gender, Sexuality, and Museums*, edited by A. K. Levin, 16–27. London: Routledge.

Scott, A. 2018. "It's a Man's World. Or is it? The 'Pilgrim Fathers', Religion, Patriarchy, Nationalism and Tourism." In *Gender and Heritage: Performance, Place and Politics*, edited by W. Grahn, and R. J. Wilson, 81–98. Abingdon and New York: Routledge.

Setlhabi, K. G. 2018. "Taller than the Rest: The Three Dikgosi Monument, Masculinity Reloaded." In *Gender and Heritage. Performance, Place and Politics*, edited by W. Grahn, and R. J. Wilson, 113–128. Abingdon: Routledge.

Smith, L. 2006. *Uses of Heritage.* London: Routledge.

Smith, L. 2008. "Heritage, Gender and Identity." In *The Ashgate Research Companion to Heritage and Identity*, edited by B. Graham, and P. Howard, 159–179. Farnham: Ashgate.

Smith, L., and G. Campbell. 2015. "The Elephant in the Room: Heritage, Affect and Emotion." In *A Companion to Heritage Studies*, edited by W. Logan, M. N. Craith, and U. Kockel, 443–460. Malden, MA: Wiley-Blackwell.

Sørensen, M. L. S. 1999. "Archaeology, Gender and the Museum." In *Making Early Histories in Museums*, edited by N. Merriman, 136–150. Leicester: Leicester University Press.

Sørensen, S. 2000. *Gender Archaeology.* Oxford: Polity.

Summers, L. 2000. "Sanitising the Female Body: Costume, Corsetry and the Case for Corporeal Feminism in Social History Museums." *Open Museum Journal* 1 (January).

Tolia-Kelly, D. P., E. Waterton, and S. Watson. 2017. *Heritage, Affect and Emotion: Politics, Practices and Infrastructures.* London and New York: Routledge.

Treaty of Amsterdam. 1997. *Treaty of Amsterdam Amending the Treaty on European Union, the Treaties Establishing the European Communities and Certain Related Acts.* Luxembourg: Office for Official Publications of the European Communities.

Treaty of Rome. 1957. *Traité instituant la Communauté Économique Européenne et documents annexes*. 11957E/TXT. Accessed 20.06.2019. https://eur-lex.europa.eu/legal-content/FR/TXT/PDF/?uri=CELEX:11957K/TXT.

Warner, M. 2000. *Monuments and Maidens*. Berkeley: University of California Press.

Waterton, E. 2014. "A More-Than-Representational Understanding of Heritage? The 'Past' and the Politics of Affect." *Geography Compass* 8 (11): 823–833.

Waterton, E., and S. Watson. 2015. *The Palgrave Handbook of Contemporary Heritage Research*. Houndsmill: Palgrave Macmillan.

Wilson, R. J. 2018. "The Tyranny of the Normal and the Importance of Being Liminal." In *Gender and Heritage: Performance, Place and Politics*, edited by W. Grahn, and R. J. Wilson, 3–14. Abingdon: Routledge.

Conclusions

Narrating Europe

The initiative "New Narrative for Europe" was launched by the European Commission in 2014. The aim of the initiative was to "give a voice to the artistic, cultural, scientific and intellectual communities to articulate what Europe stands for today and tomorrow" and to revive "a 'European' spirit" and "identify a new, encompassing narrative that takes into account the evolving reality of the European continent" (EC website, see also EC 2014). Overall, the goal was described as enabling a "New Renaissance" – a new era of rejuvenation, where art, culture, and education are leading the development of Europe. Renaissance is an interesting metaphor for contemporary Europe; the term is primarily used to refer to a specific period of cultural, artistic, and intellectual flourishing that took place in Europe between the fourteenth and seventeenth centuries. It was a time of heightened development that to some extent gave rise to what we today consider as 'Western culture'. By envisioning a "New Renaissance" of Europe, the EC aims to establish a new period of cultural and scientific progress. The emphasis is on a period of heightened awareness and cultural flowering, which would enable EUrope to move beyond the many crises it is currently facing.

However, historical metaphors are often tricky as they come with their own historical baggage. From a narrative, teleological perspective the Renaissance spurred European prosperity, enabled the Enlightenment and pawed the way towards the industrial revolution: all of which strengthened Europe's position as a global political, economic, and cultural actor. This narrative presents a European success story that the EU-AHD also mirrors. Europe's increasing prosperity, however, was not only due to internal developments (see Dussell 2000; Dainotto 2007). Behind this idea of European prosperity and progress lie other 'Europes'. Ones that build on other historical narratives and connect to what Whitehead, Daugbjerg, Eckersley, and Bozoğlu (2019) describe as other possible "dimensions" of European heritage. These different dimensions of heritage can be contradictory, but often build in relation to each other. They build connections and overlaps, but also strong juxtapositions and counter-narratives. In essence, they build on experiences that in effect construct "multiple Europes" (Whitehead, Daugbjerg, Eckersley, and Bozoğlu 2019; see also Delanty 2016). Dualities of good and bad, admiration and disregard, remembrance of and oblivion are deeply entwined in the ways these dimensions interpret the past. Irrespective of their point of view (official, banal, cosmopolitan, populist or xenophobic), these Europes seek to cherish, remember, and valorise certain aspects of our past. Although acknowledged in historical research, the darker sides of the coin, the histories no one wants to remember, are often neglected in these processes of heritagization. Especially in official contexts, the focus is often on highlighting the common ground based on the "positive sides of an argued European heritage" (Pakier and Stråth 2010, 2) and Renaissance, Enlightenment, and industrial revolution are cornerstones of this celebratory and affirmative self-narrative of Europe. At the same time the expansion of imperial domination, the trans-Atlantic slave trade, and colonialism that contributed to the European prosperity that enabled the Renaissance escape official heritagization. Together with their continuing legacies in European racism and the ongoing militarization of EUrope's borders, they are examples of European experiences and memories that do not seem to fit into the dimension of EUrope constructed through the EU-AHD.

This does not mean that all difficult histories would be repressed or forgotten in the EU-AHD. In the past decades, tragic periods regarded as formative experiences have been integrated into this canon of EUropean remembrance, most prominently the two World Wars and the Holocaust. Additionally, the EHL has had a significant role also in integrating the end of the Cold War to this canon of remembrance. Moreover, the declaration of the New Narrative for Europe (EC 2014), referred to above, has proposed that the economic crisis that started in 2008 would deserve a similar position in the narrative of difficult periods EUrope has (or will) overcome.

Despite these advances, many divisive and dark histories are still either actively repressed or passively forgotten in EUrope. This is not so much a question of absence, as the memories and traces of Europe's colonial history or Muslim influences, for example, are all around us. Rather, it is a lack of their acknowledgement and engagement. Considering the racial undertones of many of the contemporary European crises – the economic, the populist, and the 'migratory' – which have strong roots in European imperialism, these memories are more prominent now than they have been in the past. In the contemporary European social landscape, they are becoming potent enough to deserve – or even to force – recognition. These postcolonial European memories and heritages demand attention from museum and heritage practitioners across Europe on a scale that actions like the EHL seem to be unprepared for. As a heritage action expected to support intercultural dialogue and European citizens' feeling of belonging, it is, however, a challenge the EHL must arise to in order to reach its aims.

The absence of these debates from the EU-AHD make them a difficult topic for researchers and they have proved equally challenging for us when writing this book. Although we have engaged with these issues in this book only in passing, as part of our conclusions, we want to highlight the importance of these debates for future research but also for the future of EUrope. When faced with a lack of acknowledgement on the EU level, engagement in the debate becomes a one-sided plea for inclusion. There are, however, some important openings in starting the debate on the (post)coloniality of heritage in the EU context (see Settele 2015; Buettner 2018) to which the EUROHERIT has also actively contributed (Turunen 2019a, 2019b, n.d.).

After discussing the role of narratives and narration for our understanding of cultural heritage and going through the summaries of the chapters in this book, we want to return to the memories of 'multiple Europes'. We will consider the idea of transcultural heritage as a way to understand their connections and the varied voices they bring to ideas of Europe. This final debate reminds us of the need to consider what kind of European Renaissance is currently being envisioned by the EC. Building on Chapter 4, we can look at this from two perspectives. Is the "New Renaissance" going to be a renaissance of *diversity* – a celebration and transformation of national and migrant cultures in Europe seeking transcultural entanglements, inclusions, and shared mutual respect – or a renaissance of *difference* – a period of new, exclusive European cultural hegemony aimed at lifting EUrope out of its many contemporary crises at expense of migrant and minority communities?

Beyond the single story of European heritage

It's a melting pot of a lot of things that are unifying in different places and in different cultures and countries.

(P33)

It's like a ... *boule à facette* [disco ball], you know, like a ... Yes, there are many prisms, many spectrums to get to...

(P30)

You know there are all the different concepts, whether it's a type of cake, with different layers, or it is a sort of a *tiramisu*, when it goes into the different layers just melting to each other.

(E6)

The quotes above illustrate various understandings of European identity. In trying to answer a question that seems simple, but is indefinitely complex and contested, many of our interviewees found themselves resorting to metaphors – cakes, disco balls, melting pots, or even one large pizza with different toppings representing Europe's diverse cultures (P10, see also Risse and Grabowski 2008). European identities are often constructed through allegories, stories, and narratives. These narrations are crucial aspects of how we make sense of our pasts. In many ways the whole idea of history is premised on the idea of a story. As Trouillot (2015, 2) explains, "history means both the facts of the matter and a narrative of those facts, both 'what happened' and 'that which is said to have happened'". Thus, history is inseparable from how, and by whom, it is told. The past is always a representation or a construction, a subjective interpretation of what someone thinks has happened in a particular place at a particular time.

Although there are many links between history and heritage, they are not the same thing (e.g. Lowenthal 1998). Heritage is yet another narrative of the past, not chosen for accuracy, or for truth, but to tell a story about who 'we' are and where 'we' come from. These choices are not made in the past (e.g. Harrison 2013; Macdonald 2013; Lähdesmäki 2014). Rather, they reflect the values and ideologies of contemporary societies (e.g. Smith 2006). They echo the history we want to have – either as a source of pride and achievement, or as a cautionary tale of difficult times we do not want to repeat. Whereas history involves getting a full picture of the past, in academic debates, heritage is often seen as being about choices and, as a result, can at times be "cut-adrift from the anchoring historical narratives that rightly or wrongly helped shape cultural memory" (Chalcraft and Delanty 2015).

The idea of heritage as a process of choices and selections reflects recent debates in critical heritage studies. As we have noted throughout the book, there has been a shift in heritage studies from conservation and preservation to critical engagement with the politics of heritage. In these politics, the role of narratives or stories is crucial in legitimizing and sharing the choices that, when brought together, aim to define, regulate, mediate, and negotiate cultural values to future generations. But when we talk of heritage narratives, do we refer to a "single story" (Adichie 2009) or a multitude of competing narratives? Hall (1999, 5) states that:

> [w]e should think of The Heritage as a discursive practice. It is one of the ways in which the national slowly constructs for itself a sort of collective social memory [...] [N]ations construct identities by selectively binding their chosen high points and memorable achievements into an unfolding "national story". This story is what is called Tradition.

"Heritage" and "Tradition" with capital letters, both constructs of which Hall is critical, invoke a sense of heritage being singular, celebratory, official, and progressive (see authorized heritage discourse in Smith 2006): a univocal story of achievements where new layers are added on top of a canonical narrative of (national) history, but older layers are rarely reconsidered or removed (Harrison 2013, 197–198). However, the depoliticizing and 'smoothing' tendency of heritage narratives and the need to overcome and move away from single stories, has been a consistent topic in heritage studies (e.g. Tunbridge and Ashworth 1996; Hall 2005; Harrison 2013; Wu and Hou 2015; Kisić 2017). Debates on heritage dissonances (see Chapter 5) have often been attributed to conflict situations, or more recently to migrant heritages and the challenges they pose to the idea of a 'national story'. Traditionally such challenges to national heritages have been 'managed' by integrating them under a neutral and benign idea of collective heritage which has depoliticized questions of representation, visibility, and content into "technical issues of site management" (Smith 2006, 31). Although nominally including the formerly excluded, by not challenging the hegemonic narrative or interpretive frame through which a specific heritage is made meaningful, these attempts can often only make cosmetic changes to the contents and values of that heritage. Depoliticizing the epistemological and ontological challenge that including new heritages or new narratives into the 'national story' could pose is a failure to question the dominant interpretive frame and thereby to move beyond the nationalizing tendency of heritage narratives. To enable genuinely inclusive transcultural understandings of heritage, these epistemological challenges to the meaning of heritage should be taken seriously. There is a need to move from attempting to achieve a single story, towards an idea where "multiple Europes" (Whitehead, Daugbjerg, Eckersley, and Bozoğlu 2019) co-exist and are equally acknowledged as genuine experiential realities of European citizens.

Although there is increasing academic resistance to single stories, normative, depoliticized, and canonical thinking can be seen in the way many heritage initiatives have been set up – including the EHL. Harrison (2013, 168) points out how despite changing political and ideological environments that have guided the process of listing and registering heritages, "[t]here seems to be a general perception that, once objects, places and/or practices are gazetted and hence transformed into heritage, they will very rarely revert or transform into something else". Although some of these tendencies can also be identified in the EHL, it is rather different from many other heritage initiatives in that the Label places practically no value on conservation or protection of physical heritage. Rather, according to the impact assessment of the action, the EHL should be "awarded mainly on the basis of the symbolic value of sites" (EC 2010, 12) as "this symbolic would not diminish over time" (ibid. 13). While the more conventional definitions of cultural heritage emphasize the tangible aspects of cultural heritage, the EHL focuses on the symbolic meanings and intangible aspects and uses them to ensure the permanent, unchanging importance and nature of the labelled sites, and by extension of the EHL.

Once the EHL became fully operational, it quickly became clear that although the status of the EHL sites as 'heritage', might not be disputed, their status as 'European' heritage – and thereby their inclusion in the EHL – is very much up for debate. As the first monitoring report (EC 2016, 8) stated, it is up to the monitoring panel to determine "whether the European significance was fully understood, well-articulated and conveyed by the sites" (for debate, see Chapter 1; Turunen 2019a). This emphasis on articulation and ability to convey a message forces us to question the role narratives and discourses play in making something seem not only European, but also heritage.

Narrating Europe through cultural heritage

Narratives are often used to make something known: to share knowledge, teach moral lessons, or tell stories that help us understand human nature. They are part of making sense of national histories, our own lives, and where we come from. These stories do not exist in isolation but are a central aspect of social life. They are transmitted in everyday practices, where they multiply, and accumulate, constantly borrowing from and building on each other. As de

Certeau (1984, 186, original emphasis) notes "our society has become a recited society: meaning our contemporary world is 'defined by *stories* [...], by *citations* of stories and by the interminable *recitation* of stories'".

Although our lives are immersed in narratives, not all stories are equally important and potent. The idea that certain historical accounts seem 'natural' is based on the normalizing power of narratives, which is why narratives are so often used to legitimize heritages and other interpretations of our pasts. Lyotard (1993, 23; see also Lawler 2002, 242–243) states that narratives:

> determine criteria of competence and/or illustrate how they are to be applied. They thus define what has the right to be said and done in the culture in question, and since they are themselves a part of that culture, they are legitimized by the simple fact that they do what they do.

By applying this definition to the idea of European heritage, heritage narratives can be seen as constituting and legitimizing themselves: European heritage tells us who we are and where we come from, and because of who we are and where we come from, these things are our heritage. It is precisely this normative, self-referential understanding of heritages that critical scholars should attempt to investigate. As we have shown throughout this book, in the context of the EHL, neither the idea of heritage nor the idea of Europe are as self-evident or stable as they are represented to be; both are complex and continuously developing. In the following, we attempt to bring together some key points from the preceding chapters by emphasizing acts of producing a narrative, or rather narratives, of EUropean heritage.

Part I: Governing Europe

In Chapter 1, we focused on the mingled top-down and bottom-up dynamics in the governance of the EHL action in particular and in the EU's heritage policy sector more generally. The development of a specified EU policy sector makes explicit the need for heritage to be governed – in terms of the meanings of heritage and the people engaging with it. These people include both the practitioners dealing with heritage and the audiences whose belonging and sense of (European) identity heritage is supposed to promote. Our research revealed how practitioners at the EHL sites and EU officials in Brussels saw heritage policy as multilevel governance consisting of actors representing EU institutions, transnational organizations, member states, regional and local authorities, and citizens. This multilevel governance includes different networked forms of governing that mix clear top-down and bottom-up dynamics of power. In the chapter, we analysed how different governance methods function at the different levels of the EHL, emphasizing the roles that different actors take, and showing the changing, multi-layered, networked power hierarchies between these actors.

More importantly, building on a Foucauldian approach to governance, we engaged with the need to control the meanings of heritage, or the content that is used to narrate European heritage. Some of our interviewed EU officials showed a marked hesitance over claiming certain sites as European cultural heritage. This was made apparent by the way in which they strictly referred to sites as having a 'European dimension' or 'European significance', as opposed to explicitly European heritage. The chapter showed how the idea of European significance is used to condition the EHL sites to govern themselves both through and for Europeanization. This process is part of participatory multilevel governance, as it guides the sites to adopt EU-level policy discourses and to Europeanize themselves bottom-up (seemingly) on their own initiative. Hence, participation in the EHL action implies becoming part of the EU's political discourse. It enables participants to become active producers of the narrative of European heritage, but only after adopting the official and sanctioned vocabulary of the EU-AHD.

In Chapter 2, we continued to discuss forms of governance in the EU heritage sector through introducing the concept of neoliberal belonging: a form of competitive inclusion into the realm of EUropean heritage. In this chapter, we regarded neoliberalism as a cultural logic aimed at promoting self-governance and subjectification that ranges from individuals to institutions such as heritage sites, highlighting both individuality and competition. We first outlined the general trends of explicit and implicit EU funding for the cultural sector and different heritage initiatives, and then moved on to debate competition and branding as central aspects of neoliberal belonging.

A brand logic implies added value: it enables the sites to connect to stories, meanings, and contexts that normally would be beyond their reach. These connections enable the sites to place certain narratives to specific spatial environments and communicate their stories to the wider public. However, these processes take place on several scales. The EHL sites are active in multiple brandscapes functioning at different levels – local, national, regional, and, increasingly, European. Although currently rather modest, the EHL brand seeks to connect the smaller narratives (of individual sites) and broader ones (the EU-AHD). This branding is deeply entwined with the ways the EHL is used in the EC's politics of belonging. However, the EC is not sufficiently willing and able to function as a marketing agent. This positions the EHL sites as the dominant brand-makers for the EHL action. Without receiving any explicit funding, the sites are not only expected to produce the narrative content for EUropean heritage, but also ensure their own visibility, as well as that of the EHL.

Part II: Geo-graphing Europe

In Chapter 3, we approached the EHL as a geopolitical discourse and perceived scale and scalarity as central aspects of meaning-making in heritage. By focusing on the discursive means through which the practitioners create imaginaries of space and narrate their EHL site as part of 'European heritage', we identified three subject positions: EHL participant, EHL observer, and EHL creator. Although at times contradictory, these subject positions significantly overlap, and all interviewees use a combination of these discursive positions when describing their ways of engaging and making sense of the EHL and the roles of their sites in it.

Although the two first positions – EHL participant and EHL observer – reiterate the usual scalar relations (local, national, transnational), the last category of EHL creator seems to challenge this order. By actively dissolving both the power hierarchies associated to these scales and the boundaries between them, the EHL creator positions the sites as transformative actors and highlights the sites' ability to go beyond their role as reproducers of the EU-AHD (see Chapters 1 and 2). Moreover, by deconstructing the idea of scalar hierarchies, this position opens up space for new narratives that go beyond depicting Europe as a collection of its nation states.

Continuing the geopolitical analysis of the EHL, in Chapter 4, we engaged with the geopolitical border imaginaries of Europe through analysing visitor interviews conducted at the sites. Borders are a central topic to the EHL; the need to cross or overcome them is engraved in the eligibility criteria of the EHL sites. By investigating the different meanings associated with national and European borders, we highlighted the importance of heritage in processes of bordering.

Through four different categories of bordering – (1) borderless Europe, (2) internal borders, (3) external borders, and (4) borderless world – we analysed the multiple and intertwined processes of bordering from the perspective of unity, diversity, and difference. Although the interviews illustrated varied perceptions of the meaning and prevalence of Europe's internal and external borders, the analysis showed how many of the opinions expressed rather privileged understandings of borders. Ability to cross both European and global borders has a normative position either as a future or past ideal, as well as a contemporary practice. There is no acknowledgement that some people might not possess the same rights to move freely (e.g. Goldberg 2006; Van Houtum 2013; De Genova 2016). Similarly, the right-wing populist discourses on the need to close EUropean borders are absent from our data.

Although ability to cross borders and move freely has a normative position in our interviews, when debating a borderless Europe or borderless world, interviewees actively identified clear cultural differences between Europe and the rest of the world, and within Europe. Perceived cultural differences between Western and Eastern Europe were clearly expressed in some visitor interviews, especially among those from the founding members of the Union. These presumed cultural differences are viewed as a risk to the unity of EUrope: a unity that is seen both as a lost and future utopia. In a more general sense, negotiations of these borders of difference inside and beyond Europe have Eurocentric hierarchical tones, where (Western) Europe is positioned on top and the rest of the world needs to either be assimilated in order to reach unity (inside Europe) or be managed in order to claim a leadership position (outside Europe). Although not representing the official voices of the EHL, these visitor interviews highlight the unacknowledged Eurocentric biases that may be behind cosmopolitan ideas of free mobility.

Part III: Engaging Europe

In Chapter 5, we built on the discussion on participatory governance begun in Chapter 1. We brought the debate to the practical level by analysing how different EHL sites attempt to include various groups into both the physical space of the museums and the knowledge production processes at the sites. We envisaged heritage sites as change agents that have a central role in including and empowering silenced and disenfranchised groups. Our analysis builds on the ideas of heritage dissonance and inclusive heritage discourse (as opposed to the EU-AHD) as potential channels to enable participation and active contributions of citizens.

Although the majority of the practitioners highlighted the importance of participation and showcase many projects aimed at including visitor voices in the exhibitions and activities of the sites, they simultaneously (and quite contradictorily) wanted top-down processes in selecting, representing, and interpreting heritage. Many of our interviewed practitioners stressed the need for experts in guiding involved visitors to understand the importance of heritage and to engage with it 'properly'. This suggests that many practitioners have adopted the rhetoric of participatory governance and engaging the public, without challenging the top-down power dynamics that still give them the final say in interpreting the heritage in question.

Our field research revealed that in many instances, citizens are only invited to participate in heritage in pre-defined frameworks without genuine opportunities to influence. Moreover, only a handful of our interviewed visitors actively sought to challenge the story told by the EHL site. There are many potential reasons for this. The narratives available at the sites may be seen as having such a normative canonized position that they cannot be challenged by individual visitors; the exhibitions may offer such varied narratives that they are able to avoid open confrontation due to offering 'something for everyone'; most likely, those visitors seeking to challenge the narratives do so outside the actual heritage site or only in retrospect after their visit. While our data indicates some attempts to seek new audiences, not all the EHL sites necessarily engage their visitors beyond 'enlivening' the heritage on display.

Whereas in Chapter 5 we focused on participation and inclusion in concrete practices at heritage sites, in Chapter 6, we approached heritage participation in terms of constructing communities. The explicit aim to promote belonging characterizes both the EHL and other EU heritage and cultural policy initiatives. Narratives of the past have a central role in defining what kind of 'heritage communities' or 'communities of memory' are constructed, and who are perceived as belonging to them. Traditionally these narratives have been used in nation building processes but EU heritage policy, including the EHL, can be interpreted as a similar instrument of community construction.

We approached the issue from three fronts: first, in terms of analysing the relationships between the EHL sites and the local communities in which they exist; second, by investigating the sites' ways of constructing European communities, and finally, by debating affects as tools to construct communities. We showed how on the local level the sites often function as important avenues for local communities to share memories and to express feelings of attachment to the locality, the heritage site, and the past that is being narrated. The interviews with practitioners and visitors also indicate a construction of a more abstract European community is being constructed. This ongoing process builds on the narratives of the sites, but also on concrete practices like the use of multiple languages in engagement with their visitors, which is seen as an inherently European characteristic. Finally, affective communities are built in the interviews. In these community constructions, narrative elements of the exhibitions are used to create feelings of empathy for various people in the past and present. Through the narrative entanglements of various temporal layers, the heritage sites create affective experiences that cross temporal and spatial boundaries. The visitors' abilities to connect to the narratives of the sites is a crucial element in creating both local and European communities, but also in enabling people to form emotional connections to distant cultures and times.

Part IV: Embodying Europe

In Chapter 7, we started our debate on heritage and affect by outlining the development of the concept of poly-space. Based primarily on our individual experiences during fieldwork, the concept was developed to process experiences of flux or overlapping of different temporal layers of heritage. Poly-space enables us to make sense of the entanglements and relations between multiple temporal and spatial layers underlying the heritage sites and their narratives. Although the relationships between time and space have been much discussed, especially by cultural geographers, we feel that these theorizations fail to capture a crucial aspect of the way cultural heritage is experienced. Emphasizing the diverse experiential, affective, embodied, and atmospheric elements and knowledges that contribute to the way heritage sites and their layered histories are simultaneously experienced, the concept highlights the affective involvement of visitors. As active meaning-makers of heritage, visitors not only engage with the sites and their narratives but draw on their own memories and affective resources to construct experiences that facilitate plural interpretations of heritage. This experiential dimension of heritage allows a moment of flux between temporal and spatial layers; it is not necessarily linked to a concrete place or an experience that can be recreated. Rather, poly-space can be conceived as a potentiality or an abstract affective moment. It enables visitors to experience ambiguity, slippage, or alterity, and has great potential to create empathy across time and space.

In Chapter 8, we continued to focus on empathy as a crucial aspect of affective heritage narratives. It is often acknowledged that the discursive narratives and the material elements of heritage sites do not necessarily mediate the same meanings. An element of interpretation is always involved in bringing these aspects together that engages also the embodied cognitive reactions of the visitor. We approached these interpretive processes through bodies – both as representations and as cognitive tools. First, focusing on varied representations of bodies as 'sticky objects' infused with affect and emotion, we analysed the ways these representations work to enforce a normative affective narrative and thereby consolidate specific ideological positions and societal values. Drawing on representations of 'heroes' and 'victims', for example, we showed how the representations of bodies contribute to consolidating a normative discourse of who is worth being remembered through European heritage and what kind of bodies deserve to be perceived as 'European bodies'. These representations often invoke dichotomies that forcefully contribute to processes of differentiation based on looks, skin colour, origin, ability, or gender and thereby may lead to biased exclusionary narratives of Europeanness. Second, by looking at visitor bodies as 'resonating membranes' we analyzed how the visitors' bodies (often unconsciously) help them interpret various meanings embedded in the exhibitions. By analyzing both the photographs taken by visitors and their explanations of the reasons behind taking them, in the second half of the chapter we showed how meanings trickle down from the exhibitions to the visitors own narratives, but also how visitors' own prior experiences and memories work to create unforeseen associations and imaginative and creative interpretations of the heritage on display. We ultimately showed the interplay between bodies as sticky objects and resonating membranes. Both processes work simultaneously and are of equal importance for producing and absorbing affect and knowledge.

In Chapter 9, we shifted our attention to the gendered norms and biases behind European heritage. Using critical gender heritage studies, we explored the prevalence of stereotypical gender depictions and the role of gender in EUropean heritage discourses, seeking to also identify ways the dominant heteronormative male narrative is challenged by some EHL sites. Gender equality has been a defining aspect of European equality policy ever since the Treaty of Rome (EU 1957), however, in terms of EUropeanizing heritage the idea of gender equality is not explicitly emphasized. It is merely one in the abstract collection of 'shared European values' repeatedly invoked in EU cultural policies. This lack of explicit focus on gender equality is problematic, as there is a clearly identifiable (white) male biased tendency to narrate heritage, exemplified by the narratives of Europe's 'Founding Fathers' and 'Great Men' that several sites use. Moreover, some of the interviewed practitioners seemed to understand heritage narratives as inherently gendered. Although not shared by all practitioners, this understanding leads to the idea that male-centred heritage narratives are considered as neutral, whereas the interconnections of gender and heritage are reduced to questions of 'women's problems' or of 'what women do'. Associating women's perspectives with those of other marginalized groups such as minorities and migrants highlights the heteronormative, white, male dominance in European heritage narratives. Based on our data, the majority of the EHL sites still focus on grand European narratives that tend to prioritize a white, male perspective on history and heritage practices. The repetition and normalization of such gendered narratives affects political, social, and gender equality in European societies as well as the public recognition of gender beyond a binary division of male/female.

There are many actors involved in defining, maintaining, re-narrating, and challenging how the EHL, and by extension the EU-AHD, is perceived, narrated, and maintained. As we have shown throughout the book, although acknowledging the aims of the EHL, the day-to-day activities of the sites are primarily guided by their own agendas and needs. As the sites are the principal communicators of the EU-AHD to the visitors, the narratives of the sites have an important role in defining how visitors perceive the EUropean heritage. It manifests how having an existing narrative does not constitute a monopoly over its interpretation. As Smith (2006, 191) notes, "[d]ifferent groups can put these narratives and the AHD within which they are expressed to use in different ways". All actors involved have different agendas and abilities to have their voices heard in these processes. They all have a role to play in shaping what defines EUropean heritage in contemporary Europe. By the same token we, the authors, must acknowledge that in writing this book we are engaged in these heritage politics and need to take responsibility for our interpretations and the effects they may have.

Looking to the future: Towards transcultural heritage

The 2017 European Panel report (EC 2017, 7) outlines the future vision of the EHL. In addition to high ideals, many practical improvements and goals are listed in the document, such as reaching 100 EHL sites by 2030, funding network activities between the sites, and improved collaboration between the sites and academics. Some of these positive developments are already taking place. The number of labelled sites increases steadily, and new member states, for example Finland, have joined the EHL network. The vision is a testimony to the high hopes placed in the EHL. It positions heritage as a force for good, "likely to have positive impacts (and certainly no negative ones)" (EC 2010, 26; cf. Turunen 2019a). Emphasizing the positive and shared aspects of European pasts is connected to the explicit aim of EU heritage rhetoric to use heritage as a tool for integration. When seen in this way, heritage has been used to show the positive connections and similarities in Europe's past as well as to celebrate a positive cultural diversity in Europe.

Seeing heritage as a means for attaining social aims, such as integration, highlights the recent tendency to acknowledge the social value of cultural heritage. Key developments in this were the UNESCO Convention on Intangible Cultural Heritage (2003) and the Council of Europe's Framework Convention on the Value of Heritage for the Society (2005), better known as the Faro Convention. The EHL documents show influences from both conventions. The founding documents, for example, define heritage largely from the intangible perspective, highlighting the symbolic nature of the sites. Moreover, the panel reports emphasize the role of 'heritage communities' and promote an understanding of a 'European' cultural heritage as the common right and responsibility for all European citizens. As such, the EHL positions the idea of European heritage as a powerful arena to discuss the inherently transnational and entangled nature of many 'national' histories (e.g. Hall 1999; Rothberg 2009; Chalcraft and Delanty 2015; Delanty 2017) as well as a means to promote the creation of a new transnational heritage community: EU citizens.

When constructing such a European heritage community, a transnational conception of heritage can offer a multi-faceted and inclusive basis for European belonging that builds on the idea and right of participation. Indeed, scholars have proposed alternatives to national heritage narratives for a long time, such as post-national commemoration practices (Gillis 1994) or post-national, transnational and supranational models of narrating the notions of European identity and cultural heritage (Eder 2009). However, there is a need to challenge the nation-centric idea of European identity towards an understanding of heritage that emphasize trans*cultural* connections both within and across EU member states. This is not simply a rhetorical trick to move past the "national order of things" (Malkki 1995). Rather we see transcultural connections as a way to complement and deepen the transnational approach to heritage and to include various post-migrant communities and other minorities into the European heritage narrative. By bringing the plurality of cultural identities into the debates of European heritage, we can start to deconstruct the normative relationship between nationhood and European citizenship.

Through emphasizing the intangible elements of heritage, we argue that transcultural European heritage should be perceived as a fluctuating network of influences and dissonances that simultaneously contrast, challenge, cultivate, and create new layers of meaning. As such, it should be perceived as a constant process of defining topical connections between past and present, while critically examining others. Transnational and transcultural heritages can bridge geographically distinct experiences and memories to create shared narratives. It could be a particularly potent means of debating contemporary social issues, such as migration, nationhood, and citizenship. Several of our fieldwork sites also attempt to use it as such. For example, Camp Westerbork extensively uses the history of the forced migration of the Jewish communities as a tool to debate contemporary refugee issues. Such willingness to engage with difficult and contested contemporary topics and to use heritage as an intermediary in these social controversies is central to perceiving heritage sites as active change agents (van Huis 2019) and social actors.

In order to build a shared future based on a transcultural conception of heritage, EUrope will need to learn to deal with its divisive, "difficult" or even "undesirable heritages" (Macdonald 2006, 2009) more comprehensively and substantially. In Macdonald's definition, difficult heritages are pasts that are "recognised as meaningful in the present but that is also contested and awkward for public reconciliation" (Macdonald 2009, 1). As she continues, they threaten "to break into the present in distruptive ways, opening up social divisions, perhaps by playing into imagined, even nightmarish, futures" (ibid.). There have been attempts to heritagize certain difficult pasts into joint processes of remembrance. However, there are vast differences in these processes within and beyond the EU framework. The collective trauma of the two World Wars and especially the Holocaust have been a central cornerstone of EUropean remembrance. The Eastern enlargement of the EU has raised the profile of the trauma of oppressive Soviet rule (Prutch 2013). Although many museums across Europe are re-evaluating colonial histories (e.g. Thomas 2009; Dixon 2012; Kros 2014; Buettner 2018; van Huis 2019; Turunen, 2019b), for the time being both colonialism and the many mobilities it entailed are poorly represented in the EU-AHD. This contributes to the exclusion of both Muslim and post-migrant communities from the EUropean heritage community currently under construction. The intangible heritages of Eurocentrism and racism that emanate from Europe's imperial past remain a significant challenge for contemporary EUrope.

Connecting the past to the present and to the future implies a certain level of responsibility. As argued throughout the book, we see heritage as an active, presentist, and future-oriented process through which realities are being constructed from the selected elements of the past (e.g. Ashworth, Graham, and Tunbridge 2007; Harrison 2013). As such, heritage is not only open to change, but according to Harrison (2013, 198) it "requires regular revision and review to see if it continues to meet the needs of contemporary society". One central need for European society stems from the postcolonial nature of the present time. Durrant (2004, 3) notes that to define an era as postcolonial means to "attempt to think global responsibility while paying attention to the differing degrees to which we are implicated in histories of oppression".

Durrant's approach builds on a strain of thought grounded in awareness of historical injustices and their continuing effects on contemporary societies. From this perspective heritage is not only a possible cure for social crises, a tool to construct a better future, but it is acknowledged as a potential cause for them (see also Whitehead, Daugbjerg, Eckersley, and Bozoğlu 2019). The idea of inheritance can be useful in trying to figure out the responsibility that comes along our historical legacies. Building on the work of Derrida (1992, 2006) Yegenoglu asks us to interrogate Europe's past and tradition, rather than simply become its heirs. For her, considering European heritage as an inheritance comes with a double command: "It requires that we be loyal to and affirm what we inherit, but at the same time transform and deconstruct it by not letting that tradition close itself off and thereby allow that tradition to open itself to its heterogeneity, open it to a relation with alterity" (Yegenoglu 2017, 21). This is ultimately an appeal against canonization and for a heterogeneous, diverse, and plural understanding of cultural heritage in Europe – a call against single stories. It is a plea for active and critical engagement with the intangible elements of heritage, meaning the values and ideals that the EHL sites are supposed to symbolize.

The EHL offers an opportunity to reflect on both the positive and negative aspects of transcultural references and influences. It introduces alternative layers of meaning and narratives that enable a shift from a nation-state perspective to a potentially nuanced and heterogeneous view of Europe's history, past, and cultural diversity. Although this is a great opportunity, it is also a major risk of the whole idea of promoting an idea of European heritage. Unless the EHL is able to move beyond Eurocentric ideas of what a EUropean dimension of heritage might mean, there is a risk of reducing European heritage to a top-down assimilationist project that urges people to become European at the expense of forgetting or abandoning other cultural and social values and traditions. Considering the current failure to include migrant and minority communities in exclusive and assimilationist national narratives, the ability to see EUropean heritage from a transcultural perspective as pluralistic, inclusive and co-constitutive should be seen as one of the measurements of the success of the EHL.

In our opinion, it is important that actors involved in the Label show they are willing to debate all kinds of cultural influences and entanglements, including, for instance, historical Muslim influences in several European countries or the colonial histories of many EU member states. A key aspect is the development of new modes of heritage curation and management that enable equal participation and engagement of various cultural groups and heritage communities beyond the nation-state. By highlighting the importance of engaging with transnational memories and contemporary transcultural practices and values rather than tracing cultural lineages, a transcultural understanding of European heritage can accommodate 'newcomers' and help to democratize participation in cultural heritage. A European heritage should not be interpreted as a denial of the right of different groups to their own cultural practices and heritages. Rather, it should be approached as an attempt to find commonalities and connections between different cultures that enable a transcultural perspective on interpreting historical events and cultural practices beyond the national. By promoting dialogue and inviting to collaborative meaning-making, it can sensitize the public to a variety of contemporary issues such as (post)colonialism, migration, Muslim heritages or social (in)justice, and offer an opportunity to reflect upon them. Such a broader understanding of cultural heritage can make it possible to question nationalist views and interpretations, and to investigate the hegemonic power relationships and discourses that have hitherto influenced the production of knowledge on cultural heritage. As such, the concept of a common, transcultural heritage creates the opportunity for debate about what cultural heritage is. This includes questions such as who participates, who is excluded, who has a place in the society and community of Europeans, and what cultural belonging in our time means. As a heritage action aimed to support belonging and intercultural dialogue this is the kind of idea of European cultural heritage for which the EHL should aim.

References

Adichie, C.N. 2009. "The Danger of a Single Story." Speech given by author. *TED Talk*. www.ted.com/talks/chimamanda_adichie_the_danger_of_a_single_story

Ashworth, G. J., B. J. Graham, and Tunbridge, J. E. 2007. *Pluralising Pasts: Heritage, Identity and Place in Multicultural Societies*. London and Ann Arbor, MI: Pluto Press.

Buettner, E. 2018. "What – and Who – Is "European" in the Postcolonial EU? Inclusions and Exclusions in the European Parliament's House of European History." *BMGN: Low Countries Historical Review* 133 (4), 132–148.

Certeau, M. de 1984. *The Practice of Everyday Life*. Berkeley: University of California Press.

Chalcraft, J., and G. Delanty. 2015. *Can Heritage Be Transnationalised? The Implications of Transnationalism for Memory and Heritage in Europe and Beyond*. Cultural Base. http://culturalbase.eu/documents/1.%20CHALCRAFT%20&%20DELANTY.%20 Can%20Heritage%20be%20Transnationalised.pdf

Council of Europe. 2005. Framework Convention on the Value of Cultural Heritage for Society. Faro, 27.10.2005. *Council of Europe Treaty Series – No. 199*. www.coe.int/en/ web/conventions/full-list/-/conventions/rms/0900001680083746

Dainotto, R. M. 2007. *Europe (in Theory)*. Durham, NC: Duke University Press.

De Genova, N. 2016. "The European Question: Migration, Race, and Postcoloniality in Europe." *Social Text* 34 (3-128): 75–102.

Delanty, G. 2016. "Multiple Europes, Multiple Modernities: Conceptualising the Plurality of Europe." *Comparative European Politics* 14 (4), 398–416.

Delanty, G. 2017. *The European Heritage: A Critical Re-Interpretation*. Abingdon, New York: Routledge.

Derrida, J. 1992. *The Other Heading: Reflections on Today's Europe*. Bloomington and Indianapolis: Indiana University Press.

Derrida, J. 2006. "A Europe of Hope." *Epoché* 10 (2): 407–412.

Dixon, C. 2012. "Decolonising the Museum: Cité Nationale de l'Histoire de l'Immigration." *Race and Class* 53 (4): 78–86.

Durrant, S. 2004. *Postcolonial Narrative and the Work of Mourning: J.M. Coetzee, Wilson Harris, and Toni Morrison*. Albany: State University of New York Press.

Dussel, E. D. 2000. "Europe, Modernity and Eurocentrism." *Nepantla: Views from South* 1 (3): 465–478.

EC (European Commission). 2010. *Impact Assessment: Commission Staff Working Document SEC (2010) 197, March 9, 2010*. Brussels: European Commission.

EC (European Commission). 2014. *The Mind and Body of Europe. Declaration on the New Narrative for Europe*. https://ec.europa.eu/assets/eac/culture/policy/new-narrative/ documents/declaration_en.pdf

EC (European Commission). 2016. *European Heritage Label. Panel Report on Monitoring.* Brussels: European Commission.

EC (European Commission). 2017. *European Heritage Label. 2017 Panel report.* Brussels: European Commission.

Eder, K. 2009. "A Theory of Collective Identity: Making Sense of the Debate on a "European Identity"." *European Journal of Social Theory* 12 (4): 427–447.

EU (European Union) 1957. *Treaty of Rome. Treaty establishing the European Economic Community.* http://eur-lex.europa.eu/legal-content/EN/TXT/?uri¼uriserv: xy0023.

Gillis, J. R. 1994. "Memory and Identity: The History of a Relationship." In *Commemorations: The Politics of National Identity*, edited by J. Gillis, 3–24. Princeton: Princeton University Press.

Goldberg, D. T. 2006. "Racial Europeanization." *Ethnic and Racial Studies* 29 (2): 331–364.

Hall, S. 1999. "Un-Settling 'the Heritage', Re-Imagining the Post-Nation: Whose Heritage?" *Third Text* 13 (49): 3–13.

Harrison, R. 2013. *Heritage: Critical Approaches.* London and New York: Routledge.

Houtum, H. van 2013. "Human Blacklisting: The Global Apartheid of the EU's External Border Regime." In *Geographies of Privilege*, edited by F. Winddance Twine, and B. Gardener, 957–976. London: Routledge.

Huis, I. van 2019. "Contesting Cultural Heritage: Decolonizing the Tropenmuseum as an Intervention in the Dutch/European Memory Complex." In *Dissonant Heritages: Contestation of Meanings and Uses of Memory in Today's Europe*, edited by T. Lähdesmäki, L. Passerini, S. Kaasik-Krogerus, and I. van Huis, 215–248. New York: Palgrave Macmillan.

Kisić, V. 2017. *Governing Heritage Dissonance: Promises and Realities of Selected Cultural Policies.* Amsterdam: European Cultural Foundation.

Kros, C. 2014. "Tainted Heritage? The Case of the Branly Museum." *International Journal of Heritage Studies* 20 (7–8): 1–17.

Lawler, S. 2002. "Narrative in Social Research." In *Qualitative Research in Action*, edited by T. May, 242–258. London: Sage.

Lowenthal, D. 1998. *The Heritage Crusade and the Spoils of History.* Cambridge: Cambridge University Press.

Lyotard, J. 1993. *The Postmodern Condition: A Report on Knowledge.* 9th pr. Minneapolis: University of Minnesota Press.

Lähdesmäki, T. 2014. "The EU´s Explicit and Implicit Heritage Politics." *European Societies* 16 (3): 401–421.

Macdonald, S. 2006. "Undesirable Heritage: Fascist Material Culture and Historical Consciousness in Nuremberg." *International Journal of Heritage Studies* 12 (1): 9–28.

Macdonald, S. 2009. *Difficult Heritage: Negotiating the Nazi past in Nuremberg and Beyond.* Abingdon: Routledge.

Macdonald, S. 2013. *Memorylands: Heritage and Identity in Europe Today.* London: Routledge.

Malkki, L. 1995. "Refugees and Exile: From "Refugee Studies" to the National Order of Things". *Annual Review of Anthropology*, 24, 495–523.

Pakier, M., and B. Stråth. 2010. "A European Memory?" In *A European Memory? Contested Histories and Politics of Remembrance*, edited by M. Pakier, and B. Stråth, 1–20. New York: Berghan Books.

Prutsch, M. J. 2013. *European Historical Memory: Policies, Challenges and Perspectives.* Directorate-General for Internal Policies. Policy Department B: Structural and Cohesion Policies. Culture and Education. Brussels: European Parliament.

Risse, T., and J. K. Grabowski. 2008. "European Identity Formation in the Public Sphere and in Foreign Policy." *RECON Online Working Papers* 2008/4.

Rothberg, M. 2009. *Multidirectional memory: Remembering the Holocaust in the age of decolonization.* Stanford, CA: Stanford University Press.

Settele, V. 2015. "Including Exclusion in European Memory? Politics of Remembrance at the House of European History." *Journal of Contemporary European Studies*, 23 (3): 1–12.

Smith, L. 2006. *Uses of Heritage.* London: Routledge.

Thomas, D. 2009. "Museums in Postcolonial Europe: An Introduction." *African and Black Diaspora: An International Journal* 2 (2): 125–135.

Trouillot, M. 2015. *Silencing the Past: Power and the Production of History.* Boston, MA: Beacon Press.

Tunbridge, J. E. and G. J. Ashworth 1996. *Dissonant Heritage: The Management of the Past as a Resource in Conflict.* Chichester: J. Wiley.

Turunen, J. 2019a. "Geography of Coloniality – Re-Narrating European Integration". In *Dissonant Heritages: Contestation of Meanings and Uses of Memory in Today's Europe*, edited by T. Lähdesmäki, L. Passerini, S. Kaasik-Krogerus, and I. van Huis, 185–214. New York: Palgrave Macmillan.

Turunen, J. 2019b. "Decolonising European Minds through Heritage." *International Journal of Heritage Studies.* DOI: 10.1080/13527258.2019.1678051

Turunen, J. n.d. "Borderscapes of Europe: Cultural Production of Border Imaginaries through European Heritage." Unpublished manuscript.

UNESCO. 2003. *International Convention for the Safeguarding of the Intangible Cultural Heritage.* Paris: UNESCO.

Whitehead, C., M. Daugbjerg, S. Eckersley and G. Bozoğlu. 2019. "Dimensions of European Heritage and Memory: A Framework Introduction." In *Dimensions of Heritage and Memory: Multiple Europes and the Politics of Crisis*, edited by C. Whitehead, S. Eckersley, M. Daugbjerg, and G. Bozoğlu, 1–25. Abingdon and New York: Routledge/Taylor & Francis Group.

Wu Z. and Hou, S. 2015. "Heritage and Discourse." In *The Palgrave Handbook of Contemporary Heritage Research*, edited by E. Waterton, and S. Watson, 37–51. New York: Palgrave Macmillan.

Yegenoglu, M. 2017. "Cosmopolitan Europe: Memory, Apology and Mourning." In *European Cosmopolitanism: Colonial Histories and Postcolonial Societies*, edited by G. K. Bhambra, and J. Narayan, 17–30. Abingdon: Routledge.

Appendices

Appendix 1. List of sites from the inter-governmental period (n = 68)

★ has applied for the EHL label also during the EU phase
★★ has received the EHL label during the EU phase

PLEASE NOTE! Some sites that have re-applied have done so with slightly different focuses when compared to the inter-governmental period.

BELGIUM

Palace of the Prince-Bishops at Liège ★
Stoneware of Raeren (German Community) ★
Archaeological site of Ename ★
Archaeological site of Coudenberg ★

BULGARIA

Archaeological site of Debelt
Memorial Vassil Lesvki
Historic town of Rousse
Boris Christoff Music Centre

CYPRUS

Fortifications of Nicosia
Castle of Kolossi ★
Site of Kourion ★
Circuit of six churches with Byzantine and post Byzantine frescos, Troodos

CZECH REPUBLIC

Castle of Kynžvart ★
Zlín, town of Tomas Bat'a ★
Vítkovice coal mine at Ostrava
Memorial of Antonín Dvořák at Vysoká ★

FRANCE

Cluny Abbey ★★
House of Robert Schumann, near Metz ★★
Pope's Palace Court, Avignon

GERMANY

Network of places and sites of the Iron Curtain
Sites of the Reformation network

GREECE

Acrópolis, Athens ★★
Knossos Palace
Archaeological site of Poliochne
Byzantine site of Monemvasia ★

HUNGARY

Royal castle of Esztergom
Szigetvar fortress
The Reformed college and great church at Debrecen
Royal palace of Visegrád

ITALY

Birthplaces of Rossini, Puccini, and Verdi
Birthplace of Gasperi ★★
Ventotene Island
Capitole Place in Roma

LATVIA

Historic centre of Riga
Rundale Palace
Town of Kuldiga

LITHUANIA

Mikalojus Konstantinas Ciurlionis' works
Historical centre of Kaunas
Zemaitija (lowlands) region and the Hill of Crosses
Museum of Genocide Victims (1940–41) at Vilnius

MALTA

Catacombs of Rabat

POLAND

Gdańsk Shipyards ★★
Hill of Lech at Gniezno (Cathedral, church, palaces, museum) ★
Cathedral St Wenceslas and Stanislas, Krakow
Town of Lublin ★★

PORTUGAL

Braga cathedral
Convent of Jesus at Setubal ★
General library of the University of Coimbra ★★
Abolition of the death penalty ★★

ROMANIA

Archaeological site of Istria
Cantacuzino Palace at Bucarest
Roman Athenaeum at Bucarest
Park Brancusi at Targu Jiu

SLOVAKIA

Pre-Romanesque Ecclesiastical Architecture, St Margaret Church, Kopcany
The Castle of Červený Kameň
The Barrow of General Milan Rastislav Štefánik at Bradlo
Kremnica Mint (Mincovňa Kremnica)

SLOVENIA

Memorial church of the Holy Spirit at Javorca ★★
Franja Hospital at Dolenji Novaki ★★
Žale Cemetery at Ljubljana ★

SPAIN

Crown Aragon Archive ★★
Yuste Royal Monastery
Cap Finisterre ★
Students Residence, Madrid ★★

SWITZERLAND

Cathedral St Peter in Geneva
Castle of La Sarraz
Hospice of St Gotthard

Appendix 2. Labelled European Heritage Label sites by country 2013–2017 (n = 38)

For later EHL nominations, please see EC website.

AUSTRIA

Archaeological Site of Carnuntum, Petronell-Carnuntum, 2013
Imperial Palace, Vienna, 2015

BELGIUM

Mundaneum, Mons, 2015
Bois du Cazier, Marcinelle, 2017

CROATIA

Neanderthal Prehistoric Site and Krapina Museum, Hušnjakovo/Krapina, 2015

CZECH REPUBLIC

Olomouc Premyslid Castle and Archdiocesan Museum, Olomouc, 2015

ESTONIA

Great Guild Hall, Tallinn, 2013
Historic Ensemble of the University of Tartu, Tartu, 2015

FRANCE

Abbey of Cluny, Cluny, 2014
Robert Schuman's House, Scy-Chazelles, 2014
European District of Strasbourg, Strasbourg, 2015
Former Natzweiler concentration camp and its satellite camps (with Germany), multiple, 2017

GERMANY

Sites of the Peace of Westphalia (1648), Münster and Osnabrück, 2014
Hambach Castle, Hambach, 2014
Leipzig's Musical Heritage Sites, Leipzig, 2017
Former Natzweiler concentration camp and its satellite camps (with France), multiple, 2017

GREECE

Heart of Ancient Athens, Athens, 2014

HUNGARY

Pan-European Picnic Memorial Park, Sopron, 2014
Franz Liszt Academy of Music, Budapest, 2015
Dohány Street Synagogue Complex, Budapest, 2017

ITALY

Alcide de Gasperi's House Museum, Pieve Tesino, 2014
Fort Cadine, Trento, 2017

LITHUANIA

Kaunas of 1919–1940, Kaunas, 2014

LUXEMBURG

Village of Schengen, Schengen, 2017

NETHERLANDS

Peace Palace, The Hague, 2013
Camp Westerbork, Hooghalen, 2013
Maastricht Treaty, Maastricht, 2017

POLAND

Union of Lublin (1569), Lublin, 2014
3 May 1791 Constitution, Warsaw, 2014
Historic Gdańsk Shipyard, Gdańsk, 2014
World War I Eastern Front Wartime Cemetery No. 123, Łużna – Pustki, 2015

PORTUGAL

General Library of the University of Coimbra, Coimbra, 2014
Charter of Law for the Abolition of the Death Penalty, Lisbon, 2014
Sagres Promontory, Sagres, 2015

ROMANIA

Sighet Memorial, Sighet, 2017

SLOVENIA

Franja Partisan Hospital, Cerkno, 2014
Javorca Memorial Church and its cultural landscape, Tolmin, 2017

SPAIN

Archive of the Crown of Aragon, Barcelona, 2014
Student Residence or 'Residencia de Estudiantes', Madrid, 2014

Appendix 3. Unsuccessful European Heritage Label applications per year

★ Transnational applications are calculated in the total amounts as independent applications for all participating applicants.
★★ Deemed to have European significance although not meeting other criteria for the Label.

2013

(n = 9, success rate 44%)

- Carlsberg, Denmark
- Dybbøl Hill, Denmark
- Schengen, Luxembourg ★★
- "Silent Night, Holy Night!", Austria
- "The First Europeans", Denmark and Poland ★

2014

(n = 36, success rate 44%)

- Antonín Dvořák Memorial at Vysoká, Czech Republic
- Archaeological site of Kourion, Cyprus
- Archaeological site of Monemvassia, Greece ★★
- Cape Finisterre, Spain ★★
- Castle of Kolossi, Cyprus
- Castle Kynžvart, Czech Republic
- City Conservation Zone Zlín, Czech Republic ★★
- Convento de Jesus, Portugal
- Coudenberg – Former Palace of Brussels, Belgium ★★
- Ename Heritage Village, Belgium
- Hlubina mine and Vítkovice Ironworks, Czech Republic ★★
- Javorca Memorial Church of the Holy Spirit, Slovenia
- Lech Hill, Poland
- Palace of the Prince-Bishops of Liège, Belgium
- Raeren Stoneware & Raeren Pottery Museum, Belgium
- The Hajdú District Residence, Hungary
- Troyes, France ★★
- Vilnius University Architectural Ensemble, Lithuania
- Žale Cemetery "The Garden of All Saints", Slovenia
- Žiče Charterhouse, Slovenia

2015

(n = 18, success rate 50%)

- Adolf Loos interiors, Czech Republic
- Castle of Canossa, Italy
- Congress Hall, Austria ★★
- Holy Cross of Brother Mansueto of Castiglione, Italy
- Industrial Heritage of the City of Rijeka, Croatia
- Industrialisation in Upper Silesia, Poland ★★
- Mértola Vila Museu, Portugal
- Royal Palace of Visegrád, Hungary ★★
- Schunck Glass Palace, Netherlands

2017

(n = 28, success rate 31%)

- Ancient Plovdiv Architectural and Historical Reserve, Bulgaria
- Archaeological Site of Monemvasia, Greece

- Bussaco Cultural Heritage Site, Portugal
- Coudenberg Palace, Belgium ★★
- Eight Estonian and Latvian Manors, Estonia and Latvia ★
- Historical Centre of Turaida, Latvia
- Imperial Palace (Innsbruck), Austria
- Lodz – Multicultural Landscape of an Industrial City, Poland
- Mértola Historical Center, Portugal
- Oradea Fortress, Romania
- Revitalized Fortresses of Šibenik, Croatia
- Sites of Great Moravia, Czech Republic and Slovakia ★
- The Legacy of the Composer Bohuslav Martinů, Czech Republic
- Two fortresses – One Hero, Croatia and Hungary ★
- Westerplatte Battlefield, Poland ★★
- Zsolnay Cultural Quarter, Hungary

Appendix 4. Table of background information on visitor interviews

271 visitors at 11 EHL sites women (n = 142); men (n = 129)	225 EU-citizens, representing 19 EU nationalities, including:
	Austria (n = 16); Belgium (n = 33); Czech Republic (n = 1); Denmark (n = 3); Finland (n = 3); France (n = 35); Germany (n = 37), Greece (n = 2), Ireland (n = 2), Italy (n = 22), Luxembourg (n = 1), the Netherlands (n = 35), Poland (n = 9), Portugal (n = 1), Slovakia (n = 1), Spain (n = 1), Sweden (n = 2), and United Kingdom (n = 15)
	Including citizens with double/triple nationality (n = 6): Austrian-Polish (n = 1); French-German (n = 1); Russian-French (n = 1); Dutch-American (n = 1); Dutch-Swedish (n = 1); Hungarian-British-German (n = 1)
	46 visitors from non-EU countries, including: Australia (n = 3), Canada (n = 8), Chile (n = 1), China (n = 1), India (n = 2), Japan (n = 2), New-Zealand (n = 1), Peru (n = 1), Russia (n = 1), Singapore (n = 2), South-Korea (n = 1), Switzerland (n = 2), Ukraine (n = 2), and United States (n = 19)

Age group:
Visitors aged between 18–50 years: (n = 141); aged between 50 and 85+ years: (n = 130)

Group 1 age 18–25 (n = 50)	Group 2 age 26–30 (n = 27)	Group 3 age 31–35 (n = 21)	Group 4 age 36–40 (n = 11)	Group 5 age 41–45 (n = 8)	Group 6 age 46–50 (n = 24)	Group 7 age 51–55 (n = 22)
Group 8 age 56–60 (n = 21)	Group 9 age 61–65 (n = 26)	Group 10 age 66–70 (n = 27)	Group 11 age 71–75 (n = 21)	Group 12 age 76–80 (n = 9)	Group 13 age 81–85 (n = 1)	Group 14 age 85+ (n = 3)

Educational background:
High school diploma, secondary education: (n = 25)
Vocational training, apprenticeship, college: (n = 32)
University students: (n = 33)
Higher education BA, MA, PhD diploma: (n = 171)
Without information: (n = 10)

Appendix 5. Fieldwork sites

Alcide De Gasperi House Museum, Italy

The Alcide De Gasperi Home museum is located in the original birth house of the Italian statesman Alcide de Gasperi (1881–1954), who was born in Pieve Tesino. Pieve Tesino belongs to the northern Italian region of Trentino/ Alto Adige and Südtirol. The permanent exhibition in the museum tells the intertwined story of the region, De Gasperi's worldviews, and his political carrier.

The European panel describes De Gasperi House Museum's European significance in its selection report:

> The Casa Alcide de Gasperi museum, opened in 2006, is located in a traditional Alpine village house where de Gasperi was born. De Gasperi's work is fundamental to the creation of the European Union. One of the Founding Fathers of the European Union along with Robert Schuman, Jean Monnet and Konrad Adenauer inter alia, he played a formative role in the reconstruction of Europe after World War II, culminating in his election as the president of the European Coal and Steel Community in 1954. In addition to raising awareness on de Gasperi, the aim of the museum is promote the democratic values of the European Union, inspired in part by its transboundary history and location between the Italian and German cultures. The candidate site meets the criteria for European significance required for the European Heritage Label.
>
> (EC 2013, 18)

Website: www.degasperitn.it/en/museo-de-gasperi/museo/

Archaeological Park Carnuntum, Austria

The Archaeological Park Carnuntum is situated in the east of Austria. Carnuntum was an important Roman settlement founded in the middle of the first century CE at a crossing point of trade routes on the Danube and became an important city in the Roman Empire. The park includes a museum and reconstructed Roman houses, a training arena on the compound of the ancient gladiator school and the remains of the Civilian City's Amphitheatre. In the reconstructed Roman City Quarter visitors can visit the house of a middle-class citizen (House of Lucius), a high-end mansion (Villa Urbana), public baths, and the semi-reconstructed domus quarta that depicts the lavish lifestyle of the upper middle class in Carnuntum. Experimental archaeology was applied for all reconstructions and the building work was carried out using ancient building technology and craft skill as well as partly with original Roman stonework and with reconstructed Roman tools.

The European panel describes Carnuntum's European significance in its selection report:

Carnuntum is a huge archaeological site, its importance originating from its function in the Roman Empire as an important crossroads of trade routes and also due its links with emperors such as Marcus Aurelius, linked to the Edict of Milan and famous for his influence on the development of religious tolerance. Important events took place in Carnuntum such as the Emperors Conference in 308 AD which decided the future of the Roman Empire. The Roman Empire is considered by some as a predecessor of Europe, combining different cultures, religions, and geographic areas under one administrative system.

(EC 2013, 7)

Website: www.carnuntum.at/de

Camp Westerbork, The Netherlands

Camp Westerbork, located in Drenthe province, northeastern Netherlands, was built in 1939, and served as a refugee camp for Jews persecuted by the Nazis until 1942. It then became a transit camp from where approximately 102.000 Jews, Roma, and Sinti were deported to Nazi extermination and concentration camps in Germany and occupied territories of Central and Eastern Europe. After World War II, the site served different purposes. First, it was an internment camp for Dutch collaborators with the Nazi regime. Later it became a military and repatriation camp for Dutch soldiers leaving for and returning from the Dutch East Indies. After Indonesia's Declaration of Independence in 1949, it served as a repatriation camp for East Indian Dutch families and finally was used to accommodate several thousand Moluccan refugees from Indonesia until 1971. During this time the site was renamed Schattenberg. The bigger part of the former camp was demolished in 1971 to make way for the construction of radio telescopes used for astronomy research. Finally, in 1983 the memorial center was founded on the premises. The former Camp Westerbork is a historical site with original structures and historical artefacts, including two original freight cars used during World War II, the residence of the camp commander under a glass cover, and a partially reconstructed barrack (Barrack 56). The permanent exhibition at the site tells its multilayered story with a strong focus on the World War II.

The European panel describes Camp Westerbork's European significance in its selection report through listing its "layered episodes of history" (EC 2013, 8) and noting that it "gives testimony to a period of the history of the Netherlands between pre- and post-World War II in Europe" (ibid.).

Website: https://kampwesterbork.nl/en/

European District of Strasbourg, France

Since its creation after World War II, the European District of Strasbourg has been the home to the Council of Europe and its European Court of Human

Rights as well as the European Parliament of the European Union. It bears witness to European integration, the defence of human rights, democracy, and the rule of law. The site hosts a permanent exhibition of European integration in an exhibition space Lieu d'Europe.

The European panel describes European District's European significance in its selection report:

> Bilingual Strasbourg has a symbolic location in the centre of Europe. After the Second World War, European institutions created for maintaining peace were housed in an area which became the European district of Strasbourg. These institutions are the drivers of European consolidation; they are central to the strengthening of human rights and to the defence of democratic values and the rule of law. The district is also host to many events relating to Europe which underscore the candidate site's European dimension.
>
> (EC 2015, 14)

Website: https://lieudeurope.strasbourg.eu/

Franz Liszt Academy of Music, Hungary

The Franz Liszt Academy of Music was established in 1875 by Liszt himself. The site is composed of the Academy building hosting an international university of musical arts and a concert centre. In addition, the site integrates the Franz Liszt Memorial Museum and Research Centre, the Kodály Institute, and the Kodály Museum. The Academy building, designed by Flóris Korb and Kálmán Giergl and opened in 1907 in the centre of Budapest, represents Hungarian Secession.

The European panel describes Franz Liszt Academy's European significance in its selection report:

> Franz Liszt travelled extensively around Europe and the Academy he established is inherently international, from the outset. Throughout its history, the Academy has promoted an open, creative, innovative spirit, using the unbounded language of music as a living tradition. Today, it continues to foster musical talent, to motivate and support committed music teachers, to share the exemplary Kodály method of music education–named after a professor of the Academy who revolutionised the system of music education in Europe and beyond. The Academy maintains close ties with local and foreign musical institutions and orchestras. Many well-known composers played a role in the history of the Academy. A large number of its former students became key figures of the twentieth century's musical performing arts. Overall the Liszt Academy nurtures, preserves and develops a living European cultural tradition.
>
> (EC 2015, 11)

Website: https://lfze.hu/en/home

Great Guild Hall, Estonia

Located in the Old Town of Tallinn, the Great Guild Hall was built in 1410 by the Great Guild, an association of German Hanseatic merchants in the medieval times. The Guild played an important role in the framework of the Hansa for trade and cultural exchanges in medieval northern Europe. The Great Guild Hall gives the visitors an impression of medieval Hanseatic architecture. Today, the building hosts the Estonian History Museum.

The European panel describes the Great Guild Hall's European significance in its selection report:

> The history of Tallinn's Great Guild Hall is closely linked to the history of trade and cultural developments in medieval northern Europe. The Great Guild of Tallinn merchants was the most important organization in the city for centuries. The Great Guild's history of interactions with the Hanseatic League reveals the intriguing story of European "integration" in medieval times. The candidate for the award of the EHL is the Great Guild Hall together with the Estonian History Museum and its exhibition The Spirit of Survival. One section of this exhibition, "Power of the Elite," is devoted to the Great Guild Hall and its role in European history. As suggested by its title, The Spirit of Survival, the other parts of the exhibition present Estonian history as a long sequence of resistance to enemies and occupations. The recent history of Estonia creates an opportunity to present the narrative of Estonia and Estonian people within the context of European history and integration; the Panel encourages all efforts towards such contextualisation.
>
> (EC 2013, 6)

Website: www.ajaloomuuseum.ee/visiting/buildings/great-guild-hall

Hambach Castle, Germany

The medieval Hambach Castle, located in the district Hambach of Neustadt an der Weinstraße in Rhineland-Palatinate, became an important site of German's 19th century history. On 27 May 1832, around 30,000 people from Germany, France, and Poland came together at the castle to celebrate the Hambach Festival (Hambacher Fest) and to demand fundamental rights, political freedoms, equality, and democracy in Germany and Europe. The site is thus also described as the "cradle of democracy" in Germany and known in German history as a symbol of the struggle for civil liberties. The Castle hosts an exhibition of its history.

The European panel describes Hambach Castle's European significance in its selection report by emphasizing the history of Hambach Festival and noting that the Castle "stands as a symbol of the pursuit of democracy in a cross-border context" (EC 2014, 12).

Website: https://hambacher-schloss.de/index.php

Historic Gdańsk Shipyard, Poland

The historic Gdańsk Shipyard was the home for the Solidarity movement, as it is now renown, that emerged from the workers' strike in the 1970s in Poland. This strike was bloodily suppressed by the socialist authorities. Later, a new wave of strikes prompted the government to give in and sign the historic August Agreement in 1980. The site integrates several buildings and monuments: BHP Hall (the place where the August Agreement was negotiated), historic Gate no. 2 (where Lech Wałęsa made his speeches to the people), Solidarity Square with the Monument to the Fallen Shipyard Workers of 1970, a wall with commemorative plaques, and the European Solidarity Centre (that hosts exhibitions of the site's history).

The European panel describes the Historic Gdańsk Shipyard's European significance in its selection report:

> The Historic Gdańsk Shipyard has strong associations to the birth and commemoration of the Solidarity movement and to the origins of democratic transformations in Central and Eastern Europe in the late 20th century. The events that started in August 1980 at the Vladimir Lenin Shipyard in Gdańsk had a fundamental influence on the recovery of freedom by Poland and by other Central and Eastern European countries ruled by communist regimes. These events paved the way to the end of the Cold War and to changes in post-Yalta Europe and the world.
>
> (EC 2014, 19)

Website: https://ecs.gda.pl/

Mundaneum, Belgium

The Mundaneum was founded by Henri La Fontaine and Paul Otlet in Brussels. They were advocates of peace and sharing knowledge at European and international level with the means of bibliographic enquiry. The Mundaneum's original aim was to gather all information available in the world, regardless of its medium, and to classify it according to a system La Fontaine and Otlet developed, the Universal Decimal Classification. Today, Mundanuem is located in Mons and functions primarily as an archive. However, it organizes exhibitions on various topics.

The European panel describes Mundanuem's European significance in its selection report:

> The holdings of the Mundaneum trace the particular peace through culture, while the Universal Decimal Classification system and Universal Bibliographic Repertory provide the foundations of present day information science and are seen as a precursor of Internet search engines.

This combination of knowledge management and intellectual values is of European significance.

(EC 2015, 12)

Website: www.mundaneum.org/

Robert Schuman's House, France

Robert Schuman's House in Scy-Chazelles, close to Metz in the North-East of France – home of French statesman Robert Schuman (1886–1963), who is considered as one of the founding figures of the European Union. He composed the Declaration of 9 May 1950 that laid the foundation for the European Coal and Steel Community. This day is commemorated today as Europe Day. Schuman's home museum is located in the house he bought in 1926 and where he spent his retirement and died. Schuman is buried opposite of his house in the small church across the street. The site includes the museum, that exhibits Schuman as a person and politician through many objects that belonged to him, and a garden around the building.

The European panel describes Robert Schuman's House's European significance in its selection report:

> The site represents the house and grounds owned by the French foreign minister Robert Schuman, one of the Founding Fathers of the European Union. It is in this house Schuman drafted the Declaration of 9 May 1950, known today as the Schuman Declaration – the document that paved the way towards post-war European integration and the European Union. After his death, the site was taken over by a voluntary organisation to promote his memory and the values of peace and international cooperation.
>
> The role of Robert Schuman and the "Schuman Declaration of 9 May 1950" in the history of the European Union is fundamental. The location where Schuman lived is used to commemorate the Founding Fathers as well as to promote the history and values of the European Union.

(EC 2014, 17)

Website: www.mosellepassion.fr/index.php/les-sites-moselle-passion/maison-de-robert-schuman

Sagres Promontory, Portugal

Located at the South-Western tip of Portugal, Sagres Promontory was a place of myths already in ancient times. It is best known from the history related to Infante D. Henrique (1349–1460) a.k.a. Henry the Navigator, a Portuguese prince who has been credited with the onset of 'Portuguese discoveries'. As the personal fortress of Henry the Navigator, Sagres Promontory has been cemented in historical narratives as the central hub for building ideological and technological skills needed for the naval excursions and the onset of Portuguese oversees colonies. However, neither the original harbour for the ships nor an actual naval academy have been located at the site. The site hosts a broad natural park, exhibition space, and sound installation called 'Dragon's breath'.

The European panel describes Robert Schuman's House's European significance in its selection report:

> The site constitutes a rich cultural landscape that contains traces of the origins and development of European civilization dating back to the megalithic period. It was known in Roman times as the Sacrum promontorium (sacred promontory), from where it derives its name – a status that continued into the early Middle Ages with the establishment of the Igreja do Corvo (Church of the Crows), which housed the shrine of St. Vincent, and became a popular place of pilgrimage for Iberian Christians. Having been chosen by Prince Henry the Navigator as the headquarters for his projects of maritime expansion it became the privileged scenario for the accomplishments of the Age of Discoveries in the fifteenth century, a key historical moment that marked the expansion of European culture, science, and commerce both towards the Atlantic and the Mediterranean, setting European civilization on its path to the global projection that came to define the modern world.
>
> (EC 2015, 18)

Website: http://promontoriodesagres.pt/en/

References

EC (European Commission). 2013. European Heritage Label: 2013 Panel Report. Brussels: European Commission.
EC (European Commission). 2014. European Heritage Label: 2014 Panel Report. Brussels: European Commission.
EC (European Commission). 2015. European Heritage Label: 2015 Panel Report. Brussels: European Commission.

Appendix 6. Interview and survey questions

Group 1: EU actors

European cultural heritage: Concepts and actors

We will start the interview by discussing cultural heritage. This concept can be defined in different ways:

How do you understand the concept of a cultural heritage?
Who are the central actors of a cultural heritage?
    What about the role of citizens?

Can values be a cultural heritage? Why?

What do you think is European cultural heritage?

Are there some common elements or features of heritage that can be perceived as European?

What is the relation between European cultural heritage and values?

What is the connection between European cultural heritage and a national heritage?

What about a local and a regional heritage?

What about the relation to a global heritage?

What kinds of tensions can there be between these different levels?

Is it important to promote a European cultural heritage? Why?

Whose task is it to promote a European cultural heritage?

Whose task is it to safeguard a European cultural heritage?

What kind of role does / should the EU have in promoting and safeguarding a European cultural heritage?

Do you see any contradictions in a European cultural heritage?

Are there some silenced issues of the past that have not yet been dealt with in promoting a European cultural heritage?

What do you think is the role of EU actors in dealing with contradictory or silenced aspects of heritage?

European identity

Heritage is often discussed in relation to creating an identity.

How would you describe the relation between a cultural heritage and a European identity?

How would you describe a European identity? What does it mean to you?

How do you perceive a European identity in the context of migration and mobility?

Is it possible to have a European identity without having EU citizenship?

Is it possible to have EU citizenship without having a European identity?

Challenges and opportunities of a European cultural heritage

What do you see as the biggest challenges for Europe today?

Can a cultural heritage be used to tackle or solve current challenges? How?

Can it be used to increase social cohesion? How?

Can a cultural heritage and the ways of promoting it create problems or controversies?

The EU has recently created a strategy for international cultural relations and cultural diplomacy to strengthen relations between countries.

How could a cultural heritage be used in cultural diplomacy?

The EU is also emphasising intercultural dialogue to strengthen relations between different cultural groups.

How could a cultural heritage be used in intercultural dialogue?

European Heritage Label

European significance is the key criterion of the EHL: How do you understand the European significance of a cultural heritage?
How satisfied are you with the visibility and attractiveness of the EHL? What about its impact?
What can the EHL offer to different groups of people in Europe?
    What in terms of a sense of belonging?
    How about people coming from outside of Europe?
Are there any plans to engage and interact with European citizens in selecting EHL sites? How?
How is the EHL currently developing and how do you see the future of the label?

Only for the European panel + two coordinators:

How would you describe the selection process in the European panel?
    Do you have different views and disagreements within the panel in the selection process? For example the European significance?
How about the panel's interaction with the national coordinators?

Background questions

What is your nationality or nationalities?
What is your education?
What is your precise work position and in what sector? What is your DG?

Group 2: Site practitioners

Site's narrative

Could you please tell me what narratives/stories are told by this site to the public?
    What are you specifically hoping to communicate through these narratives/stories?
Are there any other narratives/stories or messages that could be told at this site?

Interaction with visitors and local people

AUDIENCE ENGAGEMENT

Who are the main visitors at your site?
    Are you interested in reaching a specific group of visitors?

How do you engage with the visitors at your site?

What kind of emotional response are you looking for when engaging with the visitors?

In your visitor engagement, how do you deal with critical aspects or different or difficult narratives/stories connected with your site? [Could you tell me more about your approach?]

LOCAL PARTICIPATION

How do the local people [people living and working around the site] perceive this site?

Could you give some examples of interaction between your site and the local people?

With whom, in particular?

Who took the initiative for this interaction?

Has engagement with the local people led to organisations of events, exhibitions or other activities?

Are you doing any advocacy work, such as public education, lobbying or participating in public debates?

COMMUNICATION AND LANGUAGES

Let's talk about the practical aspects of promoting your site and offering educational material in multiple languages.

Are you satisfied with the number of languages used at your site?

Do you have a special criterion for choosing these languages?

How do you interpret the criterion and the guidelines of the European Commission and of the EHL for promoting multilingualism at your site?

Are there any challenges connected with multilingual promotion of your site? [e.g. financing translation, finding a suitable staff; preparing the staff; language training; change of language due to an increase in a specific group of visitors etc. …]

What is your experience with multilingual brochures, tours, a web presence, signposts?

How do they contribute to increase your site's attractiveness and general competitiveness?

EHL LOGO AND SLOGAN

What do you associate with the design of the logo?
What do you associate with the slogans?

Power relations and policy

If we could talk next about the process of applying for the EHL and the impact it has had on your site .

Could you describe how the idea of applying for the EHL came about?
  Whose initiative was it?
  Who were involved?
  How did the process go?
Now that you have the label, how has the EHL impacted your site?
  Has it attracted more visitors? Also from abroad?
  For example, has it influenced the content of your exhibition or the activities you offer here?
  Has the labelling had any negative implications for you?
Could you tell more about the relationship between the different EHL actors? (for example, the EU level/expert panel, the national coordinators, the other EHL sites)
  Have there been different expectations between you and the other actors?
  Has the city/town been actively involved and, for example, used the label for marketing and branding?
What projects do you plan for the European Year of Cultural Heritage 2018?

European cultural heritage: concepts and actors

We have been talking about cultural heritage in this interview. This concept can be defined in different ways.

How do you understand the concept of a cultural heritage?
  Who are the central actors of a cultural heritage?
  What about the role of citizens?
  Can values be a cultural heritage? Why?
What do you think is a European cultural heritage?
What makes your site a European cultural heritage?
European significance is the key criterion of the EHL: How do you understand the European significance of your site?
Is your site also a national or regional or local heritage? What makes it such?
  What kinds of tensions can there be between these different levels at your site?
Is it important to promote a European cultural heritage? Why?
  Whose task is it to promote a European cultural heritage?
  Whose task is it to safeguard a European cultural heritage?
  What kind of role do the EHL sites have in promoting and safeguarding a European cultural heritage?

Do you see any contradictions in a European cultural heritage?

> Do you think a European cultural heritage is the same for all people in Europe?
> Are there some common elements or features of heritage that can be perceived as European?

What do you think is the role of the EHL sites in dealing with contradictory or silenced aspects of heritage?

European identity

Heritage is often discussed in relation to an identity and a sense of belonging.

How would you describe the relation between a cultural heritage and a European identity?

How would you describe a European identity? What does it mean to you personally?

How do you perceive a European identity in the context of migration and mobility?

Can your site affect your visitors' European identity or their sense of belonging to Europe? How? [different visitor groups]

How do you understand "Europe" at your site?

Challenges and opportunities of European cultural heritage

Let's move on to discuss the challenges and opportunities of a European cultural heritage.

What do you see as the biggest challenges for Europe today?

Can a cultural heritage be used to tackle or solve current challenges? How?

Can it be used to increase social cohesion? How?

Can a cultural heritage and the ways of promoting it create problems or controversies?

The EU has recently created a strategy for international cultural relations and cultural diplomacy to strengthen relations between countries.

Could your site be used in cultural diplomacy? [If yes, could you give concrete examples of what you have done at your site?]

The EU is also emphasising intercultural dialogue to strengthen relations between different cultural groups.

Could your site be used in enhancing intercultural dialogue between different groups within your country? [If yes, could you give concrete examples of what you have done at your site?]

Background questions

Please indicate your age group.
What is your nationality or nationalities?
What is your education?
What is your precise work position?

Group 3: National coordinators (survey)

EUROHERIT (Legitimation of European cultural heritage and the dynamics of identity politics in the EU) is an independent academic research project funded by the European Commission from its Horizon2020 Programme. The project examines the EU's recent heritage initiatives and heritage and identity politics in the context of the European Heritage Label.

As a part of our research, we invite the national coordinators of the European Heritage Label to answer the following 13 questions. All provided information will be treated confidentially and according to the highest ethical standards. Your answers will form a part of broader research data owned by the University of Jyväskylä, Finland, and managed by the project leader. Other researchers working under the supervision of the project leader may use the data for research and teaching purposes.

By answering these questions, you agree to participate in this research. Your answers are important for us. Thank you for cooperation.

Further information
Project leader: Tuuli Lähdesmäki, PhD, DSocSc, Adjunct Professor
University of Jyväskylä, Finland
Email: tuuli.lahdesmaki@jyu.fi
Tel: +358 40 805 3839
Web page: www.jyu.fi/euroherit

1.   Please state the country you represent.
2.   On the basis of your experience, what are the advantages of participating in the European Heritage Label (EHL)?
3.   Have there been some disadvantages in participating in the EHL? If yes, please specify.
4.   Would you briefly describe the process of selecting the EHL candidates in your country?
5.   Which actors are included in the selection process of the EHL candidates in your country?
6.   What kind of role do citizens have in the selection process for the EHL candidates in your country?
7.   How easy/difficult is it to find sites who are interested in applying for the EHL in your country?

8. What tasks does the position of national coordinator include in practice in your country?
9. How much influence does the national coordinator have on the final EHL selection process at the European level?
10. How do you cooperate with the EHL site(s) in your country?
11. How do you cooperate with other national coordinators and the EHL sites in other countries?
12. What do you think about the EHL selection process?
13. Can we mention your country in using your answers in our research?

Group 4: Visitors

Site

How was your visit? Was this your first time here?
How would you describe in your own words what this site/museum/place is about?

Whose past/history is this site/museum/place mainly addressing?
To whom is this site/museum/place important? Why?
What values does this site/museum/place communicate?

Could you easily relate to the story told by the site/museum/place? [Do you think this story is also your story?] Why/why not?

Heritage, scales and the European dimension

Do you know that this site/museum/place has been given a European Heritage Label?
What do you associate with the design of the logo?
What do you associate with the slogans?
What makes this site/museum/place part of a European cultural heritage?
Is it also a national or regional or local heritage? What makes it such a heritage?
Do you think that a cultural heritage is important in today's society? Why/why not?

Returning to Europe in our next question:

From your point of view, what is a European identity like?
How would you imagine a European identity to look like or what would you wish for a European identity, how should it be or look like?
Do you feel European yourself? Could you explain why?

Action and photos

Did the site/museum/place (or parts of the exhibition) raise some emotions in you? [What emotions – could you tell more about them? What caused them?]

Did you participate in some interactive activities at the site?
   If yes, how did they impact your experience of the site?
Did you take some photos at the site?
   Would you like to show us a photo that you find somehow meaningful to you?
   Please tell us about the photo.
   Would you mind giving the photo to us for research purposes?

Background questions

Please indicate your age group.
What is your nationality or nationalities?
Which country do you live in?
What is your education?

Group 5: Guides

What kind of feedback do you usually get from the visitors after the tour?
Are there some specific topics or sections of the exhibition that raise more questions or lead to discussions during/after the tour?
Are there some issues that also raise critical comments or negative feedback?
What kinds of emotions do you notice in your visitors?
Are there some particular topics that raise emotions in your visitors?

Index

For Product Safety Concerns and Information please contact our EU
representative GPSR@taylorandfrancis.com
Taylor & Francis Verlag GmbH, Kaufingerstraße 24, 80331 München, Germany